Formative Spirituality

Volume One

FUNDAMENTAL FORMATION

· ADRIAN VAN KAAM ·

Anna Loan Nguyen, S.P.
4604 N.E. Irving Street
Portland, OR 97213-2345

Pittsburgh, Pennsylvania

2002
Epiphany Association
820 Crane Avenue
Pittsburgh, Pennsylvania 15216-3050

© 2002 by Adrian van Kaam
ISBN: 1-880982-21-8

(Previously published by Crossroad, ISBN 0-8245-0544-1)

All rights reserved. No part of this book may be reproduced, stored in a retrieval system, or transmitted, in any form or by any means, electronic, mechanical, photocopying, recording, or otherwise, without the written permission of The Crossroad Publishing Company.
Printed in the United States of America

Library of Congress Cataloging in Publication Data

Van Kaam, Adrian L., 1920-
Fundamental formation

(Formative spirituality; v. 1)
Bibliography: p. 309
Includes index.
1. Spiritual life–Catholic authors.   2. Christian education–Philosophy   I. Title.   II. Series: Van Kaam, Adrian L., 1920-   Formative spirituality; v. 3.
BX2350.2.V16   1983   248   85-22079

Formative Spirituality

Volume One

FUNDAMENTAL FORMATION

Contents

Acknowledgments	xv
Preface	xvii
1. Human Life in Formation	**1**
The Emergence of the Science of Formation	5
The Ground of Consonance between Preformation and Formation	6
Manifestation of the Mystery of Formation in Initial Formation	6
Primary Foundation of All Formation	7
Prereflective and Scientific Knowledge of Foundational Formation	8
The Starting Point of Reflection on Our Formation Experience	9
Scientific Fields of Human Formation	11
Prescientific Presuppositions	12
Christian Articulation Research	14
Distinction between the Science of Formation and the Philosophy of Formation	15
2. Preliminary Questions	**17**
Six Basic Assumptions of the Science of Foundational Human Formation	18
Human Formation and Christian Formation	20
Academic Study in This Field	21
The Need for a Science of Formation	22
Why Foundational Formation?	23
Foundational and Special Theories of Formation	26
Comparison with the Field of Spiritual Theology	27

Importance of Particular School Versions of Spirituality	29
The Cultural-Personal Coloring of Christian Formation	31
The Terminology of the Science of Formation	32
The Science of Formation and the Auxiliary Science of Theology	36

3. Presuppositions of a Science of Human Formation — 42
    The Positivist View of Formation — 42
    The Rationalist View of Formation — 45
    The Foundational Human View of Formation — 46

4. Deformative Presuppositions of Formation Approaches and Sciences — 50
    The Vitalistic View of Formation — 50
    The Vitalistic-Functionalistic View of Formation — 52
    The Transcendental Autarchic Self-Actualizing View of Formation — 53

5. Foundational Dynamics of Human Formation — 57
    Four Main Form Dimensions — 57
        The Sociohistorical Form Dimension — 57
        The Vital Form Dimension — 58
        The Functional Form Dimension — 58
        The Transcendent Form Dimension — 59
    The Human Life-Form — 59
        Spirit-Mind-Body Dialectic — 60
        Vitality-Functionality-Spirituality — 61
    Integrating Formation — 61
        Spiritual Identity and Direction Disclosures — 62
        Spiritual-Functional-Vital Life — 63
    Formation Terminology — 64
        Three Centers of Formation — 65
        Human Life as Emergent and Transcendent — 65
    The Dynamics of Human Formation — 66

6. The Vital Preformation of Life and the Formation Field — 68
    Vital Preformative Presence — 69
    The Original Obscure Field of Vital Preformation — 70

Preformative Vital Life Directives	71
Scientific Reflection on Preformation	73

7. The Emergence of the Vital-Functional Dimension — 75
The Vital-Functional Relationship	76
Prehumanized Vital Dimension	*77*
The Foundational Dynamic of Emergent Human Formation	78
Emergent Human Formation and the Power of Spirit	*79*
Rupture of the Vital Impulse-Reaction Cycle	*80*
Transcendent-Functional Dimension as Mediator	*80*
Emancipation of the Functional Dimension	81

8. Functional Formation — 83
Concrete Emergence of the Functional Dimension	85
Functional Enlightenment	*86*
Functional Conscience	*87*
Exclusive Functional Dominance	*87*
The Consonant Functional Dimension	89
Conclusion	*90*

9. Distinctively Human Formation — 93
Functional Formation	93
Historical Formation	94
Historical Form Traditions	*95*
Permeation of Vital Formation by Spiritual Formation	96
Examples of Spiritualization of Vital Formation	*97*
Spiritual Formation of World and Immediate Situation	*98*
Vertical and Horizontal Interformation	*99*
Science, Technology, and Spiritual-Vital Formation	*99*
Art and Spiritual-Vital Formation	*101*
Physical and Experiential Research and Spiritual-Functional-Vital Formation	*101*

10. Spirituality and Sexuality — 103
The Dissonance of Sexuality	103
Proximate Directives of Sexual Life Formation	*104*
Excessive Sexual Security Directives	*104*
The Foundational Structure of Vital-Sexual Formation	105
Our Vital Pre- and Coformation of the World	*106*

Sexual Formation and Vital Field Formation ... 106
Spirituality and Sexuality ... 107
Adolescence and Sexual Preformation ... 109
Polymorphous Versatility of Sexual Preformation ... 110
The Integration of Vital-Sexual and Transcendent Life Formation ... 111
   Integration and Restriction ... 112
   Personalized Tradition Directives ... 114
   Change and Integration of Sexual Formation ... 115
   An Example of Misidentification of Foundational Directives ... 116
   The Reserve of the Formation Scientist as Community Consultant ... 117
   The Subcultures of the Formation Scientists ... 118
   Sexual Formation and the Foundational Structure of the Human Life-Form ... 119
   The Preparation of Formation Consultants and Counselors ... 120
   Normalcy of Formation Problems ... 121
   Conclusion ... 122

11. Ongoing Movements and Interforming Influences of the Vital-Functional Form Dimensions ... 126

Vital Dimension as Energy ... 127
   Individualization of the Vital Dimension ... 128
   Formation of Temperament ... 129
   Expression Potency ... 130
   Summary of the Characteristics of the Vital Form Dimension ... 131
Articulations of the Vital Form Dimension ... 133
   Preservation ... 133
   Growth ... 134
   Fusion ... 134
   Mortification ... 135
   Expansion ... 135
   Incorporation ... 136
   Interaction of the Articulations of the Vital Dimension ... 137
Pseudospirituality and Distortions in the Vital Dimension ... 138
   Vital Experience and the Magic Component of Pseudospirituality ... 140

Historical, Vital, Functional, and Transcendent
Spirituality in Humanity's Formation History:
A Summary 141

12. The Transcendent Dimension 145
Spiritual Experience 145
  Emergence of the Transcendent Form Dimension 146
  *The Transforming Power of the Transcendent
    Dimension* 147
  Enlightened Pulsations, Impulses, and Ambitions 147
  Transcendent Identity of Foundational Life Direction 148
  Commitment and Spiritual Life Direction 148
Transcendent Experience 149
  *Quasi-Transcendent Experiences of the Functional
    and Vital Life Dimension* 150
  Transcendent Experience of the Spirit Dimension 151
  *Sensate, Intellectual, Vital-Emotional, and Spiritual
    Intuitive Modalities of Knowing* 152
  Transcendence and Crisis 153
  Transcendence as Human Event 154
  Transcendence and Intermediate Wholes 155
  Transcendence as Less Common Contemporary Event 155
  *Limits of Vital and Functional Formation and the
    Birth of Transcendent Form Potency* 156
  Transcendent Life—Respect versus Violence 156
  The Transcendent Dimension, Integration, and Peace 158
Spiritual Presence and Religious Experience 159
  Reverence and Respect 160
  Awe, Worship, and Adoration 160
  Reverence, Culture, and Humanization 161
  Spiritual Presence as Readiness for Reverence 162
Initial Formation of the Transcendent Dimension 164

13. Transcendent Form Potency 166
Transcendent Ideals and Functional Projects 168
  Limits of Transcendent Ideals 168
  Idolized Ideals 169
  Ideals and Human Formation 170
  Projecting and Managing Operations 171
  Role of Ideals on the Spiritual Level 172
  *Ideals and the Restoration of the Unity of Life
    Formation* 173
  Dialectical Ideals 174

	Common and Personalized Ideals	175
	Peace beyond Passing Ideals	177
	Transcendentalist Formation	177
	Two Ways of Autonomous Self-Actualizing Formation	180
	Pneumatist Formation	181
14.	**The Mystery of Formation**	**185**
	The Cosmic Epiphany of the Formation Mystery	187
	Autarchic Pride-Form and Cosmic Epiphany	188
	Cosmic Epiphany of the Formation Mystery and Universal Interformation	190
	Cosmic Epiphany of the Formation Mystery and Everyday Formation	191
	Awareness Expansion beyond Everydayness	193
	Awareness of the Cosmic Epiphany in Spiritual Form Traditions	193
	Functional Formation in the Light of the Cosmic Epiphany	193
	Contemporary Physics and the Mystery of Formation	195
	Contrast and Complementarity in Cosmic Interformation	196
	Vital-Functional and Female-Male Formation Polarities	196
	The Intrinsically Dynamic, Unifying Epiphany of the Formation Mystery	198
	Static Misconception of Universal Formation Field	198
	The Formation Field	200
	Primordial Manifestation of the Cosmic Epiphany	201
	Human Life-Form and Cosmic Formation	202
	Relationship of Field and Form	203
	Distinction of Form Types	203
	Static Conception of Formation	204
	Approximate Knowledge	204
	Consonance of Cosmic Interformation	205
	Physicists and Cosmic Contemplatives	206
	The Personal-Social Epiphany of the Formation Mystery	208
	The Mystery of Personal Formation	210
	The Transcosmic Dynamic of Loving Consonance	210
	The Freedom of Transcosmic Foundational Formation	213

Formation: A Natural Analogical Concept   216
   Symbols and Human Formation   *217*
   Summary of the Anthropological Principles of
     Foundational Human Formation   *218*

15. Abandonment to the Formation Mystery   221
Foundational Formation Option   221
   Formation Matter and Freely Formative Human Life   *223*
   Knowledge of Formation Freedom   *224*
   Freedom of Foundational Response to the Mystery of
     Formation   *225*
   The Foundational Formation Decision   *227*
The Risk of Abandonment to the Formation Mystery   227
   Unavoidability of the Primordial Formative
     Alternative   *229*
   Formative Appraisal and Primordial Appreciative
     Abandonment   *231*
   The Primordial Formation Disposition of
     Depreciative Abandonment   *232*
   The Primordial Formation Disposition of
     Appreciative Abandonment   *235*
   Appreciative Abandonment and Negative Experiences   *236*
   Consistent Maintenance of Appreciative
     Abandonment in Daily Life Formation   *237*
   Obstacles to Fidelity to Appreciative Abandonment   *238*
   The Reasonableness of Appreciative Abandonment   *238*
   Affirmation and Implementation of Appreciative
     Abandonment   *240*
   Relationship of Appreciative and Depreciative
     Appraisals   *241*

16. A Foundational Theory of Human Formation: An Overview   243
The Foundational Dynamic of Human Formation   244
   Human Form Directives and Corresponding Human
     Formation Fields   *244*
   Human Formation Symbols   *245*
   Cocreation of Form Directives   *246*
   Foundational Formation Theory   *246*
   Form-Potency Maintenance   *247*
   Human Formation and Formation Field   *248*

Preformation of the Human Life-Form and the Poles of the Formation Field	249
Structural Effects of Human Formation	250
Transcendent Sources of Empirical Life Formation	252
Five Incarnational Sources of Empirical Life Formation	252
Core Form of the Empirical Life Formation	253
The Core Form and the Fourfold Potency Structure of Human Life	254
Current and Apparent Life-Forms	255
Current and Apparent Life-Forms and the Formation Field	256
Descriptive Definition of Current and Apparent Life-Forms	256
Periodical Permanence of Current and Apparent Life Formation	258
Actual Life-Form	259
Descriptive Definition of the Four Life-Form Dimensions	260
Articulations of the Functional Dimension of Human Formation	261
Dimensions of Formative Consciousness	262
Phasic Formation	263
Formative Transcendence Process	264
Form Directives	265
The Flow of Formation	266
Formation Movements in Human Life	267
Formation and Situation	269
Situational Formation Transfer	270
Formation Situation as a Point of Departure	270
Adaptative Flexibility of Foundationals	271
Key Formation Situations	272
Two Types of Formation Situations	272
Five Types of Formative Responses to Formation Situations	273
The Secondary Foundational Life-Form	274

Appendix One   **276**
The Position of the Science of Formation
within a Classification of the Sciences

Appendix Two — 284
Charts of the Science of Foundational Formation

Glossary — 299

Bibliography — 309

Index — 322

Acknowledgments

No thinker thinks alone; no writer writes alone. This is especially true of authors in a dialectical-integrational science such as formative spirituality. The primordial intentionality of this science is the perspective of spiritual formation. Such a perspective tends to transform radically the relevant contributions of other sciences. Hence, it would be a betrayal of their intentionality to ascribe to them a basic revision of their theoretical statements in light of the perspective of spiritual formation. It will not be difficult for informed readers to sense the influence of scholars and scientists such as Thomas Aquinas, Richard of St. Victor, John of the Cross, Meister Eckhart, Francis Libermann, Paul Ricoeur, Stephen Strasser, Bernard Boelen, Gabriel Marcel, Karl Rahner, Hans Küng, Johannes Metz, Karl Jaspers, Martin Heidegger, Medard Boss, Ernest Becker, Martin Buber, Jean Piaget, Maurice Merleau-Ponty. I am also indebted to such contemporary thinkers as Bohm, Bohr, Born, Capra, Einstein, Heisenberg, Ornstein, Planck, Suzuki, and Weisskopf. Although our view of spiritual formation has radically transformed the thought of these authors, we feel the need to acknowledge gratefully their inspiration.

My gratitude to the following people cannot be adequately expressed. Above all, I am grateful to Dr. Susan Annette Muto, Director of the Institute of Formative Spirituality at Duquesne University. Without her encouragement, frequent assistance, and tireless editing this book would not have been completed. In addition to Dr. Muto, the staff members of the Institute, especially Jean Feid, have been of great assistance, along with Helen Douglas and Jane Bergman. All of them helped considerably with the various drafts of the manuscript and in composing the index and the bibliography. I am also indebted to my colleague, Father Richard Byrne, OCSO, who read and commented upon the entire draft. I am grateful to our graduate assistants—Brother Romeo Bonsaint, Sister Rosemarie Carfagna, Sister Maureen Kelly, and David Nowak—who prepared the glossary and assisted in the indexing. Special gratitude is extended to Sister Rosemarie for her valuable help and to Brother Romeo and Sister Maureen for the bibliography. A final word of gratitude is extended to Marcelle West and her staff, who did such fine work on the typing of the manuscript. Last but not least, I would like to thank Richard Payne, associate publisher of Crossroad, who encouraged and supported this series.

Preface

This is the first volume of a four-volume series that aims to initiate the reader not only into a new science but also into a way of thinking that is as old as humanity, though perhaps new for many today. Our purpose here is to distinguish *informative thinking* from *formative thinking*. Most readers may be familiar with the former, but puzzled by the latter. The informative approach is customary in our culture, our sciences, our daily life. Its results are most impressive; at times, as in the technological conquest of outer space, awesome. The results of informative thinking are most useful in many fields of inquiry, including in the *science of formative spirituality*.

Formative thinking is a type of thinking that relates directly or proximately to our formation. We are always *giving or receiving form* in our life. Many experiences manifest and foster this process. Instead of denying these, bypassing them as unimportant, or merely using them as points of departure for informative thinking, we can dwell on these experiences in themselves. In doing so, repeatedly, we may disclose their unique meaning for our formation. Such discoveries enable us to gain insight into the structures, dimensions, conditions, and dynamics of the human formation process and its consonant and dissonant directions. By dwelling on our formation experiences in this way, we become better able to appraise them as good or bad for harmonious human unfolding. Moreover, since everything in life and world can serve our unfolding, formative thinking can point to one possible, universal way of thought that can be applied to all things in our lives.

Informative thinking, on the contrary, tends to be more issue-oriented than formation-oriented. The issues concerned may involve philosophical and theological thought, theoretical politics, or worldwide conflicts. Issue-oriented thinking usually starts from and leads to logical or measurable results. It does not aim primarily at the experienced art and discipline of human formation. It concerns itself with well-reasoned or well-researched information about the universe, history, and humanity. Linear and progressive, such thinking does not dwell necessarily on the implications of these issues for experiential human formation. It moves from one delineated insight to the next.

When utilized in daily life, the informative approach seeks practical solutions. It does not abide with possible experiential influences of these solutions on the spiritual unfolding of people and their environment. Informative thinking tends to be detached from such experiential implications. It has to be, if it is to reach its best results. In Western culture these results have been astonishing. Thanks to its almost amazing power, people in the West were able to build magnificent technological systems unsurpassed in any other culture. The tremendous evolution of the physical and social sciences, of medicine and law, of industry and technology would have been unthinkable without informative efforts each step of the way. The greatest minds of the West have served admirably the development of this vastly important and necessary style of thinking.

Nonetheless, exclusive dependence on informative thought alone does not seem sufficient for the full flowering of our life and world. Human thought also has to help people find ways to live more consonant, happier lives, making the world a better place for them and succeeding generations. To be sure, the majority of informative thinkers and researchers also aim at such improvement, but in a more remote or indirect way. Their insights and findings contribute greatly to its realization, but the missing link between their informative efforts and the concrete daily life of people is formative thinking.

We could depict this type of thought as the gentle master of human life as distinctively human. It respects, in relaxed detachment, the indispensable services that logical and functional thinking render to the human formation of life and world. It gathers its own wisdom by its approach of dwelling upon the formative events one encounters. It then integrates, in the light of this wisdom, any informative insights and findings that may serve the spiritual formation of humanity.

In this four-volume series, readers are introduced to the science of formative spirituality, or science of formation, and consequently to its style of formative thinking, which respectfully takes into account the relevant findings and insights of informational thought. Until now, formative thinking has been represented for the most part by spiritual masters in the East and West of various religious and ideological form traditions. All of them integrated into their writings in some measure informative insights of a philosophical or theological nature. The science of formation attempts to complement and structure this integration by doing the same for the contributions of the art and sciences that emerged more recently in history.

The distinctive character of this science lies not so much in the laborious effort of detailed analysis of a few fragmentary aspects of formation. Its students are involved primarily in the more unique area of *integrative thought and study*. This gives rise to well-grounded hypotheses regarding the foundations of all human formation. Students engage themselves in research that validates such hypotheses and leads progressively to a reliable, open synthesis.

This science focuses on the foundational themes of formation. These are taken up again and again, with slight or considerable variations, depending on the special aspect of formation being examined by the researcher in the light of the foundations. The resulting insights enrich, deepen, and concretize the foundational themes. New understandings give rise to new applications in daily experience of the primary tendency of human existence to give and receive form in life and world together with others.

Perhaps we could liken the student or scholar in this field to a spider spinning an intricate web. The points of its web ultimately clarify the whole pattern. Similarly, the unique method of foundational formation in its intricacy discloses hidden patterns in the daily formation of human life and world. It highlights first of all the *formative tendency of humanity*, its actual ongoing formation and its structures and dynamics (its essential burden and dignity);

second, the obstacles and facilitating conditions one meets on the journey; and third, the ever present threat of deformation and how to cope with it effectively.

Today we witness an eruption of old and new Eastern and Western *form traditions* and theories with corresponding prescientific suggestions regarding the scope and practice of formation. While such a variety of suggestions may contain creative leads for scientists, it can be confusing for the uninitiated. One may no longer be able to see the forest for the trees, that is, the foundations for the countless accretions. In the midst of this complexity, the formative thinker and researcher tries to ask basic questions and point to sensible solutions. All students and practitioners of this science should work in and around these integrative foundations. Particulars should by no means be neglected, but they should be reappraised in light of the foundations.

At present, findings and insights regarding the formation of human life all over the world and all though history are available to us. This has made it clear that we cannot depend on only one or the other particular approach to the formation of human life as such. No particular limited approach would be applicable to all types of people, in all possible cultures, form traditions, life situations, and formation phases.

To approximate a universally valid theory of human life formation, we should ask ourselves about the very foundations of this formation common to all people of all times and all places. This search for the foundations should take into account the contributions of the various form traditions insofar as they may have a timeless, universal relevance for human formation. We should look for similar universal insights in the arts and sciences insofar as they touch on the problems of human formation. On the basis of the integration of all such findings, we may gradually approximate a theory of formative spirituality that is truly foundational or universal.

To be sure, responsible integration demands a rigorous and complex methodology. Such a methodology will be presented in the third volume of this series, devoted to the scientific nature, principles, and methodology of the science of formative spirituality. This first volume will restrict itself to a consideration of the main presuppositions, structures, and dynamics of the formation theory.

The second volume will deal with dispositions and traditions because different form traditions emphasize different dispositions. The science tries to validate a minimum of universal foundational dispositions that a majority of people, inside and outside various *form traditions,* may eventually agree upon. The fourth volume will show how a form tradition—in this case, the Christian form tradition—can be articulated in the light of this science. This last volume will also suggest a *Christian formation theory of personality* that goes beyond a mere Christian anthropology and complements and integrates secular theories of personality.

Attentive readers will recognize that various insights of the arts and sciences have influenced the writing of this book. It is impossible to refer to each of these influences here. The Institute of Formative Spirituality at Duquesne University holds in its archives many volumes and pages of research, gathered and written by faculty members, students, and graduates in this new field of study. We hope to be able to include significant amounts of this reference material in the ongoing publications and journals of the Institute.

CHAPTER 1

Human Life in Formation

Specialists in various disciplines may turn their attention to human life. In their attempts to explain our life as a whole, they start out from one of its parts. Some may try to account for life's diversity on the basis of sexuality alone; others refer to the will to power or the physiology of the organism; still others focus on quantum theory or on the process of learning. Partial approaches, however, cannot provide a unifying insight into human life and its formation: their explanations and observations may be valid, but they are also limited; their result is more like a patchwork quilt than an integrated picture of human life as a dynamic whole. Nonetheless, specialized research in each one of these aspects is necessary, for without it there would be no sufficiently validated knowledge available that one could utilize for an integrational view of formation.

In daily life we do not experience ourselves in piecemeal fashion. We realize that we have imaginations, strivings, feelings, thoughts, dispositions, and actions. We do not usually feel that these are lived in isolation from one another. We experience them as variations of one and the same life that is ours. These aspects influence each other; they receive meaning and direction from the whole person. Each part of our life seems to be included in the formation of it as a whole. Without the dedication of countless scientific specialists, we could not know much about these interacting *formative dimensions of human life*. Without their findings, our view of formation would be relatively unreliable.

To illustrate the interaction that marks our forming presence, we shall consider the event of perception. Our eyes perceive shapes and colors. However, we do not see mere shapes or colors. What and how we see depends on many other factors in our formation, such as alertness, mood, physical well-being, biogenetic preformation, past experiences, aims, and attitudes towards others. Our whole life comes into play even in a simple act like seeing.

We are aware of life as both stable and changing. Our perception is always shifting. We see things we did not see before. There are lasting patterns in our perception as well. Our way of looking is coformed by the influence of our *transcendent aspirations*, by our life's calling and direction, by our occupation, and by our basic moods. All of these coform our perception in the same way as they coform everything else in our life. Our outlook, as it were, directs and forms our looking.

Imagine that you are a diplomat. Someone has invited you to a party of representatives of foreign countries. You walk in the room and look around. Because you have been formed as a diplomat, it is second nature for you to spot people who may give you useful information. Speaking with an ambassador, you scan his face and movements. You want to find out what he reveals or conceals as he talks about his government. You may not notice as sharply other things about him. For instance, you may not see what kind of shoes he is wearing. Were you a shoemaker, your perception would be formed in such a way that you would be more aware of his shoes, though less aware of the ways in which he tries to hide his real thoughts behind carefully chosen words.

A theory of human formation should never lose contact with life as a whole. It should not isolate one part as ultimate, but try to focus on the interwovenness of all aspects. In the examples given, it is clear that our life-form as a whole interacts with its surroundings. Let us reflect for a moment on this basically formative interaction, using the example of being college students.

When we went from high school to college, our minds were still full of the things that had formed our experience at home. Everything in college appeared both strange and familiar. Life on campus was familiar because the *formation field* of college had something in common with that of high school. Both are parts of the wider field of education in America. The students we met were similar to those with whom we had gone to high school. They displayed many of the same needs and problems. By seeing them on campus, in the classroom, dormitory, and student union, talking, studying, playing, we knew in general what they wanted. We could empathize in some measure with their lives. Not only the students, but college life as a whole was in some way familiar to us. We experienced blackboards, desks, books, papers, and sports similar to those in our high school.

Yet college was also unfamiliar. We looked at it with the eyes of freshmen, not with those of students already at home in college, or of professors who had been on campus for years, or of employees who earned their living in secretarial and maintenance jobs. The college had become a part of their daily life. It was one of the interactive settings that sparked their joy and sorrow, their boredom and interest, their success and failure, their romances, friendships, and fights.

In the beginning, college life is a new *formation situation* for us. We wanted to enter college, but no part of our formation had been rooted there. So we imparted to it a meaning made up of outside information, reading, experience, and contact with those whose lives were linked with this particular formation field. After we had spent some time on campus, we really knew the boredom of some classes and the fascination of others; the load of work towards the end of the semester and the anxiety before exams; the exhilaration when our team beat a rival college and the rhythms of dating and social life. We had walked the campus in the sunny days of spring; trudged through the snow of winter; strolled walkways during the quiet of nightfall. We had paced it in discussion with fellow students, with a girl we met in the union, with an old professor who answered our questions on the way to his office.

This whole sum of experiences makes up the formative meaning college had for us at the time. It was somehow present in each part of the campus: in the smell of the cafeteria at dinnertime, in the noises of the students before and after class, in the quiet of the library, in the test tubes and white coats of the laboratory.

Our experience of college life is limited to an aspect of our total formative experience. It does not explain the whole of formation. Wider than any particular formative experience is what we may call our global experience of our formation in its totality. It forms a living, dynamic whole, continually expanding, refining, and reforming itself. Global formative experience is made up of our experience in the family as a baby, child, and adolescent; in our schools; in our daily contacts with people and with radio, television, newspapers, and magazines; in our jobs, and in all the pushes and pulls that affected our life. Our whole past formation, including the formative residues of remembered events, make up the meaning of our formation field today.

It is evident that our formation is not confined to *inner formation,* as some form traditions have suggested. Formation is rooted in the whole of our experience and of our biogenetic *preformation.* What has not touched our experience at all is necessarily unknown to us. In other words our formation is as large as our formation field. Our emergent *life-form* expresses itself in our entire formation field. This does not mean, of course, that our life-form expresses itself in each event in the same way. To be *consonant,* forming experience must take into account the special characteristics of what is experienced. For example, we can perceive a bottle of champagne in countless ways. It can have all kinds of meanings for us, but not the same real or symbolic meanings that a jet plane or a visit to the zoo can have. Our consonant experience of the formation field is not arbitrary. It is dependent on the particular characteristics of what faces us in our formation field.

What we have discussed thus far can be summarized in the following points:

1. Our formation finds expression not only in our inner life but also in each person, event, and thing that affects our formation field and is affected by it. This field may include teachers, houses, meals, vacations, and countless other features of everyday life. Our life-form experiences itself in these surroundings. Our forming presence gives people, events, and things their formative meaning for us; it makes them what they are for us.
2. Our forming presence endows people, events, and things with formative meanings according to their own characteristics. Therefore, consonant life formation can never be totally creative, limitlessly free, or arbitrary in its life direction.
3. The formative meaning of each person, event, or thing comes from the way in which we ourselves have experienced them. If formative, they are part of our life formation. If consonant, our formation is compatible with their foundational characteristics.
4. Thus, our formation is not contained within the intraformative whole. It involves our entire formation field. Our emer-

gent life-form also exists in the people, events, and things in our daily surroundings.

Formation cannot be isolated from the people, events, and things that it animates with formative meanings and in which our life-form discloses itself. Our emergent life-form is not present in them simply as a collection of memories. At times someone or something may remind us of certain things in our past, but this is not necessarily so nor is it what usually happens. We carry our whole past formation as a lived totality that makes up all the richness of our present. This living formative experience, our own emergent life-form, brings the formation field to life for us. It is expressed in all that surrounds us. Our forming presence makes all people, events, and things what they formatively mean for us.

The Emergence of the Science of Formation

Sometimes a *congenial* and *compatible* form of life seems to emerge almost effortlessly. Formative *aspirations, ambitions, impulses,* and *pulsations* arise spontaneously in natural consonance with one another. We sense that we are growing wisely. We feel in harmony. Life flows easily. Formation is not problematic.

At other moments, however, we may feel compelled to think about what happens to us in our formation. Often what makes us reflect is some crisis that interrupts the spontaneous flow of life or a conflict that disrupts our daily routine. From whence do these problems arise? They come from a tension that seems inherent in the process of human formation itself—a tension between the spontaneous formation of life and the reflection that should guide it at crucial moments.

We are not always sure about the direction of our life. We may begin to question the sense of situations we are facing. What do these experiences and enterprises really mean for us? In short, we question our formation. We may begin to ask ourselves how consonant formation may be fostered. Can we do something about it by means of meditative reflection or recourse to formation wisdom and tradition, to formative reading, to the exercise of *appraisal*, and other means of disclosing consonant *form directives?* We wonder when and if formation may be improved in us and others.

It is not surprising that such questions arise in us. Seldom do we feel wholly at ease with the spontaneous formation of life. At crucial moments, we feel the need to appraise who we are and where we are going. The moment we begin to reflect on formation, we initiate the possibility of critically appraising our life direction. We may compare our reflections with similar reflections of others. Are their insights relevant to the problems of formation we ourselves face? In the course of such explorations, certain principles of formation may be disclosed. These may prove to be foundational. Any attempt to give form to our spontaneous human unfolding or to receive form connotes principles that could be integrated into some theory of formation. We begin to sense the possibility of the emergence of a science of formation.

The Ground of Consonance between Preformation and Formation

Our life formation is first of all preformation. Before we are able to give form to our life, we are already preformed in a certain way. Human formation could be defined as a creative tension between our human spirit as formative and our life's preformation. This tension has to be kept within the limits of tolerance; it should not become excessive.

One means to counteract excessive tension in this regard is to seek a deeper ground of formation that gives meaning to both preformation and formation. The science of formative spirituality assumes that there is a mystery of formation at the root of all formation in universe, world and history, including all forms of human formation and preformation. The *ground of consonance* between preformation and formation is to be found in this all-encompassing mystery of formation. It is the root of all life in and around us.

Within us, this mystery manifests itself in concrete form directives. Such forming directives are either preformed or adopted from our culture and its underlying form traditions. They are available as directives in the situations that coform our life from conception to death.

Manifestation of the Mystery of Formation in Initial Formation

The mystery of formation encompasses both preformation and formation in an original unity. When our response to both is consonant with this mystery, we experience their harmonious interwovenness. Both are made meaningful to us in the human love and care that are inspired by the formation mystery to which we abandon ourselves in faith, hope, and consonance.

How is this care of the mystery of formation manifested from the onset of human life? It is expressed in the faith, hope, and love of parents for their children. Human procreation of life establishes from the beginning a caring situation of human formation. This *initial formation* is exercised through vital bodily acts of nourishment, physical concern, and intimacy. Already some elementary human formation is effected through these acts. Through this vital care, the child is taken up in a special community of people living by similar preferred form directives. Parents or guardians give form to the life situation they share with their children. This shared field of formation initiates children in certain communal forms of living that are rooted in form traditions. Children search for their own *empirical life-form* in light of these concrete directions. At least in some measure their search will be influenced by these form directives, even if they oppose them later in life.

Form directives are dynamically present in parents and their form traditions. They precede any reflective appraisal and choice of life formation on the part of the children. They are a manifestation of the mystery of destiny or of foundational form direction. This original orientation precedes any later formation. It represents the dim preformative beginning of any course our life may assume. It is the mystery of the foundational life direction that allows this life to be conceived by these particular parents. This mystery allowed our life to happen in a specific moment of time and space with all the sociohistorical pressures such specifications imply.

All subsequent formation is understandable only on the basis of this mystery of initial preformation. It allows our life to be conceived, born, nourished, cared for, and guided by parents or guardians in their distinct sociohistorical milieu. Our genetic form potential, too, is a source of this foundational preformative direction of our human life in the world.

Primary Foundation of All Formation

The primary foundation of all formation is ontological; it refers to a forming direction of the universe and of humanity that cannot be controlled, manipulated, or exhaustively understood by means of clear and distinct concepts. This preformative direction does not make our formation responsibility superfluous. On the contrary, it demands that we explore its challenges freely and wisely. We are free to deny this foundational direction at our own peril, or we may disclose and appraise it progressively. We are invited to make the best of it. We should ratify unchangeable points of departure for our formation. Likewise we should contest formative meanings that are dissonant. Often these are imposed by social or cultural pressure. These swirl around us from infancy to old age. It is our calling and our responsibility to open ourselves freely in human faith, hope, and consonance to this mystery of foundational preformation. It illuminates the beginning of our life; it accompanies us to our death.

Prereflective and Scientific Knowledge of Foundational Formation

The fact that we can ask questions about formation means that we must already have a dim knowledge of what we are asking. How else could we even raise such questions? Some kind of knowledge about formation must already be ours. This knowledge emerges from our daily experiences. Human life is already a process of formation. It manifests consonant or dissonant effects. All human life reveals the tendency to find its form and to give form to its surroundings. Before any reflection, we are already familiar with formation by living it. We experience life as formation.

Life is dimly experienced as a succession of attempts to realize certain forms. Such attempts are vaguely perceived as tending to a basic unique form of life: each person feels called to formation in some mysterious way. Formation belongs to our being. It is the root of our becoming. It coforms the situations we make ours during our life's journey. Our own forming attempts change in some measure the situations in which life unfolds and expands itself.

We are prereflectively aware that formation implies a *transcendent dynamic*. We strive to go beyond the life forms we already are. We want to expand, improve, or replace the forms we have already created in and around us. We see this dynamic in the child growing from infancy, the adolescent maturing to adulthood, the middle-aged person seeking a deeper way of life, the student and scholar acquiring new knowledge, the athlete mastering new forms of muscle control, the artist transcending the forms he has already created, and the parents giving better form to the life of the child.

From all evidence, this transcendent dynamic includes an implicit awareness that one is called to a higher form of life. This dynamic manifests itself in all formation events. These events in turn can be experienced and understood in light of this dynamic. All formation of human life, whether in infancy or adulthood or in any of life's vocations, participates in the transcendent dynamic of human formation. The basic positions of the science of formation are all elaborations of the same experience of the transcendent tendency of human formation.

A fully developed life-form can only be approached gradually and partially. We grow to it along a gradient of *unfolding life dimensions, current life-forms,* and *formation phases.* Hence, the anthropology of human life as formative must include an analysis of various aspects of formation, these being, among others, form potencies, life-forms and dimensions, levels of consciousness, and formation phases of human life. Such powers and dimensions are constant in their foundational structure. However, our reflective knowledge of them is open to a continuous correction and refinement in light of new imaginative intuitions, data, and theoretical insights. The science of foundational formation starts out, therefore, from the fact that we have a prereflective a priori awareness of foundational formation.

The Starting Point of Reflection on Our Formation Experience

This science can be illumined by transcendent, imaginative formation intuitions, provided we start out from concrete formative events. We must look at them as they appear in daily life. They should be events that imply forming experiences, such as suffering, joy, anxiety, waiting, crisis, despair, appraisal, desire, understanding, love, failure, fidelity. The science of formation can emerge only as a *proximate science* by means of reflection upon concrete formation experience. In this reflection we become present to our formation. We begin to see it as an incarnation of the transcendent dynamic inherent in human life. We begin to discover that this dynamic is awakened in us by our interaction with a formation field. This field is reflected in our successive situations and by interaction with our communities and form traditions.

Our critical intelligence drives us to ask formation questions and to search for the right answers. In this asking and searching, the disposition of formative thinking develops. This deepens our power of reflection on formative events, their meanings, obstacles, and facilitating conditions. The act of *reflection* on formation is gradually perfected, corrected, elaborated, and refined. It gives rise to increasingly reliable methods of critical evaluation and validation of insights and findings. We can develop these by reflection. Such reflection should be complemented by comparison with the findings and insights of others in this field and in *auxiliary sciences* and form traditions. We conclude that the question about life as formational has to start out from concrete formative events that appear in our formation field. The science thus begins as an articulation of formative experience.

The initial awareness of human formation is spontaneous, vague, and undifferentiated. Formation happens in interaction with others, with the immediate situation, with the world, and with preformative influences. The science of formation turns this initial awareness into scientific reflection. This reflection is systematic, intersubjectively validated, and logically formulated. It purifies our spontaneous awareness from its subjectivistic and popular accretions. While such purification is necessary, we should never lose touch with our spontaneous formation awareness. Neither should we remove ourselves totally from the transcendent-imaginative source of intuitions that stimulate our creative thought in this area and keep it in consonance with the whole of formation.

We should realize that *prereflexive awareness* has its own design, language, and logic—its own coherent pattern of forming meaning. We can penetrate into this prelogical language of formative experience and analyze its structure. We can, for instance, select a formation event we experience in our life and make its structure explicit. As scientists of formation, we should try to separate its foundational elements from subjectivistic, personal, and regional or popular pulsations and accretions.

Scientific knowledge of formation emerges from and is nourished by our everyday formation awareness. Hence, we can only fully understand our scientific formulations when we grasp our primary awareness of formation in the world of everyday life. Without reference to the real world of daily formation, the science of formative spirituality would be a logical structure irrelevant to actual human formation in its richness and complexity. Foundational human formation as it really is in its dialogical fullness would evaporate. It would gradually disappear in the rarefied heights of abstraction. The forming person would be lost in such a system. The science of foundational formation would become a satire on the researchers of formation themselves. For they themselves, as living persons in formation, would find in such a system neither an explanation nor a meaningful place. There would be no relationship between the intellectual structure about human formation and the actual formation of the researchers who devised and developed that structure.

Scientific Fields of Human Formation

Initially, the awareness of the formation of human life is prescientific. Scholars and scientists reflected on this awareness and their reflection became increasingly critical and systematic. The systematization of critical reflection on the formation of human life and its corresponding world then began to differentiate itself into various sciences of human formation. Examples are the sciences of education, pedagogy, and specialized formation for various human functions. Finally, there emerged the science of foundational human formation, which is our topic here. (The term science is not meant here in the restricted sense in which it is often used by students of the physical sciences. In the context of this study, science refers to any open, systematic body of data, integrating theories and presuppositions that is validated by its own proper research methodology, including intersubjective methods of validation by acknowledged researchers in the same field of disciplined interest.)

The differentiation of the sciences dates from the Renaissance. Prior to this differentiation, many sciences were contained in the *theoretical sciences* of philosophy and theology. During the history of scientific development, the physical sciences were the first to gain their autonomy. Later, social sciences such as psychology, sociology, and cultural anthropology became independent. Especially relevant to this study is the emergence of *human-formation sciences* such as education, pedagogy, specialized formation, and the science of foundational human formation.

The science of education is concerned primarily with training teachers and secondarily with the developmental and pedagogical problems that emerge in the teaching relationship, either in the restricted sense of schoolteaching or in the wide sense of any educational effort in the family and other social institutions. Pedagogy, as a science, is not separately developed in most American institutions of higher learning. It has a respected academic position in many European universities. The interest of its doctoral students reaches beyond a primary concentration on educational methods. Its scholars and practitioners occupy themselves also with certain problems of human formation, especially as these emerge in the preadult stages of life. A newly developing field of study at certain European universities is that of "andragogy," which focuses primarily on the meanings, dynamics, and conditions of human formation as they manifest themselves in people of all ages and in all stages of personal development.

The new science of foundational formation, or formative spirituality, is related to, yet essentially distinct from, the field of andragogy. Foundational human formation directs itself primarily to a study of the transcultural universal foundations that underlie all formation dynamics, values, conditions, obstacles, and problems. The science of formation unfolds and structures itself on the basis of its investigation of foundational human formation experiences and their presuppositions. The frame of reference thus acquired is tested and enriched by means of a *dialogical and integrative* research methodology that takes into account, critically and creatively, the potential contributions of auxiliary sciences and formation traditions. (Here we usually abbreviate the term formation traditions as form traditions.)

Prescientific Presuppositions

Like all sciences, foundational formation starts out from prescientific presuppositions that should be critically clarified and evaluated. Such clarification is done in dialogue with the auxiliary sciences that are remotely directive in regard to human formation. Examples are the theoretical sciences of philosophy and theology.

Furthermore, the science of formative spirituality integrates critically and creatively within its foundational frame the relevant contributions of form traditions and of other auxiliary arts and sciences that are incarnational or proximately directive in regard to human formation. Examples of the latter are cultural history, history of ideas, medicine, theoretical physics, pharmacology, music, the representational arts, literature, history of religion, ethnology, anthropology, sociology, psychology, psychiatry, and neurology, biochemistry, education, pedagogy, andragogy, and special formation sciences.

The main presupposition of this science is that the distinctive characteristic, the foundation of the foundations of the formation of the human person as human, is the *human spirit*. The human spirit is the power to give form to our life and its corresponding formation field in a way that transcends an absolute determination by the vital-functional laws that rule the infrahuman, macro-, and microcosmic universe. The foundational forming influence of the human spirit gives rise to a unique style of typically human or spiritual formation and expression. Such styles of distinctively human life formation are called spiritualities. Underlying and permeating all such human spiritualities is an elementary foundational spirituality, a basic style of human formation that is in principle congenial to all effective human formation attempts.

Elements of such a foundational spirituality are the potentially or actually observable varied qualities and intensities found in all consonant special spiritualities. The science of foundational formation can thus also properly be called the science of formative spirituality. This foundational spiritual formation and its resultant spirituality are not necessarily bound to any specific cultural, ideological, or religious formation tradition (such as humanism, Freudianism, Buddhism, Islam, Hinduism, Judaism, or Christianity). Formation scientists will take into account the relevant contributions of such ancient or modern traditions, just as they may take into account the relevant data and insights of the auxiliary sciences.

In summary, the uniquely distinctive mark of humanity and its formation is the transcendent or spiritual nature of human life. The effect of this distinctive mark of formation is a proximate and immediate penetration by the human spirit of all formation powers, dimensions, articulations, awareness states, and phases of human life and its corresponding formation field. Such penetration is fostered by a specific style of life called a spirituality. The various styles, or spiritualities, when consonant with the essentials of human life, contain the elements of a foundational spirituality that is in principle common to all.

To offer a succinct definition: Formative spirituality is the foundational, proximate way of receiving distinctively human or spiritual formation and of humanly giving form to life and world. Once this foundational, receptive, and active formation process and its conditions and presuppositions have been researched and verified scientifically or intersubjectively, they can be articulated by complementary research in terms of classical form traditions or traditional formative spiritualities.

Christian Articulation Research

The differentiation of the sciences out of philosophy and theology is a process that continues to this day. The present development of the new science of formative spirituality demonstrates this ongoing differentiation. It also implies a differentiation in corresponding form traditions. Form traditions are usually clarified by philosophical and theological reflections and carry with them the fruits of such reflections. Hence, it is necessary to differentiate such form traditions not only from their faith traditions but also from their philosophies and theologies. The universal, foundational science of formation has in turn to be differentiated from all of them. Until recent times this final differentiation has been marked by overreaction. The scientist's search for autonomy was marked by a fear of the possible return of an exclusive domination of the human formation sciences by prescientific form traditions and their corresponding philosophies and theologies. The fear of domination was so deep that teachers of the formation sciences were inclined, even in Christian schools and universities, to eliminate all references to the Christian form tradition.

At present a shift is taking place. We witness the beginning of a new understanding. There is a growing awareness that Christian universities seem less in consonance with that name if, for instance, their departments of psychology, sociology, pedagogy, and education allow secular philosophies and other form traditions to dominate exclusively. An increasing number of Christian scholars and teachers in various *formation sciences* begin to doubt the wisdom of systematically excluding any reference to the Christian form tradition. They question the presentation of secular presuppositions and theories as the only possible integrating frame of reference for scientific data. They begin to ask why we should have Christian institutes of higher learning if they systematically fail to include any reasonable, critical reference to the Christian tradition. The same question can be asked in Buddhist, Jewish, or Islamic universities. Among some teachers in Christian universities, we observe a growing tendency to explain to students how the validated data and insights of their respective autonomous fields can be articulated also in terms of their Christian tradition.

In light of this new climate, the ultimate goal of our discussion is to show how the science of foundational formation can be articulated in terms of the Christian form tradition. The wisdom of this tradition can complement the foundational humanistic, vitalistic, functionalistic, or behavioristic theories of secular theorists of formation without neglecting their relevant insights.

Distinction between the Science of Formation and the Philosophy of Formation

As noted earlier, the foundational approach to human formation tries to make explicit its philosophical presuppositions. Every science must do the same in relation to its own presuppositions. Such necessary clarification does not mean, however, that the science concerned becomes a subdivision of philosophy. The science of foundational proximate formation is primarily and ultimately concerned with the study of concrete formative events, proximate form directives, and the solution of the practical foundational formation problems people face in their formation history. It does not aim to develop a complete philosophy of formation. Philosophical presuppositions are explicated and mutually related to one another only in so far as they affect the study of proximate concrete human formation. The style and direction of this explication is marked by its applicability to practical problems and its relevance to the development of a foundational praxis-oriented formation theory.

The scientific theoretical discourse of the practical science of formation is essentially different from that of philosophy. To be sure, the science should utilize auxiliary philosophical concepts in the clarification of its presuppositions. The further developments of the science itself, however, are necessarily guided by the particular form traditions, methods of exploration, and theory construction proper to the practical science of foundational human formation. They are fundamentally different from those of the science of philosophy. The same must be said of the relationship between Christian articulation of this science and the possible utilization of theological concepts to clarify the presuppositions of the Christian tradition.

Before preceding with the theory of formation itself, we will treat further preliminary questions and presuppositions.

CHAPTER 2

Preliminary Questions

Chapter 1 introduced us to the quest for a science of formation, but further questions pertaining to this theory necessarily arise. We will try in this chapter to answer some of them before going more deeply into the presuppositions of the science as such.

Formative spirituality is the name given to this new art and discipline. It is concerned with the foundations of the theory and practice of human formation, as well as with descriptions, explications, and analyses of formative events. It studies from a foundational viewpoint the essence, basic dynamics, consequences, and conditions of formation. It critically appraises the prescientific intuitions and experiences in this field. It integrates systematically the insights that prove to be valid and studies their meaning for the everyday life of the individual and for society.

Formative spirituality, or foundational human formation, emerges as a systematic science from prescientific maxims, intuitions, practices, and experiences that have guided humanity in its never ending effort of formation from the beginning of its history.

This science starts out from an in-depth study of two interrelated and essential characteristics of human life. The first one is our innate *formability*, or potency to give and receive form. The second is the essential human dynamic of ongoing life and world formation. Formative spirituality is studied, therefore, from the perspective of the questions that emerge from our essential formability and formation.

In this investigation we need to ask ourselves such questions as: What is the object and method of any formative spirituality, Christian or non-Christian? How is this science related to these approaches? What about its relationship to the arts and sciences and to human life in general? Are some of these approaches auxiliary disciplines of formative spirituality? Once we know which sciences are auxiliary, the methodological question arises: How can they be used in a way that is scientifically responsible?

In this chapter, it may be useful to consider not only the nature of the science of foundational formation but also its position in the academic and professional world. This consideration may be served by a discussion of some of the assumptions of this discipline. These assumptions may be understood in light of the situation that gave rise to this field of research.

Formation science emerged out of historical necessity. The need for it became evident when our world began to become a global village. The coming together of many countries led to an interdependence of their cultures. People of different cultures began to exchange ideas, including ideas about human formation. This sharing made it in principle possible to gather the best available experience, knowledge, and wisdom of all these cultures in regard to the formation of the lives of people and of their societies. Certain persons could specialize in the collection and integration of such intercultural knowledge. Together they could establish a foundational universal science of formation. Such cooperation could prevent an overdependence of less-developed nations on special form traditions that guide the particular formation of people in the technically developed nations. (This overdependency might tempt the Western nations to suppress the formation wisdom of developing countries. Such oppression would be a manifestation of social injustice in the field of human formation.) Since the purpose of this science is to identify basic dynamics and structures of human formation, these basic dynamics and structures should not be limited to Western modulations of their meaning.

A rigorous method guarantees the science's objectivity. It secures the identification and validation of foundational data and insights of Western and Eastern form traditions, arts, and sciences. It assists in the selection of data and insights that can be utilized as building stones for an internationally meaningful, foundationally formative science of life, society and the world.

Six Basic Assumptions of the Science of Foundational Human Formation

One of the science's assumptions has been that human formation, by necessity, participates in the laws of formation of the micro- and macrocosmic universe of mineral, plant, and animal formation studied in the physical and biological sciences.

Another equally important assumption has been that our formation bears a distinctively human quality. This distinctive mark manifests itself in formation abilities, demands, and desires that transcend the cosmic formation processes in which human life also shares. This distinctively human quality of formation has been acknowledged by most great cultural traditions. They have given it various names, one of which is spirit, or *spiritual formation power*.

This acknowledgement of a spiritual formation power in all humans led to a third assumption shared by the great world traditions of formation. It is that the sociohistorical, vital, and functional formation of life and culture should be directed and pervaded by the spirit power, or *transcendence dynamic*, of human life. The art and discipline of fostering such direction and pervasion of all form dimensions by the human spirit has been given various names in diverse cultures. One of these is spirituality. This universal spirituality, or basic humanization, could be called foundational formative spirituality.

The fourth leading assumption of the science deals with the social radius of this spiritualization. It holds that local and international concern for social justice and its facilitating conditions in the realm of formation is an essential and integral element of foundational human spirituality itself. The latter can never be reduced to concern for one's inner life alone. A consonant life formation for the maximum number of people is impossible to pursue in an unjust or merciless society.

A fifth assumption of the science is that the formation wisdom of humanity tends to be articulated in specific cultural form traditions of a religious or ideological nature. Such traditions may contain less or more than the original formation wisdom of humanity. The symbols and records of these form traditions are among the main sources of study of humanity's formation experience. Moreover, one of the conditions of consonant formation is participation in one or more of these form traditions. Formation scientists may first bracket such articulations to gain critical insight into the essentials of formation. Afterwards, they may return to the study of one or more of these articulations to enlighten their specific topic of research. Some formation scientists may even opt to do *articulation research* in one specific form tradition, such as the Christian, the humanist, the Marxist, the Islamic, the Jewish, the Buddhist. Their aim is to study the effectiveness of the implementation of the formation tenets of such a tradition in the light of the data and insights gained by the science of formative spirituality.

Another assumption by which this science operates is that its research should be relevant to the praxis of formation. Like the sciences of medicine, law, education, business administration, or music, this science, too, prepares not only academicians but also professional practitioners.

Human Formation and Christian Formation

Those readers who are Christians may feel at the outset a genuine concern for Christian formation. For them to know about this formation, it may seem most simple to study directly the formative dynamics of Christian spirituality.

However, another approach may serve a Christian understanding of formation indirectly. This one starts out from a consideration of the formative dynamics that operate in all people. Humans are endowed with an aspiration for transcendence. Formation scientists want to know how people respond to this aspiration. Do they allow themselves to become aware of it? Do they refuse to let it enter into their focal consciousness? Why do they respond the way they do? Do those who are aware of this aspiration engage in distinctively human or spiritual formation? If so, do they reflect on what happens to them while they are giving form to their lives? Do some of them report on these reflections? Do they try to appraise them critically? Do they validate them intersubjectively? Do they organize their reflections in a systematic way? In other words, do they try to develop a science of formation? Can we learn from their attempts? Can we in turn be of help to them?

Some Christian readers may ask themselves: Why should we be interested in the formative insights of those who do not share our Christian revelation? The answer resides in our remembering that as Christians we are called to love all people. In a spirit of justice and mercy, we should foster anything that can facilitate human goodness and happiness everywhere. Spiritual formation will make the lives of people more appreciative, joyful, whole, and effective. Human formation may be complemented and perfected by the graced formation that is the gift of the Holy Spirit. How could we in justice withhold loving interest in the formation of others and still believe ourselves to be channels of care for the mystery of formation for all people?

Another reason for our interest in human formation is the scholastic principle that grace builds on nature. Insight into the transcendent nature of human unfolding will facilitate our understanding of the accommodation of grace to this aspect of nature.

Such insight into the harmonization of human and graced formation, or of what we will later call transcendent and pneumatic formation, may help to deepen our own spiritual life. We may become holy not only in the core of our being, but also find ways to allow grace to make us more integrated, less tense and anxious, more appreciative, poised, form potent, and attractive in our whole personality. We may begin to experience and exemplify in our daily existence that the formation inspired by revelation respects, deepens, and enhances all consonant human formation.

Academic Study in This Field

People may wonder what students in the field of formation, or formative spirituality, will study. What can one expect from graduates in formative spirituality and its articulation in the Christian form tradition? What is their function, their contribution? How do they plan to make a living? Students ask themselves these questions, also.

Course work is done in the science of foundational human formation and its articulation in the various form traditions, notably the Christian tradition. In service of many possible articulations of the science, they study the art and discipline of formative reading of Scripture and the writings of the fathers, doctors, and spiritual masters of the church. They also trace the findings of ascetical and mystical theology as seen from the formative viewpoint. The curriculum also includes Christian formation theory; practical spiritual exercises, like journal keeping; formative direction and counseling; formative liturgy, and the dynamics of church, grace, and sacraments. They seek to discover how a unified science of formation and a corresponding Christian articulation can emerge from such a variety of studies. They cannot help but compare their courses with those given in similar fields of interest elsewhere. The information they gather in this way may only add to their confusion. Some tell them the study of formation is a training in techniques; others say it is a subdivision of theology; others contend that it is an anthropological, philosophical, psychological, sociological, or educational tool. The students ask themselves with some bewilderment: Who is right?

Lacking sufficient insight into the nature of this field, other questions arise: How is formation related to the various disciplines one has to scrutinize? How does this study integrate the insights and data of theoretical physics, personality theories, music, theology, literature, developmental psychology, philosophical anthropologies, and other arts and sciences? If they are auxiliary sciences of spirituality, how do they advance one's spiritual formation?

These questions are not merely academic. They are life questions for anyone committed to the study, teaching, and practice of formation. Even those who prepare themselves mainly for praxis in this field sense that they need a well-founded theory to back up their practical expertise. Is it possible to gain a unified and reliable background from the variety of readings and courses to which students must expose themselves in the graduate study of foundational human formation?

The Need for a Science of Formation

Many of us are convinced that Christianity and humanity are in need of a foundational theory of formation. Such a theory should keep central the spiritual characteristics of human life, their consonant unfolding and incarnation in all dimensions of one's world. What is needed is a view of "formation as spiritual" that integrates harmoniously the fundamental insights and data relevant to spiritual unfolding. It should take into account important findings of the arts and sciences.

The science of formative spirituality and its articulation in the Christian form tradition intends to develop the art and discipline of human formation. It hopes that such insights and data can help persons and communities find and develop their unique life-form in any phase of their history. It is evident that no one scholar, student, or publication alone could develop such a foundational approach. Formative spirituality points to a never ending, dedicated effort for generations of scholars and practitioners to come.

Why Foundational Formation?

In what sense do we use the term foundational in expressions like the science of foundational human formation, its articulation in the foundational Christian form tradition, and foundational formative spirituality?

The word foundational connotes the opposite of special. For example, when we affirm our interest in foundational Christian formation, we mean that our primary concern is not for its special types of expression. These latter expressions are perhaps more familiar to us than the foundations of Christian formation. Special modes of formation prepare persons for special tasks, life-styles, apostolates, and attitudes in Christian life. One can develop courses of formation for the apostolate of peace and justice in the world, for service in the underdeveloped countries, for nursing, or for teaching. These are only a few instances of the numerous possibilities open for special formation.

Because our age is praxis oriented, we are inclined to prepare ourselves and others for practical enterprises. Such preparation is undoubtedly of great value. Without it, Christianity could not incarnate itself concretely in the modern world. This raises the question of what foundational Christian formation means. Why is it necessary? What is its relationship to practical formation for a specific task?

As the word itself indicates, foundational formation is concerned with the basic dynamism of human and Christian life. It is not focused primarily on the attitudes and ways in which people can effectively implement a concrete calling in the world. It is concerned with the general consonant unfolding of their graced inner life. It pays attention to their basic attitudes in formative interaction with others and with their formative field as a whole, no matter the concrete task to which they are called.

To be sure, it is not enough for us to be formed only in this basic way. Once we are involved in a concrete task, we have to prepare ourselves to make a detailed response. We believe, however, that to be effective in this specialized task presupposes that we have received a foundational formation that, so to speak, puts our inner house in order. This kind of formation helps us to unfold inwardly and harmoniously, to order our faculties in a wise way, to cope with neurotic or traumatic remnants of our childhood, to facilitate our effective interaction with our formation field, and to open up in apostolic interest to the world.

In other words, foundational formation tries to provide the human and Christian basis for any other specialized formation whatsoever. Those who have experienced working with persons in concrete missions know the consequences when a splendid apostolic formation for a specific task is not supported by a deeper foundational formation. They may not have found their identity before God nor overcome inner conflicts that have perturbed them since childhood.

Perhaps we have known dedicated people, effective in a distinct apostolate or career, marvelous in their heroic fight for peace and justice, great in the administration of educational enterprises, generous in nursing the sick and caring for the poor. We may have seen these good, in some cases outstanding, people suddenly collapse or lose their way, overwhelmed by sexual or alcoholic problems, nervous breakdowns, constant conflicts, and other defeats. We witness the steady increase in counseling centers, guest houses, houses of affirmation, and similar special services to help an increasing number of people who have given themselves so generously to all kinds of contemporary apostolates.

Once they come to these centers of transformation, they soon discover that the people who assist them do not focus on concrete detailed formation for a more effective apostolate. On the contrary, they try to supply what is missing in the foundational formation of persons who could not continue their work. They try to find ways to disclose what is foundationally wrong in the human and Christian makeup of a personality. What kind of conflict was perhaps touched upon but not resolved by their special apostolic formation. The aim of this care is to assist them in laying new foundations. Often the results are remarkable. They go back into their apostolates and again become administrators of schools, ministers for peace and justice, missionaries in near or distant countries. They are now able to cope with life since a foundational transformation has taken place within them. Only now does their commitment to special groups of the population come to full flowering.

What has been missing all along was not the effective training and style of living necessary for their particular apostolate. Lacking was a foundational formation that would enable them to keep inner strength, peace, and consonance in the midst of contradiction and adversity. A deeper formation was necessary to enable them to interact formatively with people around them without a growing number of conflicts. A more foundational approach made it possible for them, with God's grace, to live with the Lord and to remain effective in spite of the suffering that any special apostolate necessarily entails.

Often when we speak with people who have been healed in one of these centers or in counseling and spiritual direction programs, we hear the same complaint. Why didn't we receive this formation in the home, school, seminary, or convent? Why did we receive our formation in a special way instead of in a foundational way? Why didn't we start out with this foundational approach that is the basis of all effective apostolic life orientations? As some put it: Why did we try to build our foundational formation on a special apostolic formation instead of the other way around? How much suffering could we have been spared if we had been initiated by wise, experienced people, prepared to pass on the wisdom of foundational formation? If we had received a sound basic formation, how much easier it would have been to acquaint ourselves with the special techniques of spirituality and human presence that we needed to accomplish the tasks given to us by God!

Similar complaints are now increasingly heard among the laity. Christian lay people today often show an interest in the spiritual life and in serving the church in its spiritual or apostolic enterprises. They may be invited to participate fully in one of these efforts or approaches. We find in the laity the same problems that are encountered by priests and religious in their special apostolates. They begin to manifest problems, anxieties, and needs that are due to inner conflicts that have not been touched on in their formation for a particular mission. Many find relief only when they receive the foundational formation that was lacking. In the light of this formation, their special orientation gains new depth and meaning. They return to their apostolates, families, and careers in far more effective, relaxed, and harmonious ways. Problems that unconsciously interfered with their prayer life and their interaction with others have finally been resolved.

Foundational and Special Theories of Formation

What is the distinction between our foundational-synthetic understanding of formation and the special theories exemplified in the *particular school versions* of human and Christian formation? We could describe a *school of spirituality* as follows: it is a categorical, in principle restrictive, lasting preorientation of a group's spiritual approach. It directs its outlook and formation in service of some specific style of life, community, work, devotion, apostolate, and shared history. It is often inspired by a part of the world population, such as Western or European. What do such preorientations of formation imply?

First of all, there is a preselected emphasis on certain foundations of formation. The followers of a particular school version are encouraged to give special attention to these favored foundations. When the particular school is sound, it does not deny or totally neglect other foundations. All are represented in some way in the school version, but they thematize especially their preferred or emphatic foundations.

The emphatic character of a particular school version of formation leads also to the preselection of a specific hierarchy of foundations. A school of spirituality usually evolves in service of a lifestyle and a task chosen by the group that originates and develops it, and it exhibits certain favored foundations that have been relevant to the personalities and aims of the people who make up the original group. The preferred foundations of such personality types form a certain inner hierarchy in tune with the hierarchy of their shared interest and attention. Naturally, a particular school version will foster its preferred foundation. This preference characterizes the approach to formation.

A preference for certain foundations over others leads necessarily to a corresponding preselection of the means of formation. A particular school version tends to favor those approaches that assure a central position for what we have called the emphatic foundations. The school version of spirituality highlights ways and means that can implement these preferred foundationals more centrally in the hearts and minds of the members of the group itself. It may do the same for outsiders who sense an affinity between the unique life-form to which they are called and the basic life-form of followers of the particular school.

This preselection expands itself, though usually implicitly, to all aspects of a particular formation system that gradually emerges.

One important aspect of our *interformation* is the influence we allow certain persons, periods, and events in formation history to exert on our formation today. A particular school of spirituality is inclined to preselect from the history of formation those persons, periods, and events that are more directly relevant to the particular formative preorientation of this version of spirituality.

Hence, we may say that the primary objective of a particular school of spiritual formation is not to form people to an equal attention to and elaboration of all foundations of the rich heritage of the church's spiritual formation. Neither is its primary objective to approach these foundations with all available relevant methods of investigation. Its main aim is not to study the foundations of formation equally under all possible conditions. Neither is it a constant and primary concern of a particular school version of spirituality to liberate itself from its own categorical preorientation. It does not necessarily foster continuous attention to the possible hardening of its categories into an absolutized version of formation. Its first concern is not necessarily to keep this version open to new input and correction. A particular school of spiritual formation does not aim to develop systematically and foundationally the universal knowledge or science of the spiritual form traditions of humanity and Christianity as they can be known and enriched at this moment of history.

Comparison with the Field of Spiritual Theology

Spiritual theology, like all theology, is essentially different from the theoretical-practical science of formation in the same way as theology is essentially different from, yet indispensable to, Christian psychiatry, psychology, education, pedagogy, and so forth. The articulation of Christian formation takes theology into account. It is one of its auxiliary sciences, just as the science of engineering is sustained by mathematics as one of its auxiliary sciences. Engineering is not thereby reduced to mathematics nor is the science of formation reduced to the auxiliary discipline of theology because it takes into account its dogmatic axioms and their explanations. Nonetheless, we can make a comparison between certain developments in the science of formation and similar developments in the science of theology. In this case, we would like to compare the basic approach to spirituality by theology and by the science of foundational formation.

Take for example the spiritual theology of Tanquerey. His book on this topic was not an attempt to develop a particular school of spirituality to be called the school of Tanquerey. A simple comparison of Tanquerey's compendium of ascetical and mystical theology with some special school of spirituality indicates the difference. For instance, we may compare his compendium with de Montfort's Marian school of spirituality. Tanquerey's compendium was an attempt to develop a universally valid, comprehensive theological science of Catholic spirituality. The particular school of de Montfort's spirituality presents us, among other things, with a way of life that enables a person to form his spirituality around the so-called act of slavery to Mary

Reading de Montfort's book on the slavery to Mary does not give us a full insight into the historical richness of Catholic spirituality as developed over all the centuries and potentially enriched today by form traditions outside the small European enclave of Catholic Christianity. Tanquerey's spiritual theology tries to give us a more comprehensive insight into the full historical richness of the foundational spirituality of the church as knowable at that time. Still, a theological science that takes into account the full richness of the foundational spirituality of the church can and should integrate within this fullness some of the basic contributions made by de Montfort in relation to the place of Mary in the spirituality of the Roman Catholic church.

This comparison may deepen our insights into the difference between the science of foundational formation and the knowledge of a particular version of spirituality. Special school versions teach ways in which a person with the right affinity can form his or her life around some preferred foundations that are elaborated in a specific way and supported by special means, thus helping to assure the central position of such foundations in one's life. The science of foundational formation takes into account the form traditions of humanity and Christianity and their potential present-day enrichment; it also integrates within this foundational frame of reference contributions made by special schools of formation. Its primary aim, however, is to establish and to keep open a universally valid comprehensive science of human formation and to articulate the Christian form tradition in the light of this science.

The comparison with spiritual theology is also significant in another respect. The study of Christian formation makes clear that most particular versions of formation were historically linked to the special schools of spirituality that developed in Christianity over the centuries, especially in the limited Euro-American enclave of spiritual formation teachings and special spiritualities.

Importance of Particular School Versions of Spirituality

Particular versions of spirituality are a great gift to Christianity. They have been an effective means for countless Christians to give form to their lives in tune with their personality, culture, life-style, or apostolic preference. An elaboration and refinement of the foundations of Christian formation took place in and through the schools of formation that concentrated on making some of those foundations the center of their attention. The formation of the church has to be personalized in each Christian. Many groups of Christians share certain characteristics with one another. Hence, they can in some measure personalize together the foundational formation principles of humanity and their articulations in the Christian form tradition. They do so by developing together a school of formation that systematizes and thematizes a special version of the foundations in tune with personality characteristics they all share.

In a sense, a special version of formation functions as a bridge between foundational and personal formation. Even Christians who form themselves in the light of such a particular school still have to personalize uniquely its special emphasis for they share it with similar but not identical personalities. Moreover, some of them may belong to different cultural form traditions.

We conclude that the merits of special versions of formation are immense both for individual Christians and for the development of foundational spirituality. Therefore, the more versions that are available the better it is, provided none of them is presented as *the* foundational way of the church, necessary or useful for all types of Christians. Another condition is that such versions ought to contain, at least implicitly, the foundations of human and Christian formation. Surely, they must not be in opposition to any of them.

The necessary and desirable proliferation of particular variants of formation could give rise to the mistaken notion that all the faithful without exception should receive their formation in and through one or another specialized rendition of spirituality. Rather, the opposite is true. Such specialization is more the exception than the rule among millions of Christians who have been initiated over the centuries in their form tradition. The overwhelming majority of Christians receive their spirituality implicitly, in and through the living wisdom of the church as expressed in the following sources: Scripture readings; sacramental life and liturgy; doctrine of Christian formation; clergy as functioning in the ministry of reconciliation, preaching, and formative direction; religious and laity as functioning in the ministry of teaching Christian formation and in other ministries that are part of their charism.

Only a small percentage of the world's Christians belongs to and feels at ease with one or another restricted, specialized understanding of the tradition of Christianity. Sometimes such small groups of sympathizers, with a specific spirituality exemplified by a religious community, may be considered different or unusual by their neighbors or fellow Christians. In these cases their special style does not seem to fit in with the everyday situation of the Christian in the world. It is interesting to note that the majority of parents whose sons and daughters entered specific religious communities were themselves not enrolled in the mode of spirituality represented by these communities. For the most part, though, they seemed to have been formed sufficiently in the foundational ways of the church to be able to plant the seed of spiritual life in their children.

Another observation could be made about Christians who identify with a particular mode of spirituality. It seems that only a small percentage of them actually restrict themselves for a lifetime to the rendition that was temporarily meaningful or interesting to them. Many of them sooner or later move into the fullness of their human and Christian heritage. It is as if this special version was formative for them at that particular passing moment of their history.

The Cultural-Personal Coloring of Christian Formation
To be sure, all Christians manifest a cultural and personal coloring in the expression of their spiritual life. Such coloring should not be confused with something quite different, namely, the lasting, categorical preorientation of one's formation by a particular variant of the form tradition of Christianity. The first is unavoidable; the second, while in certain cases desirable, is, in principle, avoidable.

Some coloring of one's expression of Christianity is normal. This coloring is least harmful when it is acknowledged. It touches more the expression than the substance and scope of one's formation. It effects less closure than a particular school of formation may do in certain instances. If it effects some closure, it usually does so over a less prolonged period of time.

Cultural and personal coloring in expression does not necessarily restrict one's openness to the richness and possible variety of approaches to the foundations of Christian spirituality. Neither does it necessarily restrict the openness of a person or a passing cultural group to many other ways of Christian life.

These ways of formation are communicated in concrete illustrations. All of them show a cultural coloring, as manifest in Scripture, in liturgy and ritual, in religious art and legend. Such illustrations in the life of Christ and the tradition of the church do have a cultural flavor, but this in no way necessarily limits the manifestation of its foundations. On the contrary, this cultural expression by Christ and his followers can support and reveal the abundance and richness of the spirituality of Christianity. This is not to deny, of course, that the further coloration of particular school versions may be most beneficial for a specific group of people who feel a genuine affinity to their ways.

The focus of a special variant of spirituality may restrict the richness and variety of approaches that have been developed over the ages. It may limit also the use of the various ways of formation that have been initiated by Christianity over the centuries. The particular school version has to focus on its preferred foundations without denying or neglecting totally the others. Cultural and personal coloring leads also to some restriction, but usually to one that is more incidental, temporary, and casual. The illustrations adopted by a school version of formation are selected on the basis of the restricted frame of that particular school. This restriction is usually more lasting. Its favored illustrations may be carried over from generation to generation, from culture to culture. By contrast, the cultural and personal illustrations typical of a certain period are a result of this passing culture. Many of them do not carry over from generation to generation or from culture to culture.

The history of the Christian form tradition is rich and dynamic. It is marked by the continual emergence of tentative particular orientations of Christian life. Some of them develop into well-formulated versions of spirituality; they are sound from the theological and psychological viewpoint. Such schools can be a great blessing for Christians who by grace, predisposition, and personality can profit from such orientations.

The Terminology of the Science of Formation

Every science develops its own vocabulary. Why cannot one use words that are simple or popular today? For instance, why does the science not say fundamental or fundamentalist instead of foundational; existential instead of formative experience; situation ethics instead of the formative potential of the life situation; conservative or conserving instead of formative memory; progressive or liberal instead of formative anticipation; evolution instead of formation history; determinants instead of formative life directives; inner devotion instead of intraformation; self-actualization or personality fulfillment instead of life formation; therapeutic encounter and group dynamics instead of interformation, and so on?

To use familiar words does not necessarily mean that people will understand better what a science is all about. Neither does it suffice to give such terms a somewhat different meaning. During the early days of this science, we tried to do just that. We used the familiar words with explanations that attempted to invest them with a wider meaning. The results were disappointing. Because it used these familiar words, the science tended to be mistakenly identified by others as merely existential, phenomenological, logical positivist, fundamentalist, behaviorist, neo-Scholastic, determinist, or evolutionist; as promoting only hedonistic self-actualization, selfish personality fulfillment, progressive liberalism, conservatism, psychologism; as unaware of social needs or overconcerned with them, and so on. The impact of familiar words was so overwhelming that people were often unable to understand that these terms were being used in a different and original way. It is only since this new science, like every other one, began to develop its own terminology on the basis of a rigorous analysis of its own formal object that such caricatures began to fade.

Why must a region of specialized knowledge develop its own terminology? The answer can be found by consulting one of the many auxiliary sciences of foundational formation—analytic philosophy, or linguistic analysis. The unfamiliar term auxiliary is used here to indicate that such sciences are only consulted in so far as they may contribute insights or facts relevant to the science of formation. As a whole these sciences may not be relevant to human and Christian formation. In this case, the science of formation does not subscribe to the restrictions of the main principles of analytic philosophy. For instance, it does not support its absolute tenet that only that which can be verified in a purely empirical-rational way can be known for sure. This demand would ban all metaphysics from philosophy since its theses cannot be verified operationally.

Nevertheless, linguistic analysis has offered some helpful suggestions for the use of language. Ludwig Wittgenstein explains that the words we use daily are by their nature ambiguous and give rise to many connotations. Disciplined thought, as exercised in a science, entails a constant struggle against the confusion engendered by the special use of language in daily situations or in related sciences, disciplines, or social movements. The only way to avoid misunderstanding is to appraise the various meanings of words according to usage, function, and role. What do they mean in daily use, in other arts and sciences, or in social, political, and religious movements nourished by a variety of cultural pulsations? Understanding this, a science can select other terms or add qualifiers to familiar words.

We should remember that when people speak they do not use words that have exactly the same meaning in all life situations, movements, and sciences. In each one of them different "language games" are developed with different rules of usage. Hence, a science can only find its precision and identity by developing its own language game. Until it establishes its own terminology and its own use of this terminology, it is not yet a reliable and identifiable science, for it has not yet sufficiently identified its focus of research. In some way, therefore, the establishment of a science is equivalent to the establishment of a language.

The historian of science, Thomas S. Kuhn, provides us with another reason for the necessity of scientific language in his highly acclaimed book, *The Structure of Scientific Revolutions*. He demonstrates convincingly from numerous well-researched examples from the history of science that each new science unfolds itself on the basis of what he calls a new paradigm. This paradigm of research and reflection embodies a new perspective on a familiar matter that may have been researched for a long period of time by means of other paradigms. In the light of this new perspective, all facts and insights already known—or newly disclosed—obtain a new dimension of relevant meaning. This dimension demands a new language, especially in those social and human sciences that deal with phenomena whose partial meanings are already expressed elsewhere in terms that have become familiar to us.

There is also a psychological explanation for the desirability of a new terminology to express expanded insights and findings. The necessity of a fresh vocabulary is due to a certain inertia and subsequent conservatism of the human mind. The human mind tends to be economical in its expenditure of energy; it is inclined to favor the neurological pathways of least resistance. Hearing a familiar term, we are not prone to engage constantly in the tiring operation of uprooting the meaning this term has acquired for us over a lifetime. After some initial attempts to invest it with a new intellectual and emotional content, we return easily to its former meaning, familiar to us and our society. This may lead to harmful misunderstanding.

Returning to the other examples cited earlier, we note that "fundamental" and "fundamentalistic" have acquired a meaning, especially in some evangelical associations, that is different from "foundational." Besides misunderstanding, these terms may evoke emotional resistance in some readers. The popular word existential bears some alien connotations because of its use in atheistic existentialism. Hence, it may be confusing to label daily formation experiences that way. The term "situation ethics" may connote an undue influence of situational factors on one's moral decisions; the "formation potential of the situation" seems to express better our reservations in this regard. "Conservative," "conserving," "liberal," and "progressive," are terms that carry too many emotional and political overtones to provide rational, exact descriptions of what we mean by *formative memory* and *formative anticipation*. The familiar word "evolution" does not convey the finer nuances of a typically human "history of formation" that complements material and biological history. The term "determinants" has a ring of determinism that diminishes the element of insight and choice always present in opting for certain "life directives." "Inner devotion," in contrast to "intraformation," neither indicates the complexity of the interacting processes between our interior powers of formation nor the necessity of complementing these by the social processes of inter and outer formation. "Self-actualization" and "personality fulfillment" have been sometimes misused in an asocial context. "Life formation" has to replace them to guarantee a more integrated understanding of this concept. "Therapeutic encounter" and "group dynamics" may have for many people a more restricted, technical, less foundational meaning than "interformation" does. Similar justifications can be given for many other terms used in this science.

The development of a terminology proper to the science of formation will enable its researchers and practitioners to utilize to the full the relevant contributions of all auxiliary sciences without themselves becoming victims of sociologism, psychologism, biologism, spiritualism, theologism, philosophical idealism, rationalism, realism, existentialism, positivism, phenomenologism, and so forth. The potential contributions of each auxiliary science—when critically translated into the wider idiom of the integrated science of proximate life formation—are significant. No one auxiliary science alone can provide a well-integrated foundational formation knowledge of the situated person as a whole. For example, an exclusively social, psychological, biological, spiritual, theological, existential, behavioristic, or phenomenological life formation would necessarily lead to some lack of insight in proximate formation in its totality. Any one of these auxiliary sciences refers to only one dimension of the total foundational formation of life. Hence, the necessity for a language that widens their respective one-dimensional contributions is clear.

Another rationale for the use of scientific terminology is its intellectual economy. It offers researchers and the interested public a kind of shorthand. This shorthand is both exact and concise. It lends itself to the coherent integration of relevant concepts. A medical specialist, for example, can communicate in such a scientific shorthand with his or her colleagues. As good practitioners, such specialists should also learn a secondary popular language to communicate with their patients in familiar images and stories. The better they have mastered the exact systematic language of their science, the less they are liable to misinform their patients in popular translations. Popular writers about medical science who fail to master its exact systematic terminology often make mistakes. The same holds true for all the sciences. Formation scientists should be at home in both types of language in this field.

The Science of Formation and the Auxiliary Science of Theology

Our special concern is to complement research in the science of formation with articulation research in the Christian form tradition. The problems surrounding this articulation are complex. They have rarely, if ever, been assessed and clarified by Christian thinkers. The consequences of this lack of clarity could be deformative, not only for the Christian community but also and especially for Christian academic life: among other things, it may make it difficult for Catholic universities to justify their existence as Catholic, beyond the limits of a theology and chaplaincy department and something as vague as a "Catholic atmosphere."

Within the limits of this chapter, we can only offer an introduction into the problematics of this Christian articulation. Other sciences taught in Christian universities face issues similar to those faced by the science of formation in relation to their Christian articulation. This similarity in problematics is well demonstrated in the lead article of *The Bulletin*, the official publication of the Christian Association for Psychological Studies, Volume 7, Number 3, 1981. The article, entitled "Beyond Integration: New Directions," is written by Michael J. De Vries, professor of psychology at Trinity Christian College, Palos Heights, Illinois. Integration refers here to the integration of psychology and theology. Since the science of formation is essentially different from the science of psychology, the terminology used by De Vries may differ from ours, yet the concerns expressed are basically the same. They apply in some way to all sciences in Christian universities that take their complementary Christian articulation seriously. The author speaks out of the Protestant tradition. Hence, he refers to the Word of God and does not explicitly complement it with the word of tradition, as representatives of a Catholic tradition would be inclined to do. For the same reason there is less awareness expressed of a living spiritual form tradition as the experiential ground of both the Christian formative experience and the numerous theological systems of conceptualization.

One of the main insights we share with De Vries is that of the absolute necessity of the independence of sciences like psychology and formation from theological systems as such. We shall both quote and paraphrase in this regard several excerpts from his article.

> Theology seeks to draw psychology into itself, to make it "theologically appropriate," to baptize it in theologically sanctified categories. I assert that the "psychological" can *never* become the "theo-logical" without losing its true character. Christian psychologists must assert the right to think psycho-logically in the name of Christ without reference to theological categories. Psycho-logic must find its truth reference directly in our personal experience of Jesus Christ as revealed through the Scriptures and not in any concept or system taken from theology.

We may say that the science of formation, when it engages in Christian articulation, finds its truth-reference directly in the formative experience of Christians of Jesus Christ as revealed through Scripture; as expressed by the living form tradition of the church in its doctrine, rituals, liturgical prayers and acknowledged spiritual masters; and as lived formatively by its committed members. The Christian formation articulation as it is lived by believers, does not find its truth-reference directly in the concepts or systems of many theologies. Indirectly, however, some of these theological concepts may have been sufficiently absorbed by the form tradition to have become formatively relevant for the Christian population as a whole, at least in principle.

> Any movement toward theology by Christian psychologists in terms of consistency between psycho-logic and theo-logic represents a step back in the real task of Christian psychology. There is too much waiting to be developed in psychology to spend time reflecting upon whether psychological concepts are consistent with a particular set of theological concepts. Our struggle is for Christian perspective *in* psychology. Our concern ought to be whether our psychologizing is faithful to a life "in Christ," and furthers the development of the kingdom of Christ in psychology as a science.

Similarly, formation scientists when engaging also in Christian articulation research, struggle to disclose a Christian perspective in the science of formation. Their concern as formation scientists, who are also interested in this Christian articulation, has been from the beginning of this science to discover if their thinking is faithful to a life of formation in Christ, as represented in Scripture and in form traditions. They also want to know whether it furthers what they like to call the transformation of the human world into the house of God, the *Domus Dei*. Since the Second Vatican Council, the deeper and more Christian understanding of the term "missionary"—an understanding which Christian formation scientists helped to foster—implies the formative Christianization of the sciences without robbing them of their autonomy and subjecting them to theology.

Professor De Vries continues:

> This is not to say that Christian psychologists must close their ears to theologians. Rather I am calling for a particular type of listening, a listening based upon a relationship of equality, independence, and mutual integrity . . . . We are first called to *be* psychologists who are Christ's representatives. In so doing we can learn much *from* theology without needing to become "integrated" with it. Our criteria must always be selective to the extent that theology assists us in creatively developing psychology. This implies, of course, a new response from theology. Theology cannot demand that psychology account for it-

self in terms of consistency with this or that theological position. Theology cannot assume a position of oneupmanship, as the authority to which psychology must prove itself "Christian." . . . theology and psychology must address each other from a relationship which is marked by "active listening," genuine confrontation and helpfulness as is befitting for brothers and sisters engaged in independent service of the same Lord.

It is for this reason that the science of formation and its Christian articulation have posited that theology is only one of its auxiliary sciences. It insisted on conducting its academic work at an institute not linked with a theology department, just as a department or school of education in a Christian university should not be a mere subdivision of the theology department. Students and scholars in the science of formation address theology from their independent scientific concerns when articulation research makes it desirable to do so in service of clarification of formation doctrine, Scripture, or form traditions.

> The integration approach in its present form does not offer a direction for psychologists which is vital, appealing, or fresh. Its attraction seems to appear only for those Christian psychologists and psychologically minded theologians who are obsessed with the authority of theology and, therefore, feel it compulsively necessary to "check up" on themselves lest they get caught indulging in "secular" pursuits such as psychological theorizing or research. Assuming that in the future Christian psychologists are able to break through the cloud of guilt hovering over psychological theorizing and research, several directions open up for the shape of our task.
> It seems to me that psychologists must first insist upon autonomy from theological categories and methods. The controls and limits to Christian thinking in psychology cannot originate laterally from another discipline, not even theology. The primary source of critique must be internal to the community of Christian psychologists as they stand before God's Word directly. Christian psychologists must make use of available theological resources, but only to the extent that they are helpful to the separate task of psychology. Christian psychologists cannot appeal to the theologians for judgments about the validity of psychological concepts. This relative autonomy under God's Word does not preclude cooperation between theology

and psychology . . . . Theologians must encourage this free development rather than persistently demanding psychology be integrated with theology.

In the same vein, the science of formation developed by necessity its own concepts and corresponding terminology. It borrowed its concepts neither from theology nor from psychology, psychiatry, sociology, or any other of its auxiliary sciences. Its conceptualization and subsequent unique, autonomous verbalization is based not on the conceptual systems of theologies or psychologies. Their source is the direct scientific observation and analysis of concrete formation events themselves *as* formational.

De Vries asserts:

> A Christian approach to psychology is not theological, but manifests itself in a willingness to penetrate to the heart of theoretical frameworks and think within each system with an aim toward the reformation of possibilities for disclosing psychologically significant insights and stimulating further theorizing and research. Inevitably such an approach will not lead to a distinctive body of concepts which can be identified as "Christian psychology."

I myself once had to interrupt my studies and publications in Holland in the field of formative spirituality to work for a while in a different field, that of psychology, in the United States and at the request of my superiors, to obtain a doctorate in that field. My work included a thorough Christian critique of two schools of contemporary psychology. My critique of existential psychology was published in the book *Existential Foundations of Psychology* and my Christian critique of humanist psychology gave rise to *Religion and Personality*. In both instances, I tried to penetrate, in the words of De Vries, to the heart of these two theoretical frameworks. I attempted to think as a critical and creative Christian from within each system. My critique of the limitations of both movements led to a wider, corrective vision of each of these systems. Yet it did not give rise to a totally new distinctive body of concepts and terminology. I utilized the unique terminology of each system as much as possible.

Returning to my original field, that of formation and its subsequent articulation in Christian spirituality, a similar approach was used in my work with scholarly colleagues and doctoral candidates in this area of research. We were and are involved in delving into the heart of the many contributions to the understanding of formation that have been made by a wide variety of auxiliary sciences and form traditions. Our aim is to disclose in them, in the light of the scientific analysis of concretely observable formative events, formationally relevant insights and form directives. As formation scientists, our approach extends itself also to the articulation of this science in the Christian form tradition. This articulation does not aim to develop a distinctive body of concepts that could be identified as a Christian formation science, for its articulated language and thinking will always in part resemble that of the science of foundational human formation. The specialized language of this science results from an analysis of its own formal object: concrete formative events *as* formational. As De Vries puts it:

> We must respect the integrity of psychology as a cultural task in its own right subject to distortion, but at the same time redeemed and claimed for us through Christ's death and resurrection. Christian psychologists must press on with the work of psychology, taking leadership and making contributions in the full range of psychological inquiry and practice. Our task is as wide as psychology itself and our future, the eternal discovery of the psychological intricacy of the creation.

Christian formation scientists respect the integrity of the science of formation as a cultural task in its own right. They are profoundly aware that this science, like all others, is subject to distortion. Their Christian articulation research helps them to disclose such distortions. Thus enlightened by revelation and the Christian form tradition, they are able, as missionaries in the deepest sense, to work to redeem the science of formation from such distortions. Our task is as wide as the cosmic, human, and transhuman *epiphanies* of the formation mystery itself. Our aspiration is the ongoing disclosure of the formation processes of God's creation. By the same token, this articulation research can enrich and expand our formative understanding of the riches handed over to us by the Christian form tradition.

CHAPTER 3

Presuppositions of a Science of Human Formation

To understand the science of formation, it is necessary to consider some of its presuppositions. A first question would be: Is the formation of human life different from that of the macro- and microcosmic world that surrounds and penetrates our existence? And if so, how? To find an answer, we should reflect on three main ways of explaining the formation of human life: the positivist view, the rationalist view, and the foundational human view.

The Positivist View of Formation

The positivist view does not distinguish fundamentally between the formation of human life and the formation of other things in the environment. In this view, formation processes and forces play blindly in the cosmos and give rise to the formation, deformation, and reformation of all forms that emerge and fall in the universe, whether those of plants, animals, minerals, or human beings. According to this view, human life, too, is formed in and through such blind powers and processes. It is merely another complex piece of matter among many similar pieces.

From the positivist perspective, it would be sheer arrogance to pretend that the formation of human life differs basically from the processes to which the things around it are subjected. The positivist sees human life as a fragile fragment of nature. Its formation is a trifle, an incident, a minute moment in the vast ocean of matter in formation. Human life is a chance event of formation similar to such events as a stone in a river, a weed in a garden, or a speck of stellar dust in expanding space.

This view of formation has been adopted by many thoughtful people; it cannot be dismissed lightly as based on mere imagination. There must be something in the formation of human life that evokes the notion that it is not different, foundationally speaking, from the formation of things around it. Indeed, when we reflect on all that plays a role in human formation, we must acknowledge that certain aspects manifest features similar to those we observe in the animals, plants, and other things around us. Auxiliary sciences of formation, such as physiology, biology, biochemistry, and neurology, are able to identify and describe a multitude of prehuman processes operative in the formation of human life.

While we recognize this fact, we are also aware that only people can reflect on both the human and the prehuman formation processes inside and outside of themselves. Stones and plants never give an indication that they reflect on the chemical or other processes taking place inside them. People, however, can establish sciences concerning their biophysical formation because they can appraise it intelligently. All formation processes can make some sense to human persons. Without people, nothing would have formative meaning. There would be nobody for whom these processes could mean processes of formation.

Moreover, when we consider the many processes that govern the formation of our organism, we feel that we are related to them differently than, for example, oil, wine, or vinegar are related to their chemical formation processes. Oil, wine, and vinegar are identified with these processes and their subsequent forms. They cannot distance themselves from them in acts of reflection and appraisal. We experience the fact that we depend on our vital processes in one way while we escape them in another, that we adapt to them congenially and yet in a certain measure may withstand them, that we are absorbed by them and yet take a stand toward them.

Even under the overpowering impact of a painful or exciting biophysical process, we are still able to experience that it is *I* who undergo this process. In an act of distinctively human formation, we can still appraise what is happening to us on the levels of prehuman formation. As relatively free, forming persons, we can still impose a variety of meanings on this prehuman formation or deformation process in our physical organism. We can still form our minds, hearts, and wills in such a way that we accept or reject, adapt hesitantly to, or withhold our assent from, a vital process.

When we freely appraise and take a formative stand toward the prehuman formation processes in our organism, we already go beyond them into the realm of distinctively human formation. No infrahuman process, nor the subsequent form to which it gives rise, is able to appraise itself or any other process of formation or any forms that may result from it. Only the human person can take such initiative.

It is true that we are able to build into a robot the practical implications of our original appraisals of the form directives we disclose in reality. We may devise a computer, a teaching machine or a robot that—within the range determined by us—may make selections among different possible directions of formative or deformative action. These selections, however, can only be variations of the pragmatic implications of the appraisals originally exercised by us and embodied afterward in our technical creations. The robot, moreover, can never become like us so long as it retains its machinelike qualities. It can never disclose and spontaneously appraise and implement a new formation value and meaning in people, nature, and things. Nor can a robot take a stand wholly in and by itself in a creatively formative, unpredictable, or surprising human fashion.

Imagine, for example, a mechanical hairstylist devised to fashion women's hairdos and to adapt itself selectively to the inexhaustible variety of female heads and tastes. Such a robot would be possible in principle, yet it could not, of itself, change its formative *value directives* and, let us say, fall passionately in love with an attractive client.

We conclude that the processlike aspect of human formation is only one essential aspect of our life. Scientists have explored and elaborated this essential prehuman formation feature. They have investigated the organismic participation of human life in the processes of formation in the universe. They have rightly demonstrated how the organismic processes of our life share in the multitude of formation processes and laws that are formulated, at least in part, by biology, biochemistry, physics, and other such sciences. In consequence, positivist thought has stimulated the biophysiological sciences to explore the degree to which the formation of human life remains subjected to the measurable impact of the constant formation and reformation of the world of matter. We can expect this magnificent and massive exploration to continue, for the physical sciences will never exhaust the richness, subtlety, and complexity of this particular profile of the formation of human life.

The Rationalist View of Formation

The positivist perspective alone cannot provide us with a full account of formation as we experience it in daily life. Biochemical *formation processes* do not fully explain to us the fact that we know ourselves as somehow also giving form to our life and world and in some measure freely refusing or accepting formative influences. Nor does the positivist view explain fully why and how we spontaneously experience that forms and formation processes make sense to us. We experience our ability to disclose and appraise formation processes as a typical ability of human formation. It manifests itself in human history as a capacity that is at least as essential and original as is the vital participation of human life in the processes of biochemical formation. Daily experience discloses to us that we are involved in the mystery of formation not only in a vital way but also in a distinctively human way.

We may become so overwhelmingly aware of this uniquely human aspect of formation that we forget or deny the prehuman vital formation processes that play such a significant role in the formation of human life. Indeed, we may be tempted to ignore the organismic-vital aspects of ongoing formation. If we were to do so, however, our description of the formation of human life would be onesided. To omit the contribution of positivist thought to our understanding of the formation of human life would be just as onesided as the denial of the distinctively human feature of our formation.

Rationalists and idealist thinkers may fall into this biased view. They unduly inflate the subjective power of people to give form to their life and world. They regard the limited human power to give and receive form as an absolute power in no way restricted by the conditions imposed on it by biophysical vital formation processes, by sense information, and by formative or deformative conditions in the world.

A rationalist or idealist view of human formation overemphasizes the distinctively human aspect. Such exclusive attention may lead in turn to a spiritualistic view of formation. This makes the distinctively human power the mysterious spring, the hidden well of all formation processes and the subsequent forms we experience. All of them are considered mere products of our formative thought, will, and imagination.

Belief in such subjectivistic power, if pushed to the limit, can lead to the illusion that human formation experiences are merely reflections of our isolated self-sufficient *formative mind*. Everything is falsely perceived as nothing but a mirage of our thoughts, decisions, imaginings. The reality and density of all objective forms and formation powers evaporates. They are dismissed as mere products of our formative consciousness.

Such exalted subjectivism has no correlation in reality. A sterile subjectivistic power, imprisoned in itself, lost in isolated *intraformation* and fully self-sufficient, is no longer a human formation power. It misses the dimensions of *preformation, interformation,* and *outer formation*. It contradicts our spontaneous perception of the daily formative life situation and the wider world it discloses. Therefore, we cannot really believe in it. Deep down, we are forced to admit that formation processes and forms that are not distinctively human are real; they are not merely the invention of formative thought, will, and imagination.

In our daily actions, we clearly take into account that the world of infrahuman forms and processes, in which we live, move, and labor, is real and inescapable. It offers density and resistance. What if we did not function in consonance with the reality of forms and formation processes in our organism and in the world? What if we tried to function only in accordance with what some idealistic thinkers claim to be reality? The answer is clear: we would soon destroy ourselves.

The Foundational Human View of Formation

Neither the positivist nor the rationalist view represents human formation as we actually experience it in daily life. Yet each of these perspectives discloses essential aspects of human formation, foundationally speaking.

Let us reflect on humanly formative events as they appear in reality. We realize that our formation is not a blind process like other processes in the universe. Nor is it a self-sufficient power of formative creation that could maintain itself in splendid isolation from the infrahuman forms and processes in our formation field. Human formation is not locked up within the mind and heart as a purely intraformative process. It is always taking place in interaction with formative and deformative actions in others and with events in our formation field. Human formation *is* a dialogue with infrahuman forms and processes in one's own organism and in one's surroundings: it gives form to life and world and at the same time lets life and world give form to it, by disclosing, appraising, and implementing the manifold potential form directives and processes in its field of formation.

In short, we really experience our formation in dialogue with pre-, inter-, and outer-formation powers and processes. Our formation is inconceivable without a human formation field. Conversely, the formation of a field, as we experience it, is imperceptible and unimaginable without our formation powers. The world is coformed as a human formation field by our perception, thought, and imagination. The human world appears to us as sky, mountains, valleys, forests, streams, and oceans. Without the formative powers of perception, thought, and imagination—of feeling and appraisal—there would be no humanized forms of sky, mountain, valley, forest, stream, and ocean. We could not even imagine them without the specific appearance and meaning with which formative presence has endowed them in an increasingly humanized universe.

Our formation is thus foundationally not only intra- but also pre-, inter-, and outer formation. It simply does not happen without this multiple interaction. It can occur only within these formative relationships. It reaches its fullness only at the gratuitous moments when all these *formation poles* are in harmony and consonance. Human formation that is not interaction would be a contradiction in terms. Subjective human inner formation cannot occur other than as the source of a formative activity, which in some way is oriented towards that which is not isolated inner formation alone.

Human formation cannot be conceived, affirmed, experienced, or imagined without the nonself, in interaction with which formation evolves in time and space. Expressions such as I think, I do, I feel, I imagine, I anticipate, I remember, I will, all imply giving form to thoughts, actions, feelings, imaginations, anticipations, memories, and decisions within one's expanding formation field. They always presuppose something that is more than isolated intraformation alone.

The assertion that human intraformation foundationally happens in relation to the poles of pre-, inter-, and outer formation cannot be demonstrated by means of formal logic alone. It is so foundational that it could not be derived from a more basic insight into the nature of human formation. If it could be deduced by mere logic from another more basic description of human life in formation, then the assertion that foundational formation is a dialogical pre-, intra-, inter-, and outer process would no longer offer the most basic description of human formation. Since there is no formal logical proof for this assertion, its truth can only be indicated.

We can indicate that no mode of human formation can be conceived, perceived, or imagined that is not at the same time implicitly or explicitly, minimally or otherwise, a mode of dialogical interaction. It is indeed impossible to describe fully any mode of foundational human formation without implying some remote or proximate interaction between past or present elements of pre-, intra-, inter-, and outer formation. In everyday parlance, this dialogical aspect is usually only implicit in our statements. I may say that I dance, walk, exercise, imagine, or fear. Such declarations always imply that I give form to my bodily movements, imaginations, or fears in ways that somehow take into account all dialogical poles of formation, no matter how vague, indefinite, and remote their coforming influence may seem.

In other words, human formation is always dialogical interaction. It is a "forming-together-with" the sacred and the secular, with organism, society, world, and history. It is not a thing closed in upon itself; it is an act of dialogical disclosure, appraisal, decision, and implementation that may progressively reveal the communal and unique life-form that one is called to realize. It is a radical formative openness for all that may manifest or support this life formation.

This balanced view of human formation unites the two aspects explored respectively by positivism and rationalism, by objectivism and subjectivism, by naive realism and idealism. Centuries of intense thought and fierce intellectual struggle were required before the precarious balance between all dialogical poles of formation could be expressed adequately.

The foundational human view thus sees formation as dialogical and integrative. Formation must be consonant with what we are preformatively called to be. It must be compatible with our life situation and with the world in which we find ourselves—compatible but not identical, for we find ourselves in society, in life situations, in the world not in the same way as chairs are in a room, cigarettes in a package, or candy in a box. These things do not experience an interformation with one another.

On the contrary, we, as humans, are coformed by the people with whom we live, by the situation and the world in which we dwell; we in turn coform our life and world. We form, cultivate, humanize, and personalize society, history, situation, and world by our formative personal and social presence. We are not in history, world, or society as stones in a wall, brooms in a closet, vegetables in a freezer. Such objects do not engage in meaningful interformation; they are subjected blindly to the nonhuman mechanical formation processes that rule the world of things.

We are formatively or deformatively engaged in history, world, and society. We are concerned about our formation as no stone, broom, or vegetable can be. Through our forming presence, we have become familiar with the situation, world, society, and history we share. We find ourselves irritated, annoyed, fascinated, depressed, bored, excited by the people, events, and things with whom we interact. In and through our forming presence, we find ourselves using, developing, organizing, accepting, rejecting, explaining, fostering, cultivating, questioning, searching, and discussing people, events, and things.

The stone, the broom, and the vegetable never find themselves in any of these formative or deformative attitudes or interactions with regard to the things that surround them. They are merely alongside other things in the same container, undergoing the same mechanical formation processes of which they are only the object—never the coforming subject. As a forming presence, we really encounter people, events, and things in our many formative or deformative dispositions and interactions. Therefore, the formation mystery only reveals itself to us in its manifold concrete manifestations when we are formatively present in the many modes of daily lived encounter.

CHAPTER 4

Deformative Presuppositions of Formation Approaches and Sciences

The preceding chapter suggested that approaches to formulation start out from presuppositions in regard to the nature of human formation as such. Such general presuppositions find expression in more articulate presuppositions that may vary in different periods of the history of humanity. These articulated presuppositions constitute a starting point that will influence all further reflections on formation. If a basic viewpoint is false or too narrow, it will falsify our formative efforts. Hence, we stress the importance of appraising contemporary presuppositions before adopting them.

The main contemporary presuppositions that pose a threat to a wholesome view of foundational formation are: the vitalistic, the vitalistic-functional, and the autonomous self-actualizing view of unfolding and formation.

The Vitalistic View of Formation

One way of looking at human formation is the vitalistic. People who take this view of humans-in-formation describe the process as a spiraling outward of what is already present as a vital, preformed life direction. In this view, what is new in formation emerges merely from vitalistic processes of differentiation, structuration, and recentralization. Crucial in this vision is that these processes are perceived as totally subject to immanent laws of the human organism. A kind of blueprint is laid down in the vital life. Structuration is a differentiation of aspects of human life that are pregiven in this vital blueprint.

This theory would not deny that the life situation also makes a contribution to human formation. Yet the decisive fact under consideration here is that people utilize life situations only in accordance with their own immanent vitalistic laws. In other words, the surrounding world is not much more than useful matter for the unfolding of the vital life. Overlooked is the fact that our formation field as human gives rise to formative value directives. These directives have an original influence on the formation of human life, but this is not acknowledged in the vitalistic-blueprint view. It holds that no manifestations of reality have any directive or formative value in and by themselves. They are useful only as nourishment or stimulation for the growth of human life. This growth is considered basically a vital process, exclusively directed by organismic laws.

It is clear that the vitalistic view is questionable for the person who studies foundational human formation. If formation were only a matter of autonomous vital growth, it would be impossible to give any distinctively human form to this growth. The vitalistic perception of self-unfolding in the human person is deduced from the organic growth biologists observe in a vegetative organism, such as a plant or a flower. When we observe the growth of a plant, it is clear that its formation can only be directed accidentally. For example, by manipulating temperature, light, and humidity, we can slow down or speed up plant formation. Such accidental form directives cannot *essentially* change the basic empirical form this plant will assume once the growth process has taken its course. In our foundational view of human formation, we believe that we can direct ourselves or other human beings in some measure by form directives to find their unique empirical form of life. This kind of formation would be excluded in the vitalistic vision.

If the formation of life is only an autonomous vital process, no real formative assistance would be possible. The only meaningful aid would be the effectuation of favorable conditions that facilitate the predetermined empirical form the human being should naturally assume; assistance would thus be only accidental and of minor importance. It would not exercise any real influence on human unfolding and would remain exterior to this process of vital formation. The only assistance one could offer the person-in-formation would be that of care, protection, and sustenance of the vital process. There is no room left for transcendent formation.

We should not underestimate the subtle influence such a vision may exert. Under the impact of this theory, people may relinquish directive foundational formation. They may only offer support for what is considered to be an autonomous vital process. In that case there could be no transcendent human formation in the true sense of this word.

The Vitalistic-Functionalistic View of Formation

More recently, there has been an attempt to go beyond this vitalistic concept of formation. This latter approach pays attention mainly to the functional dialogue between the human organism-in-formation and the environment. In the course of this dialectical functioning the person acquires certain *formative dispositions*. What is new here, in comparison to the vitalistic formation theory, is that such acquired dispositions were not present in the original preformed structure. The latter could even disintegrate under the development of such newly acquired dispositions.

This more dynamic view of formation adds something important to the vitalistic concept. Yet it does not offer us a sufficient explanation of a fully human, relatively free formation. Even these secondary dispositions have been acquired by dialectical functioning only on the basis of the preformed vital blueprint. From these secondary dispositions spring tertiary customs, habits, and character traits that enrich and expand human life. All of these patterns, including the possible functional disintegration of the basic pattern, were likewise foreseen or determined from the beginning by a vital preformation that ultimately determines one's formation. These functional possibilities were also inherent in the vital rules of human unfolding.

In this explanation life forms itself exclusively in accordance with its own immanent determinations. Such determinants may themselves be preformed or they may originate with predetermined lawfulness out of this given vital preformation. In either case, the formation of one's life is directed deterministically, without room for transcendent free direction.

The vital-functional concept that formation proceeds in accordance with a blueprint anchored in the organism does not leave room for foundational human formation. No free or inspired formative life directives can break through this deterministic process.

People who are unconsciously influenced by this vision are less able to see the need for directive formation. They are inclined to restrict themselves to the sustenance and facilitation of the vital-functional process of unfolding. While these processes should be respected and taken into account, they should also be placed in dialogue with the wisdom of transcendent formation and human form traditions.

The Transcendental Autarchic Self-Actualizing View of Formation

In our search for a balanced view of formation, we may be confronted with a vision that is exactly the opposite of the vital-functional concept. This view emphasizes the autarchy of human formation, an autarchy that transcends all vital-functional laws and determinants. Theorists—such as certain existentialists and humanists—who support this excessive view of formation freedom in humans stress that it is ultimately impossible to foresee or predict anything in formation because people actualize themselves in accordance with their own autarchic insights. They should follow their own inclinations and give form to their lives in absolute transcendent freedom. The dispositions and character traits that manifest themselves in the course of this development can only be acquired by autarchic transcendent options. In no way should they be the result of the person's vital-functional interaction with his environment. Formation is basically a matter of free self-realization or self-actualization. The emphasis is on human selfhood as exclusively transcendent and autarchic, as free from any implicit or explicit form tradition.

This existentialistic view holds further that anything which strikes people as a meaningful directive for their own life is, in and by itself, automatically meaningful for their self-actualization. The formation direction of their life receives its validity exclusively from their own subjective experience. This autonomous self-experience transcends all vital, functional, social, cultural, and religious directives, as well as all form traditions.

This view, too, seems to make superfluous the idea and practice of a foundational formation that is nourished by objective form directives and form traditions. Overreacting to past customs of upbringing and education that neglected to form people in the limited freedom that is their birthright, many people may find this concept of autarchic self-actualization attractive. They may subscribe to it indiscriminately, not realizing that, in this view, true human formation of life becomes impossible.

Foundational formation implies a *form receptivity* that enables us to surrender our lives to the formative influence of objective form directives. These directives are not simply the product of our subjective projects and desires. They are gratuitous directives that we receive in reverence and that we allow to give form to our daily unfolding. Such formative manifestations are given to us objectively. We do not invent them. We find them in cultural institutions, in the wisdom of form traditions and of simple people, and in the validated knowledge of scholars, thinkers, scientists, and practitioners in the art and discipline of formation.

Autarchic self-actualization destroys the form receptivity that is the necessary condition for consonant formation. It fosters an arrogant attitude, which is the fruit of the quasi-foundational *pride-form* of life. This pride-form cuts life off from the mystery of human formation. When people become captives of their own isolated transcendent subjectivity, everything they know, understand, possess, and encounter is valued only in relation to the isolating pride-form of life. The world around them, including their culture and its underlying form traditions, has no directive value for them. Everything is appraised as useful or useless according to the subjective criteria of their project of self-actualization. The autarchic pride-form dominates and deforms their life.

Why does this view of self-unfolding in absolute autarchy exclude consonant formation? One reason is that people would disclose, choose, and decide in arbitrary ways what they would want to do and be. This arbitrary approach would give rise to an arbitrary form of life. The direction of their life would only be the result of a series of arbitrary decisions. Their formation would not be based on consonant value directives that are formative by their own intrinsic power; it would depend merely on chance opportunities for self-disclosure, choice, and decision. Such opportunities are accidentally offered to them by the successive life situations in which they find themselves.

Decisions made in this arbitrary way may prove to be mutually contradictory. In that case, it would be impossible for people to come to a coherent form of personal and communal life. Soon they try to find some principle of unity that may integrate the variety of arbitrary and contradictory form directives that are utterly dependent on chance happenings. However, even the choice of a unifying principle of formation direction is made in an arbitrary self-centered way. The autarchic self-actualizer is not committed in form receptivity to objective form directives as they manifest themselves in people, history, culture, and form tradition.

Autarchic and exalted self-actualization could also be sought in another way. In this other style of self-actualization, the decisions, self-disclosures, and choices that form one's life would not be seen as accidental. On the contrary, these self-actualizers believe that they follow a mysterious, immanent, and subjective life direction. In no way is this direction derived from or related to universal, consonant formation directives outside one's interiority. It proceeds solely from one's inner self. Therefore, self-formation takes place autonomously. No formative law or value directive exists for such people outside the transcendent interiority of their own life. No other persons, institutions, form traditions, or form directives have any authority for them. No one could propose to them any formative value as obligatory.

We saw previously that the opposite concept of formation ascribes total autarchy to the vital-functional process of life formation. According to such a vitalistic theory, human formation would run its course with a lawfulness that results from the necessity of biophysical nature. In the autarchic, self-actualization view just described, human formation would be rooted exclusively in the absolutized autonomy of the individual's transcendent life dimension. This dimension would give direction to one's life in isolation from all other dimensions of life and world. Both views exclude any possibility of consonant human formation in the transcendent-incarnational sense.

Whereas the vital-functional concept of formation could be called fatalistic, the view of subjectivistic self-formation could be called transcendentalistic insofar as it proposes an almost divine concept of autonomy that wholly transcends the finitude and dependency of our human condition. In either view the practical consequence would be that it would be useless to engage in realistic consonant formation. One should only create conditions that facilitate the exalted autarchic self-actualization of human life, whether fatalistic in the vitalistic sense or free-floating in the transcendentalistic view. These views of formation are ultimately rooted in the autarchic pride-form of humanity.

As mentioned earlier, in overreaction to past coercive or manipulative upbringing and education, the option for autarchic self-actualization has become attractive to many people. As transcendent, it may appeal to them as so much more meaningful and spiritual than the exclusively deterministic theory of formation. Moreover, the contemporary cultural confusion in regard to right form directives fosters this retirement in subjectivism. While this option for autarchic self-actualization is seldom explicit, it still implicitly influences many permissive attitudes. Even well-established centers of formation may indulge excessively in such permissiveness. People fail to realize that this approach makes a realistic, consonant formation of human life difficult, if not impossible.

CHAPTER 5

Foundational Dynamics of Human Formation

Human life forms itself by its presence in the world. It gives form to the world and receives form from it. This forming presence does not interact with the world as such in its totality. Rather, the world contains certain opportunities for human formation. These opportunities correspond with the unique structure of the human life-form and of its form potencies. Taken together, they present us with the possibility of constituting a human formation field. When people give form to that field, deepening, expanding, and enhancing it, they give and receive form in their own unfolding life. In the meantime, they may grow in an awareness of the mysterious beyond of this evolving field.

Four Main Form Dimensions

Human life is rich in possible modes of forming presence. The science of formation has categorized these under four main dimensions: sociohistorical, vital, functional, and transcendent.

The Sociohistorical Form Dimension

The way in which we give form to life and world has been co-formed by our society, which has developed a form tradition in regard to the ways in which people should give form to various life situations. Everything we do is influenced somehow by this formation history of our people. For example, society and its form traditions instill in us the idea of regular times of labor interspersed with times of recreation and exercise. Society forms us in certain styles and skills for recreation and particular ways of enjoying nature and beauty. Were we members of an African or Indian tribe centuries ago, we might not have thought in the same way about regular work times interspersed with breaks for recreation.

Our recreation may include, for example, swimming in a lake. While swimming in this lake, we are not actually present to other scenes in our formation field, such as home, office, church, or country club. Of course, we can be present to them in memory, anticipation, or imagination, but our actual preferred form situation for the moment is the lake surrounded by tall pines, the silence of the woods, the sky above—all touched by the glow of the sun reflecting in the water. At this moment the lake is the manifestation of the actual formation field with its form potentials with which we are to interact, to which we are to give form, and by which we are to be formed. Hence, we affirm the sociohistorical situatedness of our forming presence.

The Vital Form Dimension

The embodiment of our presence in this sociohistorical situation is evident. Our senses open up to this manifestation of the formation field in which we plunge ourselves as swimmers. We see the clarity and sparkle of the water, the green moss, the beauty of the lily pads. We smell the pines and flowers surrounding the lake. We hear the buzzing of insects, the chirping of birds. The water appears resistant to our strokes, smooth and refreshing to our gliding body. Our feet touch the shallow bottom when we try to stand up. We take off again. We enjoy in our body the delightful feeling of moving swiftly through water. We savor the sense of vigor in our arms and legs. Our swimming body reacts vitally to the flow and resistance, to the freshness and coolness of the water that gently carries us.

The Functional Form Dimension

Another dimension of our forming presence plays a part in this swim in the lake. It is the dimension of functional forming presence. We had to organize many things before we could take a carefree dip into the water. We had to plan our work at the office in such a way that we would be free for a swim without betraying the traditions that give form to our workday and to the expectations of others that direct our customary performances. We had to time our stay here, to get our car ready, check the gasoline, pack the swimming gear. A measure of organization compatible with our sociohistorical position was thus necessary as a preparation for this recreation.

While we are swimming, the functional side is also present and operative. What stroke shall we use? How do we avoid bumping into loose branches that have fallen into the lake? Did we leave our glasses in a safe place? Shall we try the new stroke we have not yet mastered? These questions have to be dealt with in a functional or practical fashion.

The Transcendent Form Dimension

Floating on our back in a leisurely way, there is yet another mode of being formatively present to this lake and its surroundings. Our sociohistorical form traditions awaken us to certain experiences of peace and beauty communicated by painters and poets. The water seems to carry us peacefully. We look up to the crowns of the trees softly moving in the light summer breeze and beyond them to the blue sky with its few white puffy clouds. All around us the stillness of the forest is accentuated by the humming of bees and the twitter of birds. We begin to feel one with all of nature. There is emerging in us a serene awareness of the mysterious meaning of life and creation. This experience forms us differently from the one we felt so vividly in our body when we pushed ourselves with vital strength and pleasure through the water. The form we receive inwardly now is different from the form of control we felt when we organized our day meticulously and experienced the contentment of effectively managing our situation. This sense of oneness with all that is, this peaceful awareness of ultimate meaning and mystery, seems to touch the core of our life. It goes deeper than those dimensions of presence that enable us to form vital and functional experiences and to implement in our behavior the form directives implied in them.

From the deeper, unknown life-form that we are, there emerges an intuition, a form receptivity to the mystery of all that is. We may receive the gift of a spiritual experience. The spirit dimension of our life form, our *transcendent form potency*, is thus actuated.

The Human Life-Form

A description of this simple event of a swim in a forest lake offers us an insight into the various dimensions of forming presence that coform human life. While these dimensions may penetrate one another, they can be distinguished. It is clear that in any given moment one of them may prevail over the other. One is more in the foreground, dominating our momentary life formation. We can speak, therefore, of a sociohistorical, a vital, a functional, and a transcendent presence. Around these ranges of alertness, there develop, respectively, sociohistorical, vital, functional, and transcendent types of life, again mutually penetrating one another.

During our formation history an artificial split may occur between these dimensions and the corresponding types of life they generate. The sociohistorical life may be denied, the vital repressed, the functional neglected, the transcendent refused. People may try to cut themselves off from their situatedness and their subsequent interformation with others. They may become schizoid. Their functional life may be severely diminished in an idle attempt to live in transcendent presence, divorced from practical, everyday, effective living. In such cases of deformation, the human life-form loses its wholeness. It can only be fully effective and consonant to the extent that people live appropriately in historical, vital, functional, and transcendent presence, maintaining a dialogue between all of them.

It may be helpful to relate these four categories of the science of formation to the more philosophical, classical categories of spirit, mind, and body, which are related to, but not identical with, our four formation categories.

Spirit-Mind-Body Dialectic

Human life is complex and dynamic. It is complex because it emerges out of constant formative interaction of spirit, mind, and body. To make it more complex, spirit, mind, and body are themselves interacting with inner and outer aspects of the formation field.

Human life is also dynamic. It unfolds and expands in countless continuous and discontinuous ways. Its dynamism is due to the stimulating interpenetration of the three formative powers—spirit, mind, and body—which move in a stream of formative events. Each of these three foundational sources coforms human life. Their interpenetration is dialogical, meaning that an intraformative dialogue goes on constantly between the body and the functional mind.

This dialogue is made possible and kept alive by the human spirit, or what may be called the transcendent mind or higher reason. The possibility of dialogue between functional mind and vital body is thus rooted in the distinctively spiritual or transcendent nature of human formation.

Vitality-Functionality-Spirituality

The human body gives rise to a vital life, manifesting itself in human vitality. The functional mind calls forth an effective functional life or functionality. The vital and the functional in mutual interaction bring about a unified vital-functional life or a kind of functioning personality. The health, strength, integration, and effectiveness of this vital-functional life depends on the distinctively human or transcendent dimension, called the spirit or higher reason. This transcendent dimension gives rise to the life of the spirit, or spirituality. It tends to express itself in our vitality and functionality and in the various channels we provide and develop within the latter for such expression. This dialogue between vitality and functionality constantly nourishes human formation.

Human life is, in essence, emerging. It should not be misunderstood as a static entity. On the contrary, to the extent that life tries to become static it seems less of a human life. It resembles a remnant or a decaying residue of what it was called to be. Hence, we can say that human life is meant to be a dialogue between functionality and vitality in steady interaction with formative events emerging in one's formation field.

Integrating Formation

Human life formation tends toward integration. It fosters an increasing consonance between spirit, mind, and body, although this consonance is not achieved once and forever. *Dissonance* is inevitable at times, even desirable. In this respect, human formation follows the indeterminacy or discontinuity of elemental formation in the universe as disclosed by theoretical physics. Incidences of felt dissonance may be moments of creative discontinuity evoked by the emergence of unpredictable events in our formation field. For example, we may suddenly fall in love, experience serious illness, lose a dear friend, get fired, or start a new job. All such happenings are also formative events. They contain new directives for our life. Assimilation of such directives may occasion a relative loss of balance, at least during the initial phase of redirection of our life. We need openness of spirit to cope with such formative events and to foster their creative integration in our life.

Our spirit disturbs the provisional unity we repeatedly establish between the vital and functional dimensions of our life. It keeps pushing our life to ever wider horizons. Spirit thereby creates the never ending restlessness that is the root of our dynamic life formation.

If one grants the spirit free play, a deeper kind of peace and stability may gradually establish itself. This peace is grounded in the awareness and acceptance of our participation in the inexhaustible horizon opened up by the spirit. This deeper harmony with the universe, this consonance with the all-pervading mystery of formation, make the periods of passing through dissonance and creative discontinuity less difficult to bear.

Between repeated periods of creative discontinuity, the consonance of life can be approximated if we allow our spirit to unfold naturally. It must penetrate the vital-functional dimensions of our life in their very interaction. These dimensions in turn are uniquely preformed by genetic inheritance, a preformation illumined by the human epiphany of the formation mystery. These dimensions are shaped also by experiences accumulated during our initial formation history and by things that happen to us in childhood and infancy. The human spirit neither denies nor undergoes passively this unique preformation. On the contrary, our preformation should be one of our main guideposts on the mysterious journey we make through life, a point of departure always to be taken into account. Other guideposts are given in opportunities for consonant life formation that light up our future on the basis of what we have already become.

Spiritual Identity and Direction Disclosures

Our spirit discloses gradually what we should strive to become in the future. The human life-form as spirit is an unfolding intuition of what our own fundamental spiritual identity or life direction might be. The manifestations of our everyday pragmatic identity are the signs, shadows, and partial embodiments of a deeper spiritual identity. Without this *spiritual identity* at its core, our vital-functional identity loses its rootedness, stability, and meaningfulness. It becomes a shadow without substance, a phantom self, and we suffer a spiritual identity crisis.

Fidelity to direction disclosures is the basis of the life of formation. Life without the direction of the spirit becomes a paralyzing set of secular or pious routines. Loss of spiritual aliveness carries necessarily with it loss of effective form potency. Instead of being human participants in the drama of life, we may become only smooth functionaries. We may be technically perfect engineers, professors, parents, churchgoers, theologians, manual laborers, clerics, diplomats, or demonstrators for countless good causes. Yet we may no longer be unique, creative participants in the unpredictable formation history of humanity.

Constant disclosure and appraisal of the emergent direction of our formation is necessary. So, too, is our fidelity to the form directives disclosed in our appraising presence. Even the most original intuition of our life direction can happen and develop only in continual dialogue with all other aspects of our life. This dialogue is set in motion by our encounters with people, events, and things in successive life situations that emerge within the formation field. The dialogical nature of human formation, on the basis of transcendent presence, is one of the foundational principles of the science of formation.

Spiritual-Functional-Vital Life

The distinction between spirit, mind, and body as foundational intraformative formation powers and sources underlies this science's theory of human formation. This distinction is not new. It is as old as human thought.

Humanity at times has lost the consonance between these sources of one and the same human life-form. Periodically, this loss of unifying insight gave rise to dualistic types of thought. One or another dimension of life was no longer perceived as only a dimension of one and the same human form of life. It was lifted out of its natural context as a more or less independent entity. It was separated artificially from the other dimensions, which were also posited as independent entities. At times, the human life dimensions, like body and spirit, were considered to be at war or in competition with one another.

We have known frightful periods of spirit-body dualism. At present we often observe a split between the spirit-core of the vital-functional life of people, on the one hand, and that vital-functional life itself, on the other. This split may lead to a refusal or repression of the spirit in favor of an almost exclusive functional development. Such practical dualism undermines not only our culture but also our bodies. The more the transcendent center of life is refused, the more the vital-functional dimension becomes a person's anxious, exclusive preoccupation. A corresponding fear of defeat or failure of one's form potency ensues, making one that much more vulnerable to tensions, infections and chronic diseases.

Psychotherapy does not always take into account the transcendent center of the dimensions and articulations of life. In such a case, therapy can only bring about a vulnerable compromise within the person: a limited vital-functional integration not sufficiently illumined and mellowed by the spirit. This compromise is not without benefit. It can considerably diminish the pressures a person suffers, if he or she is constantly preoccupied with the pragmatic efficiency and adjustment of the vital-functional constellation of life. Yet this compromise remains both precarious and provisional. It does not free us from the source of social pressures and the frustration, guilt, and anxiety that they breed. The source of misery is our insulation within the vital-functional constellation of life.

Formation Terminology

The words transcendent, functional, and vital are used in the science in a special way. They represent new concepts for a foundational theory of proximate formation. While they are related to the classical spirit-mind-body concepts, they are not identical with them. Their unique meaning and function within the science of proximate formation becomes clearer when this theory is understood in its totality. Later chapters will discuss in more detail what we mean by the vital, functional, sociohistorical, and spiritual-transcendent dimensions and their intraformative interaction. In the fourth volume of ths series, we will have to add a *pneumatic dimension* to do justice to the special working of the Holy Spirit in the Christian view of the formation of life.

Formation scientists deal with spirit, mind, and body not as philosophers, theologians, or social scientists would. Formation scientists pose these concepts as integrative theorists of proximate life formation. They are primarily interested in the dynamics of concrete daily formation of human life within its *formation field*. Formation scientists are concerned with the terms spirit, mind, and body mainly insofar as they give way to a conception of concrete human formation that can always be deepened, expanded, enhanced, and integrated in its experiential and practical expressions. The consonant formation of a human life implies an enlightening, integrating dialogue between the various dimensions of human life. It is in and through this dialogue that our formation continues.

Various terms used in this theory may have been used in philosophy or in certain schools of theology, theoretical physics, or the social sciences. While there may be some relationship between the terms used by the science of formation and those found in such auxiliary sciences, their usage is not always identical.

Three Centers of Formation

The vital, functional, and transcendent formation powers are three mutually interpenetrating centers of human formation or three crystallizations of one and the same movement of human life. They represent different modes of human presence in its formation field and are the principles of actualization and integration of one's communal and unique life-form. All three foster integration within one's life and one's formation field. All three are influenced by the ubiquitous sociohistorical dimension within which human life must necessarily unfold.

The dynamic, integrating form potencies of each of these three centers and sources of formation make the human formation story possible. We should realize, however, that the functional and vital forming and unifying centers are subordinated to the unique, distinctively human, spiritual center that manifests itself in each of them.

Human Life as Emergent and Transcendent

The theory of foundational human formation has a double premise. The first is that the human life-form is emergent; the second is that the emergence of this life-form as distinctively human depends on the awakening and actualization of a person's transcendent dimension and its humanizing form potency.

The human life-form is always emerging; it is never a finished life-form. This premise means that we are only on the way to a communal and unique form of life. Our empirical life-form can always be deepened, enhanced, and integrated, reaching out to new horizons. It belongs to the essence of human life never to be static or at a final stage. Formation is the developmental, dynamic essence of human life itself. *Consonant formation* of humanness calls for an enlightening, integrating dialogue between the various dimensions and articulations of human life in the light of an inspiring spiritual openness. In and through this intraformative dialogue, in interaction with the inner and outer poles of the formation field, the human life-form is emerging continually.

The Dynamics of Human Formation

The dynamism of human formation reflects the complexity of the preformation of human life. The human life-form is preformed as fundamentally transcendent. An unknown hidden transcendence is the ground of each human life and of each of its emergent dimensions. This unknown form is disclosed increasingly through the human spirit in dialogue with the other dimensions and with successive life experiences. The human life-form is essentially preformed as incarnated spirit. This means that the vital and functional dimensions and their articulations are essential parts of the emerging human life-form as a whole.

The complexity of the process of formative emergence is due also to the fact that the historical, vital, functional, and transcendent dimensions do not develop concurrently and with the same intensity. At various times a different dimension or articulation of the life-form is emphasized in its emergence and development. For example, in early life the vital dimension is central. Later the functional dimension emerges. Successively, the individual, technical, social, and aesthetic articulations of the functional dimension come to the fore. When such a special aspect takes center stage, so to speak, in the process of formation, it tends to absorb much of our form energy.

In the meantime, the sociohistorical dimension always plays a role, no matter which other dimension temporarily prevails. This is due to the essentially situated character of human formation. Likewise, the transcendent ground of all these dimensions is always an influence, at least implicitly. This is true even when its influence is denied explicitly or unknown on the level of focused consciousness. Without a minimum of spiritual form potency, no distinctively human growth would be possible. Initially, this transcendent ground of functional-vital growth is unknown or dormant. It only gradually gains in effective form potency and is only slowly disclosed to consciousness.

When the vital-functional dimensions are sufficiently formed and coordinated, more information energy becomes available for explicit reflective attention to the transcendent ground of these dimensions. The hidden unknown source of their growth begins to disclose itself in veiled symbolic ways generated by the creative imagination. This reflective attention, supported by the symbolic imagination, facilitates the development of a more explicit spiritual life. The spiritual life in turn elevates and fosters, by means of the incarnational or functional imagination, our communal and unique functional-vital unfolding—with great benefit for the formation of culture, civilization, and its underlying form traditions.

A living, symbolizing intuition of their unique spirit and its orientation enables people to flow more freely with their preformed aspirations. By its very nature, spirit tends constantly to incarnate itself in one's vital-functional life and sociohistorical surroundings. In the next several chapters, we shall explore more thoroughly the vital, functional, and transcendent dimensions of the life-form and their underlying sociohistorical setting within the formation field.

CHAPTER 6

The Vital Preformation of Life and the Formation Field

Distinctively human formation is spiritual; the style it assumes can be called a spirituality. A restriction of the meaning of words like spiritual and spirituality may lead one to exclude the body and its vitality from the realm of human formation. Such a restriction could be deformative. Instead of fostering consonance, it could lead to dissonance. The cause of such a misconception may be spirit-body dualism which still influences many minds and hearts. Hence, it is important to highlight the role of the vital dimension in the spiritual formation of human life. In this chapter we are mainly concerned with the basic ground of the vital dimension in its independent, merely vital operation. (In later chapters, we shall deal with the content and the interaction of this dimension with the other dimensions of human presence.)

Human spirituality is embodied and vital. It is the communal and personal style of our incarnated and incarnating spirit. All modes of human formation are modes of spiritualization in and through our vital, bodily life. We interact with daily formation situations neither as disembodied spirits nor as mechanical organisms. Our forming presence to people, events, and things should be a living unity of functionality and vitality permeated by spirituality. We experience our vital organism as that in, with, and through which we receive and give form to our life and surroundings.

Our vital body is our spontaneous entrance into the formation story of the world, of history, and of humanity as it discloses itself in sensory manifestations and images. We could not give form to anyone or anything, or be formed by them, without the bridge to effective formation that is our body. Our vital life makes formation situations available to us and makes us open to them. It nourishes both our creative and functional imagination. It is in and through our vital presence that life in its immediacy becomes a concrete, effective formation situation for us. The vital dimension of our emergent life-form is thus our prereflective, spontaneously forming presence to both personal and worldwide situations. This basic dimension thus represents our initial preformative presence to life situation and world. We call it preformative in the sense that the vital dimension on a basic level does not share in our distinctively human formation of the formation field. Since these initial vital movements disclose certain sensate formation potentials of the things we meet, we can ask about the way in which they serve to form our life and world.

Take a simple example, like holding a basketball in one's hands. Our moving hands disclose to us that the ball is spherical, solid, and leathery. They show us how it may be used to give a specific form to sport and entertainment. Our throwing hands unveil the ball's bouncing quality; our pressing hands discover its elasticity. We observe similar reactions in others when they discover, through their vital senses and movements, certain formation potentials of a basketball.

Vital Preformative Presence

Vital sensing, gestures, positions, movements, images, and language constitute our immediate preformative presence to formation situations. This presence is not a secondary mediation or a symbolization; it is our formative presence itself in its preformative immediacy.

Vital *preformation* should also be studied in relation to both our formative presence and the situation to which such presence is directed. Preformative vital involvement is an act of disclosure and implementation of certain sensate form directives given in various situations. We call this vital involvement preformative, in contrast to our free, conscious human formation.

Preformative sensate *form directives* for life are not ready-made; they are not clear-cut, like a map or photograph. Neither is formative meaning and value merely an arbitrary invention of our mind or creative imagination. Sensate form directives are born in and through a vital preforming presence, which connotes bodily being and behaving in our formation field. The meaning of such preformative directives may later be illumined, via the functional dimension, by the light of our formative spirit. Our spirit may be enlightened in turn by a form tradition that is consonant with reality.

The Original Obscure Field of Vital Preformation

Vital form directives emerge in and through our formative interaction with people, events, and things in our formation field. To grasp this vital preformation process, we must first understand something of the original obscure field of the preformation of life. Our later reflective formation presupposes this field and emerges from it. So does the science of formation, which presupposes that there are preforming events that have touched our formation awareness. Formation scientists presuppose in their work the spontaneous life of vital preformative, sensate, and imaginative interaction with people, events, and things. This interaction precedes both reflexive and reflective scientific development. It is the original source of any scientific concept we may elaborate in precise description and definition. Hence, we should pay attention not only to the exact, logical development of the science of formation, but also to its obscure origin in the spontaneous, vital, preforming interaction between human life and its formation field.

Our vital life interacts with the formation field prior to our approaching it in spontaneous reflection and later, when we approach it as formation scientists in critical scientific reflection. This preforming, sensate, and imaginative presence to things is not well-delineated in our appraising mind. It refers to a vital involvement in a field of preformation in which everything is interwoven with everything else, in which one thing points to another. The field of vital preformation is a fluid field, different from the appraised, affirmed, and well-delineated formation objects in our reflective field of formation.

It would be impossible for us to view our vital preformation with precision and clarity. We could not transcribe this region of preformation into systematic concepts that together would comprise a scientific system of formation. As soon as we begin to reflect intellectually or build a scientific system, we have already ceased to consider the undifferentiated field of vital preformation. We are already beyond spontaneous sensation and imagination. In spite of such reservations and restrictions, we can still express coherently our growing insight into this obscure, vital sphere. At the same time, we must be aware that we do not and cannot know precisely and exhaustively this original ground of reflective formation. Our understanding of the vital, preforming realm of life will always be blended with not-understanding. Our perception of it will be permeated by blind spots. While it is necessary for us to devise precise concepts when we build a science of formation, it is also essential to recognize the obscurity of the primordial field from which this science emerges. This recognition prevents us from making our theory of formation inflexible, closed, or immutable. It keeps it hypothetical and provisional, always open to fertilization by sensation and imagination.

Preformative Vital Life Directives

This preconscious field of vital preformation is so obscure that ordinary reflection cannot penetrate it. Our body discloses sensate directives and images before we are aware of its preforming activity. Our vitality has already invested the formation field with preformative, directive sensate meanings and symbols before we can think about these and appraise them consciously. Preformative disclosure of directives happens spontaneously. It is different from the conscious disclosure of form directives by our power of appraisal.

Certain things in a vitally preforming formation field, signify, for example, shelter, food, or danger before we can consciously appraise them as such. We are already preforming our life on the preconscious, not-yet-free level of vital interaction with our surroundings. Numerous examples demonstrate that preforming vitality discloses anonymous life directives: we see colors; we hear sounds; we feel with our fingers the roughness and smoothness of things; we smell odors; we taste flavors, all of which predispose the formation of human life in certain directions. Sounds, odors, flavors, and colors do not exist completely in themselves, independent of our vital, preforming interaction with our surroundings. Without this vital interaction, there would be no sights, sounds, or flavors.

Experience tells us that sounds, colors, flavors, and tactile qualities do not exist for us prior to some vital interaction with our surroundings. In this interaction we know obscurely in a *preconscious* way that the sunshine itself is warm, the grass green, and the rose fragrant. We preform and direct our lives accordingly. All such directive, sensate meanings are, as it were, the face which the world shows to us and with which it directs us when we vitally interact with it.

Our bodily behavior is thus a manifold preformation question. It makes the world reply in many ways. The world itself is a field of color and shape in reply to our visually preforming interaction with it. It is a field of sound in answer to our auditory interaction. The world offers itself immediately as a field of sensate feelings in reply to our tactile preforming interaction with it.

Neither the transcendent-spiritual nor the functional dimensions of the life-form turn to our formation field to derive form directives in this way. We do not interact consciously with the world so that we may constitute it as a field of color, sound, taste, touch, or smell. This preforming interaction takes place before we consciously appraise our formation field, before we make a free formation decision to interact with it in a certain forming way.

This original vital, preforming interaction is preconscious. It is a primordial articulation of our formation field by our vital life dimension. This articulation occurs at the deepest level of vital life. There the vital dimension of our presence is still intimately interwoven with the structure of our body. There we do not choose formation. We find ourselves already involved in an ongoing vital preformation of our formation field that happens before any choice. It gives rise to spontaneous sensate images that influence our formation before reflection can intervene.

We are always in some kind of formation on the vital level. Here we are neither conscious of our preformation nor are we its free subjects. Life-directing sensate experiences and images of color, taste, sound, smell, and touch result from a preformative, vital interaction with our surroundings. This occurs at such a depth of our organismic vital presence to reality that we are unable to penetrate it with our appraising mind. Neither are we able to influence this preformation directly by means of free *formation decisions.*

Below us, as transcendent-functional persons, is a vital substratum that forms our formation field in preconscious, prepersonal ways. This substratum is our vital life dimension itself at the point where it is still undifferentiated from its organismic structures. All preformative life directives, which emerge on this level, appear to be related to the vital structure of our body. We should thus not identify our life formation and the formation of our formation field with conscious or free formation only. Vital preformation is formation, too. It is one of the foundational sources of the forming orientations of our life.

Preformative sensate meaning originates in interaction. Our vital life is not passive; it assumes an active position, making preformative interaction possible. For example, if our vital life dimension in and through the appropriate organismic structures wants to interact visually and preformatively, it must assume the correct ocular position. The pupils of our eyes, for instance, must be dilated according to the darkness of the field of vision.

In other words, the vital life dimension, working in and through our organismic structures, has to locate itself in a situation in a certain way if this preformative sense directive is to emerge. Formative mind and will are not involved in this spontaneous assumption of a position, for we are not consciously aware of what happens in our vital life dimension while we are involved in visual preformation.

Scientific Reflection on Preformation

In the science of foundational formation, we take up consciously this vital preformation process. The concepts we use presuppose the sensate meanings and images that originated in our vital, preformative interaction with the life situation. As scientists, we always start out from the meanings we find already given in reality. Such meanings originate in the preformative interaction between the vital life dimension and its formation field. The personal-reflective and the practical scientific mode of human formation refer to the prereflective mode of vital preformation.

Scientific reflection on formation is a conscious, free, planned, and selective taking up of sensate meanings, images, and relations already given in the preformative interaction of our behaving body. Our vital life dimension—in and through the organismic structures of our body—preforms our formation field.

The structures of this field depend on the structures of our body.

Our embodied vital life is a possibility of directive disclosing interaction. The appearance of a natural formation field results from preforming interaction between our vital life and the world. As scientists we take this field up in a conscious, reflective way, but we do not constitute it, for—due to the preformative interaction of our life as organismic and vital—it is already there for our formative appraisal.

The natural world as the basic formation field in which we daily move is the result of the vital dialogue between our body and the surroundings in which it finds itself. The dialogue precedes our reflective or scientific formative appraisal of our formation field as it is presented to us as a result of that preconscious interaction. This seemingly natural formation field (as it appears to awareness) antedates the conceptual world of formative reflection and of formation science. We dwell initially and formatively in our formation field before our reflective-formative minds can take up this preconscious vital dwelling. The preconscious, vitally forming body is thus the initial source of all scientific formation designs, theories, and concepts.

CHAPTER 7

The Emergence of the Vital-Functional Dimension

In this chapter we shall deal with the emergence of the vital-functional dimension of the life-form under the influence of the human spirit, or transcendent dimension. What is needed initially is some provisional understanding of the vital dimension both in itself and as an integral part of our life formation.

The first two dimensions that give rise to human formation are the vital and the functional in mutual interaction. The vital dimension, in and by itself, signifies the biophysical-reactive aspect of our formation; the functional dimension refers to the managing, ordering, organizing, and controlling responsive aspect.

Here our question is not so much about the original operation of the vital dimension, but about its contents and qualities. This treatment may help us to compare it with the other dimensions of our life with a view toward their mutual support and eventual integration.

The vital dimension includes the sensations, sensate images, impulses, and sensual feelings that flow immediately from the biophysical preformation of our life. It encompasses the relative quality, intensity, pace, and excitability of vital impulses, feelings, and sensations. Viewed together, such impulses form a unique hierarchy within our vital life. Vitality comprises, moreover, the primary orientation and primitive organization of these components, an organization which is coformed by early impulsive reactions of the vital organism to its formation field. The immediate consequence of all these factors is our temperament, which obviously plays a significant role in our human formation.

In and by itself the vital dimension is merely reactive. It does not yet share the response potency of the functional dimension of life.

Hence, we need to discuss the way in which the vital dimension comes to share in a distinctively human formation process.

The Vital-Functional Relationship

A merely reactive vital life is not yet a fully human life of formation. It is only potentially a human form of life. Persons begin to emerge as distinctively human when a minimum of reflection enters their life. Reflection implies the possibility of humanly appraising our life direction. Such appraisal goes beyond instant vital reaction. It creates room for some choice of response. Shall I or shall I not eat that delicious sundae that stimulates my vital appetite? Would it be better to pass it up because of health or other considerations?

The merely vital-reactive life is a substratum, or infrastructure, of human formation. It provides the basic vital preformation of human life. Hence, it has to be taken into account at any moment of our journey. This vital base should be taken up as a dimension of distinctively human formation. One achieves this integration to the extent that the functional dimension, under the influence of the spirit, begins to affect the orientation and organization of our vital reactions. We thus need to know more about the relationship between the functional and the vital dimension.

The vital dimension shares in human formation through a kind of delegation to it of responsible formation power by the functional dimension. This delegation grants our vital dimension a certain relative formation autonomy that enables it to contribute on its own to our human formation.

In principle, vital reactions can only be directed responsibly by our functional formation power in the light of directives from the transcendent dimension. Yet it is possible to grant the vital dimension—after sufficient formation of its impulses—a relative autonomy. This independence must always remain within the limits set by the functional dimension. To return to our earlier example, I may have trained my vital appetite in such a way that it spontaneously turns off the instant eating reaction when offered high-calorie desserts that harm my health.

The process of intraformation entails, among other things, this formation of the vital dimension by the functional. The functional in turn should allow itself to be formed by the transcendent.

Within these limits the vital dimension can operate as a center of actualization and integration of the impulses of the human life-form. In this way it participates in the emergence of human life formation.

The functional dimension achieves this kind of formation of the vital by means of authorization. It authorizes the vital dimension, as it were, to do some of its work. The functional form potency directs, reforms, adapts, and integrates vital impulsive reactions. Ideally, it would do so in consonance with the compatible and compassionate response demanded by the sociohistorical situation and by the transcendent appraisal of what is congenial for this unique form of human life. It may use reformative imagination to move the vital dimension by images that stimulate its impulses in the desired direction. The formation and reformation of these vital impulses depends for lasting results on sufficient repetition, which inclines them to remain oriented in the consonant direction fostered by the in-spirited functional dimension.

The intra-, inter-, and outer poles of the formation field, and the formative events to which they give rise, may remain relatively the same for some period of one's formation history. In that case the functional dimension does not need to review or revise the main direction it imparted already to the vital impulses by repeated practice and formative imagery.

The functional dimension will initiate a new intraformative exchange with the vital dimension when this is desirable. Practically, such a revision may occur when a significant change in the inner or outer formation field takes place. A shift in the field direction of the formation process as a whole always involves the vital dimension. Likewise, a change of this sort in formation direction depends for its consonance ultimately on appraisal in the transcendent dimension of the life-form. All this is our way of saying that the vital dimension should become integrated into the human formation process as a whole.

Prehumanized Vital Dimension

Having posited both the personalized and the prepersonalized status of the vital dimension, it may be helpful to reconsider more fully its prepersonal structure. As we have seen, the vital dimension may not yet have been elevated to participation in human life formation. In that case this substratum is not yet an acknowledged point of departure for human formation, for its operation is not directed by appraisal but by various prepersonal vital elements. Its operation is determined by the preformed hierarchy of the prevalent strengths and directions of impulses, vital strivings, sensations, sensate images, and feelings. The vital dimension is guided, moreover, by impulsive reactions to which these preformed vital powers give rise when excited by inner and outer stimuli. Other determinants include the remembered residues of former reactions that satisfied the vital impulses. Indirectly, the prepersonalized vital dimension is determined in its impulsive reactions by the pain or pleasure evoked by its impulsive reaction to stimuli.

We could say that the prehumanized vital dimension is a unity of biophysical impulses and reactions. It is not yet formed or reformed by the distinctively human life-form as such. At this stage it is governed totally by vital likes and dislikes.

The vital dimension in and by itself does not appraise and determine its own reactions in relative freedom. On the contrary, it is determined. It lives, so to speak, by its own impulses, vital strivings, and sensations, and their sediments in bodily memory, imagination, and anticipation.

Distinctively human formation, on the other hand, points to a way of life in which people take responsibility for themselves. They act instead of react. They elevate the vital infrastructure of their existence to a dimension that participates in the responsible formation of their life. In this way, the vital dimension becomes a relatively autonomous participant in human life and freedom.

The emergence of human life formation signals the beginning of a free appraisal in which people relate creatively to the vital-reactive substratum of their human formation. They initiate an intraformative dialogue with the vitally given infrastructure of their existence and its instantaneous reactions.

The Foundational Dynamic of Emergent Human Formation

How and when does vital-reactive life begin to participate in human formation? Does the power of the vital-reactive life itself give rise to this formation or does some other form potency bring it about? From whence comes the distinctive humanness that marks our formation from that of other life-forms?

Distinctively human formation announces itself in the change from merely impulsive reactivity to reflective responsibility. People no longer react to events in their formation field on the basis of the pleasure or pain that a vital reaction instantly affords their impulses. They apprehend, appraise, choose, and project a certain way of receiving and giving form in their life. They take such chosen projects into account when responding to events in their formation fields. Such a functionally directive projection cannot come from the vital-reactive life in itself. As we have seen, this dimension alone cannot generate any functional project of formation. There must be another form potency that enables people to give and receive a distinctively human form in their life and world. This power must be beyond the closed circle of vital drives and their impulsive reactions. It must be capable of opening persons to a wider horizon of their formation field, to a layer of meaning that invites them to see themselves as more than reactive organisms in a field that has a merely vital significance. This power is the form potency of the human spirit.

Emergent Human Formation and the Power of Spirit

The *spiritual form potency*, which alone makes our formation distinctively human, gives rise to the dialogue between the functional and the vital dimensions within one's formation field. In so far as our formation is grounded on this potency to receive and give form beyond the determinations of the vital infrastructure, human formation happens. To be sure, one need not necessarily be aware of this transcendent power in one's formation; it can be quite active even when its existence is denied.

The power of spirit enables us to form our life in transcendent openness. This formation includes and at the same time transcends vital, functional, and sociohistorical determinants. Foundational human formation depends ultimately on our open relation to this humanizing power of spirit, even if this intraformative relationship remains unrecognized and unacknowledged.

This spiritual form potency is identical neither with the vital nor with the functional form potencies of people. Functional potencies enable us to participate in the vital, individual, technical, social, and functional-aesthetic aspects of daily life formation. The power of spirit is the hidden ground of all these forms of human participation. It makes them possible, but it also goes beyond them because it participates in the deeper formative meaning of the formation field. It includes and transcends all other formative meanings and directives. For this reason, transcendent participation may at times have to assert itself at the expense of certain vital, functional, and sociohistorical form directives in one's life that may be dissonant and deformative. (Such transcendence in detachment is made possible by one's openness to the epiphanies of the formation mystery, as will be discussed in chapter 14.)

Rupture of the Vital Impulse-Reaction Cycle

The science of formation describes the human spirit as the transmitter of the foundational unknown life-form hidden at the center of our being. The human spirit relates this foundational form to the preformed vital-reactive substratum of the life in which it is embodied. As a result of this reminder by the spirit of an inner hidden call, the closed impulse-reaction circuit of the vital life is disrupted. The essential elements of this cycle are the stimulated, vital impulse and its instantaneous reaction. The rupture between impulse and reaction happens with the advent of apprehension and appraisal. They break the cycle of stimulated impulse and of instant reaction. These spirit powers open people to a wider horizon that calls them beyond the immediate sphere of pleasure and pain that marks the vitally attractive aspects of the formation field. Opening up to this horizon is freeing. It liberates people from their initial captivity to outer stimuli. The *horizon of the spirit* creates perspective and distance. It makes possible the emancipation of one's vital reactivity so that it may become a free power of formative response. A dynamic intraformative interaction occurs between the vital-reactive and the in-spirited functional response that interferes with the closed circuit of stimulated impulse and instant reaction. This intraformative interaction signals the beginning of human formation in the proper sense.

Transcendent-Functional Dimension as Mediator

The emergent human life-form in its transcendent-functional dimension interferes with and mediates the reaction of the stimulated vital impulse. The spirit discloses our *foundational life call*. In its light, our spirit appraises the sociohistorical, vital, and functional information provided by the other form dimensions. The human spirit both grounds emerging human formation and nourishes its growth.

Conversely, when this intraformative interaction between spiritual formation and vitality is not realized, the distinctively human life-form is arrested in its unfolding. No interruption between stimulated impulse and instant reaction occurs. Therefore, the necessary condition for the possibility of spiritual formation is not fulfilled. This explains why all great form traditions insist on detachment, asceticism, or creative delaying and distancing as an absolute condition for the very possibility of a distinctively human or spiritual life.

Emancipation of the Functional Dimension

The emergence of the functional dimension as mediator between impulse and reaction implies an emancipation of this dimension. The human spirit makes this emancipation possible. Prior to the emergence of the mediating functional dimension, the vital life was merely reactive. After this emergence, the vital life becomes responsive and responsible by participation in the form potency of the human spirit. The functional dimension is liberated from its own captivity to vital impulses and their reactions. Through the mediation of the spirit, intraformative dialogue replaces the former bondage of reactivity to vital impulses and stimulation. This dialogue happens between an emancipated, increasingly spiritualized functional dimension and the preformed vital life of impulse and sensation.

We may say in a sense that human life formation is this intraformative relationship between the emancipated functional and the impulsive vital dimension. This relationship is rooted in the human spirit and maintained by it. Should intraformative interaction drop out and should one return to the autonomously functioning circle of blind impulse and instantaneous reaction, one's human formation would be interrupted. A dissonant prepersonal formation would take its place at such moments. In some cases, such a regression may be lasting. Functionality would then become a servant of vitality.

Our preformed need for consistency in life, for some kind of centering, is so powerful that life will be centered around some other project that excludes transcendent form directives. This artificial, forced centering is not open to change. It is a fixation that closes people off from their possibility of transcendence. This dehumanizing fixation plays the role of a quasi-human formation in the stunted life of such people.

If the flow of this open intraformative dialogue is diminished, so, too, is human life itself. The vital-reactive substratum begins to encroach again upon the distinctively human formation of life. The quasi-foundational pride-form, with its arrogant isolationist tendencies, takes the place of our preformed foundational life with its hidden transformative potency, unique truth, and nobility.

CHAPTER 8

Functional Formation

The functional dimension enables us to incarnate vital impulses and transcendent aspirations into our life as a whole. It is also the source of our effectiveness in the human formation of culture, community, form traditions, world, and nature. The immediate focus of the functional dimension is the formative effectiveness of the interaction going on in our formation field between ourselves and the actual people, events, and things that confront us. (The functional dimension can be problematic if it becomes overly dominant. Formation then becomes functionalistic, a one-sided and excessive development leading to the deformation of life.)

Functional formation starts early in life. Infants, playful and impulsive, react at first instantaneously to any stimulation of their feelings. Their reactions may remind us of the way in which household pets react. Yet we sense the beginning of a more functional human response. Children begin to grasp vaguely some of the consequences of their reactions. They begin to see that restraint is important. If they wildly give in to all impulses, they soon get into trouble with adults. Perception and thought begin to precede their reactions: they are no longer merely impulsive when they learn that adults will reward their more restrained behavior.

When children begin to exercise functional control over their impulsive feelings and desires, their reactions become more like responses. What gives form to their expressions is no longer limited to vital directives that spring only from impulses. Other directives that come from another dimension are being added to those drives that still erupt from their preformed impulsive lives: the *functional mind* is being awakened. This incipient mindfulness sends out other signals, other form directives. As a result, responses to feelings are no longer formed by impulses alone. Increasingly, new directives from the functional mind begin to coform a child's deportment.

This more functional response manifests better a child's individuality. In this sense, each child has a mind of its own. There is already a difference between the impulsive reactions of individual children before the awakening of the functional mind. Even when their reactions are instantaneous, thoughtless, and impulsive, they differ from child to child. Children show a certain vital uniqueness. The strength and kinds of impulses differ because vital preformation is unique. Added to this innate uniqueness are the influences their impulses undergo from the immediate physical and psychological environments.

Almost from the beginning, both the vital vigor of preformed impulses and their unique patterns are modulated by environmental factors such as the sociohistorical pulsations to which the infant is constantly exposed. Out of the interaction of preformed impulses and sociohistorical pulsations emerge the concrete articulations of the life of the child. The vital life, thus formed, is soon called upon to function effectively.

The child learns that it has to function within its formation field. This field issues concrete demands, attractions, repulsions, and impositions. At the earliest stage, as we have seen, the interaction between the vital life of the infant and its formation field is directed mainly by its vitalistic form directives. Then a first functional direction begins to complement and modulate the vital. Initially the child's functional adaptation is mainly one of external adjustment. The child tries to adjust its impulsive life directives to outside conditions. Because there is little light available from the transcendent dimension in this phase of initial functional formation, the laws of conditioning and reinforcement developed by certain behavioristic schools of psychology are somewhat applicable.

The initial functional direction of the child's life gradually becomes more established. Formative repetition of similar functional-vital directives gives rise to the formation of more lasting dispositions. These are called customs, habits, or character traits.

Not much transcendent light floods the functional mind during these early stages of formation. Yet this light is not totally absent. It is indirectly operative. For the human spirit begins to awaken in the child, especially when it is surrounded by people who let the spirit shine forth in their own life—then transcendent enlightenment grows in strength. Soon formation of the functional dimension is deepened and complemented by directives that come from the transcendent dimension of the human spirit. This spiritual potency turns both the vital and the functional dimensions of formation into consonant, distinctively human life-forms.

People who proclaim a functionalistic view of life would not agree with this description. They do not believe in the power of the human spirit. They would restrict all formation to the initial vital-functional process and its environmental determinants. In their view, vital-functional and environmental determinants are the exclusive explanation of life's formation.

Concrete Emergence of the Functional Dimension

From this general description of the functional dimension and its initiation, we have gained further insight into this crucial aspect of formation. We realize that human life implies a potentiality for effective functional presence in its formation field. This potency implies the ability for functional apprehension, appraisal, decision, memory, imagination, and anticipation. All of these can help us to manage life practically. This functional capacity is dormant in us at the beginning. As we have seen, the vital dimension dominates initially the life of the infant. The functional dimension emerges slowly and gradually to endow the child with a more explicit sense of individuality. It promotes in children a certain ambitiousness that can be used or abused in the further formation of their life. It enables them to develop a measure of skillful control over their lives. All of these functional capacities emerge during *interformation* with other people and practical interaction with a variety of challenging formation situations.

A first training in functional control takes place during a child's exploratory handling of toys and other objects. Another matter, crucial for functional development, is the way in which a child is toilet trained. Toilet training implies the acquisition of skills in functional body control. It also gives a child some control over interaction with adults, who often reward success in this area.

Gradually, children begin to try out ways of effectively influencing others to serve their own desires or ambitions. Coincident with this development comes a sense of functional individuality.

Around the age of two this new awareness of "I am I" is reflected in the negative stance the child may take in regard to suggestions or requests. This "no" signifies the appearance of *functional identity*. It asserts that what comes from others in their functional demands is "not me."

Functional identity, control, ambitions, and skills develop from this point, signaling a growth in the ability of effective apprehension, appraisal, and management of successive life situations. Typical outgrowths of the functional dimension are analytical, logical, imaginative, and technical skills; rational abstractions; practical self-reliance, and skillful diplomacy. All of this development depends on one's effective participation in the formation field.

Functional Enlightenment

The science of formation refers sometimes to this functional or managing dimension as the executive branch of human formation. A good executive must be strong and masterful in the practical appraisal and management of a situation. The functional dimension of the life-form plays a similar executive role. It represents the form potency for effective management and practical achievement. It knows how to accomplish something effectively or how to function well in practically appraised situations, though in and by itself this dimension may not know what ultimately to accomplish or where to go. Its light and motivation have to come from outside itself.

The functional dimension as form potency receives this light from the aspirations of the transcendent dimension, from the impulses of the vital dimension, from the sociohistorical pulsations of the culture, and from the mutual formative interaction of all of these. Following appraisal and decision, the functional dimension turns these suggestions, directives, and motivations into *ambitions*. Once an ambition is set within the functional dimension, it keeps on directing practical formative action. This action pattern shifts when the person decides to increase or diminish such an ambition. When change is desired, the person incites the functional dimension to open up to new sociohistorical, vital, and transcendent *form directives*.

Once the functional dimension is enlightened, it works to implement new directives via new effective ambitions. Accordingly, the functional mind plans strategies to execute the transcendent ideals and vital desires one has decided upon after due appraisal. This ideal or desire in turn becomes a functional ambition and project.

Functional Conscience

Relatively lasting projects and ambitions adopted by the functional dimension are maintained by means of the *functional conscience*. The latter ought to be distinguished from the *spiritual conscience*. A problem arises because it is possible to absolutize such ambitions and projects: the functional dimension may cut itself off from transcendent aspirations, vital impulses, and sociohistorical pulsations. Ambitions and projects in the functional conscience may tend to become static, inflexible, and out of touch with human life formation as a whole. Compulsiveness, rigidity, perfectionism, scrupulousness, and radical conservatism may be symptomatic of a stilted functional conscience. Stubbornness, willfulness, and even fanaticism may mark this onesided, functional type of life-form. Should this happen, we would speak not of the functional dimension but of functionalism, for the functional now excludes one or more sources of necessary enlightenment.

Exclusive Functional Dominance

Imagine that my functional project is to go to a movie. As an executive officer of my firm working overtime many nights and on weekends, I have the right to take an afternoon off for recreation. While the functional dimension organizes this project, I unexpectedly receive new information: some important customers will visit the company this afternoon and they want to see me. Seeing them may clinch a large order for my company and prolong the relationship between these customers and us. If I close myself off from this information in stubborn adherence to my project of seeing a movie, the functional mode then becomes exclusive or isolated.

I can close myself off in other ways from information coming to the functional dimension from my vital life. Imagine it is winter. The snow is piling up on the walks and driveway. My ambition is to shovel it, and to show my wife, kids, and neighbors that I am young enough in heart and body to do it despite my advancing years. I turn this project into an absolute "I should." It has to be executed no matter what. I push myself in the blind, functional persuasion that anything can be done if I try hard enough. My chest begins to hurt. If I kept in touch with the message of my vital life, I would have to admit that I am overtired, that my heart may be in danger, that this sudden outburst of vital activity after weeks of sitting in living rooms, offices, and cars without sufficient exercise is too much for my body—then I could alter my ambitions and projects accordingly. What if I do not listen? What if I allow my functional conscience to guide me stubbornly and to treat my body as if it were a machine? I may end up with a heart attack.

The inclination to live an almost exclusively functional life has lately increased significantly in the West. The functionalistic tendency has been strengthened by obvious advances. Minds and machines have numerous effective ways to control nature and society. Impressive measurable results of these combined efforts give rise to a growing fascination with the power of functional formation of one's life. Ambitions, projects, and skills, as well as the tools, techniques, systems, and methods to which they give rise, often become the exclusive or main dimension of human life to be promoted and formed.

Placing the functional dimension in the forefront may be done at the expense of the other key dimensions of formation. The wholeness of the flexibly embodied, situated presence of the unique human life-form in its formation field is then lost. The excellent principles of functional control may be universally and indiscriminately applied to all aspects of life and culture. Transcendent, vital, and social directives may become subjected to the norms of the marketplace, these being efficiency, cleverness, acquisitiveness, and enhancement of status and power in the eyes of the greatest number of people.

Due to this functionalistic orientation, we may become alienated from our *spirit potency*. We may lead busy, efficient lives without deeper meaning or transcendent values. Only what is measurable means something to us; only what is productive in a material sense seems worth our efforts.

An exclusive functional orientation may shut out the claims of our vital dimension for nutrition, rest, relaxation, and recreative exercise. The excessive "shoulds" of functional performance may sacrifice health and physical vigor to the relentless pursuit of status, power, possession, and achievement, even in the transcendent realms of asceticism, charity, and detachment. These realms are easily corrupted in a functionalistic culture. So, too, are the persons serving them, for they live in forgetfulness of the fact that the highest values and form directives of human life cannot be obtained by functional skills alone.

The Consonant Functional Dimension

The functional dimension should remain focal in regard to practical matters of formation. It is only through effective functioning that the person may bring to fruition appraised pulsations, impulses, ambitions, and aspirations. A consonant functional dimension enables one to integrate and harmonize these formative movements into well-ordered effective projects of decision and action. It is in and through incarnation that our hidden foundational life-form keeps on disclosing itself.

Functional willing (or, executive will) should be activated only for service. It should not dominate any aspect of one's own or another's life, for the strength of the functional comes from the transcendent dimension, and not the other way around. We must strive for a firm yet gentle functional presence in service of our transcendent-vital ideals and needs. This service aspect of the functional dimension implies that we cannot find our identity or that of others in functioning alone. Our deepest identity belongs to our uniquely embodied spirit. Our functional identity has to be formed in dialogue with this gradual disclosure of our embodied spiritual identity. The latter becomes gradually known to us in successive situations and in many trials and errors during the lifelong adventure of self-disclosure.

We must develop faith in our functional form potency so that we can let go of any functional project when life calls for a pause or an interruption. Firmness of functional potency grants us the quiet conviction that at any time we can return and take up where we left off. This persuasion enables us to rest when necessary and prevents us from driving ourselves or others to a breakdown. We should foster a wise balance of control and serviceability to the formation field as disclosed not only functionally but also through the other dimensions and articulations of formative presence. This dynamic balance enables our *foundational life-form* to emerge via timely participation in life and world.

Like the other dimensions, the functional also has to grow by trial and error. At times we are bound to over- or underestimate the strength of the functional dimension and its openness to our embodied spirit. We must then test the limits of our functional strength and openness. We have to appraise and accept the strengths and weaknesses of our unique spiritual-vital presence at this moment and arrange our life accordingly with the help of the functional dimension.

Conclusion

We are now able to present a provisional enumeration of the main components that coform the functional dimension of our life. The functional dimension is first of all the agent of appraisal of possibilities for effective management within our formation field. It assists in the appraisal process by functional imagination, memory, and anticipation, and by acts of trial and error to test such possibilities. In practical life situations, the functional dimension of human formation is in the foreground of our forming presence. The potentiality for the development of this dimension is part of our preformation. Its actualization takes time, experience, energy, and attention.

The functional dimension is marked by individuality, ambition, and control, and by the development of a rational-analytical and functional intelligence sustained by functional imagination. It fosters functional appraisal and executive willpower, diplomatic and politic management of formative situations, and the development of practical and technical skills.

Added to the above is the development of a functional conscience. This is a depository of effective rules, ambitions, projects, and principles inspired by the transcendent dimension or borrowed from the culture.

Functional identity begins to develop early in life, first in a negative and later in a more positive fashion. It is not to be equated with our deepest identity, which is spiritual or transcendent. Functional identity should be formed and transformed in dialogue with our emergent spiritual identity. The whole structure of functionality should be open to change and development through trial and error in the light of transcendent, vital, and sociohistorical form directives.

Spiritual inspirations, aspirations, ideals, and symbols, as well as vital desires, can only become effective in the everyday formation of life and world if they are translated into functional ambitions and projects. However, the functional dimension is always in danger of absolutizing itself. In that case its ambitions and projects become exclusive or isolated. Subsequently, functional conscience may become stubborn or perfectionistic.

The functional dimension of life is the focal dimension of presence in any practical situation. Hence, the functional dimension is the principle of practical integration of the aspirations, ambitions, and impulses of the human life-form as a whole. It is the principle of effective presence to life and world, within the realistic limits and potencies found in one's formation field.

The functional dimension should be as firm, serviceable, and open as possible. It should help us to maintain the right balance between the basic polarities of our formation field. It should develop sufficient confidence to allow us to let go of functional activity or intensity when we so desire.

A consonant emergence of the functional dimension demands periodic reappraisals of its limits and possibilities as these are disclosed by trial and error in successive life situations.

We can now also enumerate some limits of the functional form potency. With our functional intelligence alone, we can never fully comprehend or imagine our own nature or the nature of the universe in which we live. Our functional intelligence and the brain evolution that sustains it allow us to deal with only a limited portion of the universe and our own human life. The functional mind with its functional imagination is designed to help us survive; it helps us mainly to understand things about ourselves and our surroundings that directly concern our physical and functional well-being and development. For this reason we do not have any direct intuitive grasp of the minute world of subatomic particles. Neither can we grasp directly the vast cosmos and the properties of space and time.

Our functional mind helps us to organize concrete daily life in nature and society. It teaches us what we need to know about nature, self, and others as they appear in everyday life. Nature did not develop our brains in such a way that they either could or need to perceive fully the micro- or macrocosmos. Science tells us that they exist, but this fact does not alter our everyday functional understanding. Our functional notions of space, time, and causality are innate, or preformed. So is our notion of human life. With our functional brains alone, we shall never be able to comprehend the formation mystery around which our foundational sense of identity is built. We can understand the human mind and social aspects of identity formation, but only our spirit intuits our basic identity as existing in this world and tending beyond it.

CHAPTER 9

Distinctively Human Formation

In the foregoing chapters, we considered the vital and the functional dimension of the human life-form. We discussed our ability to be present to our formation situations by functional and transcendent modes of presence. These take up, complete, and permeate the vital-bodily mode of preformation. The higher spiritual mode of formation is distinctively human. It is not shared by infrahuman beings, as is the vital mode.

The essential characteristic of this human mode resides in its power to go beyond mere vital directives preformatively disclosed in our formation field. The human spirit surpasses the limits of the vital. Spirit is the power to disclose and give form to life and world critically and creatively in interformative action with others. The results of such spiritual disclosure are freely appraised form directives. They complement, correct, and enhance the reservoir of vital preformative directives.

The forming presence of the human spirit is properly identified with the transcendent dimension of our life-form. We aspire to spiritually meaningful life directives that transcend the limitations of our merely vital and functional concerns. People develop more or less coherent sets of such transcendent directives. In the science of formation, these inspiring, coherent guidelines, along with the life-styles to which they give rise, are called current or enduring spiritualities and form traditions.

Functional Formation

As we have seen, the forming presence of the human spirit can be secondarily attributed to the functional dimension of the life-form. This dimension is so to speak, an in-between area. It is a center of many bridges. It functions as a bridge between the vital and the transcendent dimensions of the life-form. This function enables people to translate their *transcendent aspirations* or form directives into workable *functional ambitions*. Sober ambitions, as practical form directives, take into account the preformative signals of the vital dimension. The functional also provides the bridge between transcendent aspirations and vital impulses of people and the concrete directives of their formation field. People can only effectively give form to the world and to their formation situation if their functional ambitions are compatible with the reality around them. This reality is the necessary point of departure for their formative and reformative presence in the world.

The forming presence of the human spirit is only secondarily and conditionally attributed to the functional dimension. The emergence of this dimension is a result both of vital and transcendent life directives. The functional form potency is both illumined by the human spirit and stimulated by the vital dimension. Unfortunately, the functional can close itself off from this transcendent influence and deteriorate into an isolated, autarchic center of power. This happens under the impact of both the pride-form and the historical pulsations that glorify mere functionality. An isolated functionality may bypass not only the transcendent but also vital form directives. Life becomes functionalistic instead of wisely functional. Vital-emotional needs of the body are neglected or repressed in service of functional achievement. Transcendent aspirations are refused and replaced by functional ambitions. Functional-rational achievements may become a tyrannical concern even in religion, where anxious functional perfectionism may become the norm for some adherents. In religious studies, functional rationalistic explanation and systematization may replace all attention to transcendent experience and imagination.

Historical Formation

Historical pulsations necessarily play a role in these dimensions. They do the same in every dimension of human formation. *Transcendent aspirations, functional ambitions,* and *vital impulses* are in some measure influenced by *historical pulsations* in society. People begin to adopt them unwittingly in infancy and childhood. Hence, we identified the historical dimension of the life-form, which operates as a kind of matrix of many directives that emerge in all dimensions and articulations of the life-form as such. It is a lifelong task of formation to help people become the subject instead of only the object of their history. They must face and appraise the historical pulsations that form them. Certain contemporary pulsations favor the autarchic development of the functional dimension at the expense of the transcendent and the vital, to the serious detriment of human spirituality and vitality and the formative imagination nourished by both. This makes it much more difficult for people today to enjoy a harmonious, consonant life formation, to become resilient, joyous, peaceful, and effective (in the best sense of this word).

To be sure, some of the preformative pulsations that manifest themselves in the vital dimension are not open to transcendent-functional reformation. They are the result of the evolution of human organisms over the millennia. Yet even postevolutionary historical pulsations begin to affect people before they can freely appraise their meaning and value for life. Once they are able to appraise them, they may or may not accept them as permanent form directives for their own congenial and compatible unfolding.

Historical Form Traditions

Related to this historicity of formation is the fact that human formation is always *interformation* with those who went before us, who now live with us, and who will come after us. Such interformation has led historically to the emergence of various form traditions, usually of a religious or ideological nature. Such traditions are embedded in the customs, symbols, rituals, and resources of our formation fields. It is impossible for an individual person (or even for a few generations of people) to create sufficiently tested formation directives, symbols, and resources. Hence, individuals should either implicitly or explicitly join one of the form traditions which operate in thought, symbol, and rich imagery as a living set of preferred historical pulsations, to be assimilated, lived, enriched, and deepened by the followers of that tradition.

Each form tradition is conformed both by its foundations and by temporary accretions to such foundations. It is the responsibility of formation scientists, and to a lesser degree of each follower of a form tradition, to become aware of what is foundational and what is accretional in the tradition concerned and to appraise their respective consonance with one's life formation. This enables the follower to become not only the object but also increasingly the subject of a form tradition. One becomes the subject of these foundational preferred pulsations, and of those accretions that are still relevant, by personal participation in the basic experiences and images that gave rise to their emergence.

Such personal participation in the history of preferred formation experiences is made possible by a dwelling on the classical symbols and resources of a tradition. One has to relive and reenact experientially the past of a tradition to benefit as fully as possible from its rich and imaginative resources. By doing so, one becomes increasingly able to appraise critically other historical pulsations in one's society in the light of one's preferred form tradition.

Permeation of Vital Formation by Spiritual Formation

The preconscious vital dialogue with one's formation field should be permeated by one's human spirit and spirituality. The vital life dimension should be taken up in a spiritual manner. The functional and transcendent life dimensions should be increasingly active in the vital dimension of human formation. This does not imply that the human mind will always be able to penetrate the original dialogue between vital body and world. We will never know clearly and distinctly how this vital dialogue forms our perception of the color and scent of a rose, or of the flavor of honey. In some measure we shall be able however, to organize, expand, enhance, foster, and limit in a formative way this vital dimension of the life-form and its preformation of the formation field.

This interaction and its subsequent preformation of the formation field is the vital basis of all life-forms, perceptions, images, thoughts, and sciences. Thus vital preformation is a permanent and indispensable event. Its disappearance would mean the disappearance of the empirical life-form as a whole, for it would mean death.

The increasing permeation of the vital life by the human spirit leads to a fuller expression of communal and personal spirituality in human vitality. Such vital, image-laden expressions of the life of the spirit deepen the effective forming presence of people in formation situations and in the world. This forming presence, in and through the vital dimension via the functional, can be transcendent and rich. The capacity for spiritual presence increases with one's growth in spiritual formation and its permeation of all dimensions and articulations of life. One's organismic, vital life becomes more and more a spiritualized and personalized vital life. Even one's involuntary neuromuscular system of vital formation can be modulated by means of appropriate imagery.

Examples of Spiritualization of Vital Formation

The movements of an infant, for instance, are jerky, disorganized, and ungraceful. Anger is expressed in a primitive vital fashion: the little body may squirm, kick, and scream; the face may redden and the breathing be impaired. As children grow older, they begin to manifest in their *apparent form* of life that they as subjects are more fully present in their bodily senses, postures, and movements. They begin to transcend mere vital impulsive reactions. A first awakening of the human spirit enables them to give form to their anger more effectively. The vital expression of their anger becomes more socially compatible. It makes them more adept in interformative interaction with others and in their outer formative presence to life situations.

To take another example, an intoxicated adult may become enraged because he cannot fit his key in the keyhole. His vital fury, instead of leading him to an effective functional probing of the keyhole, erupts in unadapted movements. We can observe similar reactions in an adult who panics in an emergency. People may say that such persons forget them*selves* or are beyond them*selves*. The vital impulsive acts of infants and those of intoxicated or panic-stricken people, are ill-adapted attempts to give form to resistant life situations.

The permeation of the vital dimension by the transcendent and functional can be observed in many apparent vital expressions. The face of an infant is somewhat empty of expression. Painters prefer to depict the faces and figures of older people. In the maturing, increasingly spiritualized human body, the face, hands, movements, and posture radiate the presence of the human spirit much more fully than the not yet sufficiently spiritualized body of the child. For this reason, committed older people, such as dedicated farmers, soldiers, clergy, musicians, business persons, or teachers may sometimes be recognized by sensitive observers of the human scene, even if they have little information as a clue. Their personalized, dedicated, professional modes of life and experience have permeated their bodily appearances. Even the manner in which they move may reveal the transcendent-functional style of their professional dedication. (The term professional is used in this example not in the functionalistic sense of the word but in its original root meaning, which suggests persons who really profess in their loving labor a transcendent commitment to their specialized contribution to the effective formation history of humanity and its facilitating conditions.)

This progressive incarnation of the transcendent-functional dimensions of the life-form is observable in the body as, for instance, in the human hand. The movements of the hands of human persons and those of the paws of primates are very different. The functional and expressive quality of the paw of a primate and its movements is limited by its vital-biological needs. The spontaneous functions and expressions of human hands are of virtually infinite variety and refinement.

Spiritual Formation of World and Immediate Situation

The human spirit permeates formatively not only the functional and expressive movements and postures of the human body, but also the surroundings to which people continuously give form. The human life-form as vitally embodied leaves its formative mark wherever and whenever it emerges in nature and history. The human life-form influences, masters, takes hold of, embodies, or forms, its surroundings in countless ways. It forms them into a distinctively human world through its vitally forming involvement in reality. This is true not only of the individual person but of humanity as a whole.

The human race as an historical community of emergent human life continuously forms itself. It does so by being present to reality, and by trying to disclose consonant form directives. The spiritual possibilities of the human life-form have been prepared and disclosed in the course of millennia of evolutionary preformation and the subsequent history of humanity and its world. It is in the spiritually creative historical community that the human life-form gives rise to form traditions filled with inspiring life directives. These traditions mark humanity's erratic ascent and enlightenment.

The way in which people give form to their homes, for example, is the outgrowth of a long history of in-spirited bodily perception and formation of the world. By in-spirited acts of seeing, touching, and using, humanity has disclosed the formative potentials of stone, wood, glass, and tools; of protective walls to keep out rain, snowfall, and scorching sun; of various ornamentations of symbolic expressions of the human dwelling.

Vertical and Horizontal Interformation

Human formation is fundamentally interformation, proceeding vertically, in preformative evolution and formation history, and horizontally, in contemporary cultures. *Vertical* preformation and interformation mean that people assimilate what evolution preformed in them and what other humans have formatively disclosed before them. *Horizontal* interformation implies that they are open in personal and critical appraisal to the formation experiences, insights, and form directives of those who share with them the present dynamics of human formation history.

Both our forebears and our contemporaries disclose, in apparent vital-bodily acts and expressions, aspects of the formation mystery that are relevant, for example, to the giving of concrete form to the place in which people live and to the style of the forming culture that they share. Even rebellion against former and present directives of formation is elicited by the directives the revolt reacts against. Revolt cannot be understood without the form directives that it resists or attempts to correct.

Science, Technology, and Spiritual-Vital Formation

It is important to realize that all sciences represent central modes of human formative presence. The scientific attitude is a way of functionally utilizing in an effective and organized manner our vital-bodily encounter with life and world. This is obviously true of experimental science. For authentic experimentation implies an efficient and well-organized embodiment of searching appraisals of the hypothetical mind. This hypothetical appraisal of the exploring spirit is embodied in sense observation and in effective manipulation of microcosmic and macrocosmic formations in the universe by means of experimenting hands and their instrumental extensions.

Technology also means the organized embodiment of formative human involvement in life and world. This technical embodiment assists people in their giving form to life and world. It subdues these realities, in certain of their aspects, to the transcendent and functional powers of humanity in which the spirit shines forth. People humanize or spiritualize not only their vital life but also the world. Their culture becomes their second vital dimension, the extension of their body. Consequently, the creations of formative science and technology can be a unique expression of the spiritually enlightened functional presence of humanity in the universe.

Suppose that a sole survivor of a shipwreck is stranded on an island and feels himself to be completely forlorn. Suddenly, he spies a small house with a garden on the other side of the island. A spiral of smoke rises from the chimney. He is overjoyed and deeply moved, for this home and garden are formed by a vital-functional and transcendent presence. At this moment, the island is totally changed for him. It becomes a shared human world.

Everywhere in history we find traces of this forming embodiment of human presence. It enables us to reconstruct the formation history of a prehistoric tribe on the basis of form residues in which they expressed their formative powers. Prehistoric grottoes covered with the wall paintings of our ancestors hold a peculiar fascination for us. We realize that we are communicating interformatively with people who lived thousands of years ago. They are with us in the rocks and stones to which they gave form in terms of their functional-transcendent presence. Their human embodied spirit is not strange to us but deeply familiar. Their human spirituality speaks in their drawings.

Vital involvement in life situation and world thus means an involvement via bodily senses and movements. When people transform acres of wild prairie into fertile fields, they are involved with earth, weeds, and stones by means of their eyes, their sense of touch, and their ears. They may interact formatively with the earth by means of their measuring walk and their digging, weeding, planting hands. In such ways humanity is always reforming the world by the vital embodiment of its aspirations and ambitions. It is this continual formation event that reforms the world. The vital *embodiment of human aspirations and ambitions* appears most strikingly in our own day. Science and technology, as the incarnation of formative skills and knowledge, reform the world at a pace never possible before in the course of its preforming evolution and human formation history.

Art and Spiritual-Vital Formation

To be sure, science is only one mode of disciplined, formative engagement. Art is another vital-bodily mode of forming presence. A striking example is the dance. Primitive tribes formed their vital movements as rhythmic embodiments of their thoughts, feelings, and attitudes regarding their gods, ancestors, wars, weddings, childbirths, hunts, harvests, and other foundational dimensions of their form tradition. They attempted, moreover, to transform magically the course of formation events in their world by such vital manifestations and incarnations.

Symbolic, experiential disclosure of the *formation mystery* prevails in such ritual dances, as it does in other artistic endeavors. Some of this mystery remains as a residue in all great art. For this reason, art loses its character when it becomes too intellectual, pragmatic, or technical.

Physical and Experiential Research and Spiritual-Functional-Vital Formation

Physical scientists aim to disclose and reform the world by means of well-organized, planned, and controlled use of vital-bodily senses and movements. Experiential scientists of human life formation try to disclose and foster the congenial and compatible formation of people by means of well-structured research designs that imply sense observation and a bodily expression that makes the results available for intersubjective validation.

Both types of research, physical and experiential, make us realize that our scientific mode of forming presence is a distinctively human way of involvement in the world. It is rooted in the foundational structure of our human life-form. For the human life-form is a unity of transcendent-functional and vital life dimensions. Our human way of disclosing and giving form implies the vital-bodily as well as the transcendent-functional dimensions. Bodily sense and movements are involved when infants try out things by tasting, touching, looking, and hearing. They experiment all day long and in the course of this formative process they master their world.

Children are incipient scientists for science is always a disciplined vital participation in that which is given bodily.

The necessity of vital bodily mediation moves scientists to the formation of instruments that expand the vital and functional power of their bodily senses and movements. Such vital-functional expansion of human *formation powers* is the necessary condition for new disclosures. It gives rise to new forms of cultivation and utilization of the ongoing formation of the microcosmic and macrocosmic universe by the formation mystery. It makes humanity a more effective participant in the forming power of the formation mystery.

In modern science we are witnessing an amazing extension of the observation power of the vital dimension of the human lifeform. Indirectly this extension is also an extension of the forming power of the human spirit, which inspires this vital dimension through the functional dimension. This development is constantly stimulated and maintained by the most foundational striving of humanity, that is, by the striving to give and receive form, to share in the formation mystery, to embody oneself in reality by giving form to it in ever new yet compatible ways. Forming embodiment is a deep urge in humanity. All human activities and inventions are ultimately its expressions.

CHAPTER 10

Spirituality and Sexuality

What is the structure of the sexual articulation of our vital life? How is it related to our spiritual life? How does it interact with the historical, functional, and transcendent dimensions of our formation? These are some of the questions we may ask ourselves.

The Dissonance of Sexuality

Preoccupation with sexuality often outweighs concern for other aspects of our life. Because sexuality draws our attention so prominently, we suspect that this aspect of our life is not as consonant with the totality of human formation as it should be.

We can compare this development with other similar situations. For example, we are not particularly conscious of our fingers when we try to give form to a picture on the wall of our living room by nailing it to a selected spot. If we happen to strike our thumb instead of the nail, attention is drawn immediately to this small part of our functional life. Our thumb is no longer an unnoticed helper in the process of giving form to a picture on the wall. We may have to set aside our immediate project to seek first aid in service of vital-bodily functioning itself.

An analogous situation may emerge in society. For instance, people do not pay much attention to the water they drink. But if someone dies of typhus, water may become a main topic of conversation. In other words, when an aspect of ongoing daily life is no longer functioning in *consonance* with the whole of our unfolding, it draws disproportionate attention to itself. Something similar seems to happen in regard to the *sexual articulation* of our vital formation in our contemporary world.

Proximate Directives of Sexual Life Formation

Let us look at some proximate directives concerning our sexual life. We shall not refer here to the remote basic directives. Concern for these is the task of the philosopher, the theologian, or the ideologist of the tradition to which people commit themselves. We are primarily concerned with the proximate directives people maintain in regard to their sexual formation.

What strikes us at once is the tendency of each generation to impose on the succeeding one its own directives for safeguarding the life directives it holds sacred. The following generation may indeed adopt these protective directives. Often, however, it reacts against them and falls into an opposite extreme.

For example, one generation may insist that regardless of the occasion, exposure of the body is always a menace to the maintenance of remote directives pertaining to disciplining the sexual articulation of life. Extremists of the next generation may claim that frequent nudity is ideal. Both immoderate directives tend to isolate sex from the human formation field as a whole.

Excessive Sexual Security Directives

Some people may be saturated with excessive security directives regarding their *sexual formation*. They may have adopted such directives long before they were capable of appraising them in congenial, compatible, and compassionate ways. Our bias in regard to these directives may be either too loose or too strict. Both extremes prevent us from appraising such directives for what they are. We may assign them a position that lifts them out of their original context. They may reach unrealistic proportions. Sometimes such directives are called traditions. Appraised more carefully it appears that many of them are not really time-honored traditions, but rather the biases of a particular period of our formation history.

People may adopt the safeguards of a proper sexual life in an improper way. Protective measures have become more important to them than the directives they are supposed to protect. People may become obsessed with them. Worse than this, the way in which they appreciate them may be beset by false notions about the nature of sexuality. These misconceptions are usually not due to the basic directives of their form tradition. They are the result of a deformation of their life, of an unwholesome appraisal of sexuality.

We should first clarify the issue of the sexual preformation of life and world. Then we shall ask ourselves how people can integrate the sexual articulation of their vital life in their distinctively human or spiritual life. We shall also raise the question of how they can foster such integration in accordance with the foundational directives of the tradition to which they may have committed themselves. The main objective of this chapter remains, however, to clarify and illustrate the role of the vital life dimension in human sexual formation as seen by the science of formative spirituality.

The Foundational Structure of Vital-Sexual Formation

Many people experience a split between sexual and other aspects of their life. This rift is often rooted in a misconception concerning the relationship between the vital-bodily and the functional-transcendent dimensions of formation. One sees them as somehow separated. Ideally, however, there should be no dissonance between them. As humans we are a vitally embodied, transcendent consciousness. All our modes of forming presence act through our vital life. Our vital body is that which grasps and seizes the world. It is our spontaneous entrance into the situations we meet successively. We could not grasp, love, apprehend, or appraise our formation field and the people we meet in it without this bridge that is our body.

The vital dimension is a never absent bridge; it is a bridge that we are. It makes life situations available to our formation powers. In and through the vital dimension, a life situation becomes initially a formation situation for us; it becomes ours. Our vitally preforming presence to life situations makes them exist for us as formative before we think about them, muse over them, or reflect on them. Obscure but real, vague but factual, our vital presence is our spontaneous preforming presence in our formation field. Vital behavior discloses to us the *formation potential* of situations. As gesture, movement, touch, and language, vital behavior is our preforming dwelling in our formation field. It is our immediate preformative in-touchness with people, events, and things.

Vital preformation is thus not a mediation or symbolization of our projects, desires, or meditations. It is truly us as vital—as already embodied desire, project, aspiration, and ambition. This vital presence that we are is the locus for appropriation of preformative sense and meaning. Vital behavior is the original preforming presence by which we, as vital human beings, make life situations forming situations for us.

Our Vital Pre- and Coformation of the World

As a vitally preforming presence, we are already giving form to situations, even if we are not yet conscious of this preforming activity. Our vital-bodily presence invests life situations with formative meanings before we think much about them. It imposes a meaning on people, events, and things that is not a result of conscious appraisal. For example, certain things already assume for us, as vital presence, the meaning of shelter, food, or sexual desirability before we can consciously appraise such meanings. Spontaneously, we are a form-giving presence on the preconscious, merely vital, and not-yet-free dimension of our life.

We are thus always already giving form in our vital life. We call this *preformation* because of the prereflexive nature of our vitally forming presence. It means that we are not yet free in form appraisal and choice. The sensual forms of color, taste, smell, and sound, for example, are the results of a preconscious interaction of our vital dimension with our formation field. This extraformative interaction takes place at such a depth that we are unable to appraise it fully in the light of our reflective consciousness. Neither are we able to give form consciously to this vital interaction by means of insightful appraisals and decisions.

There is in us a vital form agency that is preconscious and prepersonal. This agency is intertwined with our body itself. All forms that emerge out of this vital dialogue with our formation field appear to correspond with the structure of our body. Hence, we should not identify our form-giving presence exclusively with our transcendent-functional conscious and free formation acts. We should realize that our vital bodily form dimension is already preforming our formation field for us before we enter it as free form agents.

Sexual Formation and Vital Field Formation

Life situations thus appear to us in manifold forms that are already preformatively given and are filled with potential form directives for our life. One of the forms that may appear in our life situation is the sexual form. A woman may have a sexual form meaning for a man, and vice versa. Men and women are vitally present to one another and they preform in and through their vital presence the sexual form potential of each other. Our culture has created the term "sex appeal" to indicate the sexual form potential people and things may spontaneously have for us.

Our body as vitally seeing is a preforming question to which our formation field replies in the form of shape and color. As vitally hearing, our body is a preforming question to which our formation field replies in the form of sound. Our body as vitally sexual is a preforming question to which our formation field replies in the form of sexual formation potential. The sexual articulation of the vital dimension of our human life-form necessarily and spontaneously evokes a formation field of sexual forms and meanings. It does so in a fashion similar to the visual modality of our vital dimension, which evokes the formation of shape and color. Our visual modality may not have developed at all or in all dimensions. Then the formation of a field of shape and color is out of reach, or it may be limited, as in the case of color blindness. If the *sexual articulation* of our vital life has not been developed, then the *preformation* of a field of sexual forms and directives does not exist for us. The field of sexual formation remains a closed book. Consequently, it cannot appeal to us or tempt us.

Such absence of a field of sexual meaning that is vitally pre- and conformed by us is neither a virtue nor a vice. Sexual virtue is only possible as a free, conscious response by the human spirit to the appeal of a preformed sexual formation field. The absence of such sexual preformation would make virtue and vice in this area of human spirituality impossible.

Spirituality and Sexuality

It is clear that our sexual preformation of life situations, people, and things is not something due to our spirit or to our transcendent consciousness. Our spiritual, or distinctively human, response toward preformed sexual appeals can make us increasingly free and conscious in this regard. Yet preformed sexual appeal itself is not a free or conscious formation. It is presented to our spirit, not formed by our spirit. We can freely foster this preforming appeal, expose ourselves to it, dwell in it or remain with it, or we can diminish its power by withdrawing our attention from certain aspects of our formation field. The initial sexual appeal offers itself to our spirit spontaneously and unexpectedly.

The first moment of the preformation of sexual appeal involves the vital dimension of our life form. The next moment involves that of our distinctively human response to this appeal. Ideally, this response should be congenial, compatible, and compassionate—one that is consonant with the uncontestable foundations of the tradition to which we may have committed ourselves. Briefly, our response should emerge out of the integrated totality of the life-form we have disclosed and realized at this moment of our history. To repeat, the first moment of sexual appeal is unavoidable; the next moment is at least minimally free. The first moment involves a particular preformation; the next moment calls for the integration of the particular preformed sexual situation into the totality of our spiritual life formation.

Sexual impulses impose themselves on us as an invitation to our freedom as spirit. In other words, the spiritual integrity of our emergent life may be thrown in question many times by our vital impulses. This vital questioning is a result of a spontaneous preformative interaction between our vital dimension and the life situation in which we find ourselves.

Whether or not we safeguard the consonance of our life depends upon the response of our spiritual freedom. It can be integrative or disruptive. We can respond in consonance with the present disclosure and implementation of our life-form and its sustaining tradition. If these conditions are fulfilled, our answer is integrative. If not, it is dissonant and disruptive and may lead to feelings of guilt and failure.

There is in our vital dimension itself an orientation or direction that preforms life situations sexually before our free appraisal and choice. Foundational formative spirituality includes the art of appraisal and integration of the results of such preforming directives of our vital life dimension. Such appraisal and integration takes time and patience. Consonant spirituality is not an instant accomplishment. Neither can it provide us with such clear insight into the sexual articulation of our life that it leaves no shade of obscurity.

Sexual preformation of life and world originates in a preconscious sphere of vital presence that is not open to the fullness of rational understanding. Therefore, this articulation of our life always remains somewhat obscure. It is impossible to say exactly where the sexual preformation of our formation field begins and where it ends. It is blended with many other sensuous and sensual preformations that originate in the same region of preconscious vital interaction between our human life-form and its formation field. Some people may strive too anxiously for a clear and distinct knowledge of all shades and nuances of their vital formation. If so, they develop an obsessive-compulsive malformation, for they willfully seek the impossible.

Adolescence and Sexual Preformation

Young people may be confused and anxious about the sexual articulation of their life. When they were children, their formation field preformed itself for them as a reply to the variety of preforming, questioning orientations, such as seeing, feeling, tasting, and hearing, that are rooted in their vital presence. One preforming question, sexuality, was not yet fully developed as a distinct articulation in their vital-bodily dimension. Therefore, their formation field did not fully preform itself for them as sexual. As a result, most children develop a formation field that is comparatively coherent, but that does not take fully into account its potential sexual meaning.

In adolescence, however, the vital dimension of life becomes sexually articulated. A new preforming question emerges. Accordingly, a new added preformed articulation of the formation field results. This new revelation of preformation is not at once clearly acknowledged, but only dimly felt. Adolescents tend to be confused. They do not know how to integrate this added articulation of their formation field into their current system of directives. Neither can they appraise all at once how it can fit congenially in the process of disclosure of their own unique life. Similarly, they do not know immediately how to cope with this emergence of a new profile of life compatibly and compassionately.

Young people may need the help of a *formation director* to understand what is happening to them. They must learn that it takes time before a new articulation of their life and its corresponding effect on the formation field can be totally and effectively integrated into their emergent spiritual life.

Polymorphous Versatility of Sexual Preformation

The sexual preformation of life within the formation field gives rise to a vague, prereflexive awareness that we are able to give and receive form as sexual beings. We are preformatively aware of the other as a possibility for sexual encounter. The same kind of awareness applies to other areas of vital preformation in relation to the formation field and our position in it.

We can illustrate this point by a consideration of other vitally preformed areas of life. We may be so much at home in our room, for example, that we can find our way around in the dark prereflexively. We know how to avoid chairs and how to find our clothes. This knowledge is not intellectual or scientific; it is not even necessarily reflective. We may not know our room in terms of square footage. We may not have worked out a system that tells us, for instance, how many inches we should move our right hand across the desk to grasp a pencil so as to prepare ourselves to perform a writing task.

Giving form to movements within a room where we are at home is more a question of vitally preformative action than of reflective consideration. As a vitally moving presence, we have preformed our room and its potentialities and limitations for action by vital activity such as walking, sitting, and reaching. This preformative vitality has appropriated this room for us as a possible field of forming movement and action. We do not experience the door of our room as precisely so many feet away from the chair or bed. We are preconsciously certain that the door is so many steps away. The preforming vital dimension thus has an understanding-in-preformation of the formation field.

In like manner, our vital life knows another person as a manifold possibility of sexual action and fulfillment. Because of this preforming vital presence, human sexuality is already on this level of formation more than an instinct. An instinct, in the precise sense of this word, does not change its pattern of action as a result of a vital preforming interaction with its formation field. An instinct follows a ready-made pattern of action.

The Integration of Vital-Sexual and Transcendent Life Formation

We have discussed thus far the structure of the sexual articulation of our vital life. Our ongoing formation should be consonant with this structure. The basic profile of the sexual preformation of our formation field is already given to us. Being a human life-form means being a foundational design of possibilities we cannot escape. Neither we nor our culture start from zero when we try to give form to our sexual life. We can only form our life in consonance or in dissonance with this dimension and articulation of the foundational design we are. Clearly, ours is a call to integration not to disintegration. Similarly, wholesome formation styles or spiritualities do not deny the unity we are called to be but facilitate the wholeness of life.

Our style of sexual formation takes shape from infancy on. It is influenced by our interformative interaction with our parents or guardians. They communicate to us in words, gestures, and actions, what people in the tradition to which they are committed find proper in this area of life. Our initial life orientation is not fashioned in isolation but in dialogue with the life-style of these representatives of one or the other form tradition.

It is thus not the case that children form their view of sexual life with a wary eye on the preformed articulation of sexuality described in the preceding sections. Children are not faced with the sexual articulation of human life as such, but with their parents' appraisal of that articulation. This appraisal is coformed in turn by the view of sexuality that prevails in the tradition to which the parents are committed. No person is an island in the great sea of life formation, especially not in the appraisal of sexual formation, which is deeply interwoven with the interests of all humanity and each human community in their formation history.

To be sure, we ought to assimilate the directives of our tradition in a unique and congenial way. They should become really and solely ours in the course of our history. The foundational formation styles or spiritualities of the great classical form traditions are ordinarily not contrary to the givenness of the human life in its main dimensions and articulations, including the sexual. They are the fruit of revered wisdom, revelation, and the experiences of generations. The sober core of such age-old wisdom is usually consonant with at least the main foundations of human life. This wisdom, however, is incorporated in directives, dispositions, and customs which change with historical situations. Its adaptive embodiment in concrete styles of life may be at odds with what we foundationally are. These concrete expressions of a form tradition are dictated not only by the foundations of the vision of generations. They are influenced also by the temporal or regional demands of the changing situations in which this vision has to be realized.

We often tend to confuse the core of the accumulated wisdom of a tradition with its historical accretions. We are tempted to such tunnel vision because of our functional practical view of situations. We are struck by immediate problems demanding swift solutions, not by long-range attitudes and ideas. How to prevent sexual disturbances here and now is a question more crucial to us than the problem of what sexuality is all about. Eager to find a solution, we develop a style we hope will safeguard the right directives in our life and in that of our children. After a while, we may forget the ultimate purpose of some of the protective aspects of that style. We no longer consider them to be safeguards or secondary security directives, but we make them ends in themselves. If we are not careful, they may take the place of the essential directives they were designed to protect. They take on a life of their own. Their growth is no longer rooted in the foundational directives of our traditions; rather they loom up before us as isolated powers. Thus the myriad sexual safeguards developed over the centuries may become a stern police force hemming in our distinctively human formation. They may have become excessive in extent and intensity. They may even come to contradict the very directives they were meant to protect.

Clearly, the integration of our vital-sexual articulation into a distinctively human style of life is not only a question of personal preference. It is also a matter of integration of each one's style of sexual life with the foundational style of the *form tradition* to which one has committed oneself.

Integration and Restriction

The integration of vital-sexual and distinctively human formation may be clarified by an analogy. The integration of a particular into a larger unity always implies a restriction of both the particular and the whole that assimilates it. When we build a house, we impose restrictions on the specific materials to be used. The bricks we use to erect the walls cannot be used at the same time for the fireplace. Even the fact that we use bricks imposes restrictions on the formation of the house itself. We must adapt the form of the house to the properties of brick. If we had used wood instead, the overall form would have been different. When there is a fault in the formation of the house, when walls begin to crumble or bricks start to fall, we may consult a form expert, like an architect, an engineer, or an experienced contractor. We expect such experts to respect our original building style. We would be startled if they advised us to rebuild our brick house in wood. The only thing we want to learn from them is *how* to reintegrate the bricks within walls that have been designed to sustain the typical form of the home in which we hope to live for the rest of our lives.

A person is not a house, a project of life is not a blueprint, and the dilapidation of a building differs from the disintegration of a style of life. Still there is an analogy between material integration in service of a chosen building design and the integration of various dimensions and articulations of human life in service of a foundational style of life. There is a likeness, too, between a form expert called in to assist people in their reintegration of a collapsing house, and formation experts who are asked to help people integrate the dissonant sexual articulation of their life with their formation as a whole.

Formation experts should carefully watch their own preconscious attitudes. They should seek to be open to key forming situations in the life of other persons. They should not depreciate the foundations of the tradition to which their advisees have committed themselves in their style of formation. They should not belittle either the value of the sexual articulation in one's life formation or the necessity of disciplining it firmly but gently in accordance with the chosen or ratified tradition to which one freely adheres.

Formation scientists or practitioners must try to help people become better aware of the *formation potential* of the foundations of the tradition they have chosen. They encourage the unique way in which persons try to implement such foundations congenially, compatibly, and compassionately. They try to facilitate the integration of the vital-sexual life with the spiritual life. If this integration is effective, the life of the spirit will become consonant with the vital dimension of the life-form and with the foundational tenets of one's tradition.

Integration of sexuality always implies integration with one's current life formation. This formation may be conscious or unconscious; wise or unwise, consistent or inconsistent, blindly adopted or personally assimilated. Whatever the case may be, a *current form* of life, which directs one's present formation, is always operative. The formation scientist, consultant, or counselor always meets a person who is already engaged in a current life direction. For the polymorphous versatility of the emergent human life-form is soon articulated in some specific direction by preforming preferences and by interformative directives. Together they initiate the hesitant beginning of a current form of life. A dialogue develops between this more or less personalized current formation and the tradition to which one feels committed. This dialogue gives rise to various layers of directives operating within one's current life formation.

Personalized Tradition Directives

A form tradition, for example, may forbid unmarried women to date men if not accompanied by a chaperon. Each woman may assimilate this expression of her tradition in a personal way.

One woman may live it in a fashion flexible enough to adapt itself to situations not covered by the present form tradition. If such a woman finds herself alone with a man, she will not panic. She will implement the purpose of the restriction in effective styles and actions.

Another woman may adopt the same custom rigidly. She does not absorb the meaning of this *security directive*. She makes it an absolute *life directive* in and of itself. Hence, she may feel unnecessarily guilty instead of creating new security devices to protect the foundational directives of her tradition.

A culture or subculture is formed gradually over the centuries. It changes with successive situations. In spite of change, however, the underlying tradition remains foundationally the same and recognizable as such. This stability of a foundational tradition indicates the existence of something deeper that undergirds the corresponding cultural customs.

In the example given above, the principle of virginity before marriage can be seen as an aspect of the infrastructure of certain cultural and religious traditions. The first woman in our example was sufficiently open to this foundational infrastructure to be able to form new protective patterns of interaction the moment the customary protective structure broke down. The second woman was not.

Traditional customs may change with new situations. For example, social change may make chaperons expendable. In such a case, the security directive may alter, but not necessarily the underlying foundational directive. It may give form to other protective customs consonant with both the functional directive and the changed situation. For example, Islamic women who discard their veils may develop other sexual safeguards consonant with their basic Islamic tradition. Such modification may be desirable, for it could be that the system of customs has suffered corrosion because of incompatibility with changed situations. Then, too, protective customs may have been proliferated over the centuries at the expense of the life directives themselves. They may have become unnecessarily restrictive, empty, functional, or purely formal.

Change and Integration of Sexual Formation

In the process of ongoing formation, there is no room for change in the truly foundational directives of one's tradition as long as one remains committed to it. Of course, it is possible that in the history of a tradition the foundational status of some of its directives may be questioned. In response to this questioning, the acknowledged authorities of the tradition may discover that the directives in question are indeed no longer foundational. After such reappraisal, there is room for changes that aim at being more congenial, compatible, and compassionate.

In any case, the formation scientist, consultant, or counselor should always be careful to distinguish between the truly foundational and the merely personal, cultural, or apparent form directives. One may discover that certain people live the foundational sexual directives of their form tradition in an unwholesome and anxious way that leads to dissonant, tense dispositions and actions. Inexperienced or uninformed formation consultants may identify this unhealthy expression of the foundational directives with the directives themselves. They may be appalled by the deforming consequences, so much so that they preconsciously communicate to their counselees that they do not appreciate the foundational directives themselves insofar as these seem to guide their lives in harmful directions. The danger of such misunderstanding and its implicit communication is that it may drain away the motivating and integrating power of the foundational traditional infrastructure of a person's life. However, it is only in the light of this structure that one may eventually be able to integrate sexual formation more wholesomely with the entire formation field. Without it, persons may lose their possibility for consonant integration.

An Example of Misidentification of Foundational Directives

Suppose, for example, that a counselee is an Amish woman whose marriage is formatively defective. A certain frigidity seems to interfere with her spontaneous form giving in sexual intimacy. We may realize during formation sessions that she feels that sex is despicable. She tells the formation counselor about the rules for dating in her Amish community. She describes the customs designed to safeguard in the young the foundations of the Amish tradition. Further exploration confirms the suspicion that these rules of dating were misinterpreted by this counselee. They came to mean to her that sexuality itself is intrinsically bad and distasteful. In the course of the sessions, however, she may become aware that this private conclusion is not justifiable, that other Amish women, subject to the same directives are not frigid, that there must be something wrong in the way in which she has appraised and adopted the customs of her tradition. Guided reappraisal helps her to reform her dissonant sexual disposition without rejecting the functional infrastructure of her tradition.

Imagine, on the contrary, that the counselor would prematurely identify the counselee's defective directives and dispositions with the foundational directives themselves of the Amish tradition. In that case the counselor may harm her possibility for effective disposition reformation by mistakenly making the Amish tradition itself the culprit, instead of her warped appraisal of its directives.

The Reserve of the Formation Scientist as Community Consultant

Formation scientists may be invited to act as consultants for a population whose subculture is conditioned by a common tradition. Serious exploration of their customs may lead to the conclusion that some of them have become *form-defective* instead of *form-effective*. A prudent reformation of such passing customs would not impinge on any foundational directives of the community.

The consultants may discover, for example, that an anxious or threatening manner of communicating security directives in regard to the maintenance of sexual life directives leads to excessive tension and fear in certain sensitive young people inclined to obsessive forms of life. At this point inexperienced formation counselors may be tempted to overstep their area of competence. They may be rash enough to suggest new directives for a subculture based on a tradition ultimately alien to them.

It is not the task of the consultants themselves to change the directives of various populations in a pluralistic society. Only the carriers of the living tradition itself can create new directives and modes of communicating them that will not betray their foundational life directives.

The consultants may respectfully suggest that a reappraisal of directives may be desirable. They may intimate, for example, that the leaders of the subculture that embodies the tradition might profitably alter the language in which sexual customs are communicated. But they will leave it up to the tradition carriers themselves to give actual form to such innovations, while remaining available for consultation if called upon. Only those who personally live a tradition within a corresponding subculture can initiate innovations in a manner that leaves its foundations intact. Sharing the subculture, they also may be able to communicate such innovations in ways that are least offensive and disruptive.

In the case of even more profound modifications, only the acknowledged thinkers and custodians of a tradition are capable of returning creatively to the sources from which their tradition sprang. This return to their sources enables them to distinguish between what is foundational and what is periodical in their directives. In the science of formation, this procedure is called a resourcing, and it is sustained by a critical and creative procedure called *foundational tracing*. When formation scientists put up the warning sign, it may be time for a tradition and the subculture that embodies it not to deny its heritage but to return to its sources.

The Subcultures of the Formation Scientists

Formation consultants are rooted in subcultures of their own, influenced implicitly by one or various form traditions. These subcultures and their underlying traditions may differ from those of the population or formation segment they are invited to advise. If they are not careful, they may implicitly impose on their advisees their own subcultural view of sexuality. An unguarded reaction, a certain look, a smile, a slight impatience or surprise may communicate better than words what they really feel. They may unwittingly suggest that their advisees should integrate their sexual formation within the subcultural structure that nourishes the consultants' own directives and dispositions. If advisees attempt to follow this suggestion, they may fail because such personal directives of sexual discipline are rooted in a subcultural ground that the advisees do not share.

The life-style that the scientist personally cultivates will be for the advisees a mere outline, without roots in their own formation history. Such an imposition of alien sexual directives may result in a new split in the advisees' dispositions. Their life-style is rooted in their own tradition as embodied in their own culture or subculture. Now they may try to develop an alien style of life, communicated to them by a tactless formation scientist or consultant. Their sexual formation will then be directed from two conflicting centers: the directives of their own subculturally embodied tradition, and those of their consultant's subculture. We presuppose, of course, that the advisees have not freely decided to change to another subculture, formation segment, or tradition.

Formation scientists can prevent such conflicts if they remain aware of the implicit impact of their own cultural directives on their communications. Simultaneously, they should try to understand the background of the counselee's life formation. This attempt to understand should be guided by the distinction made between the infrastructure of the tradition of those who consult them, its current cultural embodiment, and the personally consonant or dissonant manner in which advisees attempt to implement this structure.

*Sexual Formation and the Foundational
Structure of the Human Life-Form*

The science of formative spirituality holds that any style of sexual formation should be consonant with the foundational structure of the human life-form as such. Otherwise it would be foundationally dissonant and hence disruptive. Many of the classical form traditions humanity has developed over the centuries seem basically compatible with at least the main aspects of the foundational structure of the human life-form. Form traditions and their specific embodiments in passing cultural periods orient and limit the inexhaustible possibilities of giving form to human life.

It is one of the main functions of a wholesome culture to present people with a set of directives that respect their foundational makeup and, at the same time, help them to give form to their life in certain directions. For example, Tibetans differ in their life orientation from New Yorkers but the formation of both can be consonant with the basic structure of human life. Each member of a formation segment of the world population may personalize his or her cultural directives and their underlying traditions in one of many possible unique styles of life.

A traditional cultural set of directives gathers within itself the sexual wisdom of the past. It offers a style of sexual formation that has served countless others in an integrative way. As long as people mean to commit themselves wholeheartedly to such a traditional cultural frame of reference, they should remain loyal to its basic tenets, if not to all its incidental periodic customs. If they do not, they may suffer a split in their formation. They must either change their commitment or integrate their sexual form giving and receiving within the foundational frame of this commitment to a specific tradition. This decision is their own. No formation scientist or consultant should even suggest it to them, much less make it for them.

In short, formation consultants in a pluralistic society should understand and respect its various subcultures and their underlying traditions. They should learn to distinguish between the foundational orientations and directives of such underlying traditions and their current, protective expressions in safeguards or customs that embody such directives. They should also become increasingly aware of the variety of consonant and dissonant ways in which individuals may realize these directives and their safeguards in their own unique life formation.

Formation consultants and counselors can grow in the wisdom requisite for such insight to the extent that they are able to transcend their own excessive security directives and denigrating dispositions. They should realize that their initial formation may have instilled in them certain prejudices concerning traditions different from theirs.

The Preparation of Formation Consultants and Counselors

We have discussed the integration of sexuality and spirituality in accordance with the traditions to which people are committed. The insights gained so far have implications for the preparation of formation consultants and counselors. Such preparation should take into account that the candidates are to be prepared for dealing with normal formation problems in a pluralistic society. Certain courses and seminars should include lectures and discussions dedicated to the understanding of the varied traditions that may undergird the sexual formation of people who call upon them for consultation. Some formation sessions should enable the candidates to work through their own unconscious hostilities and self-protective misconceptions regarding form traditions that are not their own. They should be helped to see the world with the eyes of others, to feel life as others do.

An emphatic understanding of alien traditions should be the aim of such courses and seminars, especially for those participants who work in foreign cultures and countries. Such lectures should not communicate mainly the philosophical, theological, or ideological conceptualization of such traditions. They should communicate a lively feeling of what these traditions, as embodied in their current subculture, really feel like to their adherents.

Normalcy of Formation Problems

Formation consultants and counselors should be taught how to distinguish between normal formation problems and severe psychological disturbances that require referral to mental-health experts. It is a normal formation problem in a pluralistic society that people at some point in their formation history become confused about the relationship between their sexual formation and their form tradition. Many of them are simply not clear about the distinctions between the foundational directives of their tradition, its current cultural embodiment in passing customs, and the individual's own consonant or dissonant personalization of these directives. Many do not see that giving form to their sexual lives over against the foundational dictates of their own free formation commitment vitiates consonant life formation.

Most people have not clarified for themselves how they concretely experience and live the discipline implied in the integration of sexual formation in the human formation field as a whole. Discipline is essential for integration. This fact cannot be changed. The necessity of discipline is rooted in the multiform structure of the human life-form. In this case, the vital dimension of the lifeform and its *sexual articulation* should become the disciple of a gentle and respectful human spirit, enlightened by the formation wisdom of humanity as enshrined in its great traditions. Many people may thus benefit from the assistance of a science of formation in learning the art of respectful and relaxed sexual discipline.

This approach offsets a misunderstanding of the foundational directives of traditions that may lead to a depreciation of the sexual articulation of one's life-form. A misunderstanding of this sort could lead to an anxious isolation of the sexual articulation from the integral spiritual formation of one's life as a whole. It may even foster by implication an isolation of the vital dimension as such from one's spiritual life. Life becomes deformed; it turns into a dry, functionalistic, quasi-spiritual project without excitement, warmth, or charm.

In time, the isolated vital dimension and its sexual articulation may form themselves on their own, outside the transcendent illumination by the spirit. The vital dimension grows increasingly into a potentially explosive power, threatening the whole edifice of human formation. To control it demands increasing repression;

unleashed, it becomes destructive. In such a case it may take years to realign the vital dimension with the wisdom of distinctively human formation.

The opposite may also happen in a pluralistic society. Many may overappraise the role of the sexual articulation of human life. They face a problem similar to that of persons who depreciate this articulation. For example, people who lift nudity out of the whole field of formation may no longer know how to integrate the mode of being nude in the total spirituality of human life.

Formation consultants and counselors should help people to cope with such normal problems of sexual formation. They should help them see that the integration of sexuality and spirituality presupposes a wholesome concept of the foundational structure of human life, a sound appreciation of the vital dimension and its sexual articulation, and a readiness to discipline sexual formation in the light of the human spirit and the tradition that has been chosen as its guiding light.

Formation consultants and counselors should emphasize this readiness. People should realize in humility and relaxation that their will to integration does not always succeed. Periodic failures are normal. A distinctively human style of formation, or spirituality, is not a summary of what has already been achieved. It is a design for life that tries to approximate spiritual wholeness in spite of many failings. As long as people try to live the life of the spirit, they should not feel crushed by guilt and shame because of failures. A spirituality enlightened by a form tradition is a compass, not an assurance of instant achievement. It helps people to appraise where they are going, even when the going is rough.

Conclusion

The integration of sexual and spiritual formation is a lifelong venture. People begin the formation journey in polymorphous versatility. This means that they can give form to life in countless directions. However, they cannot form their lives in all possible directions simultaneously. This would result in chaos, in dissonance. Life formation becomes meaningless without consonant orientation. Some consistent form direction is necessary if formation is to have meaning.

Preformative propensities and interformative pressures combine in mutual interaction to form the beginning of such a formation orientation. Some of its directives concern the integrative or spiritual formation of the sexual articulation of the vital dimension of the life-form. A consonant formation orientation should be in tune with the foundational structure of this form. This structure implies that human life receives and gives form both within an interformative society and within a world of formative symbols.

Many possibilities of giving and receiving sexual form confront people in everyday life. The same human form structure discloses that people can transcend their vital formation dimension. People are relatively free. They can appraise, at least in principle, such vital formation invitations. After implicit or explicit appraisal, they may decide in what manner and measure they will allow these vital-sexual directives to coform their life. If they strive to integrate this vital-sexual formation into their human formation as a whole, their personal response to the sexual appeal of their formation field may become consonant with their congenial and compatible formation orientation.

In shaping a basic style of human formation, or a *foundational formative spirituality*, we are not alone. We are always sharing an odyssey of human *interformation* that stretches over millennia. Countless people before us have searched for a grand design of consonant life formation. They looked for a design that, among other things, would integrate their sexual and spiritual life formation. They tried to tune into the foundational structures, dynamics, and conditions of the human form of life. The fruit of this search has been incorporated in the great form traditions and their periodic expressions in cultural and subcultural styles of formation. No one can wisely search for a style of life that integrates sexual and spiritual formation as though no one before had ever sought for such a life of consonance.

We cannot escape the formation projects of those who have preceded us. One reason for this is that the formation of a human being is bound to a prolonged period of initial formation, or childhood. Childhood is a phase of initiation into the complex symbolic world of distinctively human formation. This first stage of formation is marked by helplessness. It is dependent on the conditioning approval of adult representatives of the symbolic universe of a human formation field. A child is rooted in some design for living during this period. This pristine design of form directives is linked with a cultural or subcultural formation style that is nourished implicitly or explicitly by one or more form traditions.

The human formation journey begins with this initial phase of conformation. It then traverses a period of lonely self-formation, and finally finds its way to congenial, compatible, and compassionate coformation. Ideally, it reaches the fully integrative stage of transformation. None of these formation phases is totally left behind. Each one keeps playing its proper role—be it diminished and subordinate—during the final transforming phase of one's formation.

In the transition stage of self-formation people may react against the form directives adopted by situational osmosis during the conformation phase of initial formation. Even this reaction will be colored by the initial formation design against which they react and by other designs suggested by other subcultures and their underlying form traditions. Human formation can never escape the influence of form traditions.

Another mark of human formation is its temporality, the relatively short life span within which formation must be achieved. It is therefore impossible for one individual or even for a few generations of individuals, to test experientially all possible styles of spiritual-sexual integration in order to choose the most effective and consonant one. The only way open to people is to make one of the already existing formation styles their own; to enrich, update, and expand it in dialogue with new insights, and to personalize it uniquely in ways that are congenial, compatible, and compassionate.

The available styles of spiritual-sexual formation are blends of form traditions and their embodiments in cultural or subcultural customs. As we have seen, the foundational directives of a form tradition cannot be changed without changing the tradition itself. However, the current customs, which incorporate such foundational directives in periodically compatible ways, can be changed. One of the conditions for such change is that it not violate the lasting directives. Other conditions would refer to the reasonable demands of congeniality, compatibility, and compassion.

We conclude that people can integrate spiritual and sexual formation consonantly when they commit themselves to at least the foundational form directives of a form tradition as embodied in a culture. This presupposes that the form tradition and its expressive culture is consonant with the foundational structure of the human form and that people in formation creatively make this style their own in a congenial, compatible, and compassionate manner. Every consonant form tradition leaves room for congenial creativity. It is like a harbor from which to venture out into the open sea of ongoing life and world formation.

The integration of spiritual and sexual formation is subtle and complex. Its dependence on form traditions means dependence on interformation from infancy on. Interformation can be fraught with disturbance and confusion, especially in the transition crises between the periods of conformation, self-formation, coformation, and transformation. It is for this reason quite normal that many people temporarily lose their way at various points during the formation journey. The science of formative spirituality, together with formation consultants and counselors, can prepare us to deal with such normal formation problems. All three can help us to find out what went wrong, how to regain consonance and trust, and how to make our own decisions.

CHAPTER 11

Ongoing Movements and Interforming Influences of the Vital-Functional Form Dimension

Preceding chapters dealt mainly with the preconscious vital preformation of our formation field and with the emergence of the functional dimension. Special attention was given to its intraformative interaction with the sociohistorical, vital, and transcendent dimensions, the latter being distinctively human. Chapter 10 focused on the sexual articulation of the vital dimension and considered the influence of form traditions on the sexual articulation of our life.

The present chapter is concerned with the relations between our social-personal development and our vital-functional life. It will emphasize the continually formative influence of vital powers on the other dimensions and events of our life. We will see that the preservation of vital vigor implies a certain enlightened asceticism of mental and physical hygiene, of exercise, diet, relaxation, and recreation—briefly, a consonant style of life.

Human formation manifests itself in every movement of unfolding. We may be most impressed with the higher expressions of formation. We cherish the signs of the expansion of our spirit, of deepening appraisal, of growing insight, and of new inspirations. The word formation may remind us mainly of such sublime marks of human unfolding. Yet these presuppose, include, and express the so-called lower movements of our life. Even the most transcendent expressions of human formation, as we shall see in chapter 12, are carried by these basic dimensions, which permeate and are part of the story of human development. If we deny their continual influence, our progress in life will become dissonant and deformative. We begin to reduce the mystery of human formation to a ghostlike spirit machine somewhere within us. We imagine that this power moves all dimensions and articulations of our emergent life in splendid isolation.

A full understanding of consonant living requires an acknowledgment of the constant influence of our vital life. Our personal life does not emerge or progress without the undercurrent of the vital form dimension. Functional-transcendent life has become aware of itself in appraisal; in this it transcends its vital ground not by denying it but by integrating it into a higher unit.

Vital Dimension as Energy

At this point it may be helpful to consider anew the vital foundations of our life. While basing this consideration on what has been discussed in preceding chapters, we shall keep in mind the aim of this chapter: to clarify the ongoing movements and forming influences of each of the life-form dimensions, starting with the vital.

We may be generally aware of the fact that many demands are made on our life and its supporting organisms. Vital energy is constantly utilized by our formation acts. This energy is limited. Our transcendent aspirations, functional ambitions, thoughts, and actions use up a great deal of vital vigor. Periodically, our energy has to be restored and replenished. Otherwise, we cannot remain effective in our formation field and we would be hindered in our ongoing formation. The formation process may become dissonant, feeble, and deformative if we do not know how to cope with a depletion of vigor. Hence, it is necessary to engage in wise asceticism of diet, exercise, rest, and relaxation; in formative love and care; in enjoyment of art and beauty; in a *gentle style of life*. When people refuse to listen to the limits and possibilities of their vitality, their life-form cannot unfold itself fully and consonantly. The fact that to be human is to be an embodied spirit makes the dialogue between spirit and body mandatory.

For example, excitableness, when not disciplined wisely in the light of the spirit, can interfere with the gracious yet economic use of energy. To be effective, we need to be formed in an approach to life that prevents premature emptying of our vital resources. The formation mystery speaks not only in our head but in our whole being. We should become sensitive to the messages for the wise direction of our formation that emanate from our experiences of fatigue, nervous tension, elevated blood pressure, irregular heartbeat, ulcers, or headaches. We must listen to the voice of formation in our bodily sensations. The body may invite us by such vital signs to quiet down or to increase our efforts when vitality is available again.

The vital uniqueness of our life-form announces itself in our body. Some are born with a capacity for hard, sustained labor; others are delicate and need to form their lives and world by a more modest style of service. During our personal formation history, changes may announce themselves in our body. If we do not listen obediently to what they tell us, we may become forced, tense, irritable. Reflection and appraisal are impaired. When we blindly resist the reality of tensions, the vital dimension may rebel against the spirit and punish it with obsessive temptations.

The form traditions of various cultures, the religious and philosophical ideologies, and the social and life sciences have enriched us with many insights into the development of a wise asceticism of the vital dimension of our formation. The science of formative spirituality researches, integrates, and, when desirable, reformulates these insights and findings in service of a distinctively human or spiritual formation.

Our vital body locates our formation at a certain point in time and space. We are born bodily into a unique period of the formation history of humanity. This insertion influences in some measure the personal and communal unfolding of our functional-transcendent life. Our bodily limits also make it impossible for us to be physically in more than one spot at the same time. They impose restrictions on the amount and kind of reflection, reading, work, study, entertainment, travel, and sports in which we can be engaged wholeheartedly.

Individualization of the Vital Dimension

Our vital dimension is individualized by our body. Our body is not a general human body. It is ours and ours only. It has its own individual assets and deformities. It may need its own kind and measure of diet, exercise, rest, and recreation. Our vital senses may be keener or weaker than those of others. The same can be said of muscular, nervous, glandular, and sexual potencies. Vital health and energy are limited and individualized by the form potency we received at birth. Our physiology influences our alertness, sluggishness, vivaciousness, tolerance, sensuality, and sexuality. Physical features make us bodily and vitally more or less attractive to others. Many more of these individualized vital potencies and restrictions inhere in the organism that is ours at this moment of organismic evolution and formation history.

This fundamental organismic structure with all its implications is the ground of our vital life in its human and sociohistorical formation. This ground depends on genetic factors we cannot choose but can only wisely appraise. We can respond to them creatively within limits we cannot deny. Because we are also functional-transcendent, we can interact with such limits personally. From the beginning of life, a spontaneous dialogue takes place between the given organism with its vital implications and our actual living in the initial formation situation. From the start the human organism and its vitality are exposed to people, events, and things that coform its initial formation field.

On the basis of this interaction the vital dimension receives its form as a constellation of reactions to the interforming influences of intial formation. This basic constellation marks our formation history for a lifetime. It is one of the influences that coform our unique spirituality. These patterns may be conducive or resistant to the overall unique spiritual form of life we are called to disclose and realize during our personal history of formation.

Ideally, consonant patterns of vital reaction become part of our emergent style of life. These reaction patterns are not at odds with the hidden form we are called to unveil in our lives. They lend a certain color and tune to our formation. They become part of our formative life-style.

Formation of Temperament

Basic *vital reaction patterns* manifest certain characteristics of a formal nature that are universal in human formation. They are rooted in one's physiological makeup. Noticeable among them are the degree or pace of flow, flexibility, coordination, speed, and intensity that one's vital reactions manifest.

Because they are rooted in physiology, people have only limited control over these formal characteristics of their reactions. Only within these limits can they change the spontaneous pace of life, response, and reaction that makes them personally most form-effective. If they become too slow or too hurried in regard to their preformed limits, they lose their peace and diminish the effectiveness of their formative presence. Peace and pace are related. All human formation should respect such limits, for limits are expressions of the mysterious direction our life is preformed to assume.

These physiologically rooted formation characteristics coform together the basis of one's temperament. One can excessively repress or conceal temperament, but this leads to dissonance and deformation. One can also take temperament into account when giving form to one's formation field. Some people let their temperament dominate their formation to the exclusion of any spiritual influence. This again fosters deformation and dissonance.

Expression Potency

Our vital form dimension is also marked by a certain power of emotional expressiveness. The *expression potency* of one's emotions should be distinguished from one's vital emotionality itself. In short, we should distinguish our basic vital emotionality, rooted in temperament, and our ease and ability to express this emotionality. Vital emotionality itself is rooted in preformed organismic factors over which we have little control.

The ease and ability to express vital emotionality depends on several factors. Important among them is *interformative interaction* with significant people and symbols in one's initial formation situation. Emotional expressiveness becomes an early, socially established articulation of one's vital form dimension. This explains similarities in expression that we may observe among members of the same culture. Formation agents in our initial formation reacted with affirmation when our emotional expressions were compatible with the customs of the form tradition and its embodiment in their particular culture. Anxiety about losing their approval, and therewith one's interformative potency and effectiveness, led to conformity. Thus we adopted a type of emotional expressiveness that would be compatible with the culture and its underlying form traditions. Later in life it is difficult to reform our adopted style of vital emotional expressiveness.

Under certain conditions, however, it may be possible within limits to grow in fluency or moderation in regard to the expressive articulation of one's unique life-form. One should be careful not to willfully exaggerate attempts to become more demonstrative and outgoing or more restrained in vital-emotional expression. Efforts to gain freedom of expression may be the result of a cultural change, a change of formation segment or of group dynamics, sensitivity training, psychotherapy, and so on. Within reasonable limits, these means may help to free our vital expressivity in service of the spirit and of the reasonable demands of new life situations. When excessive, however, such experiences may give rise to willful affectation that is more deforming than forming.

Beyond the constellation of basic reaction patterns, temperament, and emotional expressivity, the vital dimension becomes coformed by various other modes of presence. These are formed through early familial conditioning by means of affirmation or the withholding of affirmation. As already suggested, such withholding threatens the child's need for the experience of safe *form-effectiveness* within the initial formation situation.

Summary of the Characteristics of the Vital Form Dimension
Before considering other elements of vital life formation, we may summarize the characteristics disclosed thus far.
1. The vital dimension, as rooted in the human body, is the principle of organismic, spatial, and temporal limitations of one's forming presence in the formation field.
2. The vital dimension is also in and with the body as the source of energy that empowers human formation and its modes and modalities of forming presence.
3. The vital dimension is one of the main sources of individual limitations and possibilities. Hence, it is also one of the sources of the uniqueness of formative life direction, life call, life formation, sensation, and imagination.
4. The vital dimension is part of the foundational infrastructure of personal-spiritual life formation.
5. It manifests, or latently maintains, basic patterns of vital reactions as a result of interactions with significant formation agents and symbols in one's initial formation field.
6. The vital dimension is a source of temperament and of the way in which one allows that temperament to manifest itself.

7. The organismic core of this form dimension gives rise to a basic vital emotionality. As a consequence of initial interformation, the vital dimension is formed in a certain style of fluency or restraint in regard to the expression of this emotionality. Initial vital formation affects in turn one's social adaptability and the style of one's later spirituality and its expressiveness. It may possibly influence the choice of a school or movement of spiritual formation.
8. The vital dimension is marked by a specific set of modes of vital presence to people, events, and things and their symbolic formative meanings. These modes originate both in one's organismic, genetic endowment and in one's initial intraformative interaction with that endowment under the pressure of interformative reactions and responses. This set of vital modes predisposes one to a certain profile of vital dispositions which may be formative or deformative.

Our vital dimension is thus formed early in our formation history. Later in life, we may gain relative freedom in the functional-transcendent attitudes we take toward modes and inclinations that prevail in our vital life. One condition for such freedom is an increasing availability to our apprehension and appraisal power of what has coformed our individual vital dimension. Such availability enables us to appraise the vital formation dimension in light of our aspirations and ambitions. The latter originate in, respectively, the transcendent and functional dimensions of our life.

We can personalize and spiritualize the vital form dimension by integrating it within the totality of our emergent life formation. Such integration implies a transformation of the vital dimension without violating its forming function. The mystery of formation exudes its presence in universe, humanity, and history. It expresses itself also in the vital dimension of human life. Hence, we should listen to it. Otherwise, denial of this expression of the formation mystery will lead to dissonance and deformation.

From what we have observed so far, we can describe our vital form dimension as a preformed and acquired constellation of limited and limiting vital potencies of formation. It forms the infrastructure of our spiritual formation. Our personal, distinctively human presence in the world is dependent on this biophysical dimension, yet not totally determined by its laws. As spiritual expressions of the formation mystery, we escape the full determination that pertains to the universe of matter.

Articulations of the Vital Form Dimension

After considering the manifestations of the vital form dimension that are more directly observable, we must now explore the *formation energy* that enables the vital dimension to articulate itself in specific directions and to maintain its forming power. How is this flow of energy related to the flow of form energy in the cosmos? How does it relate to formation powers in other dimensions of the human life-form? How does this energy articulate itself in various basic strivings of the vital dimension of life?

The vital dimension shares in the energizing flow that interconnects the countless micro- and macrocosmic formation events. This flow manifests itself in special ways in all forms of vital life. The main manifestations of this universal formation energy are: *preservation, growth, fusion, mortification, expansion,* and *incorporation*. These six different strivings become special articulations of the vital dimension of human life. They should not be seen as separate competing powers. They are mutually interpenetrating articulations of one and the same vital formation movement.

Preservation

All life seeks to preserve itself. The vitally formative movement of preservation is a deep striving, usually preconscious, to protect, secure, conserve, and maintain one's life, the forms it has attained, and the conditions that assure their survival and expansion. It stands behind the security directives developed to protect one's valued form directives. This striving fosters vigilance against destructive and harmful agents that threaten life and its ongoing formation. It makes one look for consonant nourishment, rest, exercise, and healing so that life may be preserved. In human formation, it sustains the conserving power of formative memory and one's preservation of a form tradition.

When not transformed by the spirit into wise moderation, this urge can lead to compulsive preoccupation with one's health, to poor nutrition, to hypertension, to too much recreation or exercise.

The blind striving for preservation can also give rise to excessive security directives, brute egoism, and a type of radical, paranoid conservatism. Moderated by the human spirit, however, it will sustain *consonant formation*.

Growth

The manifestation of form energy as a striving for growth starts on the vital level of human unfolding. Later it becomes personalized on the functional level in the form of ambitions that help us grow personally and in society. In transcendent presence this energy gives rise to aspirations for spiritual growth. If not modulated by reason and spirit, it can lead to compulsive strivings both on the functional and aspirational level of human presence.

The blind urge to grow can evade or circumvent the wisdom of reason and spirit. As a result, aspiration is distorted and gives rise to a compulsive or hysterical search for *absolutized formation ideals*. People can be driven by this urge to overextend themselves to the detriment of the equally necessary vital movement of life's preservation.

Fusion

A plant has to fuse with the earth, with the light of the sun, with the fertilizing pollen of insects. Animals must mate in mutual instinctive fusion. This vital formation urge operates also in humans. We find it happening on the vital level in the tendency of the infant to fuse with the mother. The same *fusion striving* may initially destroy the development of the loving, cordial mode of personal presence. Instead of a free individual love relationship sustained also by a vital striving for fusion, fusion may take over totally. An inordinate need for fusion can make a marriage fail if the partners are unable to grow beyond this vital domination of their love life.

On the functional level, fusion is an important ingredient in the establishment of social cohesion within significant peer groups. It becomes detrimental when it takes over to such a degree that people lose their identity within the peer group. In transcendent presence, fusion helps us to participate in humanity, history, nature. If it dominates, it leads to a collectivistic or pantheistic absorption in transcendent entities.

Mortification

This is the vital striving to mortify any aspect of life that hinders its unfolding as a whole. An animal bites off its own limb to be saved from a trap. The branch of a tree dies off so that the tree may flourish. This vital urge can be personalized and spiritualized in human formation. It becomes the striving to serve the preservation, growth, and expansion of life by giving up anything that interferes with these objectives.

The *mortification striving* can take over on higher levels to such a degree that it destroys the spiritual life form. Even certain saints had to admit that they were initially excessive in mortification. Guilt and self-condemnation can be a manifestation of an unenlightened vital mortification urge, especially when the functional conscience is involved. In this way, some persons may work themselves to exhaustion. On the level of aspiration, they can wreck their lives by an unrealistic denial of life.

Expansion

All forms of life expand wherever possible. Blind expansion or proliferation seems necessary for many forms of life. Hence, we can speak of the expansion urge in vital life. In humans this urge is checked and personalized by transcendent-functional appraisal.

The *vital expansion urge* is clearly discernible in the infant's delight with its expansion of skill via crawling and walking and with its exploration of objects in its formation field. The formation of a sympathetic, cordial disposition leads to an expansion of friendly relationships with people.

Functionally, the expansion urge becomes a striving for growth in social, intellectual, and professional skills; for success in one's career; for production; for increased status, power, and possession. Unchecked by wisdom and reason, it can destroy people or fixate them on the functional level.

In transcendent presence this urge is an excellent vital companion to aspirations that point toward expansion of our daily horizon. If it predominates, we may become so dispersed in countless aspirations that we lose necessary depth. We begin to run after transcendent experiences. Our appetite for them becomes insatiable. We read wildly, travel from one formation workshop to another, unaware that it is not transcendent aspiration but the unenlightened expansion urge that goads us on.

Incorporation

A sixth manifestation of vital energy is the urge for incorporation. Life continuously strives and forms itself by incorporating what it needs for sustenance, growth, and expansion. In human formation incorporation is complemented by *transcendent participation*. The infant brings everything to its mouth, a bodily manifestation of the incorporation urge. On the level of cordial presence, this energy can sustain the striving of the heart to incorporate in one's affective life many good memories, symbols, images, and stories that evoke and maintain a loving disposition. Uncontrolled by wisdom and reason, the incorporation urge can deteriorate into an unending and unfulfilled hunt for affective experiences.

Functional incorporation should help us to assimilate useful ideas and information. It fosters studiousness. It helps us also in the acquisition of what we need to establish our place in society. If unchecked, this urge leads to functional gluttony, overexpansion, possessiveness.

On the transcendent level of presence, it fosters the steady incorporation of spiritual experience in our lives. When not illumined by reason and the transcendent powers of mind and will, it may give rise to a possessive hoarding of transcendent experiences.

In human formation at large, the incorporation striving becomes permeated and elevated by the aspiration for participation. We incorporate food into our bodily organism by destroying its original texture, structure, and appearance. Mental and cordial incorporation, however, is permeated by human participation. We do not devour but participate respectfully in the lives of those whose gifts we incorporate. There is no destruction, only an appreciative approach. The same applies to what we could call participant incorporation of spiritual values. We let things be in their goodness, truth, and beauty and participate in these manifestations. Hence, we speak not only about the emergent life-form but also about the *participant life-form*.

The incorporation striving serves wise participation in transcendent-functional values and their implied form directives. It facilitates a relaxed assimilation of the fruits of such participation. It may fall deformatively into a violent, anxious hoarding of things, ideals, and values, and their implied form directives. In that case stubbornness, rigidity, and isolation may result.

In the transcendent dimension of the life-form, the incorporation urge serves recollection and inwardness. It facilitates the nonviolent assimilation of transcendent values and their implied form directives. When the incorporation urge is not sufficiently transformed by integration, it might spawn a "spiritual collector" type of person—one who eagerly collects spiritual information but does not assimilate it in quiet reflection.

Many form traditions developed a threefold path to temper these vital strivings: the path of *obedience* to life's limitations, of *purity* as a moderation of sensual incorporations, and of *poverty* as a renunciation of indiscriminate hoarding of transcendent-functional values, images, thoughts, and directives. This threefold path assists people in the moderation and transformation not only of incorporation but also of the other articulations of the vital form dimension.

Interaction of the Articulations of the Vital Dimension

The six articulations of the vital dimension mutually penetrate each other. Take, for example, a situation of persecution. In order to survive (preservation), we may have to fuse with a group of unfamiliar people (fusion) and temporarily suspend our liking for aesthetic attractiveness in dress and behavior (mortification). To grow and unfold (growth), we have to preserve our energy and health (preservation) by incorporating right nutrition (incorporation) and expanding our muscular strength and flexibility by right exercise (expansion). Numerous examples could be given. They demonstrate the foundational unity of the vital formation striving at the core of its articulations.

These vital strivings remain operative in all dimensions of spiritual formation. Distinctively human formation is threatened when a person permits the vital urge not only to collaborate with but also to dominate the transcendent-functional formation of life. For example, a person may become greedy for spiritual knowledge and enlightenment. This attitude can be a manifestation of the incorporation urge of the vital dimension in the transcendent dimension of human formation. Mortification in the transcendent-functional dimension may be perverted into a "spiritual" masochism of compulsions and obsessions, urged on by the mortification striving of the vital dimension. The vital expansion urge may dominate the functional dimension of the human life-form, leading to a blind and exhaustive dispersion of power and energy, thereby ruining one's health, peace, and pace of life.

It may be clear from these examples that the articulations of the vital dimension can be formative or deformative in their effects on human formation as a whole. If we deny the vital functional articulations of our existence, the result is a floating, infrahuman, unrealistic life. These primordial powers should not be denied but transformed by integration into the transcendent-functional life-form to which we have been uniquely called.

Pseudospirituality and Distortions in the Vital Dimension

Pseudospirituality may result when a person becomes fixated on the vital level of human formation. This may start in childhood. The aspirations of the transcendent dimension are latent in the child. The main aspiration in this dimension is for the transcendent mystery of formation. This latent aspiration for transcendence tends to attach the child to a vital symbol of the transcendent as if it were *the* transcendent itself. The infant in the vital stage is not yet able to pass through the symbol to the transcendent that is symbolized. The symbol itself is idolized. The human father, for example, becomes a god for the infant. The creaturely experience of helplessness—as yet only experienced implicitly on a vital level—may be lived out in relation to the earthly father alone.

When in later stages the latent aspiration for the transcendent becomes gradually manifest, such children are faced with a crisis. They are invited to disclose the spiritual and symbolic meaning of the father in their life as only one of many possible pointers to the transcendent mystery of formation. In the beginning of this transition, they may be inclined to ascribe to the transcendent the traits that belong merely to one of its symbols, in this case the vital father figure of early infancy. If no higher formation takes place, they may never outgrow the confusion occasioned by their transition crisis. Their experience of God remains deeply influenced by the vital image of their father. On this shaky ground a pseudospirituality may be constructed that does not escape its vitalistic origins.

The false spirituality of total fusion is another example of pseudospirituality that originates in the vital dimension. It is a result of a settling down into or a falling back upon a primitive form of prespiritual life that emerges in infancy. It is related to the initial vital fusion of the child with the mother and her image. The tendency to fusion is nourished by a latent transcendent aspiration in the child to participation in the beyond.

Preformed in us is an aspiration to participate in all that is. Participation presupposes the experience of differentiation between me, the participant, and that in which I am called to participate as a unique person. The infant in the vital stage does not yet experience this differentiation between itself, its formation field, and the mysterious beyond. Its latent spiritual aspiration expresses itself in an experience of undifferentiated oneness with all that is, usually represented by the mother, who initially symbolizes the beyond as nourishing ground.

The first implicit experience of one's latent spiritual aspiration does not disappear. It remains alive as a foundational experience in the transconscious realm of hidden form directives. It establishes a possibility for the later experience of a mature union with the mystery of formation without being totally absorbed by it (as was the case in early infancy in relation to the mother and the formation field).

Experiences of both union and uniqueness are nourished by these early vital memories and images. This presupposes, however, that one transcends both the initial idolizing of the father and the early fusion with the mother. These early experiences and images live on in our unconsciousness. They complement one another, though one or the other may periodically prevail in life. It is harmful to repress or suppress either of these primitive experiences and corresponding images; instead, we must transform them. The original layer of vital experience is the archaic foundation of personal-spiritual formation. It must be acknowledged and expressed through our poetry, music, liturgy, and ritual. All these are means of keeping such archaic, vital experiences and images alive while transforming and reorienting them spiritually.

Spiritual formation becomes deformative if we try to build it exclusively on only one of these two original vital experiences and images while concealing or denying the other. The result can be a passive, world-denying spirituality of total absorption and immersion in an imagined divine. This would be the case if the father experience were denied. When the tendency to fusion with the mother is totally denied, we may develop a hyperactive, willful spirituality of mere performance, social activism, and perfectionism.

Vital Experience and the Magic Component of Pseudospirituality

Infants feel vitally at one with all that appears to them. Their preformed aspiration for transcendence inclines them to believe in an omnipotent source behind the changing appearances around them, but their spiritual ability to intuit and acknowledge this power is still latent. Their vital information power is predominant. Vitally immersed in the formation field, they cannot yet distance themselves sufficiently from their surroundings in a personal way. They are not yet able to imagine a mystery of formation separate from themselves and the appearances around them. Therefore, the latent aspiration for an omnipotent transcendent power becomes self-directed. Their vital presence, undifferentiated from its formation field, is pantheistically invested with divine power. Their own thoughts and wishes are felt as all powerful. Words are experienced as omnipotent. A whole system of divine magic may be postulated on the basis of this experience of universal, undifferentiated form potency.

What is correct in this vital intuition is that Someone is all powerful. What is immature is the identification of one's vital presence with this someone. In later transcendent and pneumatic formation, the gift of faith in an all powerful Someone may be granted to us. Faith makes us believe that the power of the mystery of formation is operative in our form potency, in our formation field and in the great beyond it represents and symbolizes, but that is not identical with our own form potency. This faith inspires the prayer of petition in which we ask the mystery of formation within us and within the formation field and its beyond to exert itself beneficially. We ask, but we do not try to manipulate the mystery by our rituals; the mystery is in us as a gift that eludes our personal power.

It is possible to build a pseudospirituality on the memory traces and images of the vital experience of magic power. In this spirituality of magic, we try to master and manipulate the formation mystery and the formation field and its beyond merely by thoughts, wishes, and ritual words and actions. In and by themselves, these things cannot produce the results we want, yet we falsely believe they can do so.

Related to this experience of magic in children is their tendency to see all things as vitally alive and animated. This world view is characteristic of an early current life-form that is mainly vitalistic in outlook. This view of vital equality and interwovenness deepens the belief that one's thoughts, wishes, and rituals can magically influence one's field of formation and its mysterious source.

This magic expression of latent transcendent aspirations diminishes gradually. It only loses its power when our spiritual life formation in its functional and transcendent dimension begins to assert itself. Yet, we should not underestimate the hold of these archaic experiences and images on the emergent life-form. Even when the transcendent power of the mystery of formation comes within the horizon of our unfolding life, there may still be an inclination to magic. People may try to use certain spiritual exercises as a magical means to influence and manipulate the gods. Traces of such mystifying spirituality can often be found in beginners in the spiritual life. Preconsciously, they may be tempted to use prayers, sacraments, masses, devotions, and good works mainly as a magical means to foster protection, success, healing, salvation, and sanctification. Formative direction or counseling—both with individuals and with groups—should help people to cope with the persistent power of the vital magical tendencies of infancy.

Historical, Vital, Functional, and Transcendent Spirituality in Humanity's Formation History: A Summary

Corresponding to the vitalistic phase in individual formation, we see in early humanity a phase of animistic formation and a belief in the vital magical power of people.

Functional spirituality emerges later in human history. It emphasizes functioning in this world in a more realistic way. Such realism necessitates the acknowledgment of the limitations of one's vital power. Divine powers are experienced as going beyond the individual. They are hypothesized as gods. Yet interaction with these gods is of a functional nature. One tries to placate and manage the divine powers by rituals and sacrifices. On the basis of this onesided spiritual experience, more complex religions begin to develop.

The rise of *transcendent spiritualities* is the next event in human formation history. People begin to acknowledge their powerlessness—vitally and functionally—in the face of death and nature. They become aware of an all-powerful mystery of formation that allows for the rise and fall of forms in the universe. They may develop human faith, hope, and love in relation to this transcendent source of life and formation. They may feel called upon to commit themselves to a unique formation of self and others in the formation field and hence within the historical and spatial setting allowed to them by the mystery of formation. As transcendent religions and spiritualities begin to develop, so, too, do people become aware of the call to creative formation of self, of others, and of the formation field. This call inspires one to education, art, science, scholarship, technology, ecology, and industry. This aspiration for participation in the mystery of formation becomes embodied or incarnated in the vital, functional, and historical dimensions of distinctively human formation.

This *transcendent spirituality* includes and at the same time transcends the best of the vital and the functional. Consonant spirituality is a spirituality of the whole human life in all its dimensions and articulations. Its root is transcendent experience.

In the Christian articulation of the science of formation, pneumatic spirituality completes and transforms the transcendent spirituality of humanity. According to the Christian form tradition, people discover that their own unaided powers are unable to attain the fulfillment of their spiritual aspirations. This tradition holds that God himself reveals to them that an original Fall of humanity led to this inability. He sends his own Son to help humanity overcome the Fall's consequences for human formation. The Son lives on in our formation history through the Holy Spirit. Insofar as our life of transcendent formation is the gift of the Holy Spirit, we call it a life of pneumatic transformation.

We can draw a parallel between the spiritual formation of human life in history and our individual formation. Here, too, we can distinguish five main phases of formation.

The historical phase of personal-spiritual formation. Our personal formation is embedded in the history of human formation. That history is assimilated by our parents and our early formation field in and through the form traditions available in their culture and subculture. By spontaneous vital osmosis, we imbibe this historical impact in our initial formation situation.

The vital phase of personal-spiritual formation. Early childhood is marked by a prevalence of vital strivings, by tendencies to idolizing and fusion, by a vitalistic view of the formation field, and by faith in one's own magical power within this field. The infant's primitive vitalistic spirituality is one of absorption and immersion in this field and the beyond out of which it emerges. This phase is characterized by the tendencies toward fusion with the mother and idolization of the father and by a naive centeredness on the self as the omnipotent center of its surroundings. The infant's unique life-form is not yet experienced as the nearest and most intimate symbol or image of the all-powerful formation mystery in which it participates.

The functional phase of personal-spiritual formation. Children and young adolescents develop both ambitions and skilled functional relationships with parents, other family members, and outsiders. They develop also toward God and religion functional relationships marked either by formal respect, obedience, and ritual observance, or by open or repressed rebellion against the life-style resulting from this formal observance. Religious values in their functional-ethical appearance are formally maintained or rejected, openly or secretly. At different moments of this functional phase, we may observe an appropriation or rejection of the organizational, rational, ethical, ritual, or functional aspects of religion. A critical attitude toward these mainly functionally perceived aspects of spirituality may be a sign of maturation. It may signal the announcement of a new transcendent formation dimension.

The transcendent phase of personal-spiritual formation. Late adolescence and young adulthood may be the period in which the deeper foundational life-form begins to announce to the person its unique life call and direction, its aspirations and inspirations. The growing awareness of one's unique call is experienced as a silent invitation to form self, others, and one's personal and shared formation field in obedience to one's life direction. Ideally, this stage calls forth acts of surrender to the mystery of formation. It facilitates openness for moments of contemplation and heightened transcendent aspiration. The person experiences an aspiration to integrate the historical, vital, functional, and transcendent constituents of life. There may be a felt aspiration toward a *foundational spirituality* that can guide one's effective commitment to a unique call within the formative direction of the history of humanity by the mystery of formation.

The pneumatic phase of personal-spiritual formation. The articulation of the Christian form tradition by the science of formation emphasizes that it is impossible for people to attain this transcendence in a consistent and pure way. Grace is needed, and, hence, so is the *pneumatic dimension*. At any time of life, according to the Christian tradition, the Holy Spirit is present in baptized persons and influences their unfolding. Usually, but not necessarily, the Holy Spirit adapts his gracing influence to the stage in which people find themselves. His pneumatic effect may be more obvious during the phase of *transcendent self-emergence*. The transcendent formation dimension implies the disclosure of the human spirit in which the Holy Spirit is dynamically present. In moments of grace, the Spirit creates an awareness of sinfulness and impotence, of the necessity of grace to realize transcendent aspirations. Pneumatic inspirations begin to complement and elevate the natural aspirations of the human spirit. The transcendent call may be experienced as a call of the God of revelation in the Lord Jesus. The life direction is perceived as a mystery hidden in God before all ages. Final wholeness and integration is seen as an act of the Holy Spirit. The other formation dimensions are considered now both as preparatory stages for the channels of expression and as embodiments of the transforming grace of the Spirit.

CHAPTER 12

The Transcendent Dimension

Let us recall our analogy of the swim in the lake that was introduced in Chapter 5. Floating leisurely, looking at the trees and the sky, we become aware that there is more to life than chores to be done, money to be made, status to be gained. We experience the awareness that life has a deeper meaning. We are struck by the thought that no single thing has its ultimate value in and by itself alone. We become aware of a deeper mystery that engulfs all there is. We feel immersed in that depth of reality. We may be overcome by *awe*, sensing that this mode of awareness is the deepest one we are capable of experiencing as human persons. Rarely may we be as aware of this kind of presence as we are in this lucid moment of leisure, floating in the water under a splendid sky.

Still we sense dimly that this awareness of a deeper meaning perpetually plays a role in our life. We seem to be in search of this meaning, whatever happens. We try to make it concrete, to give it a name. Other people seem to do the same, although we suspect that many give it the wrong name. They tend to make something ultimate that is only finite. Any of us may refuse to take seriously this spiritual dimension of our life. We may go so far as to deny it, to ridicule it, to flee from it. Yet it always seems to be there. It breaks through our refusal, often in disguised and distorted ways. For better or worse, it seems to be the dimension that in real or falsified fashion rules every human life. This should not surprise us, for to be human is to be spirit through and through. To be spirit is to be in need of some ultimate formative meaning of life and world.

Spiritual Experience

Imagine being deeply moved by a starry sky. Similar feelings emerge in us as those we felt during our swim in the lake. This experience is different from our everyday awareness. Usually, we take the sky and the stars for granted. Were we the captain of a ship, we might use the stars to pilot the boat. Were we scientists, we might study the stars to discover the laws that govern their course. In daily life we usually look at the sky to find out if we should put on a raincoat and take an umbrella.

When we are touched spiritually by the starry sky, we do not think about any of these things. We simply want to be with our experience. We let the sky and its sparkling beauty be. We stand there awed, in abandonment to what is beyond us and our projects. In this spiritual presence, we flow with the mystery of all that is greater than we are, a mystery of formation in which we experience ourselves as somehow sharing. We may have a feeling of oneness with the stars, the sky, the cosmos. We may begin to experience a certain kinship with all that is. In some way, we transcend our limits and feel open to the infinite.

Emergence of the Transcendent Form Dimension

The potency for transcendent presence manifests itself slowly in human life. In early childhood it seems dormant or, so to speak, in a state of latency. A deeper awakening of the spirit may happen in adolescence or early adulthood. This realization presupposes a proper arrangement of the vital and functional dimensions. The latter, as we saw in preceding chapters, is the work of the hidden spirit itself.

As an embodied presence in our formation field, we must formatively appraise, project, and manage our lives. We need to pay attention to the myriad concrete details of each situation to be dealt with in terms of maintenance, expansion, and survival. We may become so bound to immediacy, so attentive to the surface aspects of people, events, and things, that we lose our readiness to intuit their transcendent meaning. We may be lost in forgetfulness, not ready in receptivity when the transcendent begins to announce itself in daily life.

Because our culture is function-directed, it is fascinated by instant, spectacular, and measurable results. It easily tempts one to live in forgetfulness of deeper aspirations.

The Transforming Power of the Transcendent Dimension

In a functional stance, we deal with situations as occasions to be appraised in terms of effective projects and management. Pragmatic appraisal places us frequently in opposition to other people, events, and things in service of our own success, promotion, and survival. We distance ourselves from deeper intermeshed meanings as if we were lonely islands in the ocean of life.

In transcendent presence, by contrast, we allow people, events, and things to be illumined by the light of reverential awareness. We appraise them and ourselves spiritually. We see ourselves and others as emerging from a common mysterious source that lovingly embraces everything. Everyone shares a dignity, truth, and nobility that surpasses surface appearances and differences. This intuition of *oneness in uniqueness* is the ground of such spiritual attitudes as faith, hope, and consonance; receptivity, wonder, and wisdom; awe, gratitude, and sacrifice; lasting commitment, graciousness and generosity.

Enlightened Pulsations, Impulses, and Ambitions

Human life formation aspires to consonance. Its dimensions complement one another. They modulate each other graciously. Historical pulsations, vital impulses, and functional ambitions are taken up by transcendent presence. A transfiguring stance towards them modulates these dimensions without betraying them. It integrates them in one's ongoing life formation.

The transcendent dimension is thus a power of integration, a source of unification at the root of one's life. It is the source of integration binding us to reality and its mysterious source. It is a preformed capacity for openness and participation by which we experience ourselves as intimately related to all that is, yet also as unique. This uniqueness is no longer experienced as isolated or as circumscribed only by our immediate environment, family, nationality, job, political affiliation, or personal history. We begin to see ourselves and others as having a meaningful place within the mystery of formation, a noble standing not yet totally disclosed to us. Life becomes for us an assignment, a task, a mysterious call. We see the gift of uniqueness as being more than our individuality or our biophysical distinctiveness. It is more than the functional identity we have built so far. Transcendent form potency is experienced as something to be ever more disclosed and increasingly achieved, as a being called forth by destiny in ways we cannot yet fathom.

Transcendent Identity of Foundational Life Direction

Identity has many aspects. Its sociohistorical, vital, and functional sides are quite recognizable. They can be tested and measured to some degree. They determine and describe what we observably are at this moment of our life. These determinations are due to many factors. A preforming genetic inheritance plays a role in this identity. Functional history and one's position in society also contribute to an identity. In short, *functional identity* tells us what we already are. It also suggests what we may probably become if our social situation remains the same and our spirit does not intervene.

Spiritual identity is far more of a mystery. It represents a deeper, hidden aspect of life. It seems to be the most foundational aspect of our identity, its hidden base. This *transcendent identity* represents the unknown foundational life-form, or that which we are called to be. At our best moments, we may sense its hidden invitation to become who we are. This identity is so basic that it goes beyond the boundaries of one's momentary vital, functional, and *sociohistorical identity*. Because it tells us what we should become, where our life should go, we can call it our inspiring spiritual identity, our life direction, or our life call. (Terms like these seem to describe better than the static word identity the dynamic, future-oriented, mysterious nature of transcendent uniqueness.)

Spiritual direction does not disclose primarily what we already are. Neither does it tell us what we can become by means of vital inheritance and functional acquisitions. Rather, it enables us to sense what we are uniquely called to be. It suggests the direction in which we ought to go, even if this means going against certain aspects of our makeup and life situation here and now.

Commitment and Spiritual Life Direction

This awareness of a hidden, true life direction enables one to make lifelong commitments. Its scope extends beyond what one can know for sure here and now about the life situations to be faced in the future. The hidden courage that directs us to make such commitments comes from the intuitive certitude of our *life call*. This certitude of the spirit is firmer than any confidence rooted in our functional and vital dimensions. Our functional-vital identity is shaped by, among other things, the form directives, fads, and fashions that are popular in our culture. The spiritual life call implies a breakthrough to other directives. These transcendent directives may not be appreciated at this moment of history we share with others. Yet they may disclose themselves to us as form directives to be lived faithfully. They do not necessarily give us social status or fame. They may not yield economic gain. We may be ridiculed for following the rhythm of a unique drummer. Still, we have the definite feeling that if we do not follow this call, we will betray the unique epiphany of the mystery of formation in our life.

Openness to the spirit and its horizon enables us to hear an appeal to realize uniquely a certain set of form directives in our life. We feel a silent invitation to be faithful to them, no matter how much appreciation or depreciation we receive from others. These are lasting form directives for us. To be sure, we can deceive ourselves about our call. The art and discipline of enlightened appraisal of such invitations is, therefore, of crucial importance.

Spiritual experience may mean at times that we have to go on alone. Naturally, this frightens us. It may tempt us to avoid such experiences. But if we keep giving in to this dread, we may become perpetual fugitives from our deepest consonant life direction. This flight from our life call succeeds only to the degree that we refuse to be open to the transcendent dimension of our life. Bound up with this dimension is the blessing of the disclosure of who we are called to be, the burden to become who we really are, and the suffering this becoming may entail.

Transcendent Experience

Spiritual experience is transcendent. To transcend means to go beyond, which is to say that spiritual experiences go beyond our usual modes of presence. This becomes especially clear when these experiences are so-called summit experiences of the spirit and are fully beyond the world of control and manipulation. In such experiences we are absorbed by a deeper meaning and we leave the practical scene momentarily behind us.

The word transcendence may be used by some people to express a merely intellectual, abstract going beyond. Such intellectual transcendence is exemplified in stories about absentminded professors. This kind of transcendence has its own purposes and advantages, but it is not our primary interest in this theory of proximate life formation.

Our *formation theory of personality* is primarily concerned about life as it realizes itself concretely in and through experience and action. We try to look at the dynamic totality of human life as it unfolds itself in light of its accepted or rejected transcendent dimension. This dimension, no matter how much it is resisted or distorted, in some way affects our whole life in all its details. Everything in us is influenced by our spirit: our mind and heart, our thoughts and feelings, our times of rest and action, our vital and functional ways of being.

Quasi-Transcendent Experiences of the Functional and Vital Life Dimension

There is also a kind of *quasi transcendence* in the functional and vital dimensions of life. As functional people, we can go beyond our everyday routines either in functional-intellectual considerations or in functional ambitions. Unlike spiritual transcendence, these are only partial ways of going beyond. They do not leave everything behind. Such an intellectual or ambitious going beyond may lift us above everyday concerns and involvements. We may walk around as absentminded professors or live a fantasy life that fulfills ambitions far beyond our present possibilities. Yet we are still captive to our intellectual musings and ambitious dreams. We may be so preoccupied with them that they close us off from that openness to the infinite that is typical of spiritual experience in its fullness.

To ready ourselves for this experience, we must detach ourselves from even our most noble ambitions and subtle intellectualizing. This is not to say that there is no place for the thoughts and ambitions of the functional dimension. They do play a significant role in a well-integrated life. This integration implies, however, that they leave room for the spirit, that ego musings and ambitions do not obstruct the transcendent life-form, that they take the aspirations of this hidden center into account.

Vital transcendence is also only a quasi transcendence. Our daily life is filled with vital moods and emotions in response to everyday happenings. Such feelings tend to be rather pedestrian. They bind us to the immediate concerns that comprise our average day of work and play. Occasionally, however, something we read, hear, or experience may evoke feelings that take us beyond our immediate interests, worries, and daily environment. It may be an amorous or erotic experience, a feeling of anger and indignation about something far greater than our everyday concerns, an overwhelming enthusiasm for some vital cause. This kind of vital transcendence should not be confused with the spiritual sort. Like the quasi transcendence of the functional dimension, the vitalistic version does not leave everything behind. Powerful vital emotions link us with the causes that move us so violently. They encapsulate us in this vital aspect of our world and prevent our openness to the infinite.

To ready ourselves for summit spiritual experiences, we must detach ourselves from both our everyday and our quasi-transcendent vital feelings. This *detachment* does not mean that such feelings cease to have a place in the well-integrated life of the spiritual person. They surely do. Consonant people can be immensely passionate, presupposing, of course, that their vital preformation disposes them for passion. Vital passions, moods, and feelings can be spontaneously modulated by the aspirations of the spirit and by the practical knowledge and transcendent-enlightened ambitions of the functional dimension. Detachment in the consonant life is not detachment from passions, moods, and emotions as such. It is detachment from them as *ultimate*. This implies, among other things, detachment from feelings in so far as they interfere with our unique life call. This life direction is disclosed to us increasingly when we foster spiritual transcendence in our lives.

Transcendent Experience of the Spirit Dimension

Let us reflect again on the experience of beholding a starry sky. We feel drawn beyond the experience of the cosmos into a meaning, a mystery, a totality that transcends it. Such a plunge into the depth dimension of reality may happen on other occasions. The mystery of all that is may announce itself in a literary or religious text, in a painting or a musical composition, in a beautiful sunset, in a fellow human being, or in a great event in life, such as birth, marriage, or death. We suddenly feel an intimacy with the transcendent dimension of reality. In our example, it is the starry sky that evokes this intimacy. Our whole being seems filled with a peaceful presence. All the facets of our personality are drawn together in this experience of awed presence to the transcendent meaning of the cosmos in and around us.

What happens to us in this moment of presence? For one thing, we forget about our worries and interests. We feel drawn up in a deeper reality that transcends and absorbs us. We do not feel separated from the mystery that permeates sky, stars, and cosmos. We do not experience them as isolated objects outside ourselves or outside the whole of reality. We do not look on them as scientific projects to be studied in isolation or practical instruments to be utilized for space travel or navigation. We are wholly at one with the mysterious meaning of all that is, as disclosed to us by this unusual experience of the sparkling sky.

Sensate, Intellectual, Vital-Emotional, and
Spiritual Intuitive Modalities of Knowing

Outside this experience, we may relate differently to the vast universe. As persons with healthy senses, we are aware of the material dimension of reality. We perceive the empirical reality of the sky and its myriad stars. We also have adequate intelligence and education. As students, for instance, we may have taken an interest in astronomy. Education then opened our functional intelligence to the probing questions evoked by the heavens. We are able to make the cosmos intelligible in a scientific way. Moreover, as vital-emotional persons, we can experience feelings evoked by the starry sky above us, feelings perhaps of a romantic nature.

Full spiritual presence, however, engenders a knowledge that is utterly different. It cannot be compared with sensate, intellectual, or emotional knowledge. Spiritual knowledge goes beyond these other ways of knowing. It opens us to the infinite. It is an intuition that transcends other kinds of awareness and makes us feel at one with the transcendent dimension of reality. We could call this a knowledge of loving at-one-ness.

The sensate, intellectual, emotional, and spiritual-intuitive modalities of knowledge and presence are four modulations of one and the same primary human power, the power of presence to reality. Full spiritual presence happens primarily in the transcendent dimension. It is this transcendent presence that may foster a spiritual outlook and life-style. This life-style in turn facilitates a deeper spiritual presence in daily life. The same life-style prepares the way for the penetration of one's functional-vital presence by one's deeper spiritual presence.

Transcendence and Crisis

At rare moments of spiritual presence in its fullness, we are no longer involved in our usual modes of interaction. We are not preoccupied with our everyday world. We are not engaged in controlling our situation. We are not busy with the exploitation of nature. A certain amount of control admittedly is necessary for an effective human life. Humanity could not survive without some exploitation of nature. Coping with adversity as a well-developed functional presence to reality on the basis of a healthy vitality is mandatory for the necessary mastery of life and the world.

These necessities seem to be suspended during the spiritual summit experience—but not for long. Soon we come back from the mountaintop to the valley of daily existence and to the full context of daily reality. But this is not to say that the transcendent stance is betrayed. It may direct itself now to the enhanced reality of everyday living. The web of everydayness is taken up into our transcendent presence. It receives a new illumination, a glow it did not have before.

Transcendent presence to spiritual meaning in the midst of daily life requires a stance of formative receptivity. This does not mean that we deny the problems and crises that emerge in ordinary living. In *formative receptivity*, we accept crises as challenges to our creativity and courage. Yet we relativize their significance and defuse their excessive impact. We experience them implicitly against the wider context disclosed to us in our transcendent presence. We experience a more fundamental unity as spirit. This unity gives a unifying meaning to all the crises of our life.

For example, a surgeon may be exposed to many pressures in his care for patients. In his transcendent life, he may have grown to the insight that he is called to a life of gentle, effective dedication to suffering humanity. Against this horizon he meets with daily problems and crises of hospitalized people. His transcendent orientation helps him to accept creatively the tension and responsibility of life-and-death situations in the operating room. It grants him the patience to cope gently with problems of administration or with staff members who do not serve the best interests of his patients. His transcendent presence enables him on other occasions to bear the burden of a diplomatic approach to representatives of research foundations whose funding can sustain his pursuit of medical excellence in service of suffering humanity.

This attitude of going beyond the situation actually means going deeper into it by looking at it in a wider context. Transcendence in daily life does not mean running away from the everyday world and its problems. Spiritual presence is not a trancelike openness to a nebulous totality nowhere to be found. The totality that the science of formation addresses manifests itself in the concrete context of one's formation field. This context is wider than the immediate situation itself insofar as the formation field points to an even wider context, an infinite one. Transcendent people lift every problem and crisis into the light of this expanding context of ultimate meaning. This elevation relativizes their problems, or at least puts the problems in a new perspective. The awareness of this relativity enables spiritual persons to maintain their peace and equanimity.

Transcendence as Human Event

Transcendence is an event that happens to all people who allow themselves to be human. The degree of transcendence, the depth of the horizon disclosed, the emotional or mystical experiences that may or may not accompany it, are different in different persons. Much depends on each one's unique preformation, culture, form tradition, personal history, and form potencies.

The transcendent nature of the human life-form means basically that one is able to experience reality as overflowing the immediate situation in which one is involved functionally and vitally. Spirit is the human ability to experience life and its situations as part of a context so wide that it cannot be measured or exhaustively understood. Spirit is also the ability to act on this experience by allowing it to become a fundamental orientation of one's functional and vital life in one's communal and personal formation field.

Transcendence and Intermediate Wholes

Spirit opens us to a wider horizon. This horizon may initially be referred to as an intermediate whole and may be represented by social justice, family, a beloved person, humanity, country, cosmos, or nature. These are some of the more common object poles of the transcendent experience. They are definite enough to make sense and to be directly experienced as meaningful. People can connect these more specific wholes with the concrete type of dedication to which they feel invited. At the same time, such intermediate wholes are sufficiently indefinite. They allow people to sense that they in turn point to a wider horizon. This implicit pointing is essential for a truly transcendent experience. If people deny or exclude this reference to an indefinite wider horizon, they may become fixated on such an intermediate whole. They begin to absolutize it or become fanatic about it. They become victims, for instance, of a romance, a raving nationalism, a merciless ideology. They lose the transcendent openness that could set them free.

It is also possible that people may be graced with the ecstatic experience of the whole as such, of being, of all that is, without first crossing the bridge to the infinite offered by these intermediate wholes. In such cases, spiritual experience may take on an explicit religious character, that is, the experience of the whole as holy.

Transcendence as a Less Common Contemporary Event

Transcendent experience is a normal human event, yet it may not be as common in our culture today as it was in former times and still is in other cultures. Mass media, education, public information, popular literature, and the social sciences may no longer promote transcendent experience in our culture. They may emphasize instead the development of a well-integrated functional-vital life as the ultimate meaning and fulfillment of all formation.

As a result, many people may reach only incidentally a transcendent view of life. It may happen to them in special circumstances, such as death in the family, a serious illness or hardship, or a moving religious celebration. Few persons seem to live a life that allows transcendence to blossom forth and to permeate their formation as such. Consequently, their life is not functional and vital in a human way. It becomes instead functionalistic and vitalistic—thus a crippling deformation of human life. Functionalism and vitalism are harmful to the health of individuals and threatening to society and community. They are a force of dehumanization, opposed to love, openness, and integration.

Limits of Vital and Functional Formation and the Birth of Transcendent Form Potency

Transcendence implies an experience of moving beyond our limits. We realize more clearly the reality of our deficiencies while experiencing them from a new perspective. They look different to us because we see them in relation to the all-encompassing meaning to which we are mysteriously drawn. Absorbed in this embracing meaningfulness, we are able to distance ourselves from our limits. By identifying with the transcendent, we realize that these limits are no longer the whole of us. We accept our limits by transcending them. This spiritual perspective liberates us to see limits as signposts directing us toward our unique life assignment. Affirming them as meaningful pointers, we no longer feel imprisoned by them. To know and accept our limits is thus to go beyond them.

Transcendence gives birth to a form potency that is beyond our functional limits. This is not the power of potentially deformative mastery or control, but the power of formative loving presence. Transcendent formation is a power of peaceful strength and of simple, accepting presence of self, others, events, and things as they truly are in light of the transcendent. In transcendence we experience a strength rooted in our innermost being, a quiet confidence that allows us to face reality as it is. This is the source of realism, of solidity and earthiness, of fidelity to our life call, of loving commitment. This transcendent strength enables us to see more clearly what is happening in our life and surroundings. This vision is due to our participation in the inner power of all that is, in the animating source of the universe, in the all-embracing mystery of formation.

Transcendent Life—Respect versus Violence

The spiritual person is truly involved in everyday endeavors while at the same time transcending them. To be an embodied spiritual presence is to be beyond all things and yet remain in the midst of them. This stance generates a life increasingly inspired by the deepest meanings of people, events, and things. The spiritual person cultivates profound respect for any manifestation of goodness, truth, nobility, or beauty.

People who refuse any formation by the transcendent dimension of life may become so preoccupied with pleasure, power, and possession that they cannot be respectful. Anxiously immersed in a closed-off, competitive world, they tend to be aggressive, at least inwardly. Battling for the small stakes they have to share with countless others, they tend to be defensive, overly ambitious, and at times violent.

Violence implies a refusal to respect people, nature, and things in their transcendent meaning. It is rooted in a narrowing of our horizon. Instead of walking this earth in wonder, love, and admiration, we begin to live in anxious comparison. We look at others in competitive, envious ways. Such small-mindedness breeds defensiveness, anger, envy, jealousy, and rage. These in turn have to be repressed to make social functioning, or its pretense, bearable. Repression and denial foster psychosomatic illnesses and disturbances. They sap the vital life of people.

Repressed violence may turn inward against one's own life or, in veiled ways, against other people. Traditional therapeutic methods may help some people to find a compromise that makes life livable without opening up the transcendent formation dimension. This compromise is often sufficient to keep symptoms of *deformative dissonance* within manageable proportions. Yet these people remain vulnerable as long as they do not face the deepest root of their deformations. The exclusion of the transcendent dimension encapsulates them in their narrow view. If they cannot move beyond these limitations into a wider spiritual vision, violence may erupt. It may manifest itself in mild forms, such as manipulation of self or others. It may also express itself in self-rejection, self-hate, depression, excessive guilt, and self-punishment. It may result in violent discrimination against others who differ in status, wealth, class, form tradition, race, or color.

The respectfulness of the spiritual person is a spring of progress, creativity, and harmony. Violence is a source of evil, ugliness, and regression. Both forces are at work in us. Violence and respect are contesting forces of formation, constantly vying for ascendency in our life. To allow the transcendent dimension of formation to unfold itself means potentially to replace violence by respect.

What is the primal act of violence? We believe it is the defensive refusal of the potential fullness of our awareness. It is the denial of the spiritual dimension of our life. All other acts of inner and outer violence against self and others are conditioned by this primal act. This basic violence is the root cause of a blindness that refuses to face the repulsive reality of violent behavior. Primal violence is an expression of the quasi-foundational pride-form of life.

Only the spirit mitigates human anxiety, moderates defensiveness, calms envious competition, softens ambitions. Only the spirit opens us to the mystery of formation that can fulfill our deepest aspirations. Self-assurance, graciousness, peacefulness, and wholeness are given to those who have discovered the infinite in the finite. They have accepted the deepest meaning of reality as an invitation to union with their own ground. They are open to the mysterious whole that surpasses them infinitely while embracing them intimately.

To be sure, doubt, anxiety, failure, and suffering may at times mark the life of spiritual people, but the spirit will teach them how to cope effectively with these painful intrusions into their peacefulness.

The Transcendent Dimension, Integration, and Peace

Spiritual presence is a mysterious forming force at the core of human life. It is a hidden source of loving integration; it harmonizes a human being inwardly. Spiritual presence gives a new and profound meaning to other ways of living. It does not belittle the rich but partial meanings of diverse modes of life. It transforms and roots each of them in a person's deepest center. It teaches one to be truly alive in many modes of presence without becoming their prisoner.

The emergent human life-form as a whole can be seen as an ongoing *dialogical movement of formation,* a movement of *differentiation* and *integration*. Differentiation opens us to new modes and articulations of presence while integration gathers in the new and old forms of presence to which one is called at this moment of life. The human life-form is thus a unity in diversity.

The ground of such dynamic integration must be the most all-encompassing dimension of human presence. Only spiritual presence provides such a comprehensive foundation. Only the spiritual harmonizes all other dimensions and modes of life without taking away their distinctiveness. It is the spirit that centers all distinctively human formation. It recalls us from the variety of ways in which we tend to lose ourselves in our formation field. Only this holistic way of presence can be regarded as the core of the centering movement of human life.

Centering spiritual presence is the wellspring of sound realism, of energy, of relaxed persistence, of vital joy, and of quiet courage. It is a source of health and wholeness, of peace of heart and mind. Peace does not mean only tranquility. It implies also an order that safeguards equanimity. People cannot be peaceful, serene, and relaxed if they are spread out in numerous cares and concerns. They feel dismembered, fragmented, dissected, torn in various directions, no longer whole and centered or at one with themselves.

For this reason, people need to experience that horizon which surpasses and enhances all separate meanings of daily activities, gathering them together in unity. Thus centered, they will be at home with themselves in the midst of disturbances and distractions. Only transcendent presence can create this peace of centeredness in a human person.

Spiritual Presence and Religious Experience

Religious experience has given rise to worship in countless peoples, cultures, and cultural periods. This experience is related to the transcendent dimension and its spontaneous immersion in the mystery of formation.

We noted earlier that spiritual presence generates respect. In religious experience the respect of spiritual people deepens to reverence. *Reverence* may overwhelm them when celebrating love, looking at the stars, climbing a mountain, or dwelling in the silence of forest and desert. Reverent people feel small in the presence of beauty and majesty, and yet they do not feel alienated, forlorn, or threatened. They feel carried by the vast expansion of nature transcending them in space and time. Their life becomes a passing moment in the immense and continuous whole that extends itself indefinitely. Humbly acknowledging their position, they experience reverence.

Reverence is the flower of spiritualization. Its source is the sacred fascination people experience in the presence of what transcends them. Everything worthy of a person's deepest dedication receives meaning from its relatedness to that mystery which overwhelms well-disposed people in moments of silent contemplation and pure receptivity. Unrelated to this mystery, experiences lose their radiance and fail to evoke reverence.

Reverence and Respect

Facing the unknown, a person may feel fear. In spiritual presence, however, this fear is refined into awe by loving acceptance of a higher reality that embraces one as a mystery of love and generosity.

Reverence is fear that has become awe under the mitigating and elevating influence of loving surrender to a mystery that attracts people by its goodness while keeping them at a humble distance by its majesty. Reverence is an exquisite mode of spiritual presence. The more people grow in reverence, the more it can permeate their thoughts, feelings, and actions. Reverence at the root of their being fosters the mode of spiritual presence called respect.

Like reverence, respect relates the human life-form to the whole; it relates it to people, events, and things in so far as they are seen as uniquely participating in the whole. This respect, when one allows it to penetrate the functional-vital modes of presence, grants each human act the beauty of graciousness.

Awe, Worship, and Adoration

Awe can give rise to two other modes of spiritual presence: worship and adoration. This happens when spiritual presence is focused on the mysterious source of the universe that evokes awe.

A sense of worship may engulf people when they experience themselves as a source of their own activity while at the same time feeling that they emerge from a mystery that transcends them. They sense that something higher than themselves must be the ground of all personal, vital, cosmic, and cultural unfolding.

Their deepened awareness of their own limitations in space, time, and possibilities gives rise to an experience of a source of unfolding infinitely more personal than they themselves are. Their original sense of the whole deepens to an experience of the holy in and beyond themselves and everything else. They are aware of the holy as a transcosmic and transpersonal source of their own thought, movement, and being. This mysterious source is experienced as divine.

People absorbed in this mode of spiritual presence feel holy fear or awe before this divine source. They experience their personal being flowing continuously from the holy. Simultaneously, they feel irresistibly attracted to this effusive love that allows them to be and become.

Awe permeates one's being. Before the holy, one feels as nothing. Its mystery is overwhelming, fascinating, wonderful. People feel that they could not face this mystery if they did not also sense that the holy is the highest good and the origin of all goodness.

Worship thus means saying yes to this dependency, enjoying the sense that one is nothing and the holy is all. This is adoration—a mode of spiritual presence representing the highest expression of reverence and respect.

Reverence, Culture, and Humanization

Reverence, along with the respect it generates or deepens, is the root of culture and humanization. Fear not deepened to awe, and the violence to which such fear gives rise, is the *root of dehumanization.*

People may have been blessed with moments of full spiritual presence in reverence. They may cultivate a loving remembrance of what has touched them deeply and allow that reverence to penetrate all dimensions of their life. In respect, they cultivate the earth for the sake of the human community. In all persons and things they see the unfolding of a mysterious formation design. They feel called upon to assume their unique place in the history of formative evolution and human unfolding.

This awareness of a life to be lived uniquely in generous service makes reverent people builders of cultures and their underlying form traditions. Their response to life is more free, spontaneous, flexible, and creative. At the same time, it is more objective, concrete, realistic, practical, and earthy. It is this respectful, realistic, creative response that is a source of formative culture and form tradition.

Sometimes, the fear in a religious experience is not transformed into awe. Sometimes the spirit and its horizon are refused. This refusal cannot prevent the experience of the whole and holy from happening, but in such cases it evokes only fear. The holy is perceived as a threatening power. Such indeterminate fear about the great unknown may give rise to reactions that are unfree, fixated, and often violent. (We use the word *reaction* here instead of *response*. The science of formation prefers the term reaction when dealing with unfree and unspiritualized answers to reality. The term response is reserved for answers to life that are marked by a certain measure of freedom, creativity, and originality, rooted in a person's spiritual formation.)

People who refuse the transcendent usually participate in the culture in a defensive way. They are often plagued by doubts about their form potency. Their secret anxiety about formation impotence compels them to use the culture and its form traditions for the promotion of their own power, status, and defensive knowledge. Their stereotyped reactions hamper the free, daring, and creative unfolding of the culture and its underlying form traditions. They are fearful that cultural initiative may diminish their security. They also lack the leisure and playfulness that are at the heart of *cultural innovation*.

Spiritual Presence as Readiness for Reverence

Even when respect has not yet be deepened to reverence, it is a trustworthy source of culture. Respect carries in itself a possibility to become reverence. The formation mystery it respects may disclose itself as the holy. If it does so, respect is called upon to deepen itself to reverence, to root itself in presence to the holy. If people willfully refuse to answer that call, they begin to form their lives outside the formation mystery and its manifold epiphanies. They close themselves off from their own innermost possibility. They willfully refuse to walk in the light. They betray the essence of *spiritual presence*.

Spiritual presence is unconditional openness to all the ways in which the transcendent formation mystery manifests itself. To be sure, the mystery may not manifest itself as holy. It may not evoke the mode of spiritual presence called reverence. Spiritual presence can then be maintained in other ways, such as that of sheer belief in the mysterious whole that embraces us and our history. People who hold such a belief may be faithful to the light granted to them.

Though they do not experience the summit neither do they dwell in darkness. They walk in the light in so far as it shines upon them.

Imagine what may happen to people who begin to experience the mode of reverence, yet willfully refuse to allow experience to expand itself in their awareness. Such refusal necessarily paralyzes the whole spiritual dimension of their lives. The spiritual dimension is by its nature an openness to any manifestation of the transcendent. To close oneself to any form of disclosure is to deny the nature of the spiritual dimension, to nullify it as such.

Transcendent openness pushes the person to ever wider horizons of spiritual experience. This dynamic propulsion of the spirit happens whenever a human being is personally and culturally ready for a specific disclosure of the horizon of the spirit. Our presence to one disclosure of the spirit thus implies a fundamental possibility for a deeper disclosure. This spiritual potentiality must be activated by a personal readiness for this deepening of experience, for this new gift of the spirit. This personal readiness depends on the concrete inner and outer life situation in which we find ourselves.

When a favorable situation activates our form potency for deeper spiritual presence we may choose to refuse the spirit's invitation to new heights. But to maintain that refusal, we must also deny the horizon of the spirit to which we are already present. Each presence of the spirit implies an expansion of our transcendent potency and a pointing to the next phase of deepening spiritual presence. In other words, our actual spiritual presence will inevitably give rise to a deeper presence the moment we are ready for it culturally and personally. The only way for us to avoid the new horizon is to live in repressive refusal of all horizons of the spirit, to falsify them, to dwell willfully outside the light of the formation mystery.

We can thus distinguish a fundamental potentiality and a concrete *readiness for deepening*. Only when both coincide does a new disclosure take place. This readiness is usually the result of new facilitating conditions for inner deepening in our personal or cultural life and in the form tradition to which we are committed. Similarly the absence of this predisposing readiness is usually related to the lack of such facilitating conditions and their development in our functional-vital life, in our cultural surroundings, and in our form tradition.

All these dynamics of spiritual growth apply also to the deepening of respect into reverence. People can refuse to acknowledge the spiritual horizon of reverence to which they feel themselves opening up. Such denial can only be maintained by repressive refusal of the whole spiritual dimension of life. This refusal cannot do away with this dimension. It only means that the unavoidable inner aspiration to find an ultimate meaning and to live by its light seeks another outlet. This inner aspiration, when denied or distorted, moves us inevitably to find a substitute for the formation mystery. Finding a substitute for our abandonment to the mystery compels us to absolutize isolated limited objects on the functional-vital level of our formation and thus to pervert our spiritual presence.

Initial Formation of the Transcendent Dimension

The transcendent dimension is an aspiration toward that which is more than the objects of our historical pulsations, vital impulses, and functional ambitions. It is also the potency of spontaneous interest in the mystery of formation and its epiphanies. Children are preformatively directed to this mystery. They begin at a certain moment to sense the veiled meaning of sacralized movements, images, words, and songs when they are exposed to them by reverential people. Via these sounds and gestures, they begin to surmise something of that to which such symbols point. Long before any instruction, children begin to sense the invisible transcendent. Its presence is reflected in the reverential attitudes of adults who surround them.

This *preconscious formation* goes on from earliest infancy to old age, often without our focal attention. As children, we already assimilate by interformative osmosis transcendent experiences and aspirations. Our lived *transcendent aspirations* and *inspirations* are awakened first of all by our environment: the way our family prays at table; the way our mother lights a candle before a statue; the way a priest, minister, or rabbi presides at religious ceremonies; the way a teacher speaks of religion. These and other expressions of their transcendent presence affect us. We are touched not only on the level of reasoning but also preconsciously. This is possible because of our spontaneous interformative identification with them and their expressions.

We should always be open to the message of the transcendent. Such openness implies a disposition of receptivity, a gentle docility. It allows interformation to affect what is already forming us spontaneously in our emergent life. This preconscious process should be corrected, complemented, and deepened, but not replaced by reflective processes. For example, formal instruction in religion or theology can become formative only to the extent that our hearts assimilate their content in an inspirational-practical way.

Transcendent formation depends on the quality of life manifested in a child's environment. A life of aspiration evokes aspirations in others via a presence that is mostly one of wordless witnessing, of silent appeal. This power of evocation is proper to the human person as transcendent. Transcendence is a possibility we did not choose or devise ourselves; it is a call we cannot escape.

This call points to a mysterious context that goes beyond our group, culture, or life situation—even beyond ourselves. The orientation toward transcendence is always present in every human being. We can gently evoke this slumbering direction but we cannot compel its awakening. We can only promote or hinder it, foster favorable conditions or allow unfavorable ones to obstruct it. *Foundational formation* is ultimately a mystery, a gift from a transcendent source. It is unique, not in the sense that it is autonomous, insulated, or absolutely independent, but in the sense that it is a unique manifestation of an ultimate mystery.

CHAPTER 13

Transcendent Form Potency

Every human life-form is, by nature, both forming and able to receive formation. We call this potentiality for formation *formability*, or *form potency*. It is one of the most basic capacities of human life, not simply one of the many qualities we may find in people. Formability is not an ability that a human person *has;* it is an ability which one *is*. Without this potency to receive and give form, human life could no longer emerge as a *human* form and true humanity would no longer be possible.

Transcendent form potency refers to our preformed ability to allow and promote a transcendent formation of our unfolding life. It is the human ability, due to the preformation of the human person as human, to allow and promote a communal and unique formation of one's life in accordance with preformed and adopted transcendent aspirations and inspirations.

All of human life is an attempt to take the right stance toward this destiny of having to allow and foster a transcendent formation of one's unfolding life. Our whole life can be seen as a demand to disclose and implement our call to transcendence within the cultural communities whose futures we shape while being shaped by them.

Human form potency has a transcendent character. It aims at a life-form that goes beyond mere *conformity*. It invites us to rise above the immediacy of our daily surroundings, of our vital, functional, and sociohistorical determinations. *Foundational formation* aspires toward a life-form that opens us to the mystery of the beyond. Restlessness remains in the human heart as long as the form given to the emergent life is not in consonance with the mysterious ground of life, which transcends the functional context of our lives.

Jewish, Christian, Islamic, Hindu, Buddhist, and other traditions point in symbol, myth, and doctrine to this openness of life to the transcendent. In particular, *Jewish and Christian form traditions* speak of the image, or form, of God himself in which we are created. To free this divine image, or form, and to allow it to emerge in a communal and uniquely empirical form of life is the ideal of both Jewish and Christian *form traditions.*

Transcendent form potency precedes transcendent formation. It is a potentiality for formation. The potentiality for an act always precedes the act and is presupposed by the act. In other words, an act is the actualization of an already existing potentiality. All forming acts are thus actualizations of this form potency. Although we cannot observe a potentiality directly, we know it, usually implicity, in our experience of its various actualizations. An experience of our foundational form potency is, therefore, implicit in all our experiences of actual formation. This basic, distinctively human form potency is rooted in the fundamental structure of our lives as transcendent. It is precisely our transcendent life dimension that makes us human.

The call to foundational human formation that arises from the transcendent dimension is at once threatening and beckoning. We may feel threatened because we cannot yet know what that formation will do to us. We miss the certainty and security of the routines of everyday life when we have to make decisions pertaining to our future unfolding. Numerous *life directives* are available to us. We have assembled them during our past and present *interformation* and interaction. We draw on them to solve our problems. They point to the life that might be ours. We ourselves could not have chosen the number and kind of directives that history has offered us and with which it may still surprise us. In time we may come to know certain directives that seem right for us. We may allow them to form us. They point to our life process as a whole. These directives, however, far exceed our grasp; they always point beyond what we can foresee. Hence, we are aware of the threatening character of the invitation to prepare for a life whose full implications cannot be known in advance.

Nonetheless the call that issues from our form potency is beckoning, too. We realize that if we do not allow and foster some transcendence in our lives, our existence is liable to become form-

168 | FUNDAMENTAL FORMATION

less and dissipated. At the same time, life becomes imprisoned in mere vital need fulfillment, functional everydayness, and insufficiently appraised *sociohistorical pulsations*. In the end we suffer the despair of meaninglessness.

Transcendent Ideals and Functional Projects

Spiritual ideals are transcendent; they appeal to us from the beyond; they are not made by us but are given to us. Rather than allowing us to grasp them, they grasp us. Surpassing us, they unite us with the *horizon of the spirit*. They embody the call to a spiritual identity, which is a mystery that only gradually discloses to us what we are most deeply called to be. We may humbly follow, but can never lead this free disclosure. Even the ability and desire to follow the lead of the spirit is purely a gift. The transcendent ideal that calls us forth is truly an inspiration.

Inspirations have to be translated into manageable, enfleshed, and situated projects. This process implies an ongoing dialogue with concrete reality as disclosed both in the self and in the environment. As human persons, we live in and through our body in a formation field. We have to incarnate abstract ideals into concrete projects, strategies, and tactics. While trying to achieve this translation, our functional-vital presence receives information feedback from reality. This feedback gives rise to enhanced reformulations of *transcendent ideals* in terms of practicality. Briefly, an ideal on the spiritual level is transformed into a *practical project* on the functional level.

The mental, emotional, imaginary, and bodily attempts to execute various projects lead to subtle changes in muscular, glandular, nervous, and other systems of the body. These changes mark the *incarnation of ideals* into the vital dimension of human life. Similarly, the functional project, with its attendant ambitions, moods, feelings, perceptions, memories, thoughts, and attitudes, is the incarnation of the *spiritual ideal* on the functional level. Both processes are influenced by and have an influence on the sociohistoric interaction of people with their life situations.

Limits of Transcendent Ideals

The person as spirit is present to people, events, and things in this world in their mysterious ground, in their holy origin. They are experienced as emerging from the epiphanies of the *formation mystery* (as will be discussed in chapter 14). They are like the ebb and the flow of the ocean, appearing and disappearing in the waves of history. The human person as spirit centers in the infinite stillness that originates and carries all events and things. As spirit, people are inspired to accept serenely what cannot be changed and to modulate graciously what is open to wise modification. The human spirit inspires people to patience, not only in their outer actions but also in their wishing, hoping, anticipating, projecting, feeling, and planning. The human spirit and its horizon tend to tranquilize human life, to mellow its functional propensity and vital excitement, endowing it meanwhile with endurance and strength.

The spirit and its horizon may modulate the momentary orientation of our life by means of ideals. Such inspiration usually does not include the concrete details of the actualization in daily life of a new vision. It is the task of the *in-spirited functional dimension* to disclose and outline such details.

There is always the danger that ideals will become idols. The more beautiful an ideal, the greater its power to seduce us from our unique destiny, to absolutize itself. The more idealistic we tend to be, the more we should be on our guard. We should be wary of *idolatry*. Absolutized ideals make us fanatic and inflexible, scornful of those who do not follow our bent. When an ideal has become an idol, it prevents our true unfolding.

Idolized Ideals

Idolized ideals lose their dialectical quality. The functional projects they foster are idolized in turn. Soon the original inspiration is lost. The remaining attitudes and customs linger on like fossils. Idolized ideals inhibit spiritual unfolding; they calcify daily life and desiccate human culture.

Iconoclasts like *Freud, Marx,* and *Nietzsche* exposed some of the idols of our *bourgeois civilization.* Saints, heroes, and creative minds often destroy idols in their own fashion and give us ways to discern and destroy those ideals that have become idols in our own lives.

Idols in religion may assume a holy appearance that easily deceives us. Aldous Huxley, in his book *The Devils of Loudun,* gives us a novelist's view of how one woman is carried away by her spiritual idols. The beyond of the spirit should be the center of our spiritual attention; our ideals are only temporary guiding lights along the road. The more we grow in primary presence to the *horizon of the spirit* that is beyond the ideals which the spirit inspires, the more centered and simple our lives will become.

The same applies to people who cultivate a life of prayer. Discursive meditation, for instance, may be an excellent guiding ideal for the kind of prayer beginners strive to realize. But they may become fixated on this ideal as ultimate. In their functional presence, they may become so attached to meditative prayer that they do not hear the inner invitation to enter into a deeper kind of presence—the prayer of quiet. A spiritual master must often function as a gentle destroyer of *idolized forms of prayer* if they are no longer in tune with the invitation of the spirit and its horizon.

Ideals and Human Formation

Ideals play a role in our unfolding. The first question we need to ask ourselves is how ideals are related to the development of the spirit dimension of our life. Which ideals hinder the growth of the spiritual life? Which ones are compatible with its unfolding? How can functional projects be integrated with spiritual ideals?

From the viewpoint of the spirit, we should say that historical pulsations and functional ambitions would be harmful for spiritual unfolding if they were to take over totally. One principle of a consonant formation theory of personality is that our spirit should be ultimately in charge of our life over and above historical or functional ambitions and projects. The stronger our functional dimension is, and therewith our social engagement, the better for us; but it should always be an involvement in service of the spirit and its horizon. A strong functional presence with lively ambitions and well-planned projects enables us to discipline and reform our vital life; it is also a mighty force in the unfolding of the culture.

However, functionality should bend flexibly with the spirit. Our functional life should be a bridge linking the shore of the spirit with the shore of the body and world. How foolish an engineer would be were he interested in building a bridge mainly for decoration. Neglecting the structure of the bridge, he would beautify it without regard for its practical meaning and purpose. It may become an eye-catching structure, the embodiment of a proud and idle dream, but the engineer would have sacrificed solidity and usefulness to his desire to build a monument of splendor that he hopes will carry his name for generations to come. Nobody can pass over the bridge safely because its fundamental design has given way to aesthetic form. The bridge itself, not the people who use it, has become ultimate.

We are inclined to make our functional bridges ultimate, to cherish and beautify them out of proportion. Instead of making them passageways for the spirit, we let them take the place of the spirit. Our functional dimension tends to become our ultimate dimension. We have to die to our functionality and its projects *as ultimate*. This death has to occur not once but countless times. To live a fully human life is to die a thousand deaths so that we may rise as increasingly spiritual beings. Our functional bridges, when idolized, do not allow a free flow of inspirations from our spiritual life to the shore of our functional presence in the world. Our functionality and its projects become beautiful but useless tools of only our vital impulses, functional ambitions, and social pulsations. This isolated functionality begins to totalize its own exclusive projects. They are no longer illumined by ideals inspired by the spirit, which alone knows the secret of our deepest identity. These exclusive functional projects are necessarily at odds with our innermost being. They estrange us from ourselves.

Projecting and Managing Operations

The functional dimension exercises projecting and managing operations. Our functionality as projecting enables us to devise practical ventures to be realized in our daily life. In a well-integrated life, such ventures are both inspired and modulated by the human spirit. They are concretized and adapted by the functional dimension to the daily life situation. Our functionality should be in constant touch with both our vital makeup and our changing life situation.

Our *managing presence* tries to execute such objectives in daily life. Our functional mind as appraising and managing adapts the outlines and contours of projects to changing reality. If we are well-integrated, our functional mind performs this adaptation in light of our spirit. A consonant functional dimension refers to the spirit both the obstacles and opportunities met within this practical execution.

The projecting functional dimension ought to be in-spirited by our human spirit and its horizon. The managing aspect, too, must be guided by the light our spirit radiates into our functional and vital life. This necessity is based on the principle of a spiritual formation theory that the ultimate direction of our unique growth can only be disclosed to us by the spirit. We can find and realize our own truth only by walking in the truth our spirit reveals to us. Outside this truth, our functionality proceeds in darkness.

The light of the spirit must shine into the darkness of our functional-vital life. That light is always there, but we can refuse it. Instead of letting our functional-vital life participate in this spiritual power of transformation, we may put all our hopes in the managing dimension. We force ourselves blindly forward on the road to functional perfection and social relevance instead of walking humbly and in a relaxed way in the light of the spirit and its transcendent vision.

Our investigations so far have led to the conclusion that isolated projects are destructive of our consonant life formation. However, projects that are inspired or modulated by the spirit and its vision foster our wholesome unfolding to the extent that such ideals of the spirit are consonant.

Role of Ideals on the Spiritual Level

As human spirit, we are open to the mystery of all that is, the mystery that grounds us and draws us lovingly into itself, the mystery that our human spirit can never encompass or comprehend. Our spirit discloses to us at our best moments that we have a unique life to live, that we are called to radiate love and social concern within the life situations that come to us. This life call, too, is a mystery for us. At no moment will we know it completely. Only gradually is the meaning and direction of our life disclosed to us by right directives. Consonant ideals that emerge in our spirit are among such directives. Ideals point to what we should become; they outline a path of possible unfolding. We do not know at the start what we should be, for our destiny is a mystery hidden in the beyond of our lives. We do not necessarily capture at once, in one ideal, what we ought to strive after in daily life.

As emergent human life-forms, we are subjected to the laws of history. Our unfolding is a *historical unfolding*. Our emergence is a process of gradually disclosing, appraising, and implementing what life wants for us. This means that the light granted to us is always limited; it illumines only part of the way that stretches out before us. Once we have seen where the spirit wants us to journey, we can outline the best possible travel plan for this stretch of our life. This outline remains our ideal until our spirit allows us to see a new stretch of the mysterious road our life is taking. This new insight may give rise to a new itinerary, a new ideal to be realized in daily life.

One characteristic of transcendent ideals is that they require flexibility. We must never idolize an ideal. We can never be sure that a concrete ideal covers totally the way we are to go. We must always be ready to change or to adapt our ideals when we are moved to do so by new lights granted to us on our journey. Ideals are passing means, not final ends. *Consonant life emergence* implies growth in detachment. It is painful to abandon ideals that have served their purpose. We must have the courage to drop them in equanimity. Timely disengagement protects us against a sterility that would render our life uninspiring and without dynamism. Leaving burned-out ideals behind us keeps us dynamic and creative, flexible servants of vistas that the spirit calls forth in our lives.

Ideals and the Restoration of the Unity of Life Formation

In our discussion of ideals, we must again make a distinction between the transcendent, functional, and vital dimensions of the life formation that is ours. These dimensions should form a unity. Unfortunately, this unity is often lost, leaving us with the bitter taste of *inner dissonance*. It is difficult for us to live up to the unity of what we are called to realize. We can refuse the inspirations and ideals of the spirit. We can isolate our functional-vital life from this light that is in us. We can refuse to integrate our ideals concretely in our bodily-managing life in our formation field.

Our spirit is also a gentle power of embodiment, of healing, of making whole, of harmony and unification. Openness to the spirit and its vistas enables us to regain lost unity. Spiritual ideals are not meant to be stored in splendid isolation within a closed-off realm. It belongs to the true nature of the spirit to move us constantly toward the embodiment of the ideals it inspires. The embodied spirit wants us to concretize its inspirations in daily life.

Dialectical Ideals

This movement of embodiment may be halted by a propensity to abstraction. We may be inclined to create ideals tenuously related to the concrete people, things, and events we deal with daily. Such abstract idealizing can lead to destructive suffering. It gives rise to unrealistic expectations and unattainable dreams. When we fail to fulfill them, we suffer unwarranted guilt feelings that may tear us apart. As a result we may be plagued by feelings of impotence and self-rejection. We may become cynical about life and find it meaningless. We may end up in despair or become addicted to drugs or to certain meditation techniques that take us out of the world and its demand for embodiment and social involvement.

Instead of erecting impossible ideals, we must gently accept our limitations at this particular stretch of the road of our unique life formation. We should not venture out farther than our concrete formation field invites us and allows us to go. We should free ourselves from the tyranny of unrealistic ideals.

We need to try to substitute realistic, dialectical ideals for unrealistic ones. This substitution implies that we should live in dialogue with ourselves and with others as we and they are here and now. Realistic ideals are born from both spiritual inspiration and persistent dialogue with who we truly are at this moment of our life in our particular formation field.

A *dialectical ideal* is one that is attainable in principle. It is in tune with our actual ability; it can be approximated with a sustained and relaxed effort that neither exhausts nor discourages us. Yet the very notion of an ideal implies also that it is not yet reached, that its achievement demands the overcoming of resistances and obstacles, that it can only gradually be approximated in patience and endurance, and that it mobilizes the best in us and leads us to the limit of our abilities.

An ideal awakens our slumbering potency. This arousal results from the vitalizing force of an ideal in our life formation. If an ideal were fully realized, it would lose its formative potency. We would have to find a new ideal that could inspire us to new heights of emergence.

Each realistic ideal must be translated on the functional level to a concrete project to be realized in daily life. Once a project has enabled us to realize such ideals, new ideals await us to be actualized in turn. Each one of these ideals will guide us step by step to the unique form of the mystery our life is meant to express. The emergent life-form is a gradual realization of successive ideals inspired by our spirit; it leads us to approximate a mysterious life call that beckons us in and through these ideals.

Ultimately, we should pay more attention to the beyond of the spirit inspiring us than to the inspired ideals themselves. Our ultimate joy and fulfillment is not hidden in the realization of our ideals, but in the ever receding, mysterious horizon that transcends all forms. Even our inspired ideals, in tune with our life call, are not this horizon itself. Our ultimate faith, hope, and love rest in this formless beyond, not in the achievement of our project. We may often fail to realize our ideals; we may never achieve them perfectly. In spite of our failure, we must find our peace in the faithful attempt to obey our inspiration.

When we are more attentive to our ideals and projects than to the mystery of the horizon of the spirit, we may live tense, unhappy lives of compulsive willfulness and anxious watchfulness, lives of unrelieved guilt and painful impotence. Only people who live in humble abandonment to the beyond of the spirit can live with the ideals and projects they are called to realize, even when they fail in this realization.

Common and Personalized Ideals

We have seen the difference between unrealistic, abstract ideals and those that are realistic, dialectical, and concrete. We must now consider the difference between ideals that are common and those that are personalized or unique.

Religions, cultures, nations, communities, families, and associations may all develop ideals on the basis of their purpose and meaning and in dialogue with the historical situations in which they are involved. Members of such communities may only be enlisted or drafted into such ideals. In that case, they adapt to these ideals merely externally, on the surface of their life; the common ideals do not truly become theirs when they conform blindly.

They may, however, truly participate in the ideals of their community: they become involved on a deeper level and they think through the shared ideals personally. They ask themselves how they can bring the ideals of the community to realization in their own way within their own unique circumstances. The common ideal becomes for them a personal one, also. Over and above their personalization of the common ideals of a community, they may develop some ideals that are mainly personal.

One function of human formation is to facilitate the personalization of the common ideals of the community to which people truly want to belong. The means to this end are: formative reading and serious thinking about the common ideals, personal dialogue with other members of the same subculture or community, personal participation in cultural or social ceremonies celebrating the shared ideals, and examination of conscience in regard to the assimilation and personal implementation of the ideals.

The common ideals of a nation, culture, or community are developed in dialogue with human history. The personalized ideals of members of a nation, culture, or community take shape in dialogue with their unique individual makeup and with the concrete daily environment in which they find themselves. Cultures and subcultures give rise to a variety of unique life situations. This uniqueness of situation demands more than ever a uniqueness of personalization of common ideals. Any human life unfolds itself in and through a succession of life situations. A personal response to this change of situation implies a succession of practical ideals that embody the essence of common cultural ideals.

These ideals tell individuals how they can implement best the fundamental inspirations of their nation, culture, form tradition, or community in each passing period of their unique existence. People form a current life-form of modes, attitudes, perceptions, thoughts, and acts around this personalized periodic ideal to which their nation, culture, or community inspires them.

Individuals must also maintain in this regard a *radical detachment*. Such detachment readies them to give up their current incarnation of the common ideal and the current life-form it has promoted. In this way, they maintain a readiness to rise at the right moment to a new current life-form, bringing them nearer to the mystery of their unique life call as a whole. At the same time, they keep the *personalization of the common ideal* in dialogue with the changing ways in which people in the community to which they belong change the incarnation of the ideal they hold in common. For they, too, are in dialogue with the times, updating themselves dynamically, developing their own common, current, and communal ways of life.

Peace beyond Passing Ideals

Behind this multiplicity of successive and dialectical ideals, projects, and current life-forms, we rest in trust, hope, and love in the unity of the horizon of our spirit, which transcends all form and formation. In this presence, peace may come to us. All things fall together. In the moment of contemplation, we participate in the mystery of formation. As embodied spirits, we are, so to speak, condemned to be broken up into countless fragments by human history. Our life and each one of its periodic ideals and life-forms is like these fragments. They are experienced as merely fragmentary unless we see them in relation to the mystery of formation that gives unity and meaning to our entire life and our ideals.

In moments of silent presence to that mysterious beyond of the spirit, we disclose the root of our detachment from current ideals and what shapes them. This root is the peace of being present to the truly real, to unity in multiplicity, to the everlasting in the historical and the ephemeral. This is the peace that renews us via radical distancing. The radical distancing of our spirit enables us not to be seduced by any current ideal as if it were ultimate. The gift of radical detachment prevents our fixation on any current form of life during our journey to the mystery of our unique identity.

Transcendentalist Formation

We have seen the ways in which the historical, vital, and functional dimensions of life are the powers and sources behind pulsations, impulses, ambitions, and insights. The vital dimension is one main collective source of power and insight. It integrates within its own impulses, when it has been reformed into a human dimension, the pulsations and ambitions of the historical and functional dimensions.

The other main collective source of formative power and insight is the transcendent dimension of spiritual formation. Our formation can become dissonant through a onesided dominance of the historical, vital, or functional dimensions. It can also be deformed by an exclusive concern with the transcendent dimension. We call this deviation *transcendentalist formation*. It results, in fact, in deformation.

Underlying this spiritualistic deformation in some people is their feeling that they are totally free. They do not have to take into account any historical, vital, or functional determinants of their formation. They transcend them all absolutely. Hence, it is impossible to predict any unfolding of life that may take place. We can never know in advance what directive the absolutely free transcendent spirit of the person will create. For the concurrent source of any directive should not be any historical, vital, or functional condition but only one's own transcendent insight and aspiration. All formation is thus viewed as a matter of *autonomous self-actualization*. According to this thinking, the human person is exclusively transcendent and wholly autonomous.

How does the transcendentalist view of formation validate its formative directives? The only source of validation is the adherents themselves and their subjective experience of what they feel is beneficial for their formation. The autonomous experience of the person-in-formation and the directives that ensue from it transcend all historical, vital, and functional directives. In other words, human formation should cease to be nourished by objective directives. They are seen as superfluous hindrances to the free formation of the person.

We find perhaps the strongest expression of transcendentalist formation in some forms of atheistic existentialism, such as that of Jean-Paul Sartre. We find it less excessively in some humanistic psychologies, in the neo-Gnostic tendencies of Jungian formation, and in certain cultic trends of contemporary Christian formation. Rarely do we find people who ascribe explicitly to transcendentalist formation. Those who practice it do so implicitly and unwittingly. They usually suffer from unconscious overreaction against the behavioristic formation tendencies to which they were exposed in their past.

Their transcendentalism may worsen because of an underdevelopment of the disposition of humility, which is a basic condition for consonant life formation. Inner humility engenders the respectful receptivity and gentle docility crucial for consonant human formation. Consonant formation presupposes an openness to objectively valid directives that transcend our subjectivity. This means that such directives cannot be the mere product of our desires, ambitions, and projects. They are not of our making, but are gifts mediated to us by our culture, community, and form traditions. By means of transcendent symbols, we become aware of them. In humble receptivity and docility, we allow them freely to give form to our lives.

We suffer deformation if we depreciate or ignore this necessary mediation and assume a haughty, arrogant attitude toward the object pole of our formation field. Cut off from the nourishment of objective transcendent values, we fall into a kind of subjectivistic greediness. Instead of asking ourselves, What am I asked to do?, we ask ourselves, What's in it for me? All form traditions, people, things, and events are then only appreciated as potentially useful matter that may or may not feed our autonomous subjectivity. Engaged exclusively in autonomous self-actualization, we become eclectic and irresponsible. Our life formation no longer flows from the objective demands of reality but deteriorates into an isolated enterprise, an endless repetition of self-centered subjectivistic thoughts and feelings.

Transcendentalist formation excludes consonant human formation, which is essentially integral. The spiritual soul is a unity of the principles of vital, sensate, and spiritual life that gives rise to all the basic dimensions of human formation. This *unitary life principle* keeps these dimensions together and realizes human formation in and through them in unison. Consonant formation must acknowledge the hierarchical structure of these dimensions. This is to say that spiritual formation cannot be the exclusive, autonomous operation of the transcendent dimension alone. The other dimensions are necessary for the consonant formative operation of the transcendent dimension of our existence.

Consonant human formation is thus open, receptive, integral, and hierarchical. It can be uniquely nourished by objective form directives. These are mediated by the culture and its form traditions. Such objective directives do not receive their formative power from the receiving subject; they form us by virtue of their own intrinsic power. A consonant culture offers us opportunities for living, personal contact with objective value directives as conveyed by its form traditions. Such opportunities are evocative. They evoke the aspiration to interact personally with transcendent directives and the horizon of mystery to which they point. Such opportunities facilitate, but do not actualize, our formation. They are the facilitating conditions of consonant formation, not its central agent. The *central power of formation* resides both in the objective form directive and in the cooperative recipient.

Two Ways of Autonomous Self-Actualizing Formation

Not all self-actualizing formation is autonomous. Self-actualization can take place as a result of one's own form-receptive subjection to the formative power of revealed and prerevealed life directives as mediated by a form tradition through its symbols. *Autonomous self-realization,* in contrast, entails the forming self alone.

Autonomous self-formation can happen in two ways. The first way may be called arbitrary self-formation. Its exclusive source is arbitrary decisions by the subject. If there is any dependency in the formation process, it would only be a dependency on opportunities for self-disclosure, choice, and decision, not on objectively given value directives. Such opportunities are offered accidentally by the successive life situations in which persons in formation find themselves and do not encompass the objectivity and consistency of, for example, age-old form traditions in the light of which life situations are appraised. In such cases, the arbitrary decisions of the autonomous self-actualizer may be so mutually contradictory that no coherent formation of life ensues from them. Therefore, many autonomous self-actualizers search for a principle of unity of life directives. Their choice of such a unifying principle will also be arbitrary. What is missing in the autonomous self-actualizer is a humble, docile receptivity to the objective, transcendent value directives that are manifested in tradition, culture, world, nature, and history.

The second way in which self-actualizers explain their autonomy of formation seems at first more sophisticated. They do not consider their formative decisions as accidental or arbitrary. They feel that they follow unwittingly a law of formation immanent in their personal preformation. They believe in a hidden logic of personal life, an innate guide to their destiny, a sort of inborn self-direction that rights their ship like a gyroscope. This subjective orientation derives nothing from environment, form tradition, culture, or human interformation. Self-actualization is due exclusively to the law of formation written in their unique personality. It absolutely transcends everything else in their formation field and its mysterious beyond. Totally autonomous, it is subject neither to historical, vital, and functional dimensions of life nor to outside form directives, authorities, or obligations. If one complies with them, it is only because of one's subjective choice to utilize such outside matter for one's subjective unfolding.

Pneumatist Formation

The *pneumatic dimension* in the life of formation represents a graced and revealed elevation of the transcendent dimension of human life formation. Although it will be discussed in detail in volume 4, it may be helpful at this point to discuss the pneumatic dimension in connection with the distortion of the transcendent dimension previously described.

The pneumatist view sees the formation of the spiritual life as the exclusive work of one's personal inspiration by the Holy Spirit. This view does not highlight as a first criterion the objective form tradition inspired and guarded by the Spirit. The claims of form tradition and of interformation within a shared community of faith have only secondary value for pneumatists. They pay scant attention to the fact that even initially authentic pneumatic inspirations in the transconscious realm are easily distorted. Such distortions often happen when they enter the preconscious and the focal-conscious domains of attention. The most telling symptom of pneumatism is some people's easy claim that the Holy Spirit has told them in discernment or appraisal what they should do, regardless of what anybody else may think or say.

Pneumatists seem to believe that spiritual formation, at least in principle, is absolutely unrelated to cosmic laws and to the historical, vital, functional, and transcendent directives in their lives. The only source of formation is the pneumatic inspiration as subjectively received and felt in discernment or appraisal. The whole of human life becomes exclusively a pneumatic project. Formation is thus not primarily directed by revealed and prerevealed objective values that transcend subjective feeling and are mediated by form traditions and their authoritative representatives. Rather, the crucial act of formation is the cultivation of one's sensitivity to pneumatic inspirations.

Why are Christians so easily seduced by pneumatism? Many have become vulnerable due to unconscious overreaction to their onesided past formation, which may have been overly functionalistic and rationalistic. Even people who behave rationally in life may be affected by this irrational reaction. They also feel betrayed by a past training in their form tradition. They may have been victims of a behavioristic formation. They were molded instead of formed. This molding may have used mainly methods of conditioning, of behavioral modification, of stimulus-response manipulation, or reinforcement by means of reward or punishment here or in the hereafter. Some of these techniques may have a modest place in formation during the development of the historical, vital, and functional dimensions of life. Conditioning, however, can never be the exclusive or main means of distinctively human growth. It must be complemented by means of appeal to transcendent aspirations and pneumatic inspirations.

Pneumatism is fostered also by an overreaction to the activism and naturalism of our age. It may also be a flight from the complexity of the human formation process itself. People may resent the gradual and inconspicuous nature of its progress. The instant-achievement mentality of our culture is easily transferred to a desire for instant holiness, healing, or mysticism. While lack of humility was a possible facilitating condition for transcendentalist formation, the overdevelopment of a quasi-humility and quietistic receptivity may promote the pneumatist deformation. Such quasi-humility denies the importance of personal responsibility in the spiritual life and the task of dialogue with one's formation field.

The pneumatist does not understand that spiritual formation is an interaction of one's whole life with revealed and prerevealed *transcendent value directives* that are mediated by form traditions.

Form directives are not merely personal inspirations by the Holy Spirit. Most divine directives for our spiritual formation are mainly mediated by the world in which we live. We have to disclose such directives gradually by unique interaction with cultural and form traditions. We must expect a long journey of trial and error, uncertitude and questioning, interrupted by painful crises of transcendence. The Spirit enlightens and strengthens us on that journey but does not make the journey for us. The pneumatic dimension is primary and ultimate, but its presence does not cancel out the other dimensions of life formation. The Holy Spirit does not make superfluous their relatively autonomous directives. The Spirit slowly transforms but does not destroy human directives. In light of the interaction of pneumatic as well as pre- and postpneumatic directives, we have to give form to our life through much trial and error.

A crucial part of this interaction with cultural directives is our encounter with sacred texts, form traditions, and the writings of spiritual masters. This encounter must be such that we allow their communications to touch our heart in an interaction that leads to *formative meditation, affective prayer*, and *contemplation*.

What kind of deformations ensue from the pneumatist attitude? Pneumatism may lead to a floating attitude toward life, a separation from the daily directives of formation that spring from vital-functional interaction with one's concrete everyday formation field. Pneumatists may lose touch with the reality of their life situation and society. They may suffer the pneumatist greed syndrome. Their life may become an anxious hunt for inspired feelings. People, events, and things become mainly useful occasions for the discernment of quasi-inspirations or for playing the part of a pious do-gooder. Pneumatists may compulsively or hysterically climb any barricade for social-religious battles without consideration of their historical-vital-functional inclination and aptitude for the battle concerned. Exclusively engaged in the pneumatization of their life, they mistake any subjective pious feeling for divine aspiration. Instead of a pneumatic life, they develop a romanticized personal or communal life with all the compulsive and hysterical features that romanticism entails when one has lost touch with the reality of one's formation field.

We must conclude that pneumatist formation excludes consonant human formation. Such formation is integral in principle. It holds that the Spirit may direct one partly and exceptionally by personally received special inspirations. Usually, however, the Spirit directs us by deepening our human insight into what is already given in nature, history, culture, revelation, and form tradition. God created the spiritual soul as a principle of vital, functional, and transcendent life. All dimensions of life grow in unison from this soul as powers of incarnational spiritual living. All dimensions play a part in the attainment of our incarnated spiritual life-form, not only the pneumatic.

CHAPTER 14

The Mystery of Formation

This chapter deals with the deepest question about formation, a question that each of us may raise. Our response to it colors all our responses to the particular formation questions that are evoked by our daily experiences. In other words, our basic answer profoundly affects our personal history. We are thus speaking about a primordial question and a primordial response. The question is not about any one issue of everyday formation, but about formation as a whole. What is its secret, its mystery?

That there is formation is not a question for us. It is an inescapable experience. Formation exists; it goes on all the time. We see its manifestations in and around us continuously: people are born, people die; in between they grow, age, and change inwardly and outwardly in countless ways. The history, cultures, and form traditions they share are in constant flux. The changes that we observe in nature are also undeniable. So, too, are the dynamic changes that scientists observe in the micro- and macrocosmic universe. That formation goes on is thus no mystery for us. What formation means—how and why it goes on—is the mystery.

We cannot deny that the marvel of universal formation is a mystery we cannot solve. Nobody can claim to have mastered all the secrets of the ongoing formation of the universe, of humanity, history, and individual existence. We know that we are unable to penetrate the ultimate why, how, and when of the cosmic processes that we share and that still surpass us, for we can never dominate all of them in every detail; neither can we fully penetrate the secret of their hidden consonance, of their ultimate meaning and purpose, or of our role in them. No matter how far we disclose their meanings and dynamics, there remains a residue of an enigma we cannot unravel.

Does this secret of formation have any meaning? That is the

crucial question. Our whole existence and that of the globe on which we must give form to life and world is subject to the meaning of formation. We are at its mercy. We cannot evade it. It embraces and penetrates us and the world in which we live every moment. Is this mystery ultimately meaningful? If so, is it a beneficial process? Is it good for us? Can we abandon ourselves in trust to this arcane riddle of the unfolding of reality, or are we the victims of an indifferent, meaningless process? Should we look at it positively or negatively? These are basic questions. Our answers will affect our everyday formation in a foundational fashion. The form of our life and world will depend upon our response. Here are primordial questions and primordial answers.

Is the mystery of formation meaningful and beneficial? We are not compelled to answer yes or no. In principle both answers are possible. Nobody can force us to give one or the other response. Mere functional logic or scientific reasoning cannot force us to this or that position. Ultimate answers transcend the power of logic and scientific observation. They imply an option that is free. This option, however, can be rationally justified. We can show that it is not unreasonable, that it is not without reason or against reason. Our option can and should be justified rationally, at least implicitly, because we are rational human beings. Do we choose to abandon ourselves in trust to the mystery of formation or do we let ourselves feel abandoned in a meaningless formation process?

Faced with this decisive option, we may look again at the enigma of formation. Its riddle is overwhelming. It embraces and permeates all past, present, and future events in universe, history, and humanity. There is nothing that is not in constant formation. We are so much a part of it that we cannot take a stand outside it. Hence, we cannot look at it as uninvolved observers. We cannot define it by means of something else that would not be part of this mystery and with which it could be compared in order to classify it. The puzzle of formation cannot be clearly delineated within precise categories. By its all-encompassing presence and action, it transcends, comprehends, and pervades all our mental categories, while at the same time giving form to these categories and making them possible.

The formation mystery is simple in its unity and yet inexhaustibly complex and multidimensional in its appearances. Formation as a whole cannot be defined a priori. Sometimes its effects seem deformative. At other moments they seem formative from the viewpoint of our limited intellectual appraisal power. This only adds to our confusion. The mystery of formation manifests itself everywhere. It is like a never ending dance of rising and falling forms in cosmos, humanity, culture, and history.

The Cosmic Epiphany of the Formation Mystery

The formation mystery discloses itself in three main ways: the cosmic, the human, and the transhuman. We will examine first of all the cosmic epiphany of the formation mystery. This will be followed by a brief discussion of the human epiphany of the formation mystery. (Reflections on the transhuman epiphany of the formation mystery will be reserved for the fourth volume of this series. Central to that volume will be the question of the transhuman epiphany in Christian revelation and incarnation.)

What is the secret of the *consonance of the cosmos?* Recent discoveries reveal to us where that secret resides. They point to the atomic and subatomic cosmic dance of the ongoing formation and reformation occurring at every moment in the universe. These discoveries have led to the view that the cosmos is an all-embracing energy process of continuous interformation. This is not only true of the macro- but also of the microcosmos.

The findings of contemporary physics have taught us that we cannot reduce this macro- and microcosmic formation process to independently existing, changeless, minute forms that would be its building blocks. Physics points to an energy field within which forms emerge and disappear in constant energetic interformation with other merging and vanishing forms. The mystery of formation manifests itself in this field as a mystery of universal interformation between rising and falling forms. It gives rise to a subtle and complicated web of forming interactions between changing forms with a variety of life spans that appear briefly in cosmos, history, and humanity.

Our own life shares in this dance of interformation of form energies. The same mystery of formation is the source of both the cosmic and the distinctively human epiphany. This manifestation takes place in the transcendent dimension of our life-form. This human epiphany explains why we somehow surpass the merely cosmic manifestation of the formation mystery. By the same token, we realize that we can neither escape the continuous cosmic epiphany unfolding life and world nor authentically speak about human formation without constantly referring, at least implicitly, to the cosmic interformation process. We are inserted in it from conception to death. Fortunately, there is no contradiction, only complementarity, among the three epiphanies of the formation mystery.

The mystery of *cosmic interformation* thus appears as a dynamic web of inseparable formation energies. No psychophysical or physical form can survive, or keep forming itself, outside this web. This network reflects the unity as well as the intrinsically dynamic thrust of the mystery of formation in its physical epiphany. Hence, any forms that emerge in the cosmos can only be understood in terms of their surrounding field of formation. No form can be perceived as an isolated, autarchic entity. Each has to be understood as an integrated part of the universal formation process. The cosmic epiphany of the mystery is thus a dynamic, indivisible whole, which in some way always includes our own life-in-formation. All forming actions take place in time by the interweaving of form energies at play in the formation fields within which we happen to move.

Autarchic Pride-Form and Cosmic Epiphany

The autarchic pride-form may create the illusion that the person in isolation is the source of the formation of life and world within temporal, passing fields. If we can transcend such exaltations of the pride-form, we may be able to acknowledge that forming energies continuously influence one another in the cosmic and cultural fields of formation from which we emerge continuously. Increasingly, this enlightenment will enable us to appraise such form energies wisely and to enlist them firmly and gently in the service of our congenial and compatible life formation. In this way we gain freedom from the spell of exaltation. We break the bonds of the autarchic pride-form and begin to experience concretely and personally that every formation, including our own, participates in the universal manifestation of the mystery of formation.

The experience of liberation from the pride-form not only opens us to the cosmic epiphany; it also saves us from sterile isolation and inspires us to flow with foundational form energies in quiet consonance. To the extent that such consonance becomes ours, we experience inward equanimity. There are innumerable ways to facilitate such liberation. Hence, we see a variety of formation exercises developed in the form traditions of humanity.

The cosmic epiphany shows us that all forms in and around us are impermanent and transitory. The pride-form, however, gives rise to elated images of permanence, or else it makes us refuse to acknowledge the fleetingness of our life and its passing achievements. Our life-forms are also fleeting. We have to grow from current life-form to current life-form to become what we are foundationally called to be. When it is given to us to realize our own *foundational life-form*, we know that it is not permanent within this physical universe. Death comes like a thief in the night to take that form away. Certain form traditions foster the faith that this foundational life-form is transplanted after death into an eternal realm where formation continues, or that it is reborn to other forms within the physical universe. Such traditions seem to agree that the concrete life-form achieved before death does not continue as such without change. At any rate, all forms in the universe emerge and pass away.

To face the fact that flow and change are foundational features of all formation is painful as long as we live in the shadow of the pride-form. We are secretly inclined to be proud and possessive of the current forms we receive or give to our life and surroundings. For fear of losing them, we resist the flow of cosmic formation. We try to cling to fixed forms of life and world. We do not acknowledge that to attach ourselves to them as ultimate is to become enslaved to idolized exaltations that sooner or later fade away like all other forms in the universe. Such idolizing of vanishing forms makes us vulnerable to anything that threatens their continuation. It makes us vulnerable to the kind of unnecessary, deformative suffering that results from enchantment by changeable forms of life and world. Deformative suffering will be our fate when we resist the flow of cosmic formation, when we try to encapsulate ourselves in the forms of an enchanted world we have exalted beyond its limited beauty, power, and meaning.

The root of such idolizing is any frantic clinging to the exalted fantasy of the pride-form. This fantasy suggests that our functional ego is a separate power of formation, fiercely independent of any other powers in which the mystery appears and calls us forth. To cling to that exalted self-image leads to the same frustration as the idolizing of any other fixed form we have attained in life or world.

Our ignorance of the mystery of formation and its cosmic incarnation tempts us to imagine that we can receive or give form in merely functional ways of control and manipulation. We attempt to confine the flow of formation to separate categories we create in our functional mind. To realize such fixed form images, we devise inflexible paths of formation. Along these paths we try to give form to stilted images in our life and world. We lose the ability to wait respectfully for a message of the cosmic epiphany that may announce itself in the specific subfield of formation in which it has inserted itself.

This is not to say that functional-categorical thinking is not important in our giving form to inner and outer life and world. The functional dimension of our life-form is as essential as all the other dimensions for the fullness of human living. This functional power becomes deformative, however, when it begins to dominate our formation attempts. Transcendent thought, which surpasses functional-categorical thinking, should ultimately prevail. Yet it should not blot out functional apprehension, appraisal, and decision. Our mind is formed in such a way that it can only guide our relative, formative mastery of life and world functionally when it thinks categorically.

Cosmic Epiphany of the Formation Mystery and Universal Interformation

A central presupposition of the science of formation is the unity and interformation of all people, things, and events, which share in some measure in the cosmic epiphany of the formation mystery. This science, insofar as it offers a universal synthesis of all foundational factors of human formation, draws much of its inspiration from the world view of modern physics, wherein new models and theories support a vision of a universe that is a web of interformative interactions.

Cosmic formation is the intrinsically dynamic or formative essence of the universe. It is the process that keeps the world in the continuous flow and change in which all things are involved. Distinctly human formation implies a growth in the ability to appraise the patterns of those changes that influence more directly its own course of unfolding. Accordingly, humans can develop form directives that are consonant with such patterns and congenial with the foundational life-form one has to disclose and implement in consonance with the human and transhuman epiphanies of the formation mystery.

The more people are able to form their lives in consonance with the flow of universal cosmic interformation, the easier it becomes for them to relate effectively to life and world. Such coformation with the cosmic epiphany presupposes the ability to wait upon its disclosures, to go along with its expanding and contracting manifestations in equanimity—persevering in times of distress, remaining modest and cautious in times of achievement. This attitude fosters gentleness of mind and heart while avoiding excess, extravagance, and indulgence. It prefers to leave things undone rather than overdoing them. Its main concern is to remain in consonance.

Such cosmic consonance contributes to the disclosure of appropriate form directives. Impatient overdoing of things may rapidly spawn impressive accomplishments while one loses the wise and healing way of consonance. The heady winds of acclaim and applause cannot make up for the loss of consonant form direction and the tragedy of missing out on one's life call.

We must learn to live wisely with the ceaseless formation and reformation of things, events, and situations; with the rising and sinking away of forms, and with forms holding firm for some moments in time and yielding at others. The mystery of formation manifests itself as a dynamic interformation of opposites that are polar and yet united. It gives rise to the polar fields of formation. The formation of each thing, event, or person is situated in such a field. Yet human formation transcends this field because of the freedom of the human spirit. Human formation knows of its formation field but also of its beyond; it can transcend the field but it cannot escape it. There is thus no opposition between the cosmic and the distinctively human manifestations of the formation mystery.

Cosmic Epiphany of the Formation Mystery and Everyday Formation

Abandonment to the mystery of formation does not mean withdrawal from everyday affairs. The formation mystery inspires us daily to share in its forming presence, including its micro- and macrocosmic manifestations. It asks us to flow with it in everything we do. We are called to experience this epiphany of the formation mystery in the small events that bind our days together. We should be awakened to its presence in the midst of everydayness. Everyday life is our privileged opening to the mystery of formation, even in its cosmic disclosure. Human transcendent experience contains an awareness of the forming, loving energy of cosmic formation in all things. First and foremost among them are the people, events, and things that coform our immediate formation field.

Such deepened awareness is the secret of life formation, which can be at the same time highly functional and profoundly mystical (in the sense of a cosmic mysticism). It enables one to function well in the present with full attention to the seemingly small and pedestrian chores that life entails. One becomes able to experience the marvel of passing things and tasks in light of the mystery that formatively maintains their flow in the universe and illuminates their meaning in our hearts and minds. At times, one may feel like singing inwardly: How wondrous, how mysterious! I eat food, I write words, I walk, I converse, I water flowers, I clean a room, I make a bed, I wash my hands, I feel the sun, the rain, the wind, the snow. Such experiences remind us of similar ones recorded in the Psalms of the Hebrew form tradition.

Presence to the mystery of formation allows one's everyday life to be formed congenially, compatibly, and compassionately by the marvel of interactions that emerge from one's formation field. When joyful, we smile. When grieving, we cry. When tired, we rest. When rested, we labor again. But we do all of these things in consonance with the formation mystery manifesting itself in these experiences.

To gain this consonance is to transcend our *functionalistic willfulness*. Rooted as it is in the autarchic pride-form, this willfulness destroys our natural consonance with the flow of the formation mystery. It made humanity fall away from its original innocent and consonant attunement to the universal dance of formation. To regain *attunement* we need *atonement*, which implies the renewal of at-one-ment with the mystery we have lost sight of in our lives. Abandonment to this mystery helps us to disclose the foundational life-form to which we are uniquely called. We become more and more what we are invited to be from the beginning as we respond to this call.

Awareness Expansion beyond Everydayness

Awareness of the formation mystery does not limit itself to awareness of its presence in our field of daily formation. It expands itself to an awareness of the unity and mutual interformation of all things and events. All of them are radiations of one and the same formation energy. All psychophysical forms are interforming parts of this cosmic event, different manifestations of the same forming force. The mystery of cosmic formation is indeed an indivisible reality, one that manifests itself in all the unique expressions of physical and psychological formation.

Awareness of the Cosmic Epiphany in Spiritual Form Traditions

In ancient times, this view of the world in formation could not be corroborated by the findings of theoretical physics. It was the fruit of transcendent experience, which implies a direct experience of reality in its wholeness. This experience inwardly gives form to and receives form from the world, not by means of the functional but of the transcendent mind. Different spiritual form traditions may consequently stress different dimensions of the experience of the cosmic formation mystery.

Such emphasis and interpretation depends on the geographical and sociohistorical formation situation within which a spiritual tradition emerged. What all spiritual traditions essentially have in common is their awareness of a unity in the diversity of the many form manifestations of what we have called the formation mystery. They all indicate that in their experience an indivisible mystery transcends all functional concepts and categories. This mystery is the oneness of all forms in their rhythmic appearing and disappearing in time and space.

Functional Formation in the Light of the Cosmic Epiphany

In the ordinary way of functionally giving form to our life and surroundings, we are not aware of the dynamic presence of the mystery of formation in its cosmic epiphany. Effective functional formation demands that we divide the world—as it appears to our limited sense perception—into separate objects and events. This division is necessary if we are to form our everyday life and surroundings in congruity with our limited sense perceptions, concepts, and images. This functional view, however necessary, does not attune us to the foundational truth of our formation field. It is a necessary abstraction devised by our functioning mind, its categorical logic, and its sustaining sense awareness.

The isolating and autarchic pride-form strives to encapsulate us within a self-constructed world of functional formation. Pride seduces us to the elated illusion that there is nothing more to our formation field than the functional abstractions and separations that enable us to dominate and manipulate the sense-perceived world. Pride leaves no room for the epiphany of a mystery that transcends our grasp, that carries and forms our very existence and its functioning.

The binding spell of the pride-form leaves us enchanted by this illusion. We sink deeper and deeper in ignorance of the mystery of formation. What counteracts this formation ignorance? Form traditions suggest inner silence, reflection, meditation, and contemplation as ways to center and quiet the distracted and fragmented mind. Instead of being absorbed in functional thought, our mind must return to its center in its own transcendent dimension. The mind should not abdicate its necessary functional power and effectiveness. This power, however, should be centered in and enlightened by a deeper transcendent presence. Out of this wider awareness, form directives emerge to be implemented effectively by means of the functional dimension of the mind.

The foundational formative mind should be in a tranquil transcendent state from which balanced form appraisals can quietly emerge. Such equilibrium and equanimity can only be maintained if we are attuned to the mystery of formation. The mind must be purified and freed from the tyranny of functional agitation and vital impulses. The latter should play their role, but they should not dominate our forming presence. Once one enters into that purity of mind, one is ready to receive the calming gift of transcendent presence to the unifying, all-encompassing cosmic epiphany of the mystery of formation.

The Mystery of Formation | 195

Contemporary Physics and the Mystery of Formation

As mentioned earlier, the interforming oneness of the universe is one of the most striking disclosures of contemporary theoretical physics. This foundational at-oneness of ever ongoing formation is already manifest at the atomic level. The more we observe the deeper formation of matter, especially in the realm of subatomic particles, the more this interforming oneness manifests itself. There are a variety of theoretical models to explain the fascinating universe of subatomic physics. No matter how different such theories may be in detail, they all show convincingly that no form in the universe, no matter how small, can be understood as isolated from universal formation energies. No form is closed in upon itself. All are interforming. The momentary form they assume is lost or reformed when the polar field of interforming powers in which they emerge changes.

The cosmic epiphany of the formation mystery thus points to the unbroken wholeness of the micro- and macrocosmic universe. Physical formation is not an accumulation of elementary blocks that exist separately and independently. The *universal formation field* is not composed of isolated parts that explain the whole. On the contrary, the universal formation mystery explains the formation of these parts. The various forms we meet in life and world are merely particular forms and arrangements of energies made possible by the all-pervading mystery of formation. This interconnecting cosmic energy is the foundational reality of the universe: relatively independently functioning forms are merely particular and contingent points of emergence. All particular forms are subtle expressions of the cosmic epiphany of the formation mystery. They derive, disclose, and achieve their foundational form by their insertion into a polar field of formation, never in absolute isolation.

In essence, each form is a structure of forming relationships that reaches outward to a diversity of other forms. The cosmic epiphany of the mystery of formation manifests itself as a complex mosaic of events. Forming connections of various kinds alternate, overlap, or combine. In this dance of ongoing interformation, these connections determine the texture of physical and psychological reality. The formation mystery is the binding thread in this cosmic web. It weaves together all forms in formation to create a unity of interformation that the human mind cannot envisage, either in its myriad details or in its marvel of interwovenness.

Contrast and Complementarity in Cosmic Interformation

The all-embracing unity of interformation does not imply equality of all things. The forms that emerge in the universe are marked by differences and contrasts. In the light of the universal, cosmic epiphany of the formation mystery, such contrasts are not absolute but relative. All relative forms stand in a polar relationship with their opposites. Our functional mind may tempt us to conceive of polar opposites as being absolutely exclusive of any trace of one another. However, such polar opposites as joy and sadness, life and death, day and night, light and darkness, winning and losing, masculinity and femininity, success and failure, are different expressions of the same cosmic epiphany of the mystery of formation.

On the transcendent level of presence, we can take all of these into account as the polar opposites they are. In the light of the formation mystery, we can turn them into opportunities for congenial, compatible, and compassionate formation of life and world. *Virtus in medio,* virtue is in the center of extreme opposites: consonant formation takes place in us when we are able to create and maintain a dynamic balance between psychophysical opposites, allowing them to interplay in our life in service of ongoing consonant formation.

Vital-Functional and Female-Male Formation Polarities

Take for example the polarity between the vital and the functional dimensions of the basic human life-form. These two dimensions can be symbolized and experienced as, respectively, the female and male dimensions of human formation. When we do not find a dynamic balance between vitality and functionality, we may be inclined to let one or the other dimension prevail. Western form traditions have favored the functional over the vital in their striving for control and for functional categorizing in service of practical mastery of the world.

Ideally, however, formation should be balanced in the spiritual dimension, which transcends yet includes the vital and functional. The transcendent dimension integrates both in a dynamic unity. A functionalistic form tradition generates corresponding cultures and subcultures. These are often marked by an inclination to symbolize and overemphasize the functional bent of the underlying form tradition by imposing on all males the functionalistic and on all females the vitalistic stereotype. Worse than this, it may give masculine symbols of onesided functionality the leading roles and privileges in society. Such functionalistic societies may, under pressure, extend the same privileges to those women who consent to become symbols of functionalism.

Ideally, the transcendent dimension of formation should be central to any consonant society. A consonant society should manifest the dynamic unification of vital and functional form powers, of female and male symbols, thereby radiating serene tranquility. The transcendent dimension is a realm that goes beyond functional thought and language. All vital and functional opposites can appear in its light as a dynamic unity.

To live in the transcendent is to live in a higher dimensionality, nearer to the mystery of formation and its cosmic and psychophysical manifestations. The transcendent life gathers and integrates the formative experiences of the other dimensions. Hence, it is almost impossible to describe certain transcendent experiences. The mystery of formation discloses itself in this dimension precisely as a mystery that cannot be fully captured and expressed by concepts and images derived from sense perception. The transcendent mind approaches what cannot be fathomed by the functional-logical mind. In this self-disclosure of the formation mystery, the opposites in life and nature are experienced as mutually complementary. Their forming interplay is characteristic of the manifestation of the formation mystery in the universe of matter.

In an analogous way, this forming manifestation of the mystery applies also to the formation of human life and its situation. We say analogously because in the human formation situation the elements of relatively free apprehension, appraisal, and option enter into the formation process of the universe. Human life can opt to form itself in consonance or dissonance with the formation mystery. Moreover, the mystery discloses itself in unique ways in the transcendent dimension of each human life-form. Such disclosures imply unique directives for consonant life formation. There is thus no true complementarity between freely chosen dissonance and freely chosen consonance. These are ultimate moral choices, which exclude each other as ethical options.

The Intrinsically Dynamic, Unifying Epiphany of the Formation Mystery

In a state of at-oneness with the cosmic epiphany of the formation mystery, we may sense that every event is related to every other. This experience of universal interrelatedness embraces not only the present, but also the past and future; not only space but also time. From the viewpoint of the all-embracing formation mystery in which one shares experientially at a peak moment, space and time are interpenetrating.

All forms in the world are thus manifestations of the same formation mystery in its physical epiphany. This mystery underlies and unifies the multitude of things and events we observe. It transcends our functional concepts and defies description. The cosmic epiphany cannot be separated from its multiple appearances in matter. Formatively, it manifests itself in myriad forms that come into being and vanish, reforming themselves into one another seemingly without end. In its forming aspect, the cosmic epiphany of the mystery is thus intrinsically dynamic. Hence, the universe itself is a dynamically formative epiphany of the mystery. Its formation and reformation always move onward.

Movement, flow, and change are characteristic of all manifestations of this cosmic epiphany. Yet the mystery itself transcends all the forms in which it fleetingly manifests its creative presence. The cosmic epiphany is like a dance sustaining the manifold formations of the world. It unifies them all by immersing them in its rhythm and making them participate in the dance.

Static Misconception of Universal Formation Field

All forms are fluid and ever changing. Our perception of them as static is one result of the inclination of the pride-form to cling to the forms that make up our life and world as if they were fixed—whether these be people, events, things, ideas, or images. Instead, we must accept the world as a continuous flow of ongoing formation. This flow maintains the ceaseless mutation and reformation of things. We should learn to think in terms of forces, movements, sequences, and processes. The world in all its fleeting forms is incessantly in formation. No form is worth clinging to as ultimate.

A human life that had attained full consonance would no longer resist the flow of formation. It would coform itself with this epiphanous flow. It would adapt itself gently and joyously to this flow. The unique articulations of its coformation with the cosmic epiphany would be inspired by the human and transhuman epiphanies of the same mystery. The consonant human life is one that flows in peaceful coformation.

Contemporary physics has also come to conceive of the universe in terms of movement, flow, and change. It views universal formation as a network of interforming interactions. This network is intrinsically dynamic. For example, the conduct of subatomic particles can only be understood in an interforming context. Matter is marked by a formative restlessness, a mysterious readiness to give and receive form in countless ways. Matter is thus never quiescent; it is always in a state of unrest, a continuous dancing and vibrating movement of giving and receiving form. The rhythmic patterns of the formation movement in which the mystery manifests itself in matter are determined by molecular, atomic, and nuclear structures.

All forms together, and each form in relation to all others, are in not a static but a dynamic equilibrium. The rhythm of the formation mystery pervades them all in its continuous epiphany. Not only the microcosmos, but also the macrocosmic world of stars and galaxies is in ceaseless formation. Stars, for instance, are constantly formed out of interstellar clouds of gas. A star is reformed in its contraction and expansion. Finally, the star form is dissolved in other forms in the universe.

Because the word *thing* has for many people a static connotation, the formation scientist often uses the term *formation event* instead. This term points to the fact that forms are not static substances but transitory events in the ever flowing epiphany of the formation mystery. Formation scientists are more concerned with the interformation of forms than with their reduction to fundamental static substances studied in artificial isolation.

The mystery of formation discloses itself most strikingly in the interformations out of which forms emerge and temporarily maintain themselves. The foundational elements of the universe in ongoing formation are not the smallest static forms but the dynamic formation patterns. These patterns are passing stages in the constant flow of formation and reformation orchestrated by the mystery. In this orchestra of a universe in constant formation, each pattern plays its own instrument, producing rhythmic patterns of energy. Its sound, in coformation with the sounds of other patterns, creates at every moment the fragile beauty of fleeting forms under the direction of the mystery that leads the formation concert.

The Formation Field

Modern physics has developed the concept of a quantum field. This is a formation field which can assume two forms: the form of quanta or the form of particles. It is a new scientific vision of what we call the physical epiphany of the formation mystery. This view has led to a description of subatomic particles and their interformative interactions—a description which posits each type of particle as compatible with a specific field. Within this field the particle can emerge and vanish. In this sense it could be called a potential, or virtual, form within a specific compatible formation field.

There is thus no longer any validity to the concept of a separation or an absolute contrast between a field and the solid forms or particles that emerge within that field. The quantum field itself functions as the fundamental physical entity that is a manifestation of the epiphany of the formation mystery. The mystery discloses itself in its cosmic epiphany as an energy field, a continuous medium or matrix of formation and reformation, which manifests itself everywhere in space. Forms are local condensations of their formation field. They are momentary or periodic concentrations of form energy. When such forms vanish, they lose their uniqueness. They are absorbed again into the underlying field.

The primal epiphany of the formation mystery in the energy field is the only enduring reality of the universe. When the mystery in a region of space allows the field to become extremely intense, forms flow forth. All forms are transient manifestations of a foundational formation field out of which they emerge. In the course of time they will be reabsorbed in their field. Hence, a spirit of poverty and a purity of heart deepen our awareness that all of the forms to which we are so attached are transitory. Ascribing to them an ultimate solidity and endurance is wishful thinking, an illusion of the pride-form.

The formation field about which the science of formative spirituality speaks cannot be identified with the quantum field of the physicist. For the field of human formation embraces not only the cosmic but also the distinctively human and transhuman epiphanies of the formation mystery. Consequently, it is ultimately beyond all concepts, images, and symbols. It touches on the essence of the mystery itself. The quantum field, in contrast, is a well-defined concept. It refers only to the cosmic epiphany of the mystery. Even within this limitation it does not claim to touch on all cosmic formation. It accounts for only some of the forms that emerge in the cosmos.

Physicists are still attempting to unify the various physical formation fields into a single foundational field of universal physical formation that would account for all cosmic formation and for the briefer or longer form endurance that results. (At the end of his life, Einstein was in search of such a universal field.) Foundational human formation scientists, however, assume an ultimate unified field, which they consider the primary incarnation of the formation mystery: a field of created, loving energy that transcends yet includes the cosmic, human, and transhuman epiphanies of this mystery and their myriad manifestations. From this field spring not only the formations observed in physics, but all other forms as well.

Primordial Manifestation of the Cosmic Epiphany

The primordial cosmic manifestation of the mystery is beyond observable forms. It defies description and specification. One could call it formless. The word formless emphasizes that this manifestation has no form comparable to the numerous observable forms that emerge and vanish in the macro- and microcosmos. In a stricter sense, however, this primordial manifestation is not really formless. It has the elusive form of an energy flow in constant motion. Similarly, one could call this underlying formative power *emptiness*, or void. Such metaphors, while helpful, would become deceptive if absolutized. This so-called emptiness should not be misunderstood as mere nothingness, or absence of something.

We must conceive of this emptiness as a vibrant, alive emptiness, a void filled with mysterious power, the hidden, sacred spring of all material formation, the source of all cosmic life. This primordial cosmic manifestation is the living womb, the creative matrix of all material forms, like a holy grail filled with form potential. It can be likened to the quantum field of which contemporary physics speaks. For this field is also conceived as a matrix of formation. It, too, gives rise to countless forms. It keeps sustaining them during their limited life spans. Eventually, the field reabsorbs them in its undifferentiated ground-form of endlessly moving cosmic formation energy. The void is not a real void but a ceaseless dance of formation and reformation. It is the cosmic source of the continuous death and birth of dynamic and transitory sensible forms. (We call them sensible in that they can be observed by sensing forms in the universe, among them by the human form of life.)

Human Life-Form and Cosmic Formation

The human life-form itself, insofar as it is also a participant in the micro- and macrocosmic dance, is not an unchangeable constant. Physically it changes form, that is, it grows from a current life-form to a new current life-form. Spiritually, as discussed in chapter 9, it does something similar. Yet there is a difference between distinctively human formation and cosmic formation. Both the human and transhuman epiphanies of the mystery lift human life beyond all other known forms in the cosmos. This does not mean that the human life-form becomes stilted or static like a finished statue. It means that the growth through successive spiritual life-forms is guided by a unique transcendent direction. This direction operates in us as a hidden ground-form to be released either within this cosmic period or, according to certain classical form traditions, in a purification period to be experienced beyond this epiphany.

This unique transcosmic direction of the formation mystery in each of us is our deepest spiritual identity. We can compare the spiritual identity to the ego identity. The latter is formed by functional interaction with our cosmic and social world. It is only a shadow of who we really are. Hence, to live our functional ego identity as if it were ultimate and absolute is to live an illusion. Neither is our bodily life as cosmic participant lasting and ultimate. It is a subtle, condensed form of energy. Cosmic formation energy becomes visible in a body as an individual, temporary shape that disperses when its time has come. In this way the cosmic epiphany of the formation mystery condenses and disperses during the millennia of history and evolution.

We could say that the cosmic epiphany is this mystery of forming energy. This flow of energy condenses to make sensible forms appear and disperses to form once again the great primordial stream of the cosmic epiphany. This epiphanous field of formative energy carries also the interformative interactions of the emergent and vanishing forms. They are the countless threads that coform the wondrous web of universal interformation.

The Relationship of Field and Form

What is the relationship between sensible forms and the primary cosmic epiphany of the mystery as an underlying continuous field of form energy? Form and field are not opposites that mutually exclude each other. Both are manifestations of the mystery in its cosmic epiphany. These manifestations coexist in continual coformation. Sensible forms are formation energy, and formation energies, while seemingly a void, are indeed potential forms. Foundationally, the energy field manifestation of the cosmic epiphany is not different from the cosmic form manifestation to which it gives rise. These emergent cosmic forms, in turn, are not different from the forming energy. Form is epiphanous formation energy; formation energy is potential form.

The dance of the cosmic epiphany of the mystery sends pulsing waves of subtle formation through the macro- and microcosmos. The cosmos dances, as it were, around this mystery. In this dance, the cosmic epiphany sustains the manifold formations and reformations of matter. The dance of this epiphany of the mystery *is* the dancing universe; it is the ceaseless flow of forming power going through an endless variation of sensible forms that melt into one another.

Distinction of Form Types

Although the science of formation does not conceive the cosmos as a collection of isolated forms, it does distinguish types of forms that differ in their interformative patterns. What is primarily distinctive is the kind of interformative connections that are characteristic of certain types of emergent forms.

The universe appears to the formation scientist as a complicated and subtle mosaic of distinctive formation events. Interforming actions of different kinds alternate, overlap, or combine. Together they coform the texture of the whole. Consequently, an emergent form is best described not as an object, but as a formative event, an occurrence, or a happening.

Static Conception of Formation

How do we come to conceive of static, isolated forms? Is it not because we blind ourselves to the reality of the successive emergence of forms? We are usually not aware of formation phases and minute ongoing changes marking the life span of each cosmic form before its reabsorption in the endless formation flow. We tend to cut this continuous flow into static sections. We then absolutize these sections as isolated forms. We are even tempted to idolize these isolated manifestations of the incessant flow of formation, to see them as lasting, ultimate, and unchangeable, as rooted securely in themselves.

The pride-form in human life is what tempts us to idolize passing forms in self and world. The human life-form can grow to freedom and consonance only if it no longer idolizes false images or forms as if they were lasting, self-sufficient, and unchangeable.

Formation changes are not inflexible laws imposed on the cosmic world. Rather, they operate as inner form tendencies, infused by the cosmic flow of this epiphany of the formation mystery. In consonance with such tendencies, formation unfolds naturally and spontaneously. Such form tendencies can be thought of as reaction and response probabilities.

Approximate Knowledge

The world cannot be understood as an inscrutable assemblage of forms. The universe is a dynamic web of interforming formation events. None of the properties of the parts of this cosmic web of interformation are foundational in an absolutely isolated sense. All should be conceived in terms of their interforming relation to other forms and to the underlying epiphanous formation flow. The overall consonance of their mutual relationships constitutes the structure of the entire cosmic web of formation.

The laws of physics are theoretical tools invented by the human mind and are a reflection of their own intellectual map of the cosmos rather than of the cosmos itself. This mental scheme of the interforming macro- and microcosmos is necessarily limited and approximate. All cosmic formation manifestations are ultimately interformative in unison.

To explain any formation manifestation exhaustively, we would need to understand all others and their respective forming influences on this particular one. It is obvious that we cannot achieve such an all-encompassing understanding. Hence, only an approximate understanding of cosmic formation is attainable. In service of such approximation, one can describe, analyze, and explain selected formation events by means of restricted conceptual maps. To make such selection and concentration possible, one has to suspend one's attention to countless other formation manifestations that are less relevant.

In this way one can come to a significant, useful understanding of many formation manifestations in terms of a few that are typical. Thus different aspects of the cosmos in interformation can be understood approximately without an understanding of every manifestation or of the underlying primary cosmic epiphany of the formation mystery. Scientific theories and models cannot be more than approximations of the true nature of cosmic formation. The error in such approximations may be exceedingly small. Therefore, this physical approach to the study of the cosmos remains meaningful and useful.

Like physicists, formation scientists, develop a sequence of partial and approximate formation theories. Ideally, each successive theory should be more consonant with formation manifestations than the previous one. Yet none of them should claim to represent a full and final account of either cosmic or distinctively human formation.

Consonance of Cosmic Interformation

The interformation of all cosmic forms is consonant. They are all parts of a self-consistent hierarchy that flows from the cosmic epiphany of the formation mystery. They obey the form directives intrinsic to their own formation and are compatible with the formation patterns of other emergent forms in the universe and with the underlying primary cosmic epiphany of the formation mystery in an all-encompassing field of form energy. We call this phenomenon *formation consonance.*

Formation consonance is a natural and inescapable pattern of all cosmic formation. Only the human life-form, in so far as it exceeds the cosmic epiphany, can resist, escape, or improve such cosmic patterns of formation. Improvement, together with wise utilization of these patterns in service of the distinctively human formation of life and world, complements this cosmic consonance with a human, and eventually a transhuman, way of consonance.

The three epiphanies of the formation mystery are manifestations of the same forming source. They do not exclude but complement each other. The main difference is that human freedom enables us to disobey the directive patterns communicated by the formation mystery in all its epiphanies. Perfect consonance in cosmic formation means that all forms fall into place within this network of forming relations without excess or deficiency.

Physicists and Cosmic Contemplatives

In the physical formation view, everything in the universe is interforming with everything else. No cosmic form is foundational to any other. The dimensions and articulations of any cosmic form are determined not by some fundamental law of formation but by the form energies, dimensions, and articulations of all other forms that coform together in marvelous consonance and consistency.

Two kinds of people have been profoundly interested in the universe in its wondrous wholeness. These people are concerned either with intense study of the cosmos or with detached contemplation of the cosmos. Notable among the former are theoretical physicists; among the latter are the nature mystics or cosmic contemplatives. Both are aware that it would be impossible to explain exhaustively any particular form or formation because of its interformative dependency on all other formation manifestations. Each of them, however, is present to the cosmos in a different mode. The quantifying physical-scientific mode of presence leads the physicist to strive after an approximate, progressive understanding of nature by means of conceptual, quantifying maps. Cosmic contemplatives are not interested in a presence that yields only such relative knowledge. They foster inwardly a mode of presence that lifts them into an intuitive, unifying awareness of the forming cosmos as a whole.

Approximate explanations of single formation manifestations are quite possible, though seldom emphasized by cosmic contemplatives. Instead, they like to heighten in human awareness the other equally true aspect of formation. No single manifestation of the formation mystery is fully explicable in symbols or in words. Cosmic contemplatives, both inside and outside cosmic form traditions, are usually not concerned with the explanation of form and formation as is the physicist or, in another way, the formation scientist. Instead, a mode of *contemplative presence* is cultivated. It facilitates an intuitive, unifying experience of all forms in their inscrutable wholeness and mysterious interwovenness within the cosmic epiphany of the formation mystery.

Regarding other questions and their possible proximate answers, cosmic contemplatives may cultivate what they call a noble silence. They rest in the awareness that any particular cosmic form manifestation is a mysterious consequence of all form manifestations. The ultimate explanation is to explain nothing, but to surrender to this mysterious unity. This veiled wholeness itself is beyond explanation. Thus cosmic contemplatives attempt to rise above all words, symbols, images, and explanations. They try to purify and free the mind for receptive presence.

People who are predisposed to cosmic contemplation may be tempted to bypass the personal-social and eventual transhuman epiphanies of the mystery of formation. Cosmic formation traditions may foster this tendency. Cosmic mysticism should be complemented by personal-social and transhuman mysticism. If not, cosmic contemplation may lead to three foundational limitations. The first is a tendency to passive enclosure in the cosmic realm of formation. The second is an underestimation of the transcosmic human responsibility for effective formation and reformation of the macro- and microcosmic form powers in service of personal-social formation. The third is a lack of openness or readiness for any possible transcosmic and transhuman self-communication of the mystery of formation that may come to humanity.

Negligence of presence to the cosmic epiphany of the formation mystery makes our life of personal-social and transhuman mysticism less complete. Of course, all levels of mysticism presuppose our liberation from our conceptual networks as ultimate explanations of any epiphany of the formation mystery.

The Personal-Social Epiphany of the Formation Mystery

So far we have considered mainly the cosmic epiphany of the formation mystery. Let us turn now to the transcosmic appearance of human life in the cosmos. Human life, as spiritual, transcends the cosmic while participating in it. It spiritualizes its own participation in the macro- and microcosmic dance of the universe. Human life is spiritualizing, both as individual life and as the life of the human community.

As we have seen, the mystery of cosmic formation gives rise to a diversified world that is ever changing because of the interformative interaction of atomic and subatomic formation. This change is not chaotic but orderly. The universe is suffused with an order of remarkable refinement and precision. Einstein declared that the basis of his scientific search was the inescapable conviction that the world is ordered and comprehensible, not a thing of chance. A transcendent power makes everything change and grow while providing elemental structure, order, and direction. This power gives rise to a seemingly inexhaustible variety of forms and expressions. Human life, too, is called to be a manifestation of the formative power of this formation mystery. This distinctively human epiphany of the formation mystery is a call to be personal-social and yet in harmony with the overall transcendent direction of universe and evolution.

The formation mystery directs each human life toward growth and wholeness in a life-form that is shared with others and yet unique. The formation mystery sustains the formative power sources that play in the universe. It gives rise to an astonishing variety of forms, ever changing, yet ever directed. Most awesome of all is the spiritual, or human, form of life.

The play of formative power in the universe may seem capricious at first. When we look more closely, however, we see that forms always arise, disappear, and reemerge in accordance with a mysterious consistency. No person, event, or thing can escape this consistency of formation. A certain form direction seems to be infused in the very fiber of all world and life formation. This direction can be described by scientists as the laws of nature. They can also identify the forms that emerge as different constellations of atoms. They can even detect particles that are not particles in the strict sense, but energy waves. The various constellations of forms resulting from these forming waves give rise to more complex and subtle forms that keep evolving. They represent ever new forms of life and matter. But what science can neither measure nor analyze is the all-permeating source of this steady, consistent emergence of forms—the silent presence of the transcendent formative power that structures this rising and falling of forms in the universe.

This primordial formative power is alive in the epiphanies of the mystery of formation. It gives rise to all the possible forms that emerge and unfold. In the case of human life, we are formed as free, spirited persons. Hence, we are potentially free to flow with or to refuse the unique formation to which we are invited. The same is true of the human cultures and communities that are called to develop certain shared forms of life. Foundational human formation is a lifelong attempt to disclose and implement the limited form of life each of us and our cultures and communities are called to unfold.

The mystery of formation is thus, first of all, as cosmic epiphany, an unconscious process taking place in the macro- and microcosmos in which we share. It is the process of the gradual realization of the characteristic form each event, thing, or living being is tending toward in congeniality with its nature and conditions and in compatibility with its formative setting. Human life, too, shares in this universal unconscious process. This aspect of human formation could be called its cosmic, organismic, and vital preformation. It gives rise to the infraform of human life, which is the cosmic substratum of the fully human life-form and which comprehends interacting processes of organic and vital formation. The organic infraformation could be described, in turn, as the infraconscious, cosmic formation of bodily cells, tissues, organs, and systems. This aspect of infraformation is the basis of the emergence of an original, genetic, infraconscious structuring of vital impulses, needs, and strivings.

The Mystery of Personal Formation

The call to distinctively human formation is a call to the whole of our being. This call issues from the transcendent mystery that grounds us and makes us be. Uniquely called in this way, our life takes on a hidden meaning and consistency. Yet this meaning remains a mystery for us; at no moment do we have it totally in sight. Neither do we gain at once a panoramic view of all form directives that are implied in its foundational meaning.

The mystery of personal formation may gain in clarity as our life proceeds. We do not know in advance the details of the articulation of our existence. Yet we do know in faith, hope, and love that every event, encounter, and experience is meant to form us harmoniously into the foundational communal-personal life-form each of us is called to attain.

We may be at a loss for words to explain how we can believe that a disparate array of events in our life is the means of our personal formation. The formation of our communal-personal life is a mystery. We can only rest in the faith that formation goes on, filtering through seemingly unrelated incidents, choices, and events. We may be blessed with an occasional glimpse of the consistency of our formation, but such moments are rare. Most often we must live in the simple faith that we follow a call to foundational formation, though we cannot know in advance the outcome of the journey to which we are invited. Its meaning may be revealed to some degree in the course of our life of critical and creative fidelity. The only certitude we have is that the ongoing formation of our life and our work with others for a reformation of society must proceed.

Faith in the daily call to formation, and fidelity to its mystery, grant us the flexibility we need to respond to formative life directives that may unpredictably come our way. When we live in anticipation of unexpected manifestations of the mystery of formation, we live in readiness for anything that may happen to us. Formative directives may influence our life in ways we never expected. What counts is the abiding awareness of being called communally, personally, and continually to ongoing foundational formation.

The Transcosmic Dynamic of Loving Consonance

The personal epiphany of the formation mystery in our lives may be experienced as an enlightening sequence of different current forms. Each of them enables us to disclose a little more of what we are called to be. This procession of succeeding life-forms, to the extent that they are increasingly consonant, tends and points toward the possibility of a life-form that is to be uniquely ours.

The point of departure of the science of formative spirituality is *human life as relatively free formation*. We take this as an undeniable fact. Also factual is the *transcendent dynamic* of this distinctively transcosmic formation. What makes this dynamic possible? What is operative in every formative transcendent tendency? Take, for example, the tendency of a middle-aged person to seek a fuller expression of human presence, a kind of consciousness that is not determined merely by cosmic or social processes of formation. From all evidence, such a transcendent dynamic is rooted in an implicit awareness that one is called to an ever higher form of unique personal-social life.

What is that higher form of personal, transcosmic life we feel called to realize? From whence does it come? To what does it point? The answer is to a distinctively personal epiphany of the formation mystery. It draws human life transconsciously to rise above mere cosmic and social determination by increasingly personal, free, and insightful apprehensions, appraisals, and options. The transcosmic human life is, so to speak, a life of resurrection. Corresponding to this formative call is the inherent aspiration of the human person to become in some way like the mystery of formation itself in a union of consonance or, what is the same, of love and likeness, for there is a likeness between the person formed in human consonance, or love, and the mystery forming him or her in both cosmic and transcosmic consonance, or love.

Hence, the mystery of human formation involves some implicit awareness of the *transcendent call to consonance*, or to likeness, with a personal formation mystery. Humans seek a unique loving coformity with an eternal form flowing from the darkness of a divine formless beyond, which keeps drawing them above themselves. A certain form of pride may prevail against the power of consonant formation in their lives. It may tempt them to refuse the demanding and humbling attraction of the formation mystery. They may lose their lives in deformative conformity to isolated idols, or to the cosmos itself imagined as isolated from the formation mystery that is the ultimate source of its epiphany.

What constitutes this transcendent direction of the personal epiphany of the formation mystery? The answer is that there is a *foundational form direction* implied in all human formation. Every current formation of our life implies some reference to an absolutely transcendent mystery of formation. This can only be explained by the fact that there must be an absolute transcendent mystery of formation that foundationally guides and pervades universe, humanity, and history. If such a unifying formation power did not exist as an essential element shared in some measure by all formation manifestations, all current expressions of formation would be unrelated. They would indeed be so idiosyncratic that any common, foundational understanding of formation would become impossible. This is why all of the partial and passing formation sources, which enable humanity to form itself and to allow itself to be formed, point to this unifying mystery of formation.

Human formation, by its inner dynamism and its inherent aspiration, thus strives prereflexively toward consonance or likeness with the formative, transcendent, personal mystery of formation. This striving is subject to many distortions. Much dissonance may precede and accompany the hesitant and vulnerable search for consonance with the mystery of formation. Life can distort but not totally extinguish the potential search implied in the human form potency. Not that any human life, no matter how perfect, can ever be essentially like the personal, transcendent mystery of formation itself. A human life-form can be only a uniquely limited but true likeness of the form the formation mystery assumes for the human spirit.

The Christian form tradition implies that we are called beyond this limited form to participate in the "eternal formation event" that is the mystery of the Trinity, emanating from the dark and formless divinity. In this volume, however, we restrict our attention to the pre-Christian awareness that all formation points to a formative mystery that transcends us infinitely and is the source of all forms of likeness to itself. This awareness enables us to objectify and relativize the current contents of passing forms of life and matter. We can study them in their relativity and limitation because we delineate them in their finite and current appearance against the horizon of the transcendent dynamic mystery of all formation. There is thus a primordial distinction between the personal epiphany of the mystery of formation and the transhuman formative mystery to which it points.

The basic theories of the science of formative spirituality are all elaborations of the same primordial fact, this fact being the *transcendent tendency of all human formation*. This foundational tendency can be conceived as the essential aspiration of human life to disclose and realize a life-form that is a loving and lovable consonance or likeness with a mystery that infinitely transcends human formation of life and world.

The Freedom of Transcosmic Foundational Formation

The essential difference between cosmic and transcosmic human formation is that between physical constriction and spiritual freedom. Human formation is a mixture of both. The distinctively human form potency is rooted in an aspiration for transcendent formation. This aspiration is the distinctive characteristic of the human life-form. It is the privileged locus of the personal epiphany of the formation mystery. Human life aspires, at least implicitly and unthematically, in dissonance or consonance, after coformation and consonance with the source of all forms and formation in life and world. Every being longs for its own perfect form. Each such form is a limited reflection of the form that the transcendent mystery of formation assumes out of the formless darkness of the divinity.

We are foundationally in search for our ideal form of life. We grasp this ideal implicitly in our experience of aspiration for consonance with the personal mystery of formation. To the extent that we live in openness of mind and heart, life itself begins to disclose to us progressively that our human spirit, foundationally speaking, is oriented toward transcendent formation. This orientation is, in principle, if not in fact, a total openness to all directives of the human epiphany of the personal mystery of formation. Hence, human life itself could be defined as being foundationally a *transcendent formative aspiration*. All formation attempts are tentative manifestations of our aspiration to be more like the transcendent personal formation mystery that calls us forth to form our life in its image.

This dynamic movement tends a priori toward a deepening of our coformation with the formative epiphanies of the formation mystery on our way to loving consonance with that mystery itself. All of our particular concrete tendencies toward foundational formation should be understood in light of this transcendent movement of formation that we already are.

Formative tending involves an interaction between the limitless aspiration after transcendent coformation and consonance and the finite expression of this aspiration in the concrete formative events of daily life. All formative events and current forms of life—when congenial with our transcendent destiny—are but stages through which the emergent human life-form must pass in its aspiration toward the ultimate horizon of consonance already known unthematically. This insight is the key to understanding human freedom in formation.

The deepest ground of our formation freedom is a mystery that can never be comprehended. Freedom of human formation is an original datum given as such in our transcendent formative experience itself. We cannot understand it fully. We experience this inherent freedom as the ground of our possibility to be in some measure selective in our choice of directives that will guide the formation of our life. We experience ourselves as able in some degree to select from a variety of possible formation directives those that we want to be influential in our formation. We know that we can in principle transcend the fascinating power of attractive particular formation directives. By means of our spirit, we can rise above this attraction and avoid being totally determined inwardly by any particular formation directive.

Our transcendent power of formation can lift itself out of life-forms in which it has currently invested its forming energy. It can, as it were, return to itself, reasserting its original freedom of formation option. By virtue of its formative dynamism, our power of transcendent aspiration leaps toward its final goal: epiphanous coformation and consonance with the formation mystery itself.

In the course of this leap, our transcendent power frees itself from blind determination by any particular current form of life that is less than the ultimate goal. Such freeing from forms of life that are no longer meaningful involves a return of our original power of transcendent formation to itself. Thus, the possibility of a return from any current life-form to one's center of transcendent aspiration is grounded in our freedom of formation. This power of return to transcendent aspiration serves the repeated attunement of our life to the formation mystery itself. This freedom of formation distinguishes human beings from other beings in formation, such as animals, plants, or minerals.

Transcendent formation freedom precedes any objective, concrete experience of opting for a particular formation direction. This option is only possible because our transcendent freedom already exists. As such it is a more original reality in our life than the potential or factual choice of a form directive.

The ontological structure of any being-in-formation determines what its form should be. We can also apply this general principle to the human being in formation. The ontological structure of the human being should manifest the character of freedom. This means that human life will assume its form not by blind determination but through exercise of its freedom. This exercise implies also the possibility to abuse freedom, to move away from coformation with the epiphanies of the formation mystery.

Freedom of formation makes us personally responsible for the form that our life as a whole will assume. Every decision for a current form of life is indirectly, at least in principle, a decision for our final form of life, for our unique consonance with the formation mystery. Any formative option contributes to or detracts from the realization of the unique life-form to which we are called by personal affinity. Every formative decision is possible only because of the deeper dynamic of aspiration for a unique coformation with this epiphany along the way to ultimate consonance with the formation mystery itself. This aspiration is the hidden spring that continually restores and renews our freedom of formation.

Formation freedom affects our life as a whole. It calls forth an implicit option for our total life direction in each particular choice of a current form of life at any specific moment of our history. It affects our final destiny. It tends to incarnate itself in all dimensions of our human life-form and their articulations in various formation phases.

Freedom of formation thus manifests itself in the transcendent choice of our momentary life direction. This choice happens when we concretely choose life directives here and now in the light of our probable overall direction and formation. Freedom of formation thus implies responsibility for our foundational life formation. In fact, certain choices of particular life directions may extend their influence over our entire life span. Others will only be current contributions to our life direction to be replaced in time by new directives. Others again will prove to be either mistaken or unnecessary detours from our journey.

In the science of formation we speak about the incarnating tendency of the emergent life direction and life-form. This means that our life direction coforms with the formation mystery each dimension, articulation, and modality precisely as an expression of the core form of life as a whole. Meanwhile, it remains true that the transcendent dimension of formation is a superior liberating source of the whole of human life in formation. Yet this superior dimension must not be thought of in any way as separate from the other dimensions of one's foundational formation.

Formation: A Natural Analogical Concept

The *ontological basis of the science of formative spirituality* can thus be found in a natural resemblance between finite formation and the ultimate source of all formation, which is the formation mystery itself. This resemblance justifies the use of analogy or symbol when we speak about formation.

Formation, as we observe it happening in the cosmos, is discontinuous. For example, we observe a difference between the formation of the universe, of minerals, plants, and animals, and that of human persons. Evidently, the foundational formation of people is different from, yet analogous to, other kinds of formation in the cosmos. We express the specific difference between distinctively human formation and that of subhuman forms in such terms as free, transcendent, or spiritual formation.

All the different ways of formation in the universe are manifestations of an *ontological discontinuity* that is characteristic of formation as such. Our awareness of the dynamic movement of relatively free, insightful human formation provides us with the possibility of an analogous knowledge of the mystery that manifests itself in its threefold epiphany in the initial and ongoing formation of all that is. This analogous understanding is the source of a truly personalistic concept of formation. As a result, our understanding is not restricted to a concept of formation as a result of cosmic processes alone.

Symbols and Human Formation

There must be a natural resemblance between our passing current life-forms and the ultimate mystery of formation, which they symbolize and express. This resemblance is the only justification for our perception of any consonant current formation as a symbol of an all-encompassing direction and formation by a personal mystery. Hence, symbol plays an important role in formative spirituality. Symbol in human formation does not mean an artificial sign—that to which convention gives meaning, like a red traffic light symbolizes danger. Our formation of life and world is fostered and deepened by consonant symbols that are symbolic not in the artificial but in the proper sense.

A symbol in the proper sense is a person, event, or thing in which some wider meaning spontaneously manifests itself over and above a more immediate significance. Consistent high blood pressure, for example, means more than only an increase in blood pressure; it manifests some disease or irregularity in the organism of the patient. This manifestation is not due to a convention like a traffic signal; it is inherent in the person, event, or thing itself.

Foundational formation of human life happens through symbols. Our culture and the underlying form traditions in which we are embedded form us also partly through the transcendent symbols it initiates, maintains, and conveys to us. We are not automatically open to such symbols. Certain conditions must be fulfilled to foster our receptivity for the formative power of transcendent symbols.

We can illustrate the role of the symbol in foundational formation by considering again the vital dimension. This bodily aspect of ongoing formation is in no way separate from the historical, functional, and transcendent dimension of the same formation. Consider graciousness of movement. It can express the harmonious formation of human life. To the extent that this is the case graciousness becomes an expression of our life-form as a whole. It may symbolize the increasing transcendent ease and freedom of our emergent form of life. This form expresses itself consequently in the gentle flow of our bodily movements. The vital dimension of the human life-form can thus become a symbol of the ease and flow of one's foundational formation as a whole. This vital symbolizing may happen to the extent that the body is formed as the expression of one's consonance with the threefold epiphany of the mystery of formation. The vital dimension lets the transcendent shine forth. A similar relationship can be found between the functional and the transcendent dimensions of the life-form. The functional can serve the incarnation of transcendent aspirations by symbolic functioning.

Foundational human formation thus implies a lived integration of symbolizing and symbolized dimensions of our life. This integration implies that the dimensions and articulations of our life-form are not just pieces added together. Yet the expressions of this form as a whole will vary in degree as far as specific dimensions, articulations, modes, modalities, and formation phases are concerned. For example, one's speech can express the whole life-form one has attained, even though this modality of self-expression is situated in the vital articulation of larynx, lips, tongue, and oral cavity.

Hence, it is not just one or the other dimension, articulation, mode, modality, or phase of human life that is exclusively formed or deformed in the ongoing flow of its formation. Formation or deformation may pronounce themselves preferentially in one or the other specific dimension or articulation of the life-form. Still, the core form of life as a whole will announce itself increasingly in each and every dimension and articulation of life.

Summary of the Anthropological Principles of Foundational Human Formation

The anthropology of human formation displays a logical development. Its starting point is the primordial fact of the all-embracing mystery of formation in its threefold epiphany. The more specific starting point for our understanding of distinctively human formation is our grasp of human life as transcendent formability, or form potency, already involved in transcendent formation. Both starting points can be disclosed by us in thoughtful reflection on formation events we encounter daily.

To foster true formation, human life must attend reverently to the epiphanies of the formation mystery that silently direct its unfolding. Such reverent attention is nourished by an awareness that the mystery exists as a personal loving power of formation, calling us to be consonant with itself or transformed in its likeness.

Its existence can be demonstrated by unfolding the implications found in the givenness of finite formative events. Such events are manifest everywhere—in universe, history, form traditions, cultures, institutions, and, in a special way, in our personal life.

The foundational method establishes the fact that every finite formative event has a real and substantial relation to an all-permeating transcendent mystery of formation. Only the transcendent aspiration of human life enables humanity to become aware of this relation, even before a transhuman epiphany of the mystery reveals its existence with a greater certitude and deeper meaning.

Our free transcendent power of spiritual formation aspires beyond the sociohistorical, cosmic-vital, and functional limits of the partial form of our life. It is an aspiration toward an increasing coformation with the epiphanies of the formation mystery. Human life can accept or refuse this consonant formation to the extent that it has been able to actualize its potency for freedom of formative apprehension, appraisal, and decision.

The realization of our unique life-form affects and is affected by our society as formative. Each society is a web of interrelated social form directives implied in form traditions, rites, customs, conventions, and countless other formative symbols. In and through them, societies offer their members formative or deformative public-affirmation opportunities. People are inclined to doubt their formation potency, competence, and efficiency. They look preconsciously for social opportunities to prove to themselves and others that they can give form effectively to life and world. They seek to gain approval, affirmation, even applause, for their formation competence. This yearning for public potency affirmation is a source of the great forming power society holds over them. Society outlines for them the opportunities for social approval or disapproval. One had better conform, or else! Hence, our growth to spiritual formation freedom implies a growth in detachment from those popular symbols and pulsations that are dissonant with the ideal consonant life-form to which we should aspire.

Such growth in actual formation freedom implies, especially in functional-aggressive societies, a growth in the receptive dimension of one's form potency. In such societies, the productive dimension of form potency is often overemphasized to the exclusion of the far more basic potency for form receptivity. Most public-affirmation opportunities are then constituted in terms of demonstrations of a production-and-consumption potency. Spiritual formation is thus more necessary to help all persons open up to their form-receptive potency in a functional society. With spiritual courage, we can live in receptivity, even when our receptive potency tends to be negated by the prevalent productive symbols in our society.

CHAPTER 15

Abandonment to the Formation Mystery

The preceding chapter deepened our understanding of the formation mystery, especially in its cosmic and personal-social epiphanies. Now we can return to the question raised earlier: Is this mystery of formation meaningful and beneficial? Can we abandon our lives to this mysterious process in a movement of seminal faith, hope, and consonance?

The mystery of formation seems to invite us to respond to its presence in some positive or negative fashion. We feel called to take a position. We do not necessarily experience that challenge in an explicit way. Neither do we by necessity answer it explicitly. Most of the time, the response is given in the act of trusting life itself. Every person decides whether to believe and trust in the meaningfulness of the ongoing formation of life and world. No matter what we decide, this primordial option and subsequent disposition will profoundly color our formation history.

Foundational Formation Option

People are called to participate in the mystery of formation in their lives. Their first response to this call is a *foundational formation decision*. In this basic option they choose to believe in the meaningfulness or the meaninglessness of their life formation. It is a choice either to abandon themselves to this mystery or to feel abandoned in this cosmos as in a meaningless and careless system closed in upon itself. Our primordial formation decision is thus a faith option for positive or negative abandonment.

The primordial abandonment option is not totally free. Our freedom of choice can be limited by various factors. First of all, *genetic preformation* gives rise to innate predispositions that may limit our freedom considerably. For example, some people may be genetically preformed with a disposition for depression. When such depression predispositions assert themselves and begin to wear people down, it may be difficult for people to initiate or maintain their trustful abandonment to the formation mystery. They may need special medical treatment or psychotherapy to regain their freedom of felt surrender to some ultimate meaningfulness of their life.

Another limit on one's freedom of abandonment can be posed by both interformative and outer formative experiences. In the *interformation* of childhood, the child is mostly receptive in regard to its formation. Parents or other significant adults are the dominant agents in the interformative process. They are implicitly experienced as messengers of the formation field, of the beyond from which it emerges, and therewith of the formation mystery. Unfortunately, they may be without sufficient love or care or may be unable to express and symbolize these attitudes. In that case they may be inconsistent and capricious in their approval or disapproval. The freedom of the child to opt for carefree surrender may be impaired. Faith in the basic trustworthiness of life and reality may be severely restricted. Much love, friendship, counseling, or therapy may be necessary to regain the potential for spontaneous abandonment to the never fully known directions that formation may assume.

The succession of *formative life situations* one experiences after childhood may also limit one's freedom of foundational formation option. Such situations may symbolize for people either the meaningfulness or meaninglessness of the formation process. Usually both types of symbols play a part in the situations with which one is faced in life. One's predisposition to be more attentive to one or the other type of symbol may be a function partly or mainly of either genetic preformation or of formative experiences in the period of initial formation.

(In the fourth volume of this series, we will consider the articulation of the Christian form tradition, which reflects the faith Christians have that they are influenced by the ongoing divine preformation of their lives in Christ. This preformation includes yet transcends the limitations of genetic preformation of initial formation, and of ongoing inter- and situation formation. This initial and ongoing divine preformation in the Word and its incarnation through the Holy Spirit is the transpersonal epiphany of the formation mystery. It is a hidden ultimate formation that is not available to direct, unaided human apprehension and appraisal. All such influences somehow delineate our free formation potencies and our freedom of abandonment option.)

Formation Matter and Freely Formative Human Life

To understand better the unlimited freedom of the foundational formation option and its consequences, it may be helpful to make a distinction between *formation matter* and *free formation movement*. In the free, transcendent movement of formation, we participate freely in the epiphanies of the formation mystery. In this movement of form reception and form giving, we utilize our knowledge of the formation matter that is to be given form and that is available to us within our situation. Formation matter comprises all those limited horizons of human life in its formation field that in principle can be investigated from the specific perspectives of the differential proximate sciences.

On the basis of the result of the scientific exploration of these limited horizons of human life in formation, differential theories can be developed. Such theories are helpful if their validity and reliability remain appropriately restricted. Differential-proximate knowledge informs us about the limited aspect of human formation that constitutes the formal object of the scientific perspective chosen. We can distinguish, for example, those aspects of the formation of life and world that may be disclosed by such sciences as biology, economics, anthropology, sociology, or psychology, each of which represents a different approach to formation.

In relation to the human life-form as a relatively free agent of formation, all these special and proximate aspects are seen as integral parts of a rich and complex formation matter that is made more available to human freedom and insight by the factual disclosures of such disciplines. As many aspects of human life as possible should be explored by the ever increasing and differentiating factual sciences of formation matter. This effort will increasingly enable people as free formation agents to give form to this matter as it really is in all its complexity. (The third volume in this series, on the scientific nature and methodology of the science of formation, will discuss at length this aspect of the differential sciences.)

To safeguard and enhance free human formation potencies it is crucial never to absolutize such fragments of formation matter as disclosed and explored by the differential sciences. Any identification of a particular form process with the formation of human life as a whole would undermine our understanding of the formation mystery in its totality. It would disguise and falsify the distinctive essence of human life—the limited yet expanding free core of its formation—as well as the mystery of formation in which the human epiphany is called to participate freely. It is only in the light of freedom that we can become aware of what human formation most deeply is, as distinguished from the processes of formation we observe in subhuman forms in the cosmos. Only in this light can we appreciate the meaning of the free foundational abandonment option.

Knowledge of Formation Freedom

Formation freedom cannot be examined as an object similar to the other objects we observe in and around us. For this reason we cannot look at our deepest freedom from the viewpont of the physical and social sciences, for these sciences examine objective reality. From their perspective, formation freedom would appear as something unverifiable. Only one road leads to the awareness of formation freedom: the path of openness to the experiences of formation we allow into our lives by our creative action or receptivity. In other words, the awareness of such freedom can only be found in the intraformative pole of our formation experience and its history.

We are often aware that we give form to and receive form from life. Simultaneously, we have the definite experience that we could have given a different form to our life or allowed another forming influence to affect us. We are aware that we ourselves somehow decide to give or receive this specific form, which may be either relatively enduring or only a passing current form of life. We may also experience that we failed to foster a consonant form of life that we truly felt called to assume. This experience of failure in fidelity may be accompanied by the experience of formation guilt. When we look back on our life of formation, we become aware that we experience ourselves repeatedly as the source of our willingness to give form to or to receive form in this or that way and not otherwise.

Reflecting further on our formation freedom, we become aware that it is not exclusively a characteristic of this or that particular act of formative willing made here and now at this moment. We sense that it must have deeper roots in our foundational human life-form. We cannot reduce this quality of formation freedom merely to one or the other formative act of ours. Free acts of formation are, of course, evidence of and pointers to the fact of formation freedom, but this freedom itself has a far wider and deeper ground. This ground is none other than our formative life itself as a whole.

Intraformative experience teaches us also that this freedom of formation cannot be totally explained by an irresistible power of some particular motivation that would absolutely determine our formative acts. We experience that we ourselves, as free form agents, also play a significant part in what motivates us. We somehow decide how much formation power we shall allow to flow into the various motives offered to us. These motives do not take our freedom away, but neither do they ultimately determine our abandonment.

Freedom of Foundational Response to the Mystery of Formation

Our foundational response to the formation mystery is not simply a response to this or that particular formative event as meaningless or meaningful. It is a response of our entire centered being to the meaningfulness or meaninglessness of the mystery of formation as a whole. What is at stake is our foundational appreciative or depreciative disposition in regard to the riddle of the formation process going on always and everywhere in and around us: in our personal life, in the macro- and microcosmos, in the world, and in history. It is at the moment of decision that we become aware of our deeply rooted freedom to say yes or no to the inescapable formation mystery that embraces us and that we can conceive as meaningless or meaningful.

Since this is an intraformative foundational decision in regard to the overall meaning of the formation mystery, it cannot be observed or proved by the methods of differential physical and social sciences, which deal with objectifiable particulars of observable physical or social conditions, not with holistic personal experiences.

This foundational decision can be prereflexive or prereflective.

From childhood on, we grow slowly into a formative depreciative or appreciative disposition regarding the overall mystery of the formation of our life and world. (This aspect of the science of formation will be clarified more extensively in the second volume of this series.) Because we encounter the enigma of formation implicitly always and everywhere, we are compelled to take an intraformative stance in this regard. It is this overall stance that directs and colors our life as a whole in all its particular stances.

This decision is not necessarily made in its finality in the period of initial formation. It may be made later during our ongoing life formation. It can then be made either on the level of focal consciousness, in relative clarity of awareness, or it may be made preconsciously. The latter is usually the case. Most people come to the abandonment decision spontaneously, implicitly, and prereflectively in the midst of their ongoing daily formation. In periods of personal reflection, in psychotherapeutic situations, or in formation counseling, this implicit decision may be made explicit. It then becomes available to a critical, creative appraisal of its nature and its influence on one's formation history.

We may try to pass through life without formative reflection. Even then we will be repeatedly compelled to make a foundational decision of trust or distrust in life, at least on the prereflective level. Formative events of crucial importance, transcendence crises, disturbances, deaths in the family, chronic illness, disappointments, serious losses, failures, and falls from power may force us to reflection. What had been lived without reflection now becomes available to *appraisal* in such critical, creative formation moments. We feel invited to face critically, to appropriate deliberately, and to take upon ourselves resolutely the formation disposition we have been living prereflectively.

What confronts us now is the foundational question: What in principle is my disposition toward the mystery of formation in which all of my own life and all that I know and see around me is inescapably involved all the time? Is my disposition appreciative or depreciative, one of feeling abandoned to or abandoned by the mystery? How does that disposition affect my attitude toward the pre-, intra-, inter-, and outer formation events in my formation field? What do I make of the ongoing formation of the macro- and microcosmos, of human world and history? How do I respond formatively to society, its communities and its members? How is my social presence influenced by this primordial decision? What about formative courage and discouragement?

The Foundational Formation Decision

It should be clear by now that the primordial formation decision is not directly concerned with any particular formative event as such. Neither is it concerned with the more or less influential particular decisions that form the chain that binds our formation history together. Likewise, such particular decisions are not primarily concerned with the overall meaning of the mystery in our life and world.

The foundational decision and subsequent disposition is the basic response of a unique, centered human life-form *as a whole* to the mystery of formation as a whole. This response is free but not arbitrary. It is chosen in terms of the assumed meaningfulness or meaninglessness of the formation processes that govern life and world. This response can be appreciative or depreciative, made in abandonment *to*, or in a spirit of abandonment *by*, this riddle of formation. It can be prereflective or reflective.

This foundational decision and its subsequent disposition underpins all particular formation decisions and subsequent dispositions. In some way it coforms and colors all the daily decisions we make. The primordial decision implies a basic choice of meaning pertaining to the ongoing formation of one's own life and that of other people, universe, world, and history. As such, it provides the foundational formation theme of one's style of appraisal. This theme repeats itself in all particular appraisal themes. All other decisions are influenced by this primordial foundation. We cannot stress this point too strongly. Our life formation hinges on it. This underlying decision coforms all our perceptions, feelings, thoughts, memories, images, anticipations, and actions. Other formation decisions and dispositions may seem to be in some way foundational to our personal and communal life formation. They are, however, secondary to this radical formation decision.

The Risk of Abandonment to the Formation Mystery

The primary formation decision in favor of the beneficial meaningfulness of the all-embracing mystery of formation implies an abandonment to this mystery in seminal faith, hope, and consonance, in trusting appreciation. Appreciation, in turn, is the root of contemplation.

The formation mystery in and by itself does not extort an appreciative or depreciative primary decision in regard to its beneficial meaningfulness. This quality of the mystery of formation is not transparent or self-evident. Otherwise it would no longer be a mystery. Indeed what is most mysterious about the formation processes is their ultimate meaning. Their beneficial meaningfulness is by no means obvious, calculable, or demonstrable by the methods of the physical and social sciences. It is veiled in secrecy. Only an act of abandonment in faith, hope, and consonance enables us to decide in favor of the beneficial meaningfulness of the enigma of formation. This abandonment has to be maintained, often in the face of seemingly meaningless and disappointing formation events. Without some elementary seminal triad of human faith, hope, and consonance, it would be impossible to make or maintain this primary decision.

In this appreciative abandonment, we take a risk; we are without security or guarantee. We can surrender in peace only when we believe that the mystery of formation in all its apparent ambiguity is somehow ultimately meaningful and reliable for the formation of our life. In the opposite choice, that of depreciative abandonment, we must believe that the formation processes are ultimately meaningless and indifferent. It is a question of belief here as well because their final meaninglessness is impossible to demonstrate by means of mere functional logic or the methods of the proximate sciences.

The risk of appreciative abandonment must be sustained by an elementary human hope that the mystery of formation will ultimately benefit the present and future formation of our life and world. Depreciative abandonment implies the collapse of hope. A silent foundational despair about the meaninglessness of it all may take over.

Our seminal faith and hope in the mystery sustain and are sustained by a disposition of consonance, of elementary sympathy, of in-tuneness and partnership with the cosmic and transcosmic processes of formation. The belief that these enigmatic processes are somehow in consonance with our final beneficial life formation enables us to flow with them in creative fidelity, at least in principle. If we opted for depreciative abandonment instead, we would feel no consonance with these ambivalent forces and processes. We would begin to live a life of dissonance.

Unavoidability of the Primordial Formation Alternative

Our foundational human life-form distinguishes itself from other known forms in the universe by its relative freedom. This freedom makes the primordial formation decision unavoidable. It becomes impossible for us to keep hovering indefinitely over a decision between meaningfulness and meaninglessness. We may try to escape this decision for a lifetime by simply not choosing at all. However, the decision not to choose, if final in intention, is itself a choice. For we actually say no to the mystery of formation. In fact, we deny its beneficial meaning. In this decision for no choice at all, we even refuse to leave open the possibility that we may grow to an appreciative abandonment. We cut out of our life even the possible meaningfulness of formation. Factually, we choose an agnostic formation indifference. In reality we do not abandon ourselves to the mystery of formation as ultimately meaningful and beneficial in seminal faith, hope, and consonance.

The *final beneficial meaningfulness* of the enigma of formation does not manifest itself obviously and conclusively. Thus we remain free to interpret this enigma as meaningful or as meaningless. The way in which the mystery of formation appears to us will depend on our primordial decision in regard to its meaning. If we allow it to emerge for us in the light of a seminal triad of faith, hope, and consonance, it will appear as filled with a hidden ultimate harmony, consonance, and consistency in regard to the formation of life. It will manifest itself as ultimately beneficient, in spite of the dissonance, disharmony, inconsistency, and cruelty of countless intermittent events of formation.

This seminal human faith, hope, and consonance will dispose us to openness for any disclosure of its beneficial meaningfulness in our life and world, no matter how small and seemingly insignificant. This is for us a glimpse of the ultimate goodness of the formation mystery. It affirms and deepens our appreciative abandonment. Each tiny disclosure strengthens that disposition of human hope that inclines us to strive for a more consonant formation of our own life, and of our society and world.

If, on the contrary, we decide to apprehend the mystery of formation as meaningless or even malignant, it will appear to us as pointless, worthless, or inimical. This decision for a depreciative abandonment will dispose us to a cynical apprehension of any signs of apparent meaninglessness or maliciousness in the formation process that may seem to manifest themselves in life and world. It disposes us to skepticism and despair in regard to attempts to foster the consonant, meaningful formation of humanity and society.

The primordial alternative is thus a prereflective or reflective yes or no to the formation mystery. It is the choice of a willingness either to abandon ourselves to or to feel abandoned by the seemingly ambivalent processes of formation. One or the other conviction cannot be forced upon us or proven conclusively by means of mere functional logic or by the methods of the proximate sciences.

When we speak about the foundational triad of faith, hope, and consonance as *the root of appreciative abandonment*, we do not mean particular dispositions of faith, hope and consonance toward certain people, events, or things. We mean this threefold disposition as a basic orientation of the whole person toward the formation mystery as a whole. This disposition, so to speak, "founds" all other foundational and nonfoundational formation dispositions toward particular people, events, and things. It alone makes possible any other act or disposition of faith, hope, and consonance. As a primordial disposition, however, it by no means excludes the possibility that this seminal triad may be inactive in one or the other particular situation.

This foundational triad should not be confused with floating romanticism, naive credulity, blind optimism, or utopianism in regard to actual formation situations in all their meanness and cruelty. Similarly, the absence of the primordial triad in regard to the mystery of formation as a whole does not necessarily exclude some experiences of faith, hope, and consonance in particular situations. When an experience of faith, hope, consonance, or love, in a limited situation is affirmed, it may strengthen and expand its tenuous hold over the person. Eventually the experience of appreciation may grow so strong and consistent that it awakens in one the potentiality for an enduring, unconditional, primordial appreciative abandonment to the mystery of formation as a whole.

Formative Appraisal and Primordial Appreciative Abandonment

Our life formation is guided by form directives. The human mind appraises possible directives that emerge on its horizon. We can only be at ease with this appraisal when we are convinced that our power to appraise is essentially reasonable and trustworthy. Our conviction of the essential reasonableness of our appraisal power rests ultimately on faith. It is rooted in the belief that the mystery of formation appearing in cosmic and transcosmic epiphanies has formed well the human mind. We live in the implicit conviction that the mystery took care to gift the human mind in such a way that one can believe in one's appraisal power to guide the history of human life effectively and realistically. (The actualization of this essential reasonableness presupposes, of course, the fulfillment of many conditions, but these do not concern us in the context of this section. We are dealing here mainly with the essential reasonableness itself of the human appraisal power, not with the precise conditions for its effective actualization.) This radical reasonableness cannot be proven by means of mere functional logic alone or by the methods of the proximate sciences.

Our implicit conviction of this reasonableness can only be affirmed by our experiences and by observations of formative acts that implement human appraisals. Effective, well-adapted actions attest to the reasonableness and effectiveness of the appraisals that direct them. Such well-chosen actions incarnate in daily life our appraisals via formative decisions and subsequent actions and dispositions. Repeated incidences of reasonable action convince us that our appraisal power can be effective when the proper conditions are met.

By the same token, we can trust wholeheartedly such formative appraisals, decisions, actions, and dispositions only if we abandon ourselves to the mystery of formation that has formed our human appraisal power and its underlying brain formations over the millennia.

The Primordial Formation Disposition of Depreciative Abandonment

We must now consider the disposition of depreciative abandonment. Like all enduring form dispositions, it is a disposition of the formative heart, the *core form of life*. In this regard, it is like the disposition of positive "abandonment to." The depreciative abandonment disposition, however, is an enduring inclination to feel basically abandoned and forlorn in the meaninglessness of the formation processes that play in our life and world. A primordial depreciative disposition closes the heart to potential disclosures of the ultimately beneficial meaningfulness of the formation mystery. The directives that flow from the appreciative abandonment disposition can be consistently incarnated in everyday life. However, the directives to which the depreciative disposition gives rise cannot be implemented in the praxis of daily life, at least not consistently.

Daily reality resists the consistent implementation of this refusal of the heart. The disposition of depreciative abandonment implies an exclusive, usually prereflective, attentiveness to any possible manifestation of either the meaninglessness or harmfulness of the foundational processes of formation of life and world. This negative attitude of constant depreciation presupposes the paralysis of the seminal formation triad of human faith, hope, and consonance. It gives rise to the disposition of depreciative appraisal or depreciative thinking. It results in dissonance.

To feel basically and enduringly abandoned in life and world is not consonant with the foundational communal and personal form of life we are called to disclose and unfold during our formation history. We are preformed to resist a depreciative decision that would favor the ultimate meaninglessness of all formation. While we are free to do so, we are not preformed to prefer such a depreciative appraisal of the enigma of formation. We are basically inclined to flow with the foundational processes that govern universe and humanity. If the majority of people were not spontaneously inclined in this way, no progress in life would be possible. Everyone would lose his life, time, and energy in refusals to flow with the processes of formation. Human life would become chaotic.

Our inclination to flow with the mystery is deeply anchored in the human life-form itself. Protests against the meaninglessness of the foundational processes of formation are like a cry for meaningfulness. They signify the desperate moaning of a tortured heart for a disclosure of the ultimately beneficial meaning of life in the midst of an overwhelming experience of abandonment and forlornness.

Nevertheless, we remain free to allow ourselves to sink away in the abyss of perceived abandonment by the mystery of formation. Our faith and hope are challenged by countless events that seem ruthless and oppressive. The temptations to feel lost and abandoned within a meaningless whirl of blind formation processes should not be taken lightly. They are genuine and serious. Those who succumb deserve our compassion, not our condemnation.

The depreciative abandonment disposition is based in part on the fact that our formative attentiveness to reality is perspectival, that we are unable to take in everything at once. We cannot be present simultaneously to all aspects of a situation. At any one moment we can only look at life and world from a certain perspective. Ideally, our appraisal of the formative meanings and implied form directives of a situation should be the fruit of successive apprehensions of the many aspects of that situation by means of mutually complementary perspectives. It is this radical perspectivity of our formative attention, apprehension and appraisal that enables us to choose to be focused enduringly on only one aspect of reality. Instead of shifting our attention continuously, so as to gather in as many complementary aspects as possible, we can stay with only one side of a situation.

In this case, we may have decided to be present selectively and exclusively to the many apparently absurd or pointless manifestations of the enigma of formation. *Yet we have a preformed inclination to the contrary.* Already in infancy we are predisposed to flow spontaneously with the process of life formation. If this predisposition is not thwarted, frustrated, or disappointed, it may grow to a gentle willingness to form life in consonance with the epiphanies of the mystery of formation as sources of meaningful life directives.

In spite of favorable childhood influences, we can still close our hearts to formative manifestations of the beneficence of this mystery. Our spontaneous predisposition to consonant living may be thwarted later in life. Often, however, it is an unfriendly period of initial formation that has paralyzed one's original spontaneity. Paralysis in this sense implies sleep, not death. The gift of the inclination to consonance may always be awakened by loving interformation later in life.

Even if we live in depreciation, we may not always be able to escape the manifestations of sense and direction in formation events. Unfortunately, we can always come up with an explanation that fits our depreciative life direction. We may explain away such manifestations of beneficence as deceptive projections. We may reduce them to illusions of a heart yearning to create some consoling signs of an imagined benevolent direction of the powers of formation that in reality are indifferent to us.

We are as free to make the wager of a primordial faith in depreciative abandonment as we are to make the wager of appreciative abandonment to the mystery of formation. We are free *in principle*—as noted earlier, our actual freedom may be seriously curtailed by negative childhood experiences or similar ones later in life. The wager of depreciation may lead to a life of silent desperation, the appreciative one to a life of hope.

When we live in depreciative abandonment, we see only senseless processes of formation and deformation repeating themselves in endless cycles. We cling basically to the conviction that there is no ultimate believable meaning in the form processes that rule reality. We may only admit that certain formation processes at certain moments seem to benefit life and world. In this stance what seems apparent to us is the patent absurdity of formation in its totality.

We may believe that formation is basically senseless. In accordance with this foundational depreciative appraisal, any manifestation of formation seems pointless and void. We try to implement this appraisal in the way we give form to everyday living. It is then that we run into difficulties. It soon becomes evident that we cannot give form to life and world in a consistent fashion on the basis of this negative conviction. Some formation processes demand our positive abandonment if we want to be effective.

Take, for example, the cosmic formation processes that account for changes in climate and weather conditions or the human formation processes that we observe in people who are close to us. If we do not abandon ourselves to these changes and flow with them, we are unable to live in effective, loving, and reasonable cooperation. What about the microcosmic formation processes that affect our body chemistry over a lifetime? If we do not take them into account and abandon ourselves to their reality, we may seriously harm our health.

In other words, we are forced to develop false compromises between our primordial depreciative disposition and our daily formation praxis. Our life formation as a whole may become ambiguous, unreasonable, unpredictable, dissonant, and distorted because we are torn between our depreciative, negative stance and the necessity of adapting often to certain demands of daily formation as if they were reasonable, meaningful, and realistic.

The Primordial Formation Disposition of Appreciative Abandonment

As mentioned previously, appreciative abandonment is a disposition of the heart, or core form of life. It is a basic inclination to strive for consonance with the mystery of formation. This inclination is fostered by and fosters in turn a conviction that one is ultimately cared for by the formation mystery. One result of that conviction is the faith that formation events carry potential beneficial meanings that imply valuable form directives for one's life.

Such a disposition of positive abandonment opens the heart to potential disclosures of the beneficial meaningfulness and direction of the mystery of formation. It is then possible to implement this abandonment consistently in daily acts and dispositions in one's formation of life and world. This positive outlook generates a spontaneous attentiveness to, an expectant waiting for, any manifestation of beneficial form directives that the mystery of formation may communicate.

Such positive attitudes presuppose the presence and unfolding of the seminal triad of faith, hope, and consonance in regard to people, events, and things as manifestations of the threefold epiphany of the formation mystery. This stance gives rise to the disposition of appreciative thinking. This disposition of appreciation grants one a foundational assurance in regard to the ultimately beneficial meaning of one's unique formation history. This firm, unshakable assurance persists in the face of the constant permeation of one's history by menacing events that may seem deformative and demeaning.

Appreciative abandonment to the mystery of formation is consonant with the foundational communal and personal form of life we are called to disclose and unfold. Nonetheless, we always remain free to allow our formation to be overwhelmed by a depreciative mood or by a feeling of being abandoned by the mystery. The flowering of seminal faith, hope, and consonance may be stifled by scepticism, cynicism, discouragement, anxiety, anger, and negativity. At any moment we may lose our form receptivity, which is rooted in surrender to the mystery.

Form receptivity presupposes a gentle willingness to appraise appreciatively the formative events that come our way. We try to discover in them any formation potential that can benefit the receptive or creative unfolding of life and world, at least in the long run. Some classical form traditions articulate this aspect of the science by pointing also to the possibility of an afterlife, a life of purgation. In that afterlife, people can still find the form to which they believe they are called.

We may have chosen the "abandonment to" disposition in appreciative faith, hope, and consonance. Yet we should remember that the temptation to give way to a feeling of "abandonment by" may emerge at any moment of our formation history. One reason for that temptation is the hiddenness of the beneficial meaningfulness of formation. In a sense, this hiddenness protects our formation freedom. It means that we are never compelled by undeniable clarity in one or the other direction.

Appreciative Abandonment and Negative Experiences

In the light of faith, hope, and consonance, we may recognize and acknowledge the signs of genuine beneficial meaningfulness in many formation events. To be sure, there is much deformation, too. Abandonment to the formation mystery does not mean that we deny such deformation in facile optimism. Neither do we succumb to it in pessimism. We acknowledge the deformation of people and societies, of form traditions, formation segments, and communities. We see it starkly in all its horror and darkness. Yet abandonment to the formation mystery inspires us to believe and hope that we will be able to turn some of this darkness into light, that is, into means of receptive and productive formation for ourselves and for others, now or in the future. Appreciative abandonment sustains our faith in the concealed, unifying mystery of formation, despite seeming inconsistency, emptiness, deformation, cruel fate, and death.

The practice of this abandonment deepens our primordial certainty about the beneficial presence of the mystery. Doubt, fear, failure, and disappointment may challenge this certainty, but they cannot conquer it against our will, even if our moods and feelings are darkened by negative experiences. We alone can withdraw our appreciative abandonment in faith, hope, and consonance. Deep down, in the core of our life-form, the light of courage can burn brightly when everything seems lost and our moods and feelings are marked by despondency.

Consistent Maintenance of Appreciative Abandonment in Daily Life Formation

We have seen how negative abandonment becomes entangled in contradiction when we try to implement it in daily formation. If we were to deny consistently the possible meaning of all formation events and exercises, we could not survive in society. To give only one example, we could not take seriously any efforts directed toward training or education.

Appreciative abandonment, however, can survive and endure through all experiences of deformation of life and world, of people and society. It is quite possible to combine primordial faith in the ultimate beneficial meaningfulness of the mystery of formation as a whole with the numerous particular experiences of maliciousness, meanness, absurdity, and deformative stupidity manifested abundantly in passing formation situations. We say this because the dynamic formation triad of faith, hope, and consonance can disclose an element of potential beneficial formative opportunity in every deformative or nonsensical situation. The depreciating stance, if made absolute, would be unable to find any element of meaningful formation in situations, no matter how sensible they may be. Only the disposition of appreciative abandonment opens us to the concealed meaningfulness of the mystery of formation in every situation. It readies us for the art and discipline of what we could call "opportunity thinking."

Obstacles to Fidelity to Appreciative Abandonment

Fidelity to appreciative abandonment cannot be maintained without continuously withstanding the obstacles of doubt, disillusion, betrayal, and misunderstanding. Obviously, the beneficial meaningfulness of the mystery of formation discloses itself only gradually and incidentally to our believing, hoping, consonant appraisal. This meaningfulness can only be glimpsed through the veil of seemingly meaningless deformation that abounds in all societies.

This fidelity presupposes the foundational hope that carries and inspires us to transcend all particular functional-vital events and their meanings. This primordial hope is not any particular hope for this or that well-delineated goal. It is a *transcendent hope* that our life as a whole is ultimately meaningful in a way we cannot foresee or predict. All other projected hopes and their passing fulfillment are only pointers to the ultimate fulfillment of a life that will be meaningful as a whole. This transcendent hope is the condition for the possibility of the distinctively human transcendent formation of life as a whole. The opposite of this hope is despair.

The Reasonableness of Appreciative Abandonment

Before considering the reasonableness of appreciative abandonment, we should ask ourselves if the decision for its opposite, depreciative abandonment, could ever be reasonable. Could we say that people are reasonable in a formative sense if they choose a life of depreciative abandonment? Initially, it may seem reasonable to them to make this decision. Those who decide that all formation is ultimately meaningless, just a foolish stab in the dark, may be learned and intelligent. They may be able to amass all kinds of reasons for their primordial stance in regard to the ambiguous enigma of world and life formation.

However, when we look at the history of formation as it unfolds itself in a person's life, this option begins to appear less reasonable. As we have seen already, the foundational preformation of human life seems to incline us prereflectively to flow with the epiphanies of the mystery of formation in faith, hope, and consonance. Careful reflection on formation history makes us aware that formative meanings, opportunities, and occasions are disclosed to us only to the extent that we live in this stance of appreciative appraisal.

Allowing ourselves to sink into a negative mood, to feel lost and abandoned within meaningless processes of formation, hides for us the potential beneficial meaningfulness of the numerous formation events woven into our formation history. As a matter of fact, the history of human formation seems to disclose to us that only a disposition of appreciative abandonment in faith, hope, and consonance can be consistently and effectively implemented in our daily life formation. We conclude, therefore, that a foundational formative reasonableness is characteristic only of an appreciative abandonment to the processes of formation as manifestations of a threefold epiphany of the formation mystery.

It is quite possible that some kind of reasonableness may be involved in one's initial decision that one is lost and abandoned amidst the formation processes and hence that one should depreciate any attempt to depict these processes as ultimately meaningful. This initial reasonableness is due to the mysteriousness and hiddenness of the formation mystery itself. Without it, the mystery would no longer be a mystery, nor would we be free to affirm or reject it. Because it is a mystery, it cannot be known exhaustively and immediately as either meaningful or meaningless. Initially we may only be able to be agnostics in this regard. In so far as it cannot be known compellingly, the human decision either to feel embraced or abandoned by this mystery is an act of at least elementary human faith.

The apparently reasonable initial faith in the ultimate meaninglessness of formation may be affirmed by our experiences. Early in life we may painfully sense the absence of consistent faith, hope, and sympathy in regard to our own beneficial form potency. This lack of consistent affection and affirmation manifests itself in interformative relationships with significant formation agents, such as parents, siblings, and teachers. The doubt in one's own form potency that results from lack of affirmation by others may expand itself to all form potency in the universe. It may lead to a *feeling of abandonment*. The unsupportiveness of parents in regard to the form potency of the child may give rise to a distrust of the mystery of universal form potency, which parents represent to children.

The all-pervasive mood and disposition of depreciative abandonment makes the formation processes in and around us appear senseless, untrustworthy, chaotic, absurd and illusionary. Hence, depreciative abandonment, if rigidly maintained, does not foster the power of rational appraisal. Formative reason itself can only function as a rational and realistic appraisal power by the grace of an a priori appreciative acceptance of the potential meaningfulness of the formation processes that govern life and world. Primordial, appreciative, formative abandonment is thus the condition for the possibility of the effective functioning of our powers of rational formation appraisal.

Affirmation and Implementation of Appreciative Abandonment

Before discussing the implementation of appreciative abandonment, let us first look again at the attempt to implement the depreciative abandonment disposition. In principle, an initial faith decision not to put trust in enigmatic formation powers and processes is possible. It is not immediately and absolutely contradicted by reason as embedded in concrete formation experiences. Yet this initial decision to appraise all formation processes as basically meaningless and irrational leads to consequences in everyday formation that contradict the apparent rationality of this initial appraisal. This decision does not seem to offer us the same opportunities for consistent, effective living as a positive appraisal does. We soon discover that it is not really a choice between two equally effective possibilities for consonant formation. Ultimately, it becomes a choice for the possibility or impossibility of real, rational life formation itself.

We may choose to take the risk of appreciative abandonment to the mystery of formation in its foundational epiphanies and manifestations. Our choice implies that we allow this appreciative stance to illumine in faith, hope, and consonance our mind, will, heart, memory, imagination, and anticipation in daily vital-functional encounter with formation events.

When we choose appreciative abandonment we begin to experiénce the unmistakable concrete affirmation of our rational appraisal. In experiencing the effective compatibility between this positive stance and daily formation demands, we experience the rationality and rightness of our primordial appreciative appraisal. We discover for ourselves the effectiveness of appreciative abandonment to the foundational process of formation in its incarnation in the daily formation of life and world. Such affirmation does not come to us prior to this act of concrete abandonment. Neither does it come to us afterward. We learn it in formative functioning.

The rightness and reasonableness of positive abandonment can neither be proved nor experienced in advance. There is no positive formation experience nor any formation argument that precedes the first primordial act of appreciative abandonment to or depreciative abandonment by the formation mystery. If there were, this act would no longer be the primordial formation act presupposed by all subsequent acts.

The formation mystery discloses itself as real and beneficial, as consonant with reason, as meaningful in the incarnation of our appreciative decision in its favor, in our concrete everyday life of formation. Every new implementation strengthens this affirmation, in spite of the veil of mystery, the apparent inconsistency and persistent incomprehensibility, that surrounds, hides, and obscures the beneficial meaningfulness of the mystery of formation.

Relationship of Appreciative and Depreciative Appraisals

An attitude of foundational appreciation by no means excludes numerous particular depreciative appraisals. On the contrary, it depends on them for its functional-incarnational decisions and actions. We should realize that the transcendent appraisal of the ultimately beneficial meaningfulness of the mystery of formation as a whole is essentially different from the particular appraisals of formative or deformative events and situations. Depreciative appraisals of this or that aspect of formation must be made in service of this primordial appraisal of the beneficent direction of the formation mystery. It is the formation mission of humanity to disclose increasingly this ultimate intent of the mystery and to unmask personal and social conditions that interfere with its realization.

Formative appraisal made in the light of the mystery of formation rightly resists anything in self, others, society, and the world at large that diminishes, obscures, distorts, depletes, or demeans the radiance of the beneficial meaningfulness of the mystery and its epiphanous disclosures. Formative appraisal depreciates in service of appreciation anything that interferes with human faith, hope, and consonance in regard to this mystery. Appreciative appraisal makes its home in particular expressions of appreciation and in functional form directives that have been disclosed as consonant with the threefold epiphany of the formation mystery. They are elevated to enduring appreciations and directions in the core form, or heart, of life.

(While the disposition of appreciative abandonment is a most foundational one, it is by no means the only one. The second volume of this series will take up the topic of dispositions and form traditions in humanity. It will deal at length with the foundational disposition structure that supports human formation and depends on form traditions for its consonant unfolding.)

CHAPTER 16

Foundational Theory of Human Formation: An Overview

Human life, like all forms in the universe, is always in formation. The dynamism of formation is a basic assumption of the science of formation. Human life is the steadily emergent, flexible outcome of a continual formation process.

The science of formative spirituality elaborates its formation theory in close interaction with already established arts and sciences. Especially helpful were the discoveries and theories of contemporary physics. These studies gave rise to the presupposition that the formation of human life could be envisaged in terms of a field theory. Human formation is not an isolated, self-sufficient, or autarchic event. It is a dynamic participation in a formation field. In this respect it reflects the formation dynamics of the micro- and macrocosmos.

Formation is an evolutionary process characteristic of the universe known to us as a formative energy field. The cosmos is like an ocean of merging and submerging forms. These falling and rising forms may be complex or simple, physical or organic, atomic or subatomic. Each of them tends to realize, maintain, and enhance its own particular form. This form is meant to remain in consonance with its own unique ground or nature.

Human formation shares in this universal process even while transcending it. It also tends to reach a characteristic form, which is at the same time communal and unique. People realize this form in a dialogical interaction with all polar forces of their formation field.

The Foundational Dynamic of Human Formation

All forms in the cosmos emerge and attain their proper form because of their *foundational form potency*. As long as they are able to maintain that potency, their form persists and develops. This potency enables them to assimilate whatever can serve their preservation and differentiation. The moment their effectiveness to receive or give form is exhausted, these specific forms disappear again in the energy field of formation or emerge as other forms. The principle of *form-potency maintenance* in human formation is related to this discovery.

Form potency and its maintenance implies by necessity a *form direction*. Without a preformed direction, the formation process would become erratic. Its particular form would be dissolved. Form direction enables specific forms to initiate and develop directives that are congenial, that allow the formation process to stay in tune with one's foundational form direction. Yet form direction is flexible enough to adapt compatibly to changing form situations. Minerals, plants, and atomic and subatomic particles form themselves congenially and compatibly in natural consonance with their form direction. They are endowed with a built-in formation readiness.

Among the wide variety of forms in the cosmos, we find sentient, organismic ones that come equipped with instinctual form directives. These preformed directives correspond with certain form appearances in their environment. Such matching appearances provide them with a restricted formation field. This field is exclusively relevant to the survival and differentiation of these specific organisms.

Human Form Directives and Corresponding Human Formation Fields

The human life-form appears on the cosmic scene with almost no instinctual form directives. Devoid as it is of sufficient preformed directives, it has to disclose its own. In the process of this development, the human life-form emerges as distinctively human. This distinctive form of life has to stake out its own formation field. Appearances in the cosmos that are meaningful for human formation are not articulated in nature as such. The seeming chaos of the universe has to become a meaningful cosmos, a human field of formation highlighted by human symbols.

Our life-form highlights certain form appearances in the cosmos. It puts them into relief, as it were, as formationally relevant. These forms correspond with the life directives of our life-form. Subsequent networks of enhanced, compatible appearances constitute human formation fields. They make it possible for us to give form to life, humanly speaking, in accordance with our own form directives. Our formation is both a continuous and a discontinuous process of disclosure and implementation of receptive and creative form directives and their formation fields. In this process human societies develop universes of symbols pointing to traditionally shared formation fields.

Human Formation Symbols

The human life-form needs symbols to disclose and maintain its transinstinctual form directives and their corresponding formation fields. Only by means of symbols can it set them apart in human mind, heart, and imagination. Through symbols, the human life-form can also externalize form directives. Symbols may then become part of the interconscious realm. This treasure of symbols is available to all participants in a form tradition or culture.

A universe of formation symbols and their implied form directives can be interiorized by people. It begins in them a life of its own. It participates in their intraformation. Human life is inwardly formed in part by the countless experiences we can draw from that symbolic universe. We can play with these symbols imaginatively, combining and recombining them in endless new associations. We reflect on them thoughtfully. We structure and restructure them in numerous ways in their mutual relationships. We can do so with focal attention, but mostly this happens prereflectively in pre-, infra-, and transfocal conscious presence and interaction.

We may be tempted to withdraw into this inner world of symbols. This inclination may emerge at moments when the interformative world and our life situation seem to let us down or threaten to overwhelm or destroy our feeling of form potency. Such a threat to our sense of formability may be real or imaginary. When real, strategic momentary withdrawal from an overwhelming situation may be beneficial.

Cocreation of Form Directives

No other life-form on this planet has created such a rich and subtle universe of form-directive meanings. The human life-form has overlaid cosmos and history with a wealth of these meanings. These directives make up our sociohistorical formation fields. People of many generations disclosed together symbolic directives. In the light of experience, experiment, and dialogue, they appraised them as effective for the formation of human life and its expanding fields. Neither a single life-form by itself alone nor a few generations of life-forms would have been able to accomplish this. How could they amass sufficient experience and knowledge? How would it have been possible for them to develop a set of symbolic form directives, a balanced formation field, and a refined style of distinctively human formation? It takes millennia to make a contribution to the consonant formation of human life in present and future generations.

One human life or the life of a few generations is too short, too encapsulated in a restrictive set of formation experiences and sociohistorical pulsations, to design a validated consonant vision of human formation. The limits of time, energy, and environment make it impossible to disclose and test a sufficient selection of form directives. To be truly foundational and universal, they would have to be consonant with the foundational form structure, field, and dynamics of each human life.

Moreover, emerging form traditions themselves have to be constantly purified critically and creatively by many generations. Each generation must separate anew the accidental, historical accretions due to particular historical situations from the disclosure of foundational conditions. The latter must be universally applicable to all human formation. To be sure, such transcultural form directives may lie concealed within particular, less universal directives handed over by former generations. It is the task of formation scientists to free these enduring directives from their temporary encasements.

Foundational Formation Theory

Foundational formation theorists are mainly interested in directives that can be scientifically appraised as truly foundational and universal. They aim at the establishment of a theory of foundational formation on which consensus can eventually be reached among a significant number of students of this process.

The overall structure of the theory is supported by substructures or subtheories. *Ten intertwined subtheories* have been proposed. They are the subtheories of *formation sources, formation dynamics, initial form dimensions, integrational form structures, formation fields, formation mystery, form traditions, formation dispositions, social presence formation,* and *phasic formation.* Each subtheory is based on its own specific assumptions, yet it is intimately related to the assumptions of the other subtheories.

The critical and creative disclosure of such integrational principles is rooted in the structural analysis of significant numbers of relevant experiences and empirical observations. This analysis is kept in rigorous dialogue with the factual findings and theoretical insights of both form traditions and auxiliary sciences so that a theorist may be able to propose workable integrative concepts or constructs. Such hypothetical constructs should be able to unify groups of similar findings and insights. The constructs should be broad enough to categorize such findings without betraying their distinctive contribution.

Formulations should be synthetic in regard to past and present knowledge. They should also be seminal or deductive. This means that they must allow us to remain open to new or related formation insights and observations. Such hypothetical constructs can only be maintained as long as they are not conclusively proven to be ineffective. Their rejection should be the result of new disclosures of the sciences or of new intersubjectively validated experiences and observations.

Form-Potency Maintenance

Form potency and its related principle of maintenance are central in the subtheory of formation dynamics. This hypothetical construct tries to express an irreducible primary property of all forms in the universe. Form potency and implied form maintenance can be analogously predicated of every form in the cosmos. It applies also to all forms of life. Subhuman forms are initiated into the use of their specific form potencies not by form genetics *and* form tradition but by form genetics *only.* They inherit the form potencies of their species by a genetic code that preforms their instincts, affinities, propensities, and subsequent form directives. Hence, they do not have to form effective formation styles that are at the same time cultural and unique. Neither do they need form traditions built into a culture and communicated by representatives of such traditions.

Children are long in need of parents because they lack instinctual form directives. They have to be formed in an effective style of human formation. Subhuman life-forms do not need traditional form directives for consonant living. They share genetically the accumulated information obtained through trial and error during the evolution of their species. The genetic code of the human life-form, however, must be complemented by human form traditions. Together with unique personal appraisal, they give rise to a life-form that is at the same time communal and unique.

The principle of form potency extends analogously to all rising and falling forms in the universe—from atomic and subatomic particles to the human life-form. They can only be themselves as long as they maintain their form potency. The universe itself is a large energy field, an unimaginable storehouse of form potency. Out of this free-floating mystery of form potency, new forms emerge in an unending dance of emergence and submergence of forms.

The principle of form potency, with its implied principle of maintenance of, at least, the sense of one's form potency, is integrational. It enables us to synthesize a vast variety of observations and partial theories in regard to formation dynamics that have been formulated in particular formation and personality theories, in various sciences, and in form traditions. The same principle equips us to make deductions in regard to the conditions, consequences, and dynamics of human formation. Hence, we may hypothetically identify form potency as an infrastructural principle of the foundational theory of human formation.

Human Formation and Formation Field

A foundational formation theory, as we have posited throughout this book, starts out from the concept of human formation as a field. This field of formation is made up of five poles. They are the poles of *pre-, intra-, inter-,* and *extra-, or outer, situational formation* and the *world pole. Preformation* points to those organismic vital aspects of formation that initially do not fall under the appraisal power of the human life-form. *Intraformation* refers to inner formation dynamics. *Interformation* refers to the formative influences of people on one another. The *situational pole* relates human life to immediate formative situations. The *world pole* is concerned with the impact of the mediated cosmic and cultural world situation on formation. This mediation happens in and through one's immediate environment.

These poles constantly interact with one another by means of formative dynamic relationships. The theoretical outline of this formation field has to be refined and made concrete by checking it against actual formation fields as they appear in the history of human formation.

The study of such fields increases the knowledge of formation theorists. They begin to understand how these field relationships are concretely manifested; how they vary in different cultures and their underlying form traditions, in formation segments of their populations, and at various stages of human formation, and how this variation is reflected in differential formation studies and theories. These insights may enable them to disclose further the realm of *universal directives of formation*.

Such directives, if and when disclosed, may hasten the moment in which some planetary consensus may become possible in regard to at least a minimum of universally valid conditions for human formation. A foundational formation theory has the potential to gain in universal, transcultural relevance. It could enable all people to respect and foster numerous concrete variations and expressions, in different form traditions and cultures, of the same accepted essential conditions for formation. The science of formation would be able to present a basic theory that could be uniquely refined, augmented, and deepened by each form tradition in turn.

*Preformation of the Human Life-Form
and the Poles of the Formation Field*

A universal, evolutionary, unconscious process of formation is characteristic of the micro- and macrocosmos. In so far as human life shares in this cosmic, initially unconscious process, the science of formation posits the preformation of human life. This preformation provides the substratum of one's ongoing formation.

Preformation depends on two interrelated processes: organic and vital formation. *Organic formation* refers to the infraconscious, biogenetic formation of bodily cells, tissues, organs, and systems. This organic formation sets the stage for an initial structuring of vital impulse, needs, and strivings of various intensity.

Vital formation refers to the infraconscious preformation of the direction of vital impulses. These impulses emerge from the biogenetic and evolutionary preformation of the human organism. Such impulses gain their vital direction by a process of interformative exchanges with significant persons, events, and things in the earliest life situations.

Organic and vital formation in unison give rise to formative temperament. At the root of both processes, the science of formation postulates a transcendent preformation effected by the formation mystery that directs all formation in the universe.

This vital infraform does not develop in isolation from other aspects of emergent life. An *intraformative process* unfolds within the human life-form itself, hence the term intra- (within) formation. This process brings the vital infraform into forming interaction with other inner modalities of human life, such as sensing, perceiving, imagining, remembering, anticipating, appraising, deciding.

Interformation of people refers to formative processes that happen in our interaction with other persons and communities of persons. *Extra-, or outer, formation* refers to processes that result from interaction with the life situation and the wider world beyond one's immediate surroundings.

These processes of formation are usually not the object of prolonged *focal consciousness*. They remain *preconscious* most of the time. Some are even infra- or transconscious. *Infraconscious* refers to certain organismic vital processes of formation, *transconscious* to certain transcendent processes.

Structural Effects of Human Formation

The integrational structures effected by formation are respectively, the foundational, core, current, apparent, and actual forms of life. The foundational potential form of the human personality is the lasting effect of transcendent and biogenetic preformation. This foundational form is preexperiential. It is unique, like fingerprints; it tends to manifest itself gradually during one's history of formation. It concretizes itself in the emergent core form, or heart, of human life and, via this core form, in the provisional current, apparent, and actual forms. This distinction between the initially unknown and foundational life-form and other forms of life implies a distinction between preempirical and empirical life formation. The foundational embodied life-form is a preempirical basic formation structure. It has a transcendent quality, yet is embodied in one's biogenetic preformation. (In the fourth volume of this series, we will discuss the Christian belief that this foundational life-form is created in the image, or form, of God.)

Our empirical formation refers to the lifelong task of giving consonant form to the unique general direction that is contained in our initially unknown preformation. Our foundational life-form cannot be experienced directly in itself. Hence, we call it preempirical.

The empirical life-form we are called to develop is not predetermined in detail. The unknown foundational form is gradually disclosed to us. This disclosure reveals increasingly that this unknown form is only a basic indication of the overall unique direction that the unfolding of our life should take. We could compare this to a road sign telling us that our direction is, for instance, toward the city of New York. While this sign indicates our destination, it does not explain how to dress for our journey; how to interact with fellow travelers, where to rest, where to eat, or how to drive under different weather and road conditions. How we concretely travel will depend on the dialogue we maintain with the circumstances we meet on our trip. We keep in mind our basic direction but realize that our response to such circumstances will have an influence on how we will look, feel, and express ourselves when we arrive at the end of our journey. How we give form concretely to our journey and to ourselves as travelers is not contained in our awareness of the general direction our travel should take.

As any comparison, this one is imperfect. Our adventure of daily formation can be compared to a journey and the foundational life-form may be likened to a road sign. There our comparison breaks down. A road sign is a clear indication of where we are going. But the foundational life-form is preempirical. This means we do not know our unique life direction in advance. It takes a lifetime to disclose what this unknown direction is to be. We only become progressively aware of whether our ongoing formation is compatible with the successive situations in which we find ourselves. It takes a lifetime to know how congenial our journey is with the hidden foundational form that gradually begins to announce itself.

The empirical life-form develops by a kind of implicit dialogue between the foundational form and the formative communities, situations, and formative events that emerge in our formation field.

Transcendent Sources of Empirical Life Formation

Reflecting on the formation structures that lead to the emergence of the empirical life-form, we distinguish two kinds. The first is transcendent, the second incarnational. These structures give rise to the core, current, apparent, and actual empirical life-forms.

The *transcendent sources of formation* are first the *formative transcendent mind* with its powers of higher reason and of transcendent and intuitive imagination, memory, and anticipation. The transcendent mind apprehends and appraises potential formative life directives. The second transcendent formation source is the *formative transcendent will*, which decides the direction to be taken in the light of the appraisal of the transcendent mind.

Five Incarnational Sources of Empirical Life Formation

Once the will as transcendent has made its final decision, mind and will as functional come into play. The functional will, enlightened by the practical appraisal of the incarnational and formative mind, engages in the many practical decisions that have to be made in accordance with the demands of the situations in which the transcendent decision to follow a certain direction has to be concretely incarnated.

We speak of incarnational or functional sources because they assist the implementation of transcendent ideals in daily life. The incarnational sources are functional formative intelligence, will, memory, imagination, and anticipation. *Functional formative intelligence* is the potency to apprehend and appraise the concrete ends and means and the rational logic of actual or possible projects of life. *Functional formative will* concretely decides on and executes this apprehension and appraisal. It sustains our perseverance in this execution. *Functional formative memory* enables us to remember concrete past events and our ways of dealing with them as formative or deformative in similar situations. We recall how past happenings influenced us and how we handled them and what concrete direction they seemed to indicate. As such, these memories of formation offer necessary information to our functional intelligence when we are engaged in the appraisal of how to implement our transcendent life directives. Functional formative remembering is accompanied and supported by *formative imagination*. As the companion of memory, it presents the functionally appraising intelligence with concrete pictures and symbols that put us in the midst of concrete life situations. A final source of incarnational insight is the power of *functional formative anticipation* of the concrete future of our life. The incarnational appraisal of the functional intelligence sustained by the formative will is facilitated by the power of concrete anticipation of the situation in which we hope to implement our transcendent direction. This lively anticipation is facilitated in turn by our power of functional formative imagination. Imagination as the companion of anticipation makes available to the appraising mind and deciding will the potential concrete life situation in which we have to realize the transcendent life direction we have chosen.

Core Form of the Empirical Life Formation

The result of the formative operation of transcendent and incarnational formation sources is the progressive formation of the integrational core, current, apparent, and actual forms of life that are congenial with the foundational life-form and compatible with the situations in which we have to express the basic direction of this form in so far as it is disclosed to us.

The core form of life is often called the heart. The heart symbolizes the global and relatively lasting directives of our life that are no longer mere conceptions but convictions. They give form to our current, apparent, and actual ways of interacting with people, events, and things. We call them global because they represent basic convictions. These have to be translated in special formative acts. Such acts are meant to express global convictions in particular current circumstances. For example, the heart of a faithful and dedicated wife is marked by a lasting disposition of love for her husband. This global love direction that has given form to her heart has to be expressed in different concrete ways. Such current expressions should be in accordance with the circumstances of their life together. For instance, the expression of this global love of the heart will differ from the exciting form of the honeymoon period to the more sober form of the mid-life crisis both may later experience.

The core form is thus the relatively enduring ground form of one's empirical life. It is formed mainly during the period between birth and early adulthood. In later life, it is not often changed fundamentally. More often than not, the core form may be modulated in many ways. This modulation is due to the various current, apparent, and actual forms life assumes during one's formation history.

Many form traditions represent the core form by the image of the heart. This metaphor points to certain properties of the core form. The heart signifies the fact that the core form functions, among other ways, as an integrative center of global formative affects. As such, the core form gives a unique vibrancy and color to the personality when it tries to express concretely the foundational form with which it is endowed by biogenetic and transcendent preformation. In the metaphorical sense, the heart is the more or less harmonious, sensible, and responsible core of affective dispositions directing one's life formation.

The core form, or heart, concretizes in its palpable movement the tendencies of the foundational life-form as disclosed, understood, or misunderstood at any given moment of one's formation history. The core form, or heart, in turn further concretizes its forming tendencies in the more specified formative motions of the current and apparent forms of the emergent life-form. Ideally, our core form functions as the guardian of the consonance between the current and apparent aspects of life and the foundational form, which is the biogenetically incarnated transcendent ground of our life.

The Core Form and the Fourfold Potency Structure of Human Life

The formation theory relates the heart, or core form, to the original form potency structure of human life. Our core form basically structures itself in accordance with the fourfold initial differentiations or dimensions of human life as sociohistorical, vital, functional, and transcendent. The heart as integrational form structure integrates these original form differentiations. It actualizes them in its structure in basic formative proclivities corresponding to each of these human formation potentials.

The core form of life is thus an integrating, responsible, and sensible structure of sociohistorical pulsations, vital impulses, functional ambitions, and transcendent aspirations. All formative affects of the heart are marked by a specified yet global moving towards, away from, against, or with. In other words, they are marked by hope, longing, desire, (moving toward); withdrawal, beneficial recollection, fear, suspicion, rejection, resistance (moving away from); firmness, fortitude, courage, anger, hate, rebellion, protest (moving against); fusion, servility, sympathy, compassion, mercy, love, acceptance, union, benediction (moving with).

Such global formative affects of the heart tend to concretize themselves in one's current life as lived here and now in one's everyday world. These global tendencies coform the affective modality of one's current, apparent and actual everyday life. This is a coformation in so far as the affective modality is modulated by the more refined tendencies of the current, apparent and actual structures of our emergent life-form.

Current and Apparent Life-Forms

Current and apparent forms of human life can be seen as the bridges between the core form and the inter- and outer dimensions of the formation fields in which the human life-form unfolds. These forms are subservient to the core form in two ways. First, they concretize the basic inclinations of the heart into everyday life as lived here and now within one's concrete formation field. Second, the current and apparent forms of life serve the heart indirectly. They provide our functional and transcendent appraisal powers with concrete information from the inter- and outer poles of our formation field.

This information can influence not only our appraisal power but also the subsequent formative powers of option and execution of certain form directives. Such information is the result of situational interaction of the human life-form with its formation field. Information thus gained may point to the possibility of enriching and deepening modulations of the basic inclinations of the heart. In some instances it may even suggest a basic change of heart.

The appraisal and acceptance of current formative information may lead also to a new disclosure of the unique, biogenetically incarnated ground form of our life. This may effect also a better understanding of our organismic-vital infraform and its formative inclinations.

Current and Apparent Life-Forms and the Formation Field

The current and apparent life-forms are necessary integral constituents of our life as a whole. This necessity flows from the field character of human formation. The four initial dimensions of human life-form—sociohistorical, vital, functional, and transcendent—have to be actualized within the formation field. Such actualization happens in a basic integrative way in the core of our life. In this core, they are actualized only as specific global directions. They would remain latent in their generality and without distinct and tangible influence were they not evoked in and through concrete actualizations in everyday endeavors.

Such evocation by the inter- and outer poles of the formation field takes place by means of current, apparent, and actual interactions with people, situations, and the larger world as they are made meaningfully available to human formation via one's concrete formation field. These interactions not only give form to one's current, apparent, and actual living, they also present new possibilities for the inner formation of one's core form, or heart.

Descriptive Definition of Current and Apparent Life-Forms

The formation theory describes the current form as the provisional integrational form our life assumes in reaction and response to each new disclosure of the unique transcendent and biogenetic potential of the person. In response to such disclosures, the current form may effect some modulation of the core form itself. In other words, each current life-form is also an opportunity for a more refined disclosure of the uniqueness of one's formation potential.

In this light, it is possible to describe the apparent form of life. It is the integrational manifest form life assumes in reaction and response to real or imagined expectations of others. Part of one's current life situation implies the need to adapt in some measure to the expectations of one's culture, family, colleagues, or neighbors, even if this adaptive behavior does not express the basic preferences of what one experiences to be the core of one's life.

This is not to say that the manifest aspect of our everyday life is necessarily dissonant with our core form. While adaptative, this does not have to be at odds with the core. We can respect and wisely accommodate the expectations of others without betraying our convictions. It is possible to allow our heart to shine through wisely and selectively in these accommodations. The apparent life-form would only be dissonant and deformative if it were dictated by the merely imagined expectations of others, or if it were in absolute contradiction to our deeper integrational form structures, or if it were willfully deceptive and manipulative.

The heart, as we have seen, plays a main role in the formation of the core form of life. The life of the senses seems to function importantly in the formation of the current life-form. What a current situation concretely looks like is initially perceived by our inner and outer senses. They present this information to the feeling heart, the appraising mind, and the deciding will. Such information enables us to appraise and decide how the global dispositions our of our heart should be adapted to the concrete nuances of our current life situation. We are called to implement in them the transcendent directives that have become global dispositions and convictions of our heart. To be sure, not all directions given to the current formation of life are translations of the global dispositions of the heart. Certain current directions of life flow directly from the appraising mind and deciding will, even if their concepts have not yet become heartfelt, lasting convictions.

The current life-form represents the compatibility of our formation. It helps us to make formation not only congenial with the foundational life-form, but also compatible with the current demands implied in the concrete situation that invite our realistic adaptation.

Another element of the situation that should be taken into account is the fact that any human situation and all the people involved in it manifest flaws and frailties. This means in practice that we will often be faced with faltering situations and with people who are not only limited and irresolute, but vulnerable. It is not enough to respond to the realistic and rational aspects of the current life situation; we must also respond to the aspects of form impotence and faintheartedness that mar the human condition. Awareness of this vulnerability compels us to go beyond forms of expression that are merely functional, rational, and reasonable. Compassion for the failings and illusions of our own life formation and that of others inspires a certain caution and concern with the way in which we express ourselves and execute our projects.

No matter how rational and functional our current feelings may be, we begin to realize that we cannot let them appear in our expressions without taking into account how they affect our own and others' formation in its vulnerability. This insight signifies the birth of a consonant apparent life-form, one that is nourished by compassion and yet does not deny what we currently feel. It functions as a screen, that is, it lets shine forth only what is desirable, wise, and compassionate in any specific interaction with people and situations. The apparent life-form can also be dissonant. It can be used for deception and manipulation in service of the projects of the autarchic pride-form of our life.

Periodical Permanence of Current and Apparent Life Formation

Formation theory describes the integrational structures that are the current and apparent forms of life as *periodically* permanent. As such, they are distinguished from the relatively lasting empirical core form.

The structures of the current life-form are constituted by consistent reactions and responses of people to the characteristic manifestations of inter- and outer poles of their *formation field* during a certain prolonged period of their formation history. This relative consistency gives rise to a structure of appraisals, decisions, attitudes, strivings, motivations, and perceptions that are compatible with the current life situation of a person. This formation structure, both as latent and manifest or as apparent, is adaptive. Current formation adapts the four original dimensions of our formation potential, and their subsequent chosen core directions in the heart, to the practical, flexible directives that are suggested by the period of life and its characteristic situations in which we find ourselves.

The current and apparent forms enable us to make our unique life congruent and compatible with the here and now situation. At the same time our current life-form helps us to keep our public life congenial with its foundational preformation. It also attunes this public expression to the affects of our heart. Hence, any current latent or manifest form of personality can help us to disclose and concretize in our personal life specific potential aspects of our unique biogenetic and transcendent preformation. If consonant, it does so in ways that are compatible with and effective in the totality of our present formation field.

Actual Life-Form

In the course of this book we distinguished the initial differentiations of the human life-form. We called them form dimensions. They are the initial actualizations of corresponding basic form potentials that are inherent in our form of life. We identified them as the sociohistorical, vital, functional and transcendent dimensions. They are always operative in our formation. In childhood and adolescence these dimensions can be more easily observed as distinct in their initial emergence and structure. Even then they soon begin to appear as coordinated with one another in the three integrational form structures we have just discussed, namely, the core, current and apparent integrational forms of life.

These three integrational form structures provide an initial integration of our four original form dimensions. They integrate these dimensions in service of our congenial, compatible and apparent presence in our formation field. This initial integration is complemented by an "intermediate integration." It gives rise to our actual life-form. We call this integration intermediate because it is only an approximation of full integration. Full integration would mean full consonance of our life-form and all poles of its formation field with the formation mystery substantially at its center.

The actual life-form integrates both our historical, vital, functional and transcendent dimensions and the core, current and apparent integrational form structures that provided these dimensions with an initial integration. The *actual life-form* integrates all of them selectively in service of an actual integrated form of life.

Core, current and apparent life-forms integrate our form dimensions in an initial basic way. This integration of our dimensional *form potencies* provides us with an appropriate, general response-readiness in our typical formation field. These three integrational form structures attune us basically to the life situations we are lastingly, currently and apparently living. In concrete everyday life, however, we are faced with events, people and things that demand a holistic approach which integrates relevant responses contained in each one of these three integrational forms of life. Our *actual life-form* is a flexible integration of our relevant lasting core convictions, of our usual current reactions and responses to our present day situations, and of the ways we have disposed ourselves to appear to others. Hence our actual life-form not only has to select what is appropriate from the three initial integrational form structures. It must add to this its own inventive adaptations in order to deal effectively and creatively with each new emergence. Our actual life-form thus both draws upon and transcends our usual core, current and apparent life-forms and their dispositions.

Gradually our actual life-form begins to stabilize itself in its own right. It begins to manifest a certain consistency in its selective integrative and adaptive endeavors. It influences and modulates in turn the three integrational structures it draws upon. The more we mature in the life of the spirit, the more our actual life-form begins to approximate full integration or consonance. It is a consonance with our transcendent and biogenetic preformation. It is also consonance with the formation mystery itself substantially united with our foundational life form. This substantial union becomes increasingly a union of likeness of our actual empirical life-form with the formation mystery at the root of our being.

Descriptive Definition of the Four Life-Form Dimensions

At this juncture it may be helpful briefly to describe again the four basic dimensions and corresponding potentials, of the human life-form. They are the sociohistorical, vital, functional, and transcendent dimensions of human formation. These are the actualizations of similar basic form potentials inherent in the human form of life.

The sociohistorical form potential refers to the potency and tendency of our life to be formed by and to give form to the movements, trends, feelings, ideals, appraisals, and pressures—*the pulsations*—in our sociohistorical environment. This is the receptive and creative historical formation potential of human life.

The vital form potential refers to the potency and tendency of human life to be formed by and to give form to *impulses* emerging from our biogenetic vital life. This dimension represents the receptive and creative vital formation potential of human life.

The functional form potential is the potency and tendency of human life to be formed by and to give form to *ambitions* emerging from our functioning in life situation and world. This is the receptive and creative functional formation potential of human life.

Finally, the transcendent form potential refers to the potency and tendency of human life to be formed by and to give form to *aspirations* and *inspirations* emerging from the transcendent inclination of human life.

These dimensions of foundational formation influence the structure of the core form as well as that of the current latent or apparent form.

Articulations of the Functional Dimension of Human Formation

All four dimensions of formation draw forth specific articulations. In this overview, we will restrict ourselves to those of the functional dimension. This dimension serves as the link between the vital and transcendent dimensions of human life. It is a bridge between the impulses of the vital dimension and the aspirations and inspirations of the transcendent dimension, on the one side, and the everyday life situation, on the other. The functional dimension can translate these impulses, aspirations and inspirations into workable, concrete ambitions that can be realized in relation to the other poles of the formation field.

The functional dimension articulates itself in an individual, technical, social, and functional-aesthetic presence to its formation field.

The deliberate individual character of formative functioning completes in praxis its sociohistorical, vital, functional, and transcendent modes of presence in their uniqueness.

Technical articulation refers to the formation and integration of mental, sensory, and manual skills and their extensions in logical and scientific systems, in tools, machines, and organizations as invented, fostered, or assimilated by a human life-form. This formation and use of the logical mind and manual dexterity distinguishes the functional dimension from the sociohistorical, vital, and transcendent dimensions.

Social articulation refers to the personal formation of social skills, which enable the human life-form to interact effectively and smoothly with others, to establish itself in the sociohistorical networks of its formation field. It facilitates also the realization of one's functional ambitions in so far as one's accomplishments depends on effective social interformative interactions.

Functional-aesthetic articulation refers to the formation and utilization of aesthetic skill, feeling, and sensitivity. It enables one to refine and to make attractive, appealing, and elegant one's functional style of striving and its expressions. The formation theory distinguishes functional aesthetics from transcendent aesthetics, the latter being one of the articulations of the transcendent dimension of the life-form.

Dimensions of Formative Consciousness

In formation theory, we distinguish five dimensions of formative human consciousness in relation to life formation. These are *focal, pre-, inter-, infra-,* and *transconsciousness.*

Focal, or focused, consciousness comprehends the fully aware concentrated dispositions and acts of attentiveness of a human life form.

Typical preconscious patterns of nonfocal, peripheral attention influence in some measure the perceptions and rational processes that mark the direction of this focal awareness and attention. This preconscious dimension of the life-form is marked by a continuous interplay of dynamic interests that are alive in one's formation. These interests are partly due to peripheral daily perceptions and to residues of focal attention, both of which are characteristic of this specific life-form.

Another formative influence on all dimensions of consciousness is interconsciousness. It is the sociohistorical consciousness, externalized in the customs, symbols, myths, form traditions, arts, and writings of a culture, subculture, or family. The theory calls it interconsciousness because all participants in the same sociohistorical formation field can share in some way in this externalization of consciousness.

Other influences entering the preconscious dimension of the human life-form are those of the infraconscious. These are the vital, functional, individual, and sociohistorical pulsations, impulses, and ambitions that the person does not know or acknowledge focally or preconsciously as realistic points of departure for further formation.

The transconscious dimension contains the aspirations and inspirations typical of a particular life-form. Human life may be formed in such a way that it denies these aspirations and inspirations to its focal consciousness. A person may refuse to own them as actually forming influences, even on the preconscious level. Nonetheless, like the unknown or unacknowledged tendencies of the infraconscious dimensions, they may at times penetrate the porous barriers that separate the preconscious dimension from the infra- and transconscious dimensions that surround it. Once they penetrate this barrier, they will interact with all the other dynamic forces that are constantly in fleeting interaction with one another within the field of preconscious energy. This preconscious dimension surrounds the dimension of focal consciousness at all times.

In relation to these dimensions of consciousness, we may introduce the idea of *formation conscientization*. This is the act of bringing to focal awareness at appropriate times the directives that actually in some measure give form to one's life, be it on a pre-, inter-, infra-, or transconscious level.

Phasic Formation

Another characteristic affecting all structures and dimensions of one's empirical life formation is that of formation phases. Human formation is marked by the necessity to progress through various discontinuous phases of formation. Each phase may benefit the emergence or the enrichment of one or a few specific dimensions and articulations of the formation structures mentioned previously. The successive accentuation of each dimension affects at least indirectly the whole formation structure. This structure as a whole may be temporarily out of balance in each formation phase, but form potency tends to restore the equilibrium as it tries to integrate the new or more richly developed dimension. This integration leads to a deepened and enriched synthesis of the empirical life-form.

The phasic character of human formation gives rise to moments of transition from one periodic life-form to another. Such periods may evoke a transcendence crisis. This crisis occurs when one leaves behind a former periodic form of life and ventures out into a new, unfamiliar, and unknown form. Such a periodic form is a special type of current life-form. The emergence of this periodic current form is due to the phasic, discontinuous progress of human formation. Other types of current life-forms are the result of other changes in one's formation field. These changes are not necessarily linked with formative phasic events in one's life.

The science of formation uses the term *phasic formation* only when the formation events involved are related, at least implicitly, to some vital biological change in the forming organism. Otherwise it refers to the process of formative transcendence, which applies both to phasic and other decisive changes.

Formative Transcendence Process

The process of formative trancendence is one of going beyond a current life-form. The form left behind has been congenial and compatible in a life period or life situation that is now passing. This transition implies mourning for what was and searching for a partially or totally new mode of presence. This renewal should be compatible with the changed life period or situation. At the same time, it should remain faithful to the emergent uniqueness of the person.

The process of transcendence or formative transition often evokes a trancendence crisis, an experience of danger and opportunity. A threat to one's sense of form potency may be felt. This might be a consequence of the feeling of a structural weakening of a familiar, trusted life-form. The familiar current form no longer supports one's feeling of form potency; it no longer upholds one's effective and sure coping with newly emerging life situations. Doubt of one's potency may be deepened by one's uncertainty about appropriate directives for a new, more effective mode of life. This doubt may lead to an anxious search for a new style of presence that is more compatible with the changing life period or situation and more congenial with the preformed roots of one's life as they increasingly manifest themselves.

The transcendence crisis may be solved in a congenial and compatible way. The solution is congenial if one is able to surpass the crisis effectively without the betrayal of one's foundational life-form. One can modulate and integrate one's foundational life-form, and its congenial expressions, in one's core form, in one's past current and apparent forms, and in the sociohistorical, vital, and functional determinants of one's life. This might be achieved in such a fashion that the new integration fosters increasing disclosure and realization of one's unique life call, which is partly hidden in preforming influences. The solution of the transcendence crisis is compatible when it insures momentarily the best possible integration of the new current life-form with the relevant form directives of one's present life situation and the people, events, and things that coform it.

Form Directives

Human life is guided and maintained in its emergence by form directives. Such directives are not invented or developed in isolation from the formation field as a whole. This field, insofar as it is shared with others, is permeated by form traditions. People live by such traditions consciously or preconsciously. A human formation directive can be affirmed by one's emergent life. In that case, the directive is raised to focal consciousness and opted for both rationally and transrationally. If it was already lived beforehand preconsciously, it is now ratified in a focally conscious way. Such personal affirmation is based on insightful appraisal of one's experiences.

The structure of one's emergent life may imply a free commitment to one or more form traditions available in one's formation field. In that case, life experiences are usually appraised in the light of such form traditions. The more the life-form develops rational and intuitive astuteness, the more it raises to focal consciousness the foundations of such form traditions and their accidental accretions, distinguishing them increasingly from one another. After the process of appraisal and subsequent affirmation, the affirmed direction is allowed to sink back into the preconscious dimension of one's life, where it remains operative until the life situation calls for its reappraisal.

Formation theory points to the availability of sedimented sociohistorical form directives for human life formation. These are directives for possible formation available in the formation field in its inter- and outer dimension. Such directives are contained in the language, customs, form traditions, expressions, myths, symbols, and monuments of the sociohistorical situations in which human life emerges and unfolds. As an integral part of one's formation field, these cultural factors may influence, at least preconsciously, the direction of the formation of one's life. In formation theory, we distinguish the preconscious sharing of such sociohistorical formation models from the participation in the same models that is ratified after focal-conscious appraisal. In the latter case, these directives may be flexibly and freely assimilated within the uniquely emergent form of human life.

The Flow of Formation

The free unfolding of human life depends on the unhindered flow of its formation energy. Under the impact of certain sociohistorical pulsations that happen to be alien to the unique preformation of a person, one may form a counterfeit form structure that is uncongenial. This counterfeit form of life is fostered by the pride-form, which tends to bind the formation power and to turn it into a *power of erratic deformation*. Deformation manifests itself in a concentration or imprisonment of formation powers and energies that become fixated in a proudly absolutized core or in a current or apparent life-form. Our actual life-form will be similarly affected by such fixations.

This encapsulation of the foundational form energy in any aspect of life leads to exaltation, insubordination, and isolation of a partial, fixated formation manifestation. It blocks the free flow of ongoing formation. It distorts and hampers spontaneous, creative functioning in everyday life. Encapsulation can give rise to emotional hypertension that may adversely affect the organismic ground of wholesome life.

The free flow of spontaneous formation may be repeatedly lost, especially in the beginning of one's formation history. This loss is due to continual reassertion of the exalting, greedy, grasping, clinging, manipulating, absolutizing, and fixating counterform of one's life as alienated. The dissonant, quasi-foundational prideform of life is always at war with the consonant foundational lifeform within us.

Formation Movements in Human Life

The foundational unique preformation, in which one's congenial life-form is rooted, animates and energizes one's consonant formation action. It does so by an ongoing flow of formative movements. The primary movement of consonant personality formation is identified with the foundational, transcendent, biogenetically incarnated life-form itself as formative. The foundational movements of life formation mediate the animating power of the foundational life-form on the spiritual, functional, vital, expressive, life-situational, and world levels of human presence.

Before discussing these foundational form movements, it is important to distinguish them from other aspects of the life-form expressed in other constructs of the theory. The foundational formation movements of our life are preempirical expressions of the formative life force. They stimulate human life to form both incidental and enduring forms of life. The enduring basic forms of human life, as we saw earlier, are the *core, current, apparent, and actual forms* and their structural dimensions and articulations.

The foundational formation movements of life should not be confused with the *four formation potentials* (sociohistorical, vital, functional, and transcendent). These potentials are the basic prefigurations of the directions and corresponding predispositions that human formation will assume once it is animated and energized by the flow of the foundational formation movements.

The first formation movement is called foundational in so far as it founds and directs the form expressions on various levels of human life. This movement proceeds from the unique foundational life-form at the root of congenial formation. This initial movement is preempirical. In order to shape the empirical life-forms, it needs the mediation of the human spirit.

The human spirit refers to mind and will as illuminated by the *transcendent dimension of consciousness*. This spirit must form itself in congeniality with one's foundational life-form and in compatibility with the life situations that help translate the seemingly chaotic world into a concrete formation field. The spirit then becomes increasingly able to give a directive impetus to the distinctively human expression of life on the other form levels.

The functional form of life develops when one begins to realize concretely one's foundational life-form under the impetus of the human spirit. This realization happens through interformative encounters with the persons, events, and things of everyday life. It comprises all modes of consciousness and all experiences, dynamics and conditions related in any way to human functioning. Sociohistorical pulsations, vital impulses, and funtional ambitions become increasingly integrated with transcendent aspirations and inspirations.

The vital, or bodily, form is inwardly and outwardly affected by human formation. Congeniality and compatibility of ongoing formation will lead to a more relaxed flow of organismic powers and energies. It will also manifest itself in the formative movements and expressions of the body. The gentle yet firm style resulting from such formation will make the bodily form more gracious and less subject to symptoms of stress and overexertion.

The verbal and nonverbal expression form of the congenial life corresponds to the spiritual, functional, and vital form if the latter are congenial to the foundational form and compatible with the consonant communities and situations in which human life participates within its formation field. The more the ongoing formation of life is congenial and compatible, the more its expression form will become gracious, peaceful, and joyful. It will manifest openness and an inner relaxed attentiveness. Facial expression, language, gesture, movement, and bearing will become relaxed yet animated manifestations of our uniquely human, congenial life in its playful interaction with all the polarities of the formation field.

The situation form, too, will be affected by one's unique congenial formation history. If feasible, the life-form will express itself in its surroundings. The way in which people arrange and organize their home, work, and recreational environments, as well as their interformative actions with others, will increasingly carry the signature of their uniqueness.

Finally, the physical and human world, as mediated to people via their living situations, will be affected by each human person.

For persons form themselves and their surroundings within their own formation field in a world formation task that spans the generations.

Formation and Situation

The foundational *polarity paradigm* of the science of formation is constituted not only by the poles of pre-, intra-, and outer formation but also by *situational formation*. (See Polarity Chart, Appendix One.) Life situations exert an essential influence on one's giving and receiving of formation. The science of formation calls these formation situations, in view of the potential form directives they imply for human life. Like the other formation poles, this one too is rooted in the sociohistorical dimension of the life-form.

The term formation situation refers to the fact that the personal and communal formation of each human life is coformed by external sociohistorical conditions that manifest a certain connection in space and time. They imply potential form directives for human unfolding. Such situational directives may facilitate or hinder one's consonant formation. Situational formation conditions are brought about by familial, communal, cultural, educational, and traditional symbols and by other factors in one's environment, including technological, industrial, economic, and sociopolitical events that are formationally relevant.

We should realize that situational formation also affects inner formation, or *intraformation*. Some situational conditions become interiorized and hence play a significant role in the intraformative history of the person. Interiorized situational directives shape to some extent one's appraisal dispositions, appraisals, form directives, and form decisions. They affect also the corresponding dispositions of both the transcendent-intuitive and the incarnational powers of memory, imagination, and anticipation.

In the course of one's formation history, interiorized form directives may be uniquely modulated by personal assimilation. Fully personalized formation dynamics can no longer be adequately categorized under the situational pole; from now on they fall mainly under the intraformative pole for their further unfolding. There is thus a transitional flow from the process of situational formation to that of its interiorization and congenial assimilation.

Situational Formation Transfer

One of the most enlightening areas of research in foundational formation involves the relation between outer and interiorized situational form directives in the formation history of populations, communities, and individuals. One interesting insight gained from such research is that of *situational formation transfer*. Such transfer refers to the fact that intraformative dispositions and directives resulting from formation situations tend to be transferred to other situations. Some analogous situations are formed or reformed in the image of the original influential situation.

For example, excessive functionalistic intraformative dispositions may have been engendered by one's daily participation over many years in functional administrative situations. Such intraformative situational dispositions may affect not only one's interiority and the situation concerned. They may also begin to affect the formation style of the family, community, recreational, or learning situations that one is coforming with others. Similarly, one's coforming influence on the improvement of world conditions may be colored by this functionalistic disposition. However, this disposition was initially the interiorized effect of a specific functionalistic life situation to which one was exposed for many years.

We should realize that formation situations cannot be reduced to an enumeration of the various apparent surface aspects that make up a life situation. Far deeper forming powers are operative in most formative situations. Some of them are form traditions, contemporary pulsations, and popular appraisals and directives. These are embedded, as it were, in various formation situations. People are situated not only in webs of formative customs but also within contemporary structures of formation appraisals, directives, and dispositions. Thus contemporary formation appraisals and dispositions are a situational given. They provide data for formation research and reflection. They are one of the empirical presuppositions of research in this field.

Formation Situation as a Point of Departure

Another presupposition of the science of formation is that no situation can determine irrevocably the formation of people in their appraisals, form directives, dispositions, imaginations, memories, and anticipations. The spiritual nature of human life enables it to transcend sociohistorical situatedness during its history of formation. The formation situation is a *point of departure for formation*. One has to accept it as such. It is only a starting point; it does not determine in detail where the mystery of formation may lead when one is open to the possibility of ever new current forms of life that prove to be increasingly congenial with one's foundational life-form. Neither does it exclude a life of dull determination if one prefers uncritical conformity to congenial compatibility in regard to the formation situations one encounters on life's journey.

One must transcend the tyranny of the formation situation. Even when one has chosen or ratified a form tradition as one's key situation in life, one must increasingly distinguish between its foundational constituents and its accidental accretions. Such appraisal liberates personal formation from the despotism of passing accidental form directives that may be hailed as essential by obsessive-compulsive or hysterical personalities.

Adaptive Flexibility of Foundationals

Another type of liberating appraisal concerns the potential flexibility in adaptation of the foundations of one's chosen form tradition. How well and how far can they be attuned to one's inward congeniality, to compatibility with one's various life situations and with the world, to compassion with others? This appraisal serves a wise, effective personalization of foundational directives. It may save one's originality without betraying the central meaning of the tradition. To be sure, the power of such appraisal differs among people. The probabilities of transcendence of formation situations are different in different persons.

The formation situations in which people find themselves provide them potentially with form directives for life. The science of formation should try, therefore, to clarify the foundational formative meanings of such situations. It must help people to refine their sensitivity to what these situations may communicate. Beyond this proximate clarification, the science leaves people on their own, allowing formation situations themselves to be their personal guide.

The science of formation assists people also in the unmasking of exalted, idolizing appraisals of a situation. Such uncritical exaltation limits their openness for the formative message of a situation.

Such exaltation is usually due to the pride-form of life. The science helps people transcend standardized meanings of formative situations imposed by historical pulsations that were not critically and creatively appraised. It counteracts the tendency to fit the situation into one's own schemes and projects instead of allowing the truth of the situation itself to direct one regardless of self-centered inclinations and individual or shared stereotypes.

Key Formation Situations

The human life-form is always situated. From conception on, people are located somewhere in time and space. They are inserted formatively in human history. Basic formation situations, such as one's family, formation segment of the population, and form tradition, lastingly affect one's life formation. Such situations may permeate life from the beginning. They infiltrate one's structure of form directives. In the science we refer to them sometimes as key formation situations, meaning that they offer us a key to the formation history of people. Initial formation is marked by the fact that certain key situations almost totally determine at that time of life one's appraisal and implementation of form directives.

Ongoing formation is in part a critical and creative lifelong dialogue with the key situations of one's initial formation. This dialogue is usually implicit and preconscious. It plays an important role in ongoing formation. For such historical key situations are implicit in one's form tradition, which underlies the cultural or subcultural situation into which one is born.

Ongoing formation should enable people within the limits of their congenial possibilities, to dwell personally on the foundational experiences that gave rise to the form tradition that became theirs in initial formation. They may either ratify or contest the foundations of their form tradition. When ratified, they may increasingly distinguish between these foundations and accidental accretions and determine what power, if any, the latter should exercise in their ongoing formation.

Two Types of Formation Situations

After these considerations, it might be easier to clarify the distinctions made by the science of formation in regard to the various types of formation situations. The science distinguishes basically between two main types of formation situations: current and persistent.

Current formation situations are those people face in various immediate environments. Their daily life currently forms itself within such situations while they themselves also give form to the situations. Such situations can be distinguished further as communal, occupational, and socioperiodical formation situations.

Persistent situations are the real or symbolic, at least partially interiorized life situations that form one's life more lastingly. Such persistent situations can be distinguished further as the initial sociofoundational formation by nation and culture; the initial familial formation; the initial, implicit or explicit, syncretic or monolithic form tradition, and the initial formation segment of the population to which one belongs.

Such key formation situations initially became part of one's life-form mainly through situational osmosis. The same cannot be said of other key situations that later influence one's life formation in a relatively lasting fashion. The science of formation distinguishes them as the single, marital, or communal life-form one chooses; the formative professional and educational life-form that is one's by choice and self-exertion; the style of one's life-form that has been freely developed, and the personally ratified or newly adopted sociohistorical cultures or subcultures, form traditions, and formation segments.

Five Types of Formative Responses to Formation Situations

The science of formation distinguishes between the kinds of formative responses that can be given to various formation situations. Five main types of responses are identified: *blind identification, ratification, contestation, consonant ratification-contestation,* and *consonance.*

The reaction or response of blind identification with a formation situation without critical and creative appraisal may be due to anxiety, indifference, apathy, immaturity, or other negative causes.

The ratification of a past or present formation situation has as its object the foundational and accretional constituents of the situation. A discerning ratification may extend itself to all of these elements or only to those that are appraised as both objectively deserving ratification and subjectively consonant with the ratifying person. This subjective consonance, its quality and intensity, can be experienced on various levels of formative consciousness.

Contestation is a reaction or response extending itself to the same foundational and accretional elements. Instead of ratifying them, it contests their directive value for one's life partially or totally. Many people spend their whole life, for example, in the contestation of their initial formation, form tradition, or formation segment. The contestation response, like that of ratification, can be experienced on various levels of formative consciousness and can be in consonance or dissonance with what one is foundationally meant to be.

The consonant contestation-ratification response seems most effective from the viewpoint of wholesome life formation. It transcends the stultification of blind identification. It escapes a life of form ratification that may not be sufficiently critical in its formation appraisal. It does not get bogged down negatively in a life of mere contestation. Rather it critically and creatively contests in its ongoing process of appraisal all current and persistent formation situations. It firmly and gently ratifies what seems consonant with objective form directives, congenial with one's foundational lifeform, compatible with the foundationally and accretionally consonant elements of the life situation, and compassionate with oneself and with those with whom one must live the life of interformation.

Finally, the gift of a full response of peace-filled, accomplished consonance, beyond any contestation and ratification, may be ours only at privileged peak moments of life or at its peaceful end.

The Secondary Foundational Life-Form

The preempirical foundation life-form should be expressed, via the spirit and its subordinated form potencies, in one's empirical life and world. Consonant and dissonant attempts at such expression progressively result in a basic empirical life-form.

Unlike the primordial foundational life-form, this one is in principle open to experience and change; it can be influenced by *appraisal, decision, reformation,* and *transformation.*

This secondary form of life "founds" in an empirical fashion our concrete formation of life and world. Hence, it can be appropriately called a foundational life-form. The primordial, preempirical foundational life-form should thus be complemented by a secondary, empirical foundational life-form. This secondary foundation of our life formation may be wholly or partially consonant or dissonant with the primary foundation.

This secondary foundation is a flexible constellation of dynamically interacting form dispositions. These dispositions formatively qualify, refine, and define the form potencies of all structures, dimensions, and articulations of the empirical life-form. Their potencies receive and give form within the formation field, usually not directly but through the form dispositions inherent in or acquired by the structures of the empirical life-form. The formation of such dispositions in turn is influenced by the form traditions developed by humanity during its formation history.

(Our secondary foundational life-form of dispositions, and their dependence on form traditions, is basic to our actual life formation. The second volume in this series will focus on the topic of dispositions and traditions.)

APPENDIX ONE

The Position of the Science of Formation within a Classification of the Sciences

Before introducing our classification of the sciences, we should clarify the distinction between the science of foundational formation and its possible complementary articulation efforts in various form traditions. The two efforts are intimately related but not identical. In this series, we are not only concerned with this science itself but also with complementing its research by articulation research, especially in terms of the Christian form tradition.

The science of formation is also called the science of foundational formative spirituality. The reason for the latter title is based on the central presupposition of this science: human formation should be based on what is distinctively human. This distinctive mark is to be found in the transcendent nature of our existence.

Accordingly, formative spirituality is the art and discipline of receiving distinctively human formation and of humanly giving form to life and world. It is the art of penetration by the spirit of all powers, dimensions, articulations, awareness states, and phases of human life and its corresponding formation fields. This process and its conditions must be researched and verified scientifically or intersubjectively.

For now, let us turn to the position of this science within a classification of contemporary sciences. Such classification serves their distinct organization and functioning in any institute of higher learning. It protects us against an imposition by experts trained in other fields of inquiry seemingly similar to this science, at least for uninformed outsiders.

Accurate classification clarifies and protects the special character of various groups of sciences. It also guards against a distortion of our own particular field of science within such a group. We must always be on our guard against scientific imperialism. It tempts specialists to impose aggressively their own method of inquiry upon other sciences. The following classification of the sciences is guided by the intentionality to relate the human formation sciences, among them particularly the science of foundational human formation, to the whole field of scientific inquiry.

Formation is a universal event, embracing universe, world, and humanity. It is the universal process of the gradual realization of the characteristic form each living being, event, society, or thing is tending toward in accordance with its nature and conditions. From the macrocosm of the entire universe to the microcosm of the subatomic particle, we see a dynamic tending toward shape, form, and direction. Human beings, endowed with spirit and with the relative freedom and insight that forms them as human and distinct from the rest of creation, share in the receptive and active process of formation and at the same time transcend it. Human beings manifest free formability. That is, as spiritual beings they are consciously and freely able in some measure to receive and give form in their own and others' lives, and in history, world, and universe.

Eightfold Classification of the Sciences

All classifications of science necessarily proceed from an initial guiding perspective. Hence, in the light of the perspective of formation, we can discern eight main divisions within the sciences: theoretical, theoretical-formative, physical, physical-formative, conceptual, conceptual-formative, experiential, and experiential-formative.

Theoretical Sciences

Every group of sciences in some way arises from human experience. The primary element, however, that distinguishes theoretical sciences as a group is the prevalent attention involved in their operations. This attention is not concentrated in experience as such, which functions chiefly as their point of departure. While also excluding knowing for the sake of living, the main intentionality of the scientific act in this group of sciences is knowing for the sake of knowing and for the conceptual understanding of the experience of life and world. Examples are philosophy and philosophical and symbolic, or dogmatic theology.

Theoretical-Formative Sciences

This group of sciences is theoretical in its mode of operation, but its theory is at the service of the intentionality to assist humanity in giving form to its life in the world and to the world itself. It is theory about formative praxis in a specific sense: it seeks to disclose universal norms that may offer remote directives for formation within a specific sector of human life or world. Typical examples are philosophical ethics and the various disciplines of applied, or practical, theology. Chief among them in the Christian tradition are moral theology and spiritual theology. Spiritual theology, for instance, aims at insight into the normative means and methods Christians employ to live the inner life of faith, hope, and love through the gift of the Holy Spirit. Other examples are pastoral theology or the theology of ministry; homiletics; missiology; and liturgics. All of these seek to establish directive theoretical norms for the expression of faith symbols in various specific sectors of Christian formation.

Physical Sciences

Like the theoretical, conceptual, and experiential sciences, the physical sciences originate in an initial attention to some aspect of the sense-perceptible world. However, their object is not the world of human experience as such, but the physical dimension of life and world. Under this physical dimension of reality falls also what is material in human life. Hence, the physical sciences are relevant as auxiliary sciences for the science of foundational human formation. Physical sciences seek to obtain theoretical insight into the physical manifestations of life and world. In the physical sciences the method ought to be both strict and exact, whereas in theoretical and experiential sciences methods must be equally strict but cannot be exact in the same way the methods in physical sciences are. In the realm of human experience, for instance, the element of the unpredictable and the unmeasurable is more at play; human experience cannot be subject totally to the same type of exact experiment and analysis that apply to certain dimensions of physical reality. The goal of physical science is ever more exact theory to explain the physical dimension of reality. Examples of physical science include physics, chemistry, astronomy, geology, biology, physiology, and physical anthropology.

Physical-Formative Sciences

These sciences are intimately related to the physical sciences. However, while the physical sciences' proper role is the ongoing expansion of theoretical explanations of the physical dimension of reality, physical-formative sciences are more concerned with the formative applications of already established physical laws and theories to concrete ongoing formation of the somatic aspects of human life and the material structures of world and universe. Accordingly, their research methods seek means and methods for the effective implementation of physical-scientific theories that will assist humanity in its task of formative stewardship over the material world. Physical formative sciences that assist the formation or reformation of the somatic dimension of human life include such sciences as medicine, nutrition, physical therapy, and pharmacology. Examples of sciences that serve the task of giving effective form to the material world are engineering, architecture, industrial design, and the applied nuclear sciences.

Conceptual Sciences

These sciences are sometimes also called ideal, or formal, sciences. The basis for the emergence of these sciences, like that of all sciences, is ultimately found in human interaction with the world of experience. For example, the conceptual science of geometry emerged from prescientific geometrical intuition in the course of the practical art of surveying land. The main intentionality of these sciences, however, is the creation of a world of concepts, idealities, or symbolic forms that are mutually interrelated and have a mathematical existence of their own. These mathematical symbols may be employed as a mode of interpreting certain relative structures of the world as perceived and experienced by humanity, or they may be a world unto themselves where only probabilities and imaginative variations are investigated in different relationships to one another. Hence, the concept itself, or the "ideality," is the proper object of the conceptual sciences and distinguishes them from other sciences. Examples of the conceptual sciences include all forms of mathematics and some forms of logic.

Conceptual-Formative Sciences

While the main objective of the conceptual sciences is a conceptual or ideal world in and for its own sake, there is an ongoing formative intent present in many branches of conceptual science. Mathematics and logic serve the human organization and development of the everyday world and of many different scientific worlds as well. Therefore, aside from certain branches of computer science that may be classified as conceptual-formative, the conceptual sciences as such become formative when they are employed by other groups of sciences, especially formative sciences, as part of their methodological means of inquiry.

For example, the statistical methods of behavioristic psychology require mathematical expertise in order to assess behavior with the intention of giving more effective form to the functional dimension and apparent life-form of people. Mathematics becomes conceptually formative in this context. The formative engineering sciences use several disciplines within the mathematical sciences in order to construct airplanes, bridges, and buildings, or to accomplish any other physical formation project. Indeed, the mathematical and logical sciences offer a necessary means for the exact execution of the projects of the physical and the physical-formation sciences. They may serve similarly in some of the experiential-formation sciences and logical theoretical sciences.

Experiential Sciences

This group of sciences is marked by its attention to the sense-perceptible world of the expressions of human experience. These sciences start out from observation of the expressions, conditions, effects, and dynamics of experience. These expressions and the experiences which they reflect are subjected to the critical methods of identification, description, explicitation, analysis, and validation that are proper to each type of experiential science. Theories are hypothetically formulated, tested, and intersubjectively validated. In this case, theory is always at the service of explanation of meaning-structures, dynamics, and facilitating or interfering conditions and effects of the concrete realm of human experience, its nature, and its emergence and unfolding in different sectors and phases of human life. Theoretical thinking in these experiential sciences is, therefore, closely bound to the ongoing examination of intersubjectively observable and comparable expressions of the life of experience.

Examples of sciences that may be included in this category are cultural history, phenomenological psychologies and sociologies, psychoanalysis, cultural anthropology, and the spirituality of interior experience. The latter, for instance, identifies, describes, explicates, and obtains insights into the experiential aspect of the spiritual life. It studies the experiential expression of the self-communication of the formation mystery. Within this content attention is paid to the experiential aspects of a person's readiness for that self-communication. The experiential response in various phases of spiritual unfolding is described and appraised. This science finds its sources, among others, in classical expressions of the experiences concerned, such as can be found, for example, in the works of Far Eastern masters of the spiritual life and those of Western masters, such as Teresa of Avila, John of the Cross, Meister Eckhart, and Ignatius of Loyola. Another source is contemporary expressions of interior experiences from various cultures and religions.

Experiential-Formative Sciences

Like the other groups of formative sciences, this group is marked by its intentionality not only to identify, describe, and understand but primarily to give form. As formative, their research of dynamic human experience is circumscribed by its orientation toward the assistance of humanity in its foundational movement of constantly receiving form and giving form to life and world in concrete interaction with the corresponding human and social experiences in one's formation field. Formation theory seeks to formulate concrete proximate form directives that explicate the means and methods that assist the purposeful striving of humanity to realize its formation of life and world in a specific sector of human formation.

Included in this group of sciences are those that are oriented toward the formation and reformation of pathological human experience and those that are oriented toward formative development or transcendent transformation of human experience and formation with all its potentialities. Examples of the former are the many forms of psychotherapy and counseling. Examples of the latter are the sciences that may be called the sciences of human formation. We can distinguish five major sciences of human formation: training, education, pedagogy, andragogy, and foundational human formation. All of them originate out of concern for a specific profile of the experience of the human formation process and its dynamics, conditions, and effects.

Role of the Science of Formation

The science of foundational human formation, also called the science of foundational formative spirituality, directs itself to the study of the necessary and sufficient conditions for the possibility of any distinctively human or, what is the same, spiritual formation. It studies the foundations, dynamic conditions, and problems of this formation by the human spirit from a perspective that is in principle transcultural and transtemporal.

Foundational human formation is primarily an empirical science, but it has certain transempirical presuppositions, as do all other sciences. This science maintains a critical and creative dialogue with the relevant, validated findings and insights of religious and ideological traditions and with the formationally relevant contributions of other sciences. It seeks to create a unifying theory of human formation that is sufficiently foundational to be potentially relevant to all people in all cultures. Hence, its essential and ultimate intent is formative, even in its most theoretical statements.

Such a unifying theory of human formation will in turn be helpful as an auxiliary science to many other sciences, both to sciences of human formation and to other types of science. It can inspire and enlighten, moreover, a corresponding complementary research attempt among students of various religious, humanistic, and ideological form traditions. It may help them to reexamine their tradition in light of the concepts developed by this science. Such research may suggest a reformulation and enrichment of both formation science and tradition, insofar as this can be accomplished without betrayal of the foundational tenets of the tradition concerned or of the validated data of the science.

The position of the science of foundational human formation within a classification of the sciences has been clarified here from the perspective of the universal event of formation in humanity, world, universe, and history.

No classification can be regarded as absolute. Elements that distinguish one group can be found in some measure in other groups as well. For example, theory is present in each group, even though one group is identified as primarily theoretical. Each group has some aspect of initial emergence out of human experience. Variations occur in how each approximates, relates to, and remains or does not remain attentive to such initiating experiences. All divisions of science are differentiations of the all-embracing unity of human knowledge. The unifying ground of this multifaceted knowledge is the mutual reciprocity between the human striving for knowledge and the world as capable of disclosing itself. This helps to explain why the science of foundational human formation can benefit from all other sciences as auxiliary to its own quest and can be in turn auxiliary to all others: it is rooted in the universal event of formation that marks all events in our universe.

APPENDIX TWO

Charts of the Science of Foundational Formation

The following charts are designed to clarify the organizational coherence of the foundational formation theory, which underlies the science in its present stage of development.

Chart I
Empirical Chart

This chart emphasizes the preempirical and empirical aspects of foundational human life formation. Preempirical formation is that aspect of our human life formation which is not directly available to experience. Empirical formation represents dimensions of our life formation potentially available to experience; their actual availability, however, may be dependent on special means such as formative direction or psychotherapy. Empirical formation embraces two constantly interacting poles of formation: empirical life formation and empirical world formation.

Empirical life formation is influenced not only be preempirical formation and by empirical world formation but also by three other intrinsic factors potentially available to human experience. They are respectively:
1. Four essential horizons of all human formation.
2. Five degrees of human attention and inattention that affect formation.
3. A succession of formation phases that mark decisively human formation history.

The four essential horizons or basic orientations of all empirical formation are the human preformed tendencies to form life through a formative striving after transcendent, functional, vital and historical values offered to our formation potentials by our formation field. Each category of these four basic formative value-strivings gives rise to its unique type of striving called, respectively, aspirations and inspirations, ambitions, impulses, and pulsations.

Our formation is influenced by the degree of conscious or unconscious attention. Empirical life formation is furthermore affected by formation phases.

At the bottom of the chart we position empirical world formation, which is an integral part of the always ongoing foundational human process.

Chart II
Structure Chart

This chart presents an overview of the essential structures that play a role in the process of foundational human formation. The reader will find reexpressed here all the dimensions of the former empirical chart, now defined and named from the structural viewpoint of the foundational formation science. Added are the transcendent and incarnational sources of empirical life formation. Another addition to this more detailed structural chart is the expressions of the empirical life form, which are the core, current, apparent and actual life forms.

Chart III
Action and Disposition Chart

The various structures of formation form human life foundationally by means of their appropriate acts and dispositions. These will be defined and explained in the second volume of this series. When studying them, it may be advisable to return to Chart III to visualize their exact position and function in the foundational human formation theory.

Charts IV(a), IV(b), and IV(c)
Chart of Foundational Formative Energy Flow

The science of foundational human formation and its Christian articulation must ask questions pertaining to the what and how of the foundational formation energy and its flow. It is evident that a certain power or energy must be available for the actualization of structures, acts and dispositions that keep the human and Christian formation processes moving. Hence, this chart outlines the general direction channels of human and Christian strivings that energize and animate foundational human and Christian formation.

Chart V
The Formation-Polarity or the Formation Field Diagram

The formation-polarity diagram situates the five formation poles between which the foundational human and Christian formation process unfolds itself in a constant dialogical tension. The polarity diagram visualizes by means of arrows the mutually formative directions of this interaction. The various formation poles are, respectively, those of pre, intra, inter, immediate and mediate outer formation. The three latter poles highlight the typical social conscience orientation of foundational formation. Some spiritualities are mainly intraformation-oriented. In foundational formation only one pole is intra and discernment-oriented; three poles are social conscience and appraisal-oriented. This chart represents the totality of the human and Christian formation field.

Chart VI
Input Chart

The science relies on a basic and an auxiliary input. Basic are lived formation events. The social consciousness of foundational formation specifies as its proper object not only intra but also inter and outer formation events. They are researched at the various levels of their prereflexive and reflective impact. Auxiliary are the formationally relevant insights of the auxiliary remotely and proximately directive sciences. The third volume of this series on the science and the scientific method will discuss this chart in more detail.

Chart VII
Integration Chart

This chart is designed to clarify the integrational movement of our life formation as complementing its differential movement. It starts out from the formation mystery of the center of our life formation. The chart then indicates the various differentiations of our empirical life-form due to the incarnational movement of the formation mystery. It ends with a return to the formation mystery at our center by a participative union with this mystery. Such a union would integrate in full consonance all differentiations of our empirical life-form. The chart distinguishes between an initial, intermediate and full integration. The initial integration is that of the original differentiations or dimensions of our life-form into the three integrational structures of our core, current and apparent life-form. The intermediate integration is accomplished by the actual life-form which selectively and creatively integrates the relevant responses of our core, current and apparent form in an increasingly consonant actual form of life. Full integration may be increasingly approximate by an ever more consonant actual form of life, which assists in turn the core, current and apparent forms in their own growth in consonance. Full integration or consonance would mean a complete union of likeness with the formation mystery at the center of our being. We would have come full circle in our formation journey.

Chart I

EMPIRICAL CHART

Preempirical Formation

1. Preformation of the embodied soul which we cannot experience directly.
2. What is given: The foundational embodied life form.

Empirical Life Formation

Horizons of human formation: A. *Transcendent:* Aspirations and Inspirations
B. *Functional:* Ambitions
C. *Vital:* Impulses
D. *Historical:* Pulsations

Along a gradient of attention and inattention:
A. *Transconsciousness*
B. *Infraconsciousness*
C. *Preconsciousness*
D. *Focal Consciousness*
E. *Interconsciousness*

Through a succession of formation phases

Empirical World Formation

1. I find myself as an embodied foundational life form within my formation field in which I am called to embody myself empirically in compatibility and compassion, peace, mercy and justice with the inter and outer poles of my formation field and in congeniality with my foundational life form.
2. In this interaction I develop an empirical life form which is in principle open to relevant formation events in my formation field.

Chart II

STRUCTURE CHART

Foundational Embodied Life Form: Soul

1. The soul is considered from the viewpoint of formation.
2. The soul is the principle of life and the principle of formation. *Anima Forma Corporis*—Soul is the form of the body, that is, of the whole empirical form.
3. The soul cannot be known directly.
4. The soul is incarnated and incarnating.

Empirical Life Form: Result of dialogue between Foundational Life Form and Formation Field.

Empirical Life Form Sources:
  A. *Transcendent:* Spirit
    1. Formative Transcendent Mind
    2. Formative Transcendent Will
    3. Formative Transcendent Memory, Anticipation, Imagination
  B. *Incarnational:* Functional
    1. Formative Functional Mind
    2. Formative Functional Will
    3. Formative Functional Memory, Anticipation, Imagination
  C. *Incarnational:* Vital

Empirical Life Form Expressions:
  A. *Core Form:* Heart
  B. *Current Form:* Senses. How do I adapt *Compatibly* to the perception of the current life situation?
  C. *Apparent Form:* Body Expressions: How do I express my life *Compassionately* in response to the imperfection—and vulnerability—aspects of people and situations?
  D. *Actual Form:* Momentary Action: My actual integrated form of life selectively integrating and creatively complementing the relevant response of my core, current and apparent forms.

Shared Horizons of Human Formation:
  A. *Transcendent*
  B. *Functional*
  C. *Vital*
  D. *Historical*

Along a gradient of Attention
and Inattention: A. *Transconsciousness*
　　　　　　　　B. *Infraconsciousness*
　　　　　　　　C. *Preconsciousness*
　　　　　　　　D. *Focal Consciousness*
　　　　　　　　E. *Interconsciousness*

Through a succession of Formation Phases

Within Empirical Formation Field: *Formative*
　　　　　　　1. *Form Tradition*
　　　　　　　2. *Community*
　　　　　　　3. *Situation*
　　　　　　　4. *World*

Approached in Interformative:
　　　　　　　A. *Faith-Hope-Consonance Triad*
　　　　　　　B. *Peace*
　　　　　　　C. *Mercy*
　　　　　　　D. *Justice*

Chart III

ACTION AND DISPOSITION CHART

Foundational Embodied Life Form: Animating formation

Empirical Life Form

Empirical Life Form Sources: A. *Transcendent*
  1. Formative Transcendent Mind: Apprehension and Appraisal
  2. Formative Transcendent Will: Decision and Perseverance
  3. Formative Transcendent Memory, Anticipation, Imagination

  B. *Incarnational:* Functional
  1. Formative Functional Mind: Functional Apprehension and Appraisal
  2. Formative Functional Will: Functional Decisions and Executions
  3. Formative Functional Memory, Anticipation, Imagination
      a) Memory: Recall what functionally was done in past
      b) Anticipation: Projects; what functionally should be done
      c) Imagination: Symbolizes and concretizes relevant functioning of past, present, future

  C. *Incarnational:* Vital
  1. Formative excitability of voluntary and involuntary neuromuscular system, glandular system, cardiovascular system
  2. Formative selection excitability and reactivity of these systems due to vital memory, anticipation, imagination
  3. Incarnationally formative selective reactivity of cells and organs

Empirical Life Form Expressions:
  A. *Core Form:* Heart
  1. Formative global, felt inclination and striving
  2. Acts and Dispositions forming *Congenially* the core form

  B. *Current Form*
  1. Formative periodic adaptation of the global strivings
  2. Acts and Dispositions *Compatibly* forming the current life form

  C. *Apparent Form*
  1. Formative periodic expression of both global and current life form

      2. Acts and Dispositions forming *Compassionately*
       the current expression form
     D. *Actual Form*
      1. Formative creative/adaptation of global, current and apparent strivings and dispositions to an integrated consonant actual form of life.
      2. Acts forming *Effectively* the actual form of presence and action

Shared Horizons of Human
Formation: A. *Transcendent*
        B. *Functional*
        C. *Vital*
        D. *Historical*

Along a gradient of Attention
and Inattention: A. *Transconsciousness*
        B. *Infraconsciousness*
        C. *Preconsciousness*
        D. *Focal Consciousness*
        E. *Interconsciousness*

Through a succession of Formation Phases

Within Empirical Formation Field: *Formative*
       1. *Form Tradition*
       2. *Community*
       3. *Situation*
       4. *World*

Approached in Interformative
       A. *Faith-Hope-Consonance Triad*
       B. *Justice*
       C. *Peace*
       D. *Mercy*

Chart IV A

CHART OF FOUNDATIONAL FORMATIVE ENERGY FLOW

Foundational Formative Energy flows by necessity into the only available general direction-channels of foundational formative human and Christian striving. Possible expressions of each striving:

Emotions: initiate our striving toward or away from
Desire: is protracted emotion
Passion: is enduring and intense desire
Will: is mind directed and decisive desire or passion

There is always a global energy that comes from the embodied soul that animates life to give form to itself. Certain channels direct the *foundational formation flow*:

Formative Energy Channels: *Historical-Cultural* Pulsations
 Vital Impulses
 Functional Ambitions
 Transcendent Aspirations and Inspirations
 Pneumatic Inspirations and Aspirations

Foundational formative direction channels of energy can be considered from the viewpoint of their:

Source, Object Pole, Structure, and Act of Striving

Chart IV B

Energy Flow Channel:	Socio-Historical	Vital	Functional
Source:	The historical cultural movement of human life as participating in the historical formative flow of human communities as formative.	The vital movement of the human life as participating in the physical, biological life force animating all living creatures.	The ambitious movement of human life as participating in the ongoing concrete matter linked formation of human formation fields.
Object Pole:	The socio-historical aspect of human communities as affecting the direction of communal and personal formation of human formation fields.	The organismic vital aspects of life and its impact on the ongoing formation of human formation fields.	The concrete matter-linked aspect of the ongoing formation of human formation fields as demanding effective skill and action.
Structure:	The socio-historical dimension of all human formation. The historical dispositions of memory, imagination, anticipation, and of the core, current, apparent and actual forms of the empirical life to which this dimension gives rise.	The human organism with its vital formative drives and vital dispositions to which this organism gives rise in mind, will, memory, anticipation, imagination, and in the core, current, apparent and actual forms of life.	The functional formative mind, will, memory, anticipation, imagination and the functional formative dispositions to which they give rise on all levels and structures of formation.
Act:	Pulsations	Impulses	Ambitions

Chart IV C

Energy Flow	Transcendent	Pneumatic
Channel:	The ideal movement of human life as participating in the ongoing ideal formation of the human formation field as "more than" its physical, concrete appearance.	The graced movement of human life as participating in the ongoing healing and elevating transformation of the human formation field in Christ.
Object Pole:	The "more than" aspect of the ongoing formation of the human formation field as demanding or inviting ideal vision and action.	The divinely revealed aspect of the ongoing formation of the human formation field as demanding or inviting to pneumatically inspired vision and action.
Structure:	The human spirit as the transcendent direction of mind, will, memory, anticipation, imagination and the transcendent disposition to which the spirit gives rise on all other levels and structures of life.	The human spirit as transformed by the Holy Spirit, the pneumatic direction of mind, will, memory, anticipation, imagination to which the Pneuma gives rise and pneumatic dispositions on all other levels and structures of life.
Act:	Aspirations and Inspirations	Inspirations and Aspirations

Chart V
THE FORMATION-POLARITY DIAGRAM OF THE HUMAN FORMATION FIELD

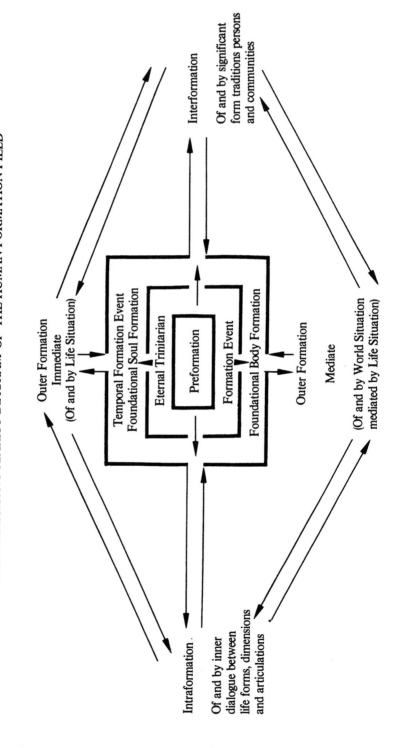

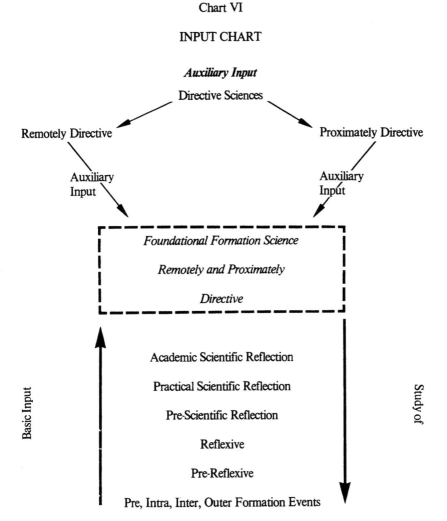

Chart VII

INTEGRATION CHART

FORMATION MYSTERY

Preempirical Preformation

	Transcendent	Substantial		Transcendent
Initial	Biogenetic	Union	Ongoing	Biogenetic

Primordial Embodied
Foundational Life Form

Ongoing Transconscious

Inspirations   Aspiriations

Incarnational Movement

― ―

Abandonment Option

― ―

Empirical Life Formation

Formative Differentiation   +   Formative Integration

Through
Dialogical
Intra
Inter   Formation
Outer

Original Dimensions

Sociohistorical (Pulsations)
Vital (Impulses)   Initial Integration
Functional (Ambitions)
         Inspirations
Transcendent   Aspirations

Core
Current (Periodic)
Apparent (Appearance)

Intermediate Integration
Actual Life Form

Approximating Full Integration
increasingly finding consonance
with preformation, both initial
and ongoing, and with the
formation mystery itself
substantially at its center.
(Union of Likeness)
(Empirical Ideal Life Form)

THE FORMATION FIELD

Glossary

The terms here have been selected from a series of over one thousand entries published in the scholarly journal *Studies in Formative Spirituality* (Volumes 1, 2, 3 and following). Back copies and subscriptions can be ordered from the Institute of Formative Spirituality, Duquesne University, Pittsburgh, PA 15282.

Apparent Life-Form The manifest form life assumes in reaction and response to real or imagined expectations of others.

Appraisal Mature final appraisal of a consonant formation directive or set of directives is usually preceded by provisional formation appraisal. Provisional formation appraisal gives rise to a plurality of formation directives which at that stage of the appraisal process are selected as equal potential formation directives.

Appraisal Function of Formative Mind Within every human formation act an infraformative interaction takes place between formative mind and will. The formative mind, by means of comparative formative appraisal and appreciation, can indicate—at least in principle—which formation act seems effective, congenial, compatible, and compassionate at this moment of one's situated formation history.

Conscientization The bringing to focal awareness of formation directives that actually give form to life, be it on a pre-, infra-, inter-, or transconscious level.

Consonant Life-Form The empirical life-form manifests its overall consonance with the mystery of formation in four specific ways. It is congenial, or in tune, with the embodied foundational life-form; compatible with, or attuned to, inter- and outer formation; compassionate, or in empathy, with the consequences of the fallen state of formation and the vulnerability it entails for human life, and it is effective in concrete formation acts.

Ultimately, human life formation aspires toward the peace and joy of consonance with the divine life form to which humans are called from eternity. In the Christian form tradition, the empirical life-form attains a Christian consonance insofar as it is in tune with all the manifestations of the Christ form in the soul, of the Holy Spirit in the human spirit, of the mystery of grace and redemption in the church and in humanity. This consonance does not destroy but heals and elevates human consonance with the cosmic and social-personal epiphanies of the created mystery of formation.

Core Form of Life The relatively enduring ground form of life formed during the period between birth and early adulthood. In later life, it is usually not changed fundamentally, but is continuously modulated by the succession of provisional current forms life assumes.

In the Christian view, the core form or heart, of life becomes the integrative responsible-sensible center of global formative affects, which tend to give a basic concrete form to the soul's image of Christ, under the guidance of the Holy Spirit.

Cosmic Epiphany of the Formation Mystery The cosmic epiphany of the formation mystery enables all forms in the cosmos to emerge, expand, and maintain themselves until they are submerged in the cosmic energy field to emerge again as other forms. This epiphany of the formation mystery as forming energy field grants all forms their own foundational form potency.

Critical and Integrational Approach of the Science of Formation The science of foundational formation respects and welcomes the relevant contributions of all differential approaches. It is critically aware that each one of them in isolation can lead to a certain onesidedness of emphasis in the study of formation. Hence its scientific, integrational, and dialogical method aims at granting each contribution its rightful place in the total view of human life formation. Christian foundational formation, in turn, tries to complement and correct contributions from the viewpoint of Christian revelation and theological and philosophical auxiliary sciences while trying also to do justice to all scientifically demonstrated findings that are truly relevant to the science of foundational formation.

Cultural Pulsations Partial and pragmatic formation approaches may be supported by an exciting formation pulsation in the culture or subculture. On the basis of that pulsation, a culture as a whole may be effectively coping with the deformative side effects its members exhibit as a result of formerly shared partial and pragmatic formation approaches. (A culture also provides its members with pulsations that are either beneficial or neutral.)

Current Life-Form The provisional form that life assumes in reaction and response to a life situation and/or to a new disclosure of a person's uniqueness. This change usually implies a modulation of the core form of life and offers an opportunity for a more refined disclosure of the uniqueness of one's life.

The articulations of the current life-form consist of the main nuances of one's current dimension of presence in differentiating reactions and responses to nuances in the reality to which one is present.

The dimensions of the current life-form are the current actuations of historical, vital, functional, transcendent, and pneumatic formation potentials into dimensions of presence to reality.

Decision Function of the Formative Will Because the formative mind is not determined absolutely by any finite particular formation pole, it needs the decisive power of the will to make final its incarnational appraisal. The formative will, being a blind formation power, cannot appraise by itself but has to follow or refuse the formation directives that are proposed to it by the apprehension, appraisal, and appreciation process of the formative mind.

Dimensions of Consciousness Formative spirituality distinguishes five dimensions of consciousness: focal, pre-, infra-, inter-, and transconsciousness. Focal consciousness is fully aware, concentrated attentiveness. Prefocal patterns of attention and inattention influence to some extent the perceptions and rational processes that mark the direction of focal awareness and attention. Prefocal attentiveness is marked by a continuous interplay of dynamic interests tending to exert a directive influence on attention and inattention in service of formation. These influences on the patterns of prefocal attention and inattention are our peripheral daily perceptions and the residues of focal attention. Other interacting influences are the shared historical pulsations, vital impulses, and functional ambitions that are either residues of focal conscious attention or emerge—masked or unmasked—from infrafocal attentiveness.

Aspirations and inspirations keep interacting with the influences in the prefocal attentiveness. They are either residues of focal aspirations and inspirations or the result of transfocal attentiveness that managed, like those of the infrafocal life of attention, to penetrate the barriers of the prefocal domain of formative influences. Interconsciousness refers to the monuments, symbols, writings, and traditions that represent the publicly available exteriorizations of the inner consciousness of the participants in a culture or form tradition. Participation in this interconsciousness can be focal, pre-, infra-, and transconscious.

Empirical Life-Form The emergent fourfold life-form, which, unlike the life-form principle in the soul or foundational life-form, is in principle open to experience. The fourfold empirical life-form consists of the core, current, apparent, and actual life-forms.

Expression Form The expression form is not one of the four main forms of life. It is a style of life corresponding to our spiritual, psychic, and vital orientation. The expression form should be congenial to the foundational life-form and compatible with the foundational forms of our communities and situations. The more our ongoing formation is congenial and compatible, the more our expression form will become gracious, peaceful, and joyful and reveal openness and an inner relaxed attentiveness. Facial expression, language, gesture, movement, and bearing will become relaxed yet animated manifestations of the partial divine form we are called to express uniquely in our life.

Form Directives The main personal and prepersonal formation of human life finds its source in human form directives, also called formation directives or life directives.

Form Potency and Form Direction A given form potency implies a form direction. This given form direction can give rise to form directives that are congenial with this foundational form direction and compatible with the formation situation.

Form Tradition Form tradition refers to the form directives that have been handed over from generation to generation in a specific culture, religion, or ideological movement; they give direction to the concrete receptive and creative formation of life and formation fields within the culture, religion, or ideology. Form traditions are intimately related to the faith traditions in which they are rooted. They should, however, be distinguished from such faith traditions. (The word *tradition* comes from the Latin *tradere* which means handing over.

Formation Director, Role of The obstacles to global form-directive identification constitute one of the reasons why the guidance of a formation director, in common or in private, may be advisable or necessary. Well-prepared, sensitive, and experienced formation directors are inclined to look for signs of positive, negative, or conditional exaltation in the expressions of their directees. Such signs may open for the directors avenues along which they can trace the exalted subdirectives from which such signs arise. (These signs may disclose the exalted global form directives that are the ultimate source of such subdirectives and their diversified expressions.)

Formation Mystery as Manifested in Human Formation The formation mystery manifests itself in the embodied foundational life-form or soul, in the interformative processes in the communities to which one belongs, and in the formative interaction with the outer world of culture and nature. Briefly, the formation mystery discloses itself in the pre-, inner, intra-, inter-, and outer formation.

Formation of Ego-Identity To be human means to function effectively as an individual in society. Individual functioning is moved and guided by directives of personal thought, performance, achievement, production, consumption, expression, and appearance. Stimulated and consolidated by a corresponding cultural and historical pulsation, this functioning forms gradually a functional ego-identity. This individual articulation of our life in its functional dimension is good and necessary in ongoing human and Christian formation.

Formation Polarity The concept of formation polarity that underlies the science of foundational life formation emphasizes the social dimension. In this regard, the science differs from formation traditions that focus mainly on interiority and the discernment of inner spirits. In contrast, the polarity concept of foundational life formation regards one-quarter of a full empirical life formation in Christ as inner formation, while three-quarters are regarded as social formation.

Formational Power of Human Life The overall global formation power of human life is intrinsic to and coextensive with human life as such and with its formation field. It cannot be restricted to one of its particular manifestations, such as the formative power of the mind or will or of one of the other formation dispositions.

Formation Symbols Formation symbols exercise a form directive influence on the formation history of a human life-form or of a society of such life-forms. Not all human symbols exercise this influence on all people. For example, mathematical symbols may not have this formative impact on each human life-form. In that case, it is still known as a symbol, but not experienced as a formation symbol.

Formative Detachment The initiation or ratification of privations that are appraised as desirable in a new period or situation of life seen in the light of one's emergent uniqueness and chosen formation tradition.

Formative Directive Disposition Directive dispositions are formative if they direct human formation powers habitually to formation acts that are congenial, compatible, compassionate, and effective.

Formative Life Directives as Personalized Human and prehuman form directives may be elected or affirmed by free personal appraisal and choice. Only then can they be called personal or personalized human form directives. Otherwise they remain prepersonal directives, which may be either prehuman or human.

Formative Memory The residues in human life of past formation and deformation that potentially or actually still influence the present direction and formation of that life. These formation memories, while differing in availability, content, and meaning, tend to organize themselves in formative memory configurations under the influence of the present formative direction of life. In accordance with their availability, formation memories maintain themselves on the corresponding infra-, trans-, pre-, and focal levels of consciousness.

Formative Modes of Core and Current Life-Forms Formative modes of presence (as distinct from formative modalities of presence) are fundamental overall orientations of one's core and current presence to reality.

Formative Thinking An experiential, open style of thinking characteristic of the human person as open to transcendent formation. Dwelling reverently on familiar formative events, it discloses the transcendent and pneumatic meanings they conceal. This gentle formative presence makes human life available to the transforming created and uncreated powers that pervade the universe, humanity, history, and one's interiority. Engagement in formative thinking fosters personal transformation.

Foundational Christian Life-Form The foundational Christ form of the Christian life. Under the influence of the Holy Spirit, it inspires, directs, and moves the ongoing formation of Christian life. It moves the Christian life freely to disclose and incarnate in empirical life the image of Christ in the soul. This incarnation gives rise to empirical forms of life that are at the same time communal and unique expressions of the body of Christ, or the church. If lived in faith and love, they express progressively the graced, transfigured principle of human life and its divine direction.

Foundational Compassion Foundational compassion and mercy refer to the deepest poverty of self and others. This most profound indigence entails the abandonment of the soul or of one's unique foundational life-form. This abandonment of soul is facilitated by the lack of those pneumatic, transcendent, functional, vital, cultural, or historical conditions that protect and foster the foundational formation triad of faith, hope, and love, and the subsequent trust and appreciative abandonment to the formation mystery.

Foundational Human Life-Form The dynamic ground-form, or foundational formation principle, of human life. It inspires, directs, and moves the ongoing formation of human life. It moves human life to freely disclose and realize its ground-form. This realization gives rise to empirical forms of life that are at the same time communal and unique. If congenial and compatible, they express progressively the inherent formation principle and its direction.

Functional Anticipation The availability, meaning, and configuration of anticipated functional formation aspects of future formation events that potentially or actually influence the formation of one's present ambitions and operational dispositions. This anticipation enables one to surmise tentatively the functional component of one's life direction in the near and distant future.

Functional Dimension of the Life-Form The functional dimension of presence serves as the link between the vital and transcendent dimensions of presence and as the bridge between their impulses and aspirations and the everyday life situation. The functional dimension translates impulses and aspirations into workable, unified concrete ambitions that can be executed in one's formation field.

The functional dimension of current presence to reality articulates itself in an individual, technical, social, and functional-aesthetic presence to the life situation.

The individual articulation of the functional dimension is the deliberate individual character of formative functioning in life situation and world that sets it apart from mere vital presence and from the presence of union typical of the transcendent and pneumatic dimensions.

The technical articulation of the functional dimension consists of the formation and use of mental, sensory, and manual skills; their extension in logical and scientific systems, tools, machines, and organizations. This formation and use of the logical mind and manual dexterity distinguishes the functional dimension from the mere vital dimension and from the holistic presence of the transcendent and pneumatic dimension.

The social articulation of the functional dimension consists of the formation of social skills that enable one to interact effectively and smoothly with others, to establish oneself in society, and to realize functional ambitions.

The functional-aesthetic articulation of the functional dimension consists of the formation and use of aesthetic skill, feeling, and sensitivity enabling a person to refine and make attractive, appealing, and elegant the functional style of striving and its expressions, whether or not this functional aesthetic is in service of the transcendent beauty of aspirations and inspirations.

Functional Formation Potential The potency and tendency of all human life to be formed by and to give form to ambitions emerging from one's functioning in life situation and world.

Functional Formative Imagination Those shared and personal formative images that result from and point to one's ambitions and operational dispositions and that potentially or actually influence the direction and formation of one's present ambitions and operational dispositions.

Functionalism To function well in competitive societies of autarchic self-fulfillment and self-exertion, it is silently assumed that it is necessary to live as if one had settled or eliminated the great enduring questions of the transcendent formation of life. The longer formation questions are delayed or denied, the more any emergent awareness of them evokes irritation, anxiety, and guilt. To escape such anxiety by return to ignorance, functionality, and vitality in and by themselves may be preconsciously exalted as the main or only meaning of life's formation. This leads to deformation.

Functional Memory The availability, meaning, and configuration of past functional formation truths and events, shared and personal, that once formed one's ambitions and operational dispositions and that still potentially or actually influence the direction and formation of one's present ambitions and operational dispositions. This memory enables one to disclose the functional component of one's shared and unique life direction.

Historical Formation Potential The potency and tendency of all human life to be formed by and to give form to the pulsations of movements, feelings, and ideas that pulsate in one's period of history.

Ideal Formation Source of Human Life The initially hidden directive call of the unique life-form which the soul, or unique life, principle is transconsciously tending toward. This inner call takes form gradually as a series of successive life ideals. These life ideals emerge in our prefocal and focal attentiveness through interformation and interaction with life situations and cultural form traditions. Such ideals give rise to daily directives of formation.

Immersion in Vitalism and/or Functionalism The pride-form captures formation energy and invests it in accordance with its own exalted design for the autarchic form of human life. It tends to invest this formation energy in the limited, tentative, vital, and functional manifestations of the human Christian foundational striving for transcendent fulfillment and corresponding self-exertion. Such exclusive investment is deformative. It presupposes, maintains, and deepens formation ignorance. Formation ignorance manifests itself here in ignorance of the transcendent aspirations for human and Christian fulfillment and self-exertion. These aspirations should not paralyze but enlighten, penetrate, modulate, and gradually transform the vital and functional manifestations of the human and Christian fulfillment and exertion strivings.

Incarnation The process of gradually fleshing out in all dimensions and articulations of the personality the directives of one's life formation. (The word incarnation is derived from the Latin word for flesh, *caro*, *carnis*.)

Incarnational-Directive Sources of Human and Christian Formation There are five incarnational-directive sources of human and Christian formation: functional-formative memory, intelligence, will, anticipation, and imagination. They are incarnational insofar as they assist transcendent mind and will in their task of directing the concrete incarnation of transcendent ideals in daily life. These should be distinguished from transcendent-formative memory, mind, will, anticipation, and imagination.

Informative Thinking An issue-oriented style of thinking that, in service of functional achievements, aims primarily at information rather than formation. It leads to definite measurable results. Linear and progressive, it does not dwell or recollect itself like formative thinking; it moves from one logical and functional insight and its practical realization to the next. When it becomes exclusive and excessive, it abandons the soul by not allowing it to be nourished by creative contemplation of the transcendent meanings hidden in formative events.

Inframation of Human Life The organismic and vital preformation of human life; it shares in the universal unconscious process of gradual realization of a characteristic form of organic life; it forms the infraform of organismic human life, which is the substratum of the fully human life-form.

Integrational Proximate Thinking A type of thinking that focuses attention primarily on the potential and actual integration of differential facts, experiences, and their proximate causes into an open-ended, synthesized body of proximate knowledge.

Intraformation Formation that takes place by the interaction of formative processes within the human person. Intraformation is distinguished from interformation and from extra-, or outer, formation. Interformation refers to formative processes that happen in the interaction with other persons and communities of persons. Extra-, or outer, formation refers to formative processes that result from interaction with the life situation and the wider world beyond the immediate life situation.

Memory of Deformation Our partial and pragmatic formation approaches may be fueled by the painful memories of suffering under the deformative side effects of former formation approaches. They feed into a deep-seated anxiety of being victimized again. This anxiety may emerge when a life situation reminds us of the potential limits of our present effective partial and pragmatic formation approaches.

Openness of the Vital Infraform The vital infraform of human life is in principle oriented toward intraformative interaction with the historical, vital, functional, transcendent, and pneumatic powers of formation in the human person.

Organic Infraformation The infraconscious formation of bodily cells, tissues, organs and systems. Organic formation provides the base for the emergence of an original structuring of vital impulses, needs, and strivings of varying intensity. This structure is the ground of a formative temperament that coforms all life structures, dimensions, articulations, acts, and dispositions.

Pneumatic Dimension of the Life-Form The pneumatic dimension of the life-form is not the Holy Spirit itself. Rather, it consists of the inspirations and aspirations of the Spirit given through the Scriptures as explained by the church and personalized in the pneumatic orientation of life in consonance with the church.

Pneumatic Formation Potential The infused potency and tendency to be transformed by and to serve the transformation of inspirations and aspirations of the Holy Spirit.

Pride-Form As the counterfeit form of life, the autarchic pride-form tends to dominate formation, at least initially. Its first line of defense against true transcendent formation is to foster ignorance of the true nature of formation and to create the illusion of autonomous self-formation and fulfillment. True formation, fulfillment, and self-exertion are only possible when we rise beyond this ignorance and participate in the mystery of formation that infinitely transcends life in formation.

The quasi-foundational pride-form is always secretly and subtly seducing us to push ourselves beyond the limited gifts of grace and nature granted to us in regard to our limited possibilities of gentle and firm participation in the reformation and transformation of the world. It pushes us beyond our providential life situation.

Primordial Decision All of our life decisions are related to our primordial formative decision and disposition. This primordial decision is either for appreciative abandonment to the mystery of formation in faith, hope, and consonance (love) or for depreciating and despairing abandonment to the meaninglessness of the formation processes that seem blindly to form evolving life and matter, individual and shared history and culture.

Receptive and Reverential Appraisal Receptivity and reverence should give rise to a well-informed respectful appraisal and appreciation which would serve: (1) the identification of formatively dissonant expressions of our vital impulses and functional ambitions; (2) growing recognition of how such dissonant emotional directives obscure and deform the deepest foundational thrust of these impulses and ambitions themselves; (3) growing relaxed recognition of a deformative identification of our foundational strivings with their limited, tentative manifestations (vital and functional strivings—not yet penetrated by transcendent appraisal—are exalted in their isolated promise of fulfillment. The limited, tentative, relative vital and functional strivings for fulfillment and exertion are mistaken for these foundational strivings themselves in their transcendent totality and directedness. This unconscious identification tends to totalize any life directives implied in such impulses and ambitions. Such unconscious absolutizing withdraws these directives from gentle transcendent appraisal. Totalized in this way they become deformative, even destructive.); (4) growing insight into the art of gently mitigating and mortifying not the vital and functional strivings themselves, but their felt directives that are formatively dissonant; (5) appreciative appraisal of consonant emotional directives that can be interwoven with the higher directives of corresponding aspirations and with the emergent totality of the ongoing consonant formation of life; (6) integration of the vital impulses and functional ambitions in the enlightened formation process—slow and progressive integration that tempers the unbridled explosive force of blind impulses and ambitions yet does not paralyze their vitality into rigid, stilted, and compulsive patterns; gradually, these impulses and ambitions begin to operate with that spontaneous lively consonance characteristic of spiritually enlightened formative striving and behaving.

Reformation of Formative Imagination The images that direct our life may be partly deformative. A reformation of imagery is often necessary. Such reformation is only possible in the measure of our awareness of images that are preconscious or unconscious. A crucial change in one's life direction and formation demands a corresponding reformation of the life of formative imagination. Formative imagery has to be apprehended and appraised in the light of the new life direction; imagery should become compatible with the new current life-form, which in turn should be congenial with the core and foundational form of life.

Situation Form The gradual incarnation of the foundational life-form into our empirical life will affect the form we give to our life situation. Our surroundings will express who we are uniquely called to be. The way in which we arrange and organize our home, work, and recreation environments, and our interformative interactions with people, will increasingly carry the signature of our unique calling.

Social Justice Formative social justice aims at the elimination of all deformative coercive, manipulative, and seductive acts, dispositions, and social or political structures in family, community, and society that militate directly or indirectly against fidelity to one's primary right and duty of congenial life formation (personally as well as socially). It aims at the development of acts, dispositions, and social and political structures that foster and facilitate freedom of communal and personal congenial life formation. Formative social justice is rooted in the transcendent dimension. It goes beyond the social articulation of the functional dimension and the emotional sympathy of the vital dimension. It includes both of them while reforming them.

Spirit Form The foundational life-form unique in each person is preempirical. In order to form the rest of life, it needs the mediation of the human spirit. The human spirit—mind and will as illuminated by the transcendent dimension of the mind—must form itself in congeniality with the foundational life-form and in compatibility with the providential communities and life situations in and through which one has to form one's life and world. In Christian formation the Holy Spirit acts as the deepest pneumatic dimension of the human formative spirit. The Holy Spirit directs us in such a way that we may progressively emerge into the communal and unique image of Christ to which we are called by our foundational life-form.

Spiritual Formation The preconscious and conscious process of a search for and tentative realization of a unique human form of life guided by directives of formation opted for or ratified in relative freedom on the basis of insightful appraisal of the directives concerned. After such option or ratification and reinforcement by initially focal-conscious repetition, the spiritual formation process continues on the level of prefocal formative disposition.

In the Christian form tradition graced formation power discloses and implements—in the light of pneumatic-transcendent presence—congenial and compatible life-forms that express in unpredictable and creative ways the foundational Christ form of the soul and that approximate progressively the final transcendent and transparent self-forgetful form of life.

Thrust of Formation History The integrative science of foundational life formation concludes—partly on the basis of the findings of the sciences, arts, and disciplines that it integrates—that the thrust of formation history is not toward homogenizing but toward diversifying, with a consequent tendency to uniqueness of the diversified phenomena. Such a tendency implies fidelity of phenomena to their initially given design potential. The foundational formation theory calls this fidelity a tendency toward congeniality.

Transcendence In formative spirituality, transcendence implies, among other things, the process of "going beyond" a current life-form that has been congenial and congruent in a specific life period or situation. The process implies the search for a partially or totally new current life-form that is at the same time congruent and compatible with the changed life period or situation and congenial with the emergent uniqueness of the personality insofar as this uniqueness increasingly manifests itself during the journey from current life-form to current life-form.

Transcendence Crisis A period of basic insecurity due to the structural weakening of a no-longer-effective life-form. This insecurity is deepened by the uncertainty about appropriate directives for a new current life-form more congruent with the changing life period or situation and more congenial with the foundational life-form as it increasingly discloses itself.

Transcendent Anticipation The availability, meaning, and configuration of anticipated transcendent meanings of future formation events that potentially or actually influence the present formation of one's life of aspiration. Transcendent anticipation enables one to surmise tentatively the transcendent component of the unique direction of one's shared and personal life direction in the near and distant future.

Transcendent Formation Potential The potency and tendency of all human life to be formed by and to give form to aspirations and inspirations emerging from the transcendent nature of human life.

Transcendent Formative Imagination Those shared and personal formative images that result from and point to transcendent aspirations and inspirations that potentially or actually influence the formation of one's concrete incarnational life.

Transcendent Memory The availability, meaning, and configuration of past transcendent formation truths and events that once formed one's life of aspiration and that, as aspirations, potentially or actually continue to influence the present formation of one's life as transcendent. It enables one to disclose the transcendent component of the unique direction of one's shared and unique life direction.

Vital and Bodily Form The form we give our lives affects our inner and outer bodily form. Congeniality and compatibility of ongoing formation will lead to a more relaxed flow of our organismic powers and energies. It will also manifest itself in the formative movements and expressions of our visible bodies. The resulting gentle yet firm life-style will make our bodily form more gracious and less subject to symptoms of stress and overexertion.

Vital Formation Potential The potency and tendency of all human life to be formed by and to give form to impulses emerging from one's organismic life.

Vital Infraformation The infraconscious preformation of the direction of the vital impulses by a process of interformative exchanges with significant persons and things in the earliest life situations.

World Form in the Christian Form Tradition In expressing our foundational life-form in a unique yet communal way in our successive life situations, we contribute to the formation of the world. Because there can be no opposition between the form God wants to give to our lives, and the form God wants to give to the world, we are clearly called—each in his or her own way—to shape the world in the likeness of the divine. Together with others who appear on this earth over the millennia within their own cultures and life situations, we are called to this task of world formation.

Bibliography

Books

Adler, A. *Social Interest: A Challenge to Mankind.* Translated by J. Linton and R. Vaughn. New York: Capricorn Books, 1964.
Aelred of Rievaulx. *On Spiritual Friendship.* Translated by M. E. Laker. Washington, D.C.: Cistercian Publications/Consortium Press, 1974.
a Kempis, T. *The Imitation of Christ.* Edited by H. C. Gardiner. Garden City, N. Y.: Doubleday and Co., Image Books, 1965.
_____. *Truth.* Chicago: H. Regnery, 1952–54.
Alexander, E., and French, T. M. *Studies in Psychosomatic Medicine.* New York: Ronald Press Company, 1948.
Allport, G. W. *Becoming.* New Haven, Conn.: Yale University Press, 1968.
Andreach. R. J. *Studies in Structure: The Stages of the Spiritual Life in Four Modern Authors.* London: Burns and Oates, 1964.
Angyal, A. *Foundations for a Science of Personality.* London: Oxford University Press, 1958.
Anonymous. *The Cloud of Unknowing and The Book of Privy Counseling.* Edited by W. Johnston. Garden City, N. Y.: Doubleday and Co., 1973.
Ansbacher, H. L., and Ansbacher, R. R., eds. *The Individual Psychology of Alfred Adler: Systematic Presentation in Selections from His Writings.* New York: Harper and Row, 1964.
Aquinas, St. Thomas. *De Anima.* London: Routledge and Kegan Paul, 1951.
Argyle, M. *The Scientific Study of Social Behavior.* London: Methuen Press, 1957.
Argyris, C. *Personality and Organization: The Conflict between System and Individual.* New York: Harper and Row, 1970.
Arnold, M. B. *Emotion and Personality.* New York: Columbia University Press, 1960.
Atkinson, J. W., and Feather, N. T. eds. *A Theory of Achievement Motivation.* New York: John Wiley, 1966.
Augustine, St. *The Confessions of St. Augustine.* Translated by John K. Ryan. Garden City, N. Y.: Doubleday and Co., 1960.
Barnett, L. *The Universe and Dr. Einstein.* New York: Harper and Row, 1948.
Barnett, S. A. *Instinct and Intelligence.* Englewood Cliffs, N. J.: Prentice-Hall, 1967.
Barron, F. X. *Creative Person and Creative Process.* New York: Holt, Rinehart and Winston, 1969.
Becker, E. *The Denial of Death.* New York: The Free Press, 1973.
_____. *The Structure of Evil.* New York: The Free Press, 1968.
Beckett, S. *Waiting for Godot.* London: Faber and Faber, 1956.
Benedict, Ruth. *Patterns of Culture.* Boston: Houghton Mifflin, 1961.
Bennett, J. G. *A Spiritual Psychology.* London: Hodder and Stoughton, 1964.
Benson, Herbert. *The Relaxation Response.* New York: William Morrow and Co., 1975.
Berger, P., and Luckman, Thomas. *The Social Construction of Reality: A Treatise in the Sociology of Knowledge.* New York: Doubleday and Company, 1966.

Bergson, H. *Essai sur les données immédiates de la conscience*. Paris: Presses Universitaires de France, 1889.
———. *Matière et mémoire*, 46th ed., Paris: Presses Universitaires de France, 1946.
———. *L'évolution créatrice*, 62nd ed., Paris: Presses Universitaires de France, 1946.
———. *The Two Sources of Morality and Religion*. Translated by R. A. Audra and C. Bereton with the assistance of W. H. Carter. New York: Doubleday and Co., 1935.
Bernard of Clairvaux, St. *The Steps of Humility and Pride and On Loving God*. Translated by A. Conway and R. Walton. Washington, D.C.: Cistercian Publications/Consortium Press, 1976.
Binswanger, L. *Einführung in die Probleme der allgemeinen Psychologie*. Berlin: Springer, 1922.
Blondel, M. *L'action: essai d'une critique de la vie et d'une science de la pratique*. Paris: Presses Universitaires de France, 1950.
Bloom, Anthony, and Lefebvre, George. *Courage To Pray*. New York: Paulist Press, 1973.
Bohm, D. *Causality and Chance in Modern Physics*. Philadelphia: University of Pennsylvania Press, 1957.
———, and Hiley, B. *On the Intuitive Understanding of Non-locality as Implied by Quantum Theory*. London: Birkbeck College, University of London, 1974.
Bohr, N. *Atomic Theory and the Description of Nature*. Cambridge, England: Cambridge University Press, 1934.
———. *Atomic Theory and Human Knowledge*. New York: John Wiley, 1958.
Born, M. *Atomic Physics*. New York: Hafner, 1957.
———. *The Restless Universe*. New York: Dover, 1951.
Brentano, F. *Psychologie vom empirischen Standpunkt*, Vol. I. Leipzig: Dunker and Humblot, 1874.
Bronowski, J. *The Identity of Man*. London: Heinemann, 1966.
Brown, C. W., and Ghiselli, E. E. *Scientific Method in Psychology*. New York: McGraw-Hill, 1955.
Buber, M. *Between Man and Man*. Translated by R. G. Smith. New York: Macmillan, 1965.
———. *I and Thou*. Translated by W. Kaufmann. New York: Charles Scribner's Sons, 1970.
Bucke, R. M. *Cosmic Consciousness: A Study in the Evolutions of the Human Mind*. New York: E. P. Dutton and Co., 1969.
Bugenthal, J. F. T. *The Search for Authenticity*. New York: Holt, Rinehart and Winston, 1965.
Calon, P. J. A., and Prick, J. J. G. *Psychologische grondbegrippen*. Arnhem, Holland: Von Loghum Slaterus, 1962.
Capra, F. *The Tao of Physics*. Berkeley, Calif.: Shambala, 1975.
Carnell, E. J. *The Burden of Soren Kierkegaard*. London: The Paternoster Press, 1965.
Carrel, A. *L'homme, cet inconnu*. 2nd ed., Paris: Librairie Plon, 1935.
Chakravarty, A., ed. *A Tagore Reader*. Boston: Beacon Press, 1966.
Chang, C. *Creativity and Taoism*. New York: The Julian Press, 1963.
Chautard, Dom Jean-Baptiste. *The Soul of the Apostolate*. Translated by A Monk of Our Lady of Gethsemani, Trappist, Ky.: The Abbey of Gethsemani, 1946.
Chiang, H. M., and Maslow, A. H. eds. *The Healthy Personality: Readings*. New York: Van Nostrand Reinhold, 1969.
Ciszek, W., with Flaherty, D. L. *He Leadeth Me*. Garden City, N. Y.: Doubleday and Co., 1973.
Cole, P. J. *The Problematic Self in Kierkegaard and Freud*. New Haven, Conn. and London: Yale University Press, 1971.
Collins, W. J. *Out of the Depths: The Story of a Priest-Patient in a Mental Hospital*. Garden City, N. Y.: Doubleday and Co., 1971.
Crom, S. *On Being Real: A Quest for Personal and Religious Wholeness*. Wallingford, Pa.: Pendle Hill Publications, 1967.

Crowne, D. P., and Marlowe, D. *The Approval Motive: Studies in Evaluative Dependence.* New York and London: John Wiley, 1964.
Cuzzort, R. P. *Humanity and Modern Sociological Thought.* New York and London: Holt, Rinehart and Winston, 1969.
Dabrowski, K. *Personality Shaping through Positive Disintegration.* London: J. and A. Churchill, 1967.
David, H. P., and VonBracken, H., eds. *Perspectives in Personality Theory.* New York: Basic Books, 1957.
de Caussade, J. P. *Abandonment to Divine Providence.* Translated by John Beevers. Garden City, N. Y.: Doubleday and Co., 1975.
de Chardin, P. T. *The Divine Milieu.* New York: Harper and Row, 1960.
De Coninck, A. *L'unité de la Connaissance Humaine et le Fondement de sa Valeur.* Louvain. Institut supérieur de philosophie, 1943.
De Greef, E. *Notre Destinée et Nos Instincts.* Paris: Plon, 1945.
———. *Les Instincts de Défense et de Sympathie.* Paris: Presses Universitaires de France, 1947.
de Unamuno, M. *The Agony of Christianity.* Translated by K. F. Reinhardt. New York: Frederick Unger Publishing Co., 1960.
———. *Tragic Sense of Life.* Translated by J. E. Crawford Flitch. New York: Dover, 1956.
Dewey, B. *The New Obedience: Kierkegaard on Imitating Christ.* Washington, D.C.: Corpus Publications, 1968.
De Witt, Bryce S. and Graham, N. *The Many Worlds Interpretation of Quantum Mechanics.* Princeton, N. J.: Princeton University Press, 1973.
Dilthey, W. *Descriptive Psychology and Historical Understanding.* Translated by R. M. Zaner and K. L. Heiges. The Hague: Nijhoff, 1977.
———. *Le Monde et L'ésprit.* Paris: Aubier, 1947.
———. *Pattern and Meaning in History.* Translated by H. P. Rickman. New York: Harper and Row, 1962.
Dondeyne, A. *Contemporary European Thought and Christian Faith.* Pittsburgh, Pa.: Duquesne University Press, 1958.
Drucker, P. F. *The Age of Discontinuity: Guidelines to Our Changing Society.* London: Heinemann, 1969.
Dubos, R. "Biological Determinants of Individuality," *Individuality and the New Society.* Edited by A. Kaplan. Seattle, Wash., and London: University of Washington Press, 1970.
Durckheim, K. G. *Daily Life As Spiritual Exercise.* Translated by R. Lewinneck and P. L. Travers. New York: Harper and Row, 1972.
Durckheim, K. G. V. *Hara, the Vital Center of Man.* Translated by S. M. von Kospath and E. R. Healey. London: Allen and Unwin, 1962.
Eckhart, M. *Meister Eckhart: A Modern Translation.* Translated by R. B. Blakney, New York: Harper and Row, 1957.
Einstein, A., and Infeld, L. *The Evolution of Physics.* New York: Simon and Schuster, 1961.
Eisley, L. *The Unexpected Universe.* New York: Harcourt Brace Jovanovich, 1964.
Eliade, M. *The Forge and the Crucible.* Translated by S. Corrin. New York: Harper and Brothers, 1962.
———. *Patterns in Comparative Religion.* Translated by Rosemary Sheed. Cleveland and New York: The World Publishing Co., 1963.
———. *The Sacred and the Profane: The Nature of Religion.* Translated by Willard R. Trask. New York: Harper and Row, 1961.
Eliot, C. *Japanese Buddhism.* New York: Barnes and Noble, 1969.
Eliot, T. S. *Four Quartets.* New York: Harcourt, Brace and World, 1971.
Elsenhans, T. *Die Eigenart des Geistigen.* Leipzig, 1921.
Enzler, C. J. *My Other Self.* Denville, N. J.: Dimension Books, 1958.
Erikson, E. H. *Childhood and Society.* New York: Norton, 1963.

Farber, M. *Basic Issues of Philosophy: Experience, Reality, and Human Value.* New York: Harper and Row, 1968.
Ferguson, M. *The Aquarian Conspiracy: Personal and Social Transformation in the 1980's.* Los Angeles: J. P. Tarcher, 1980.
Fernandez, R., ed. *Social Psychology through Literature.* New York: John Wiley, 1972.
Fordham, F. *An Introduction to Jung's Psychology.* Middlesex, England: Penguin Books, 1966.
Franck, F. *The Zen of Seeing.* New York: Vintage Books, 1973.
Frankl, V. E. *Man's Search for Meaning: An Introduction to Logotherapy.* Translated by L. Lasch. New York: Washington Square Press, 1963.
Fremantle, A., ed. *The Protestant Mystics.* New York: Mentor, 1965.
Friedman, M. *To Deny Our Nothingness: Contemporary Images of Man.* London: Macmillan, 1958.
Frings, M. S. *Max Scheler: A Concise Introduction into the World of a Great Thinker.* Pittsburgh: Duquesne University Press, 1965.
Fromm, E. *Man for Himself: An Inquiry into the Psychology of Ethics.* London: Routledge and Kegan Paul, 1949.
Gadamer, H. G. *Truth and Method.* Translated by G. Barden and J. Cumming. New York: Seabury Press, 1975.
Gardner, J. W. *Self-Renewal: The Individual and the Innovative Society.* New York: Harper and Row, 1963.
Gates, J. A. *The Life and Thought of Kierkegaard for Every Man.* London: Hodder and Stoughton, 1961.
Geertz, C. *The Interpretation of Cultures.* New York: Basic Books, 1973.
Gide, A. *La Porte Entroite.* Paris: Livre de Poche, 1966.
Gjerlov-Knudsen, C. O. *The Philosophy of Form.* Translated by C. Campbell-McCallum. Copenhagen: G. E. C., 1962.
Glass, D. C., ed. *Neurophysiology and Emotion.* New York: Rockefeller University Press, 1967.
Goffman, E. *The Presentation of Self in Everyday Life.* New York: Doubleday, 1969.
Goldbrunner, J. *Individuation: A Study of the Depth Psychology of Carl Gustav Jung.* Notre Dame, Ind.: University of Notre Dame Press, 1964.
Gratton, C. *Guidelines for Spiritual Direction.* Denville, N. J.: Dimension Books, 1980.
———. *Trusting.* New York: Crossroad Publishing Co., 1982.
Greeley, A. M. *Ecstasy: A Way of Knowing.* Englewood Cliffs, N. J.: Prentice-Hall, 1976.
Guardini, R. *Sacred Signs.* Translated by G. Branham. St. Louis, Mo.: Pio Decimo Press, 1956.
Gurwitsch, A. *Field of Consciousness.* Pittsburgh, Pa.: Duquesne University Press, 1964.
———. *Phenomenology and the Theory of Science.* Edited by L. Embree. Evanston: Northwestern University Press, 1974.
Hall, C. S., and Gardner, Lindzey, eds. *Theories of Personality.* New York: John Wiley, 1970.
Hammarskjold, D. *Markings.* Translated by L. Sjoberg and W. H. Auden. New York: Knopf, 1969.
Hansen, W. *Die Entwicklung des Kindlichen Weltbildes.* 6th ed. Munich: Koesel-Verlag, 1965.
Happold, F. C. *The Journey Inwards.* London: Darton, Longman and Todd, 1968.
Haughton, R. *On Trying to Be Human.* London and Dublin: Geoffrey Chapman, 1966.
Heidegger, M. *Being and Time.* Translated by J. Macquarrie and E. Robinson. New York: Harper and Row, 1962.
———. *Discourse on Thinking.* Translated by J. M. Anderson. New York: Harper and Row, 1969.

———. *The Piety of Thinking*. Translated by J. G. Hart and J. C. Maraldo. Bloomington: Indiana University Press, 1976.
Heisenberg, W. *Across the Frontiers*. New York: Harper and Row, 1974.
———. *Physics and Beyond*. New York: Harper and Row, 1971.
———. *Physics and Philosophy*. New York: Harper and Row, 1958.
———, et al. *On Modern Physics*. New York: Clarkson Potter, 1961.
Hengstenberg, H. E. "Das Band Zwischen Geist und Leib in der menschlichen Person." In *Christliche Philosophie in Deutschland 1920–1945*, edited by P. Wolff. Regensburg: J. Habbel, 1949.
Henrici, P. *Hegel und Blondel: Eine Untersuchung über Form und Sinn der Dialektik in der Phänomenologie des Geistes und der ersten Action*. Pullach bei München: Verlag Berchnonskolleg, 1958.
Herrigel, E. *Zen and the Art of Archery*. New York: Vintage Books, 1971.
Heschel, A. J. *Who Is Man?* Stanford, Calif.: Stanford University Press, 1965.
Hillman, J. *Emotion*. Evanston, Ill.: Northwestern University Press, 1961.
———. *Insearch*. New York: Scribner's, 1967.
Horney, K. *Neurosis and Human Growth*. New York: Norton, 1950.
Husserl, E. *The Crisis of European Sciences and Transcendental Phenomenology*. Translated by D. Carr. Evanston: Northwestern University Press, 1970.
Huyghe, G. *Growth in the Holy Spirit*. Translated by Isabel and Florence McHugh. London and Dublin: Geoffrey Chapman, 1966.
Jacobi, J. *The Way of Individuation*. New York: Harcourt, Brace and World, 1967.
James, W. *The Principles of Psychology*. New York: Holt, 1890.
James, W. *The Varieties of Religious Experience: A Study in Human Nature*. New York: Collier Books, 1961.
Jaspers, K. *Reason and Anti-Reason in Our Time*. Translated by S. Godman. New Haven: Yale University Press, 1952.
———. *Truth and Symbol*. Translated by J. T. Wilde, W. Kluback, W. Kimmel. New York: Twayne, 1959.
John of the Cross, St. *The Collected Works of St. John of the Cross*. Translated by Kieran Kavanaugh and Otilio Rodriguez, Washington, D.C.: Institute of Carmelite Studies, ICS Publications, 1973.
Johnston, W. *Christian Zen*. New York: Harper and Row, 1971.
———. *Silent Music: The Science of Meditation*. New York: Harper and Row, 1976.
———. *The Still Point: Reflections on Zen and Christian Mysticism*. New York: Fordham University Press, 1970.
Jourard, S. *Disclosing Man to Himself*. Princeton: Van Nostrand, 1968.
Jung, C. G. *Modern Man in Search of a Soul*. Translated by W. S. Dell and Cary F. Baynes. New York: Harcourt, Brace and World, 1933.
———. *Psychology and Religion*. New Haven: Yale University Press, 1938.
———, and Pauli, W. *The Interpretation of Nature and the Psyche*. Princeton, N. J.: Princeton University Press, 1955.
———. *The Undiscovered Self*. Translated by R. F. C. Hull. Boston: Little, Brown and Company, 1958.
Kahler, E. *The Tower and the Abyss: An Inquiry into the Transformation of the Individual*. New York: Braziller, 1975.
Kaplan, A., ed. *Individuality and the New Society*. Seattle and London: University of Washington Press, 1970.
Kelly, T. R. *A Testament of Devotion*. New York: Harper and Row, 1941.
Kierkegaard, S. *The Concept of Dread*. Translated by W. Lowrie, Princeton: Princeton University Press, 1969.
———. *Concluding Unscientific Postscript*. Translated by D. F. Swenson and W. Lowrie, Princeton, N. J.: Princeton University Press, 1941.
———. *Purity of Heart Is to Will One Thing*. Translated by D. Steere. New York: Harper and Row, 1956.
Klages, L. *Der Geist als Widersacher der Seele*. 3 vols. Leipzig: Bouvier, 1932.
Kraft, W. F. *The Search for the Holy*. Philadelphia: Westminster Press, 1971.

Krech, D., Crutchfield, R. S., and E. L. Ballachey. *Individual in Society: A Textbook of Social Psychology.* New York: McGraw-Hill, 1962.
Kuhn, T. S. *The Essential Tension: Selected Studies in Scientific Tradition and Change.* Chicago: University of Chicago Press, 1977.
Kung, H. *Does God Exist?* Translated by Edward Quinn. Garden City, N. Y.: Doubleday and Co., 1980.
Kwant, R. C. *Encounter.* Pittsburgh, Pa.: Duquesne University Press, 1960.
―――. *Phenomenology of Social Existence.* Pittsburgh, Pa.: Duquesne University Press, 1965.
Lawrence of the Resurrection, Brother. *The Practice of the Presence of God.* Translated by Donald Attwater. Springfield, Ill.: Templegate, 1976.
Leclerq, D. J. *Alone with God.* Translated by Elizabeth McCabe. New York: Farrar, Strauss and Cudahy, 1961.
Lepp, I. *The Ways of Friendship.* Translated by Bernard Murchland. New York: Macmillan, 1966.
Le Senne, R. *Obstacle et valeur.* Paris: Aubier, 1934.
―――. *Traité de caracterologie.* Paris: Presses Universitaires de France, 1957.
Levi-Strauss, C. *The Savage Mind.* Chicago: University of Chicago Press, 1966.
Lewis, C. S. *Surprised by Joy.* New York: Harcourt, Brace and World, 1955.
Libermann, F. *Spiritual Letters to Clergy and Religious.* 3 vols. Translated by Walter Van de Putte. Pittsburgh: Duquesne University Press, 1963, 1964, and 1966.
Longchenpa. "The Natural Freedom of Mind." Translated by H. Guenther. In *Crystal Mirror*, Vol. 4, 1975.
Luijpen, W. A. *Existential Phenomenology.* Translated by H. J. Koren. Pittsburgh, Pa.: Duquesne University Press, 1969.
―――. *Phenomenology and Metaphysics.* Translated by H. J. Koren. Pittsburgh, Pa.: Duquesne University Press, 1965.
Mackenzie, C. S. *Pascal's Anguish and Joy.* New York: Philosophical Library, 1973.
Macquarrie, J. *Paths to Spirituality.* London: SCM Press Ltd., 1972.
Makkreel, R. A. *Dilthey, Philosopher of the Human Studies.* Princeton, N. J.: Princeton University Press, 1975.
Marcel, G. *Being and Having.* Translated by Katherine Farrer. Boston: Beacon Press, 1951.
―――. *The Decline of Wisdom.* New York: Philosophical Library, 1955.
Marcel, G. *Homo Viator: Introduction to a Metaphysics of Hope.* Translated by Emma Craufurd. New York: Harper and Row, 1962.
Marechal, J. *Studies in the Psychology of the Mystics.* Albany, N. Y.: Magi Books, 1964.
Maritain, J. *Approaches to God.* Translated by Peter O'Reilly. New York: Harper and Brothers, 1956.
―――. *The Degrees of Knowledge.* Translated by G. B. Phelan. New York: Charles Scribner's Sons, 1959.
Martin, P. M. *Mastery and Mercy: A Study of Two Religious Poems.* London: Oxford University Press, 1957.
Maslow, A. H. *Motivation and Personality.* New York: Harper and Row, 1954.
―――. *The Psychology of Science.* New York: Harper and Row, 1966.
―――. *Motivation and Personality.* New York: Harper and Row, 1954.
May, R. *Man's Search for Himself.* New York: The American Library, Signet Books, 1967.
McConnell, T. A. *The Shattered Self: The Psychological and Religious Search for Selfhood.* Philadelphia: Pilgrim Press, 1971.
Mead, G. H. *Mind, Self and Society: From the Standpoint of a Social Behaviorist.* Chicago: University of Chicago Press, 1938.
Merleau-Ponty, M. *Phenomenology of Perception.* Translated by C. Smith. London: Routledge and Kegan Paul, 1962.
―――. *La Structure du comportement.* Paris: Presses Universitaires de France, 1942.

Merton, T. *The Sign of Jonas.* Garden City, N. Y.: Doubleday and Co., 1956.
Metz, J. B. *Poverty of Spirit.* Translated by J. Drury. Paramus, N. J.: Newman Press, 1970.
——. *Faith in History and Society.* Translated by D. Smith. New York: The Seabury Press, 1980.
Meyerson, E. *Identity and Reality.* New York: Dover, 1962.
Miller, D. L. *Individualism: Personal Achievement and the Open Society.* Austin and London: University of Texas Press, 1967.
Minkowski, E. *Vers une cosmologie. Fragments Philosophiques.* Paris: Aubier-Montaigne, 1946.
Missildine, W. H. *Your Inner Child of the Past.* New York: Simon and Schuster, 1963.
Montessori, M. *The Absorbent Mind.* New York: Dell, 1967.
Moustakas, C. E. *Creativity and Conformity.* Princeton, N. J.: Van Nostrand, 1967.
Mullahy, P., ed. *A Study of Interpersonal Relations: New Contributions to Psychiatry.* New York: Science House, 1967.
Mumford, L. *The Transformations of Man.* New York: Macmillan, Collier, Brooks, 1962.
Muto, S. A. *Approaching the Sacred: An Introduction to Spiritual Reading.* Denville, N. J.: Dimension Books, 1973.
——. *Blessings That Make Us Be.* New York: Crossroad Publishing Co., 1982.
——. *Celebrating the Single Life.* New York: Doubleday and Co., 1982.
——. *The Journey Homeward: On the Road of Spiritual Reading.* Denville, N. J.: Dimension Books, 1977.
——. *A Practical Guide to Spiritual Reading.* Denville, N. J.: Dimension Books, 1976.
——. *Renewed at Each Awakening: The Formative Power of Sacred Words.* Denville, N. J.: Dimension Books, 1979.
——. *Steps Along the Way: The Path of Spiritual Reading.* Denville, N. J.: Dimension Books, 1975.
——, and van Kaam, A. *The Emergent Self.* Denville, N. J.: Dimension Books, 1968.
——, and van Kaam, A. *The Participant Self.* Denville, N. J.: Dimension Books, 1969.
——, and van Kaam, A. *Practicing the Prayer of Presence.* Denville, N. J.: Dimension Books, 1980.
——, and van Kaam, A. *Tell Me Who I Am.* Denville, N. J.: Dimension Books, 1977.
Newman, Cardinal John Henry. *Apologia Pro Vita Sua.* Garden City, N. Y.: Doubleday and Co., 1956.
——. *The Idea of a University.* Garden City, N. Y.: Doubleday and Co., 1959.
O'Doherty, E. F. *Religion and Personality Problems.* Dublin: Clormore and Reynolds, 1964.
Ornstein, R., ed. *The Nature of Human Consciousness.* New York: Viking, 1974.
Otto, R. *The Idea of the Holy.* Translated by John W. Harvey. London: Oxford University Press, 1958.
Pannenberg, W. *Theology and the Philosophy of Science.* Translated by F. McDonagh. Philadelphia: Westminster Press, 1976.
Pascal, B. *Pensées.* Translated by W. F. Trotter, New York: E. P. Dutton, 1958.
Pears, D. *Wittgenstein.* London: Collins, Fontana Modern Classics, 1971.
Piaget, J. *La répresentation du monde chez l'enfant.* Paris: Alcan, 1947.
Pieper, J. *In Tune with the World: A Theory of Festivity.* Chicago: Franciscan Herald Press, 1973.
——. *Leisure, The Basis of Culture.* Translated by Alexander Dru. New York: New American Library, 1963.
Planck, M. *The Philosophy of Physics.* New York: Norton, 1936.
Platt, J. R. *The Step to Man.* New York: John Wiley and Sons, 1966.
Plessner, H. *Lachen und Weinen.* Bern: A. Francke, 1950.

Popper, K. R. *Conjectures and Refutations: The Growth of Scientific Knowledge.* New York: Basic Books, 1965.
―――. *The Poverty of Historicism.* New York: Harper and Row, 1964.
Rahner, K. *Foundations of Christian Faith.* Translated by W. V. Dych. New York: The Seabury Press, 1978.
Reich, C. A. *The Greening of America.* New York: Random House, 1970.
Richard of Saint-Victor. *Selected Writings on Contemplation.* Translated by Clare Kirchberger. New York: Harper and Brothers, 1957.
Richards, M. C. *Centering in Pottery, Poetry and the Person.* Middletown, Conn.: Wesleyan University Press, 1962.
Ricoeur, P. *History and Truth.* Translated by C. A. Kelbley. Evanston: Northwestern University Press, 1965.
―――. *The Symbolism of Evil.* Translated by Emerson Buchanan. New York: Harper and Row, 1967.
Rogers, C. *Client-Centered Therapy.* Boston: Houghton Mifflin, 1965.
Ruitenbeek, H. M. *The Individual and the Crowd.* New York: New American Library, 1965.
Sartre, J. P. *The Emotions.* Translated by B. Frechtman. New York: Philosophical Library, 1948.
Schachtel, E. G. *Metamorphosis: On the Development of Affect, Perception, Attention and Memory.* New York: Basic Books, 1959.
Scheler, M. *Wesen und Formen der Sympathie.* Frankfurt: Schulte-Bulmke, 1948.
Schillebeeckx, E. *World and Church.* Translated by N. D. Smith, New York: Sheed and Ward, 1971.
Schhapper, E. B. *The Inward Odyssey.* London: George Allen and Unwin, 1965.
Schneider, L. *Religion, Culture and Society.* New York: John Wiley, 1964.
Schoeck, H. *Envy: A Theory of Social Behavior.* Translated by Michael Glenny and Betty Ross. London: Secker and Warburg, 1969.
Schrag, O. *Existence, Existenz, and Transcendence: An Introduction to the Philosophy of Karl Jaspers.* Pittsburgh: Duquesne University Press, 1971.
Schultz, A. *The Phenomenology of the Social World.* Translated by G. Walsh and F. Lehnert. Evanston: Northwestern University Press, 1967.
―――, and T. Luckman. *The Structures of the Life World.* Translated by R. Zaner and H. T. Engelhardt. Evanston: Northwestern University Press, 1973.
Scott, N. A., Jr. *The Broken Center: A Definition of the Crisis of Values in Modern Literature: Symbolism in Religion.* New York: George Braziller, 1960.
Selye, H. *The Stress of Life.* New York: McGraw-Hill, 1956.
Shand, A. F. *The Foundation of Character.* New York: Macmillan, 1914.
Solzhenitsyn, A. *One Day in the Life of Ivan Denisovich.* New York: Bantam Books, 1963.
Spitz, R. *A Genetic Field Theory of Ego Formation.* New York: International University Press, 1959.
―――. *Nein und Ja; die Ursprunge der Menschlichen Kommunikation.* Stuttgart: Klett, 1957.
Strong, F. J. *Understanding Religious Man.* Belmont: Dickenson Publishing Co., 1969.
Strasser, S. *Das Gemüt.* Utrecht: Spectrum, 1956.
―――. *The Idea of Dialogical Phenomenology.* Translated by H. J. Koren. Pittsburgh, Pa.: Duquesne University Press, 1969.
―――. *Phenomenology and the Human Sciences.* Translated by H. J. Koren. Pittsburgh, Pa.: Duquesne University Press, 1963.
―――. *The Soul in Metaphysical and Empirical Psychology.* Translated by H. J. Koren. Pittsburgh, Pa.: Duquesne University Press, 1957.
Suzuki, D. T. *Mysticism, Christian and Buddhist: The Eastern and the Western Way.* New York: Harper and Row, 1971.

Suzuki, S. *Zen Mind, Beginner's Mind*. New York: Weatherhill, 1970.
Tanquerey, A. *The Spiritual Life: A Treatise on Ascetical and Mystical Theology*. Translated by H. Branderis. Westminster, Md.: Christian Classics, 1930.
Teresa of Avila, St. *The Way of Perfection*. Translated by E. Allison Peers. Garden City, N. Y.: Doubleday and Company, 1966.
Therese of Lisieux, St. *Story of a Soul: The Autobiography of St. Therese of Lisieux*. Translated by John Clark. Washington, D.C.: Institute of Carmelite Studies, ICS Publications, 1975.
Thoreau, H. D. *Walden and Civil Disobedience*. Edited by P. Sherman. Boston: Houghton Mifflin, 1957.
Toffler, A. *Future Shock*. London: Bodley Head, 1970.
Toulmin, S. *Human Understanding: The Collective Use and Evolution of Concepts*. Princeton, N. J.: Princeton University Press, 1972.
Tournier, P. *A Place for You: Psychology and Religion*, Translated by Edwin Hudson. London: SCM Press, 1966.
―――. *The Whole Person in a Broken World*. Translated by John and Helen Doborstein. New York: Harper and Row, 1964.
Tyrell, F. M. *Man: Believer and Unbeliever*. New York: Alba House, 1974.
Underhill, E. *Mysticism: A Study in the Nature and Development of Man's Spiritual Consciousness*. London: Methuen and Co., 1949.
Van Croonenburg, B. *Gateway to Reality*. Pittsburgh: Duquesne University Press, 1963.
Van der Leeuw, G. *Sacred and Profane Beauty: The Holy in Art*, Translated by David E. Green. New York: Abingdon Press, 1963.
Van der Post, L. *The Lost World of the Kalahari*, Middlesex, England: Penguin Books, 1962.
Van Kaam, A. *Am I Living a Spiritual Life?* Denville, N. J.: Dimension Books, 1978. Co-author.
―――. *The Art of Existential Counseling*. Denville, N. J.: Dimension Books, 1966.
―――. *The Demon and the Dove*. Pittsburgh, Pa.: Duquesne University Press, 1967.
―――. *The Dynamics of Spiritual Self Direction*. Denville, N. J.: Dimension Books, 1976.
―――. *Dynamisme du Quotidien*. Sherbrooke, Quebec: Les Editions Paulines, 1973. Paris: Apostolat des Editions, 1973.
―――. *The Emergent Self*. 1st American ed. Denville, N. J.: Dimension Books, 1968. (2nd rev. ed., 1968). Co-author.
―――. *Encuentro e Integracion*. Ediciones Sigueme, Apartado 332, 1969.
―――. *Envy and Originality*. Garden City, N. Y.: Doubleday and Co., 1972.
―――. *Existential Foundations of Psychology*. Pittsburgh, Pa.: Duquesne University Press, 1966.
―――. *Existential Foundations of Psychology*. Garden City, N. Y.: Doubleday and Company, 1969.
―――. *In Search of Spiritual Identity*. Denville, N. J.: Dimension Books, 1975.
―――. *A Light to the Gentiles*. Pittsburgh, Pa.: Duquesne University Press, 1959. Expanded ed., Denville, N. J.: Dimension Books, 1979.
―――. *Living Creatively*. Denville, N. J.: Dimension Books, 1978.
―――. *Looking for Jesus*. Denville, N. J.: Dimension Books, 1978.
―――. *The Mystery of Transforming Love*. Denville, N. J.: Dimension Books, 1982.
―――. *On Being Involved*. Denville, N. J.: Dimension Books, 1970.
―――. *On Being Yourself*. Denville, N. J.: Dimension Books, 1972.
―――. *The Participant Self*. Denville, N. J.: Dimension Books, 1969. Co-author.
―――. *Personality Fulfillment in the Religious Life: Religious Life in a Time of Transition*. Denville, N. J.: Dimension Books, 1967. (Also in Vietnamese and Japanese)
―――. *Personality Fulfillment in the Spiritual Life*. Denville, N. J.: Dimension Books, 1966.

———. *Practicing the Prayer of Presence*. Denville, N. J.: Dimension Books, 1980. Co-author.
———. *Religion and Personality*. New York: Prentice-Hall, 1964.
———. *Religion and Personality*. Garden City, N. Y.: Doubleday and Co., 1968.
———. *Religion and Personality*. Expanded ed. Denville, N. J.: Dimension Books, 1980.
———. *Religion et Personnalité*. Gasterman-Paris-Tournai: Editions Salvator, Mulhouse, 1967.
———. *Religione e Personalita*. Brescia: Editrice La Scuola, Officine Grafiche La Scuola, 1972.
———. *Spirituality and the Gentle Life*. Denville, N. J.: Dimension Books, 1974.
———. *Tell Me Who I Am*. Denville, N. J.: Dimension Books, 1977. Co-author.
———. *The Third Force in European Psychology*. Greenville, Del.: Psychosynthesis Research Foundation, 1960. (Also in Greek)
———. *The Transcendent Self: Formative Spirituality of the Middle, Early, and Late Years of Life*. Denville, N. J.: Dimension Books, 1979.
———. *The Vocational Director and Counseling*. Derby, N. Y.: St. Paul Publications, 1962.
———. *The Vowed Life*. Denville, N. J.: Dimension Books, 1968.
———. *The Woman at the Well*. Denville, N. J.: Dimension Books, 1976.
van Laer, P. H. *Philosophico-Scientific Problems*. Translated by H. J. Koren. Pittsburgh, Pa.: Duquesne University Press, 1953.
———. *Philosophy of Science: Part One, Science in General*. Translated by H. J. Koren. Pittsburgh, Pa.: Duquesne University Press, 1956.
———. *Philosophy of Science: Part Two, A Study of the Division and Nature of Various Groups of Sciences*. Translated by H. J. Koren. Pittsburgh, Pa.: Duquesne University Press, 1962.
van Melsen, A. G. *Science and Responsibility*. Translated by H. J. Koren, Pittsburgh, Pa.: Duquesne University Press, 1970.
van Peursen, C. A. *Phenomenology and Analytical Philosophy*. Translated by Rex Ambler. Pittsburgh, Pa.: Duquesne University Press, 1972.
van Zeller, D. H. *The Current of Spirituality*. Springfield, Ill.: Templegate Publishers, 1970.
von Hildebrand, D. *The New Tower of Babel*. London: Burns and Oates, 1954.
———. *Transformation in Christ*. Chicago: Franciscan Herald Press, 1973.
Watkin, E. I. *A Philosophy of Form*. London: Sheed and Ward, 1935.
Watts, A. W. *The Book: On the Taboo Against Knowing Who You Are*. New York: Collier Books, 1967.
Weil, S. *Attente de Dieu*. Paris: Edition Fayard, 1966.
Weisskopf, V. *Physics in the Twentieth Century*. Cambridge, Mass.: M.I.T. Press, 1972.
Wessman, A. E., and Ricks, D. F. *Mood and Personality*. New York: Holt, 1966.
White, Winston. *Beyond Conformity*. New York: The Free Press of Glencoe, 1961.
Whitehead, A. N. *Modes of Thought*. New York: Putnam, 1958.
Williams, R. J. *Biochemical Individuality*. New York: John Wiley, 1956.
Wittgenstein, L. *Notebooks 1914–1916*. Translated by G. E. M. Anscombe. Oxford: Basil Blackwell, 1961.
———. *Briefe und Begegnungen*. Translated by P. Engelmann. Munich: 1970.

Articles

Buber, M. "Urdistanz und Beziehung." In *Werke*, Vol. 1, Munich: Koesel-Verlag, 1962.

Byrne, R. "On Doing What We Can: Good Will as an Origin of Contemplative Living." *Studies in Formative Spirituality*, Vol. 1, No. 1 (1980).
De Vries, M. J. "Beyond Integration: New Directions." *The Bulletin*, Christian Association for Psychological Studies, Vol. 7, No. 3, 1981.
Gratton, C. "Approaching a Formative Context for Direction of the Original Self." *Studies in Formative Spirituality*, Vol. 1, No. 1 (1980).
———. "Summaries of Selected Works and Selected Subject Bibliography on Automation and Leisure." *Humanitas*, Vol. 3, No. 1 (1967).
———. "Summaries of Selected Works and Selected Subject Bibliography on Creative Response to Customs and Traditions." *Humanitas*, Vol. 7, No. 1 (1971).
———. "Summaries of Selected Works and Selected Subject Bibliography on the Crisis of Values in Contemporary Culture." *Humanitas*, Vol. 4, No. 3 (1969).
———. "Summaries of Selected Works and Selected Subject Bibliography on the Human Body." *Humanitas*, Vol. 2, No. 1 (1966).
———. "Summaries of Selected Works and Selected Subject Bibliography on Lived Space and Time." *Humanitas*, Vol. 12, No. 3 (1976).
———. "Summaries of Selected Works and Selected Subject Bibliography on Society and Self Emergence." *Humanitas*, Vol. 5, No. 3 (1970).
———. "Summaries of Selected Works and Selected Subject Bibliography on Spirituality and Originality." *Studies in Formative Spirituality*, Vol. 1, No. 1 (1980).
———. "Summaries of Selected Works and Selected Subject Bibliography on Spirituality and Sexuality." *Studies in Formative Spirituality*, Vol. 2, No. 1 (1981).
Muto, S. A. "Richer at Each Awakening." *Cross and Crown*, Vol. 27, No. 1 (1975).
———. "Solitude, Self-Presence and True Participation." *Spiritual Life*, Vol. 20, No. 4 (Winter, 1974).
Sarfatti, J. "The Physical Roots of Consciousness." Mishlove, J. *The Roots of Consciousness*, New York: Random House, 1975.
Walker, E. "Nature of Consciousness." *Mathematical* Biosciences, 7 (1970).
Van Kaam, A. "Addiction and Existence." *Review of Existential Psychology and Psychiatry*, Vol. 3, No. 1 (Winter Issue, 1968).
———. "The Addictive Personality." *Humanitas*, Vol. 1, No. 2 (1965).
———. "Anger and the Gentle Life." *Humanitas*, Vol. 12, No. 2 (1976).
——— and I. V. Pascoe. "Anthropological Psychology and Behavioristic Animal Experimentation." *Festschrift Dr. Straus*, ed. R. M. Griffith and W. von Baeyer, Berlin, Heidelberg, New York: Springer-Verlag, 1966.
———. "Assumptions in Psychology." *The Science of Psychology: Critical Reflections*, ed. D. P. Schultz, New York: Appleton-Century-Crofts, 1970.
———. "Clinical Implications of Heidegger's Concepts of Will, Decision and Responsibility." *Review of Existential Psychology and Psychiatry*, Vol. 1, No. 3 (1961).
———. "Commentary on 'Freedom and Responsibility Examined'." *Behavioral Science and Guidance*, ed. Lloyd-Jones and Westervelt, New York: Teachers College, Columbia University Press, 1963.
———. "Counseling and Existential Psychology." *Harvard Educational Review*, Fall Issue. (This article was later published in *Guidance—An Examination*. New York: Harcourt, Brace and World, 1965.)
———. "Counseling from the Viewpoint of Existential Psychology." *Counseling and Psychotherapy: An Overview*, ed. D. S. Arbuckle. New York: McGraw-Hill, 1966.
———. "Die Existentielle Psychologie als eine Theorie der Gesamtpersönlichkeit." *Jahrbuch fur Psychologie und Medizinische Anthropologie*, 12 Jahrgang Heft 4 (1966).
———. "Differential Psychology." *The New Catholic Encyclopedia*. Washington, D.C.: The Catholic University of America, 1966.
———. "The Dynamics of Hope and Despondency in the Parents of Handicapped Children." *Humanitas*, Vol. 13, No. 3 (1977).
———. "Dynamics of Spiritual Self-Direction." *Spiritual Life*, Vol. 21, No. 4 (Winter Issue, 1975).

———. "Education and Human Motivation by Harry Giles." *The Catholic Educator* (January, 1958).

———. "Education to Originality." *Psychologia Pedagogica Sursum*. Barend Frederik Nel, Stellenbosch/Grahamstad, South Africa: University Publishers and Bookseller, Ltd., 1970.

———. "Encounter and Its Distortion in Contemporary Society." *Humanitas*, Vol. 2, No. 3 (1967).

———. "Existential and Humanistic Psychology." *Review of Existential Psychology and Psychiatry*, Vol. 5, No. 3 (1965).

———. "Existential Crisis and Human Development." *South African Journal of Pedagogy*, Vol. 3, No. 1 (1969).

———. "Existential Psychology as a Theory of Personality." *Review of Existential Psychology and Psychiatry*, (Winter Issue 1963).

——— and R. May. "Existential Theory and Therapy." *Current Psychiatric Therapies*, Vol. 3 (1963).

———. "The Fantasy of Romantic Love." *Modern Myths and Popular Fancies*. Pittsburgh, Pa.: Duquesne University Press, 1961.

———. "The Field of Religion and Personality or Theoretical Religious Anthropology." *Insight*, Vol. 4, No. 1 (1965).

———. "Freud and Anthropological Psychology." *The Justice*, Brandeis University (May, 1959).

———. "Francis Libermann." *The New Catholic Encyclopedia*. Washington, D.C.: The Catholic University of America, 1966.

———. "The Goals of Psychotherapy from the Existential Point of View." *The Goals of Psychotherapy*, ed. A. R. Mahrer. New York: Appleton-Century-Crofts, 1966.

———. "A Guide to Pondering Scripture." *Sign*, Vol. 56, No. 6 (1977).

———. "Humanistic Psychology and Culture." *Journal of Humanistic Psychology*, Vol. 5, No. 3 (1965).

———. "Human Potentialities from the Viewpoint of Existential Psychology." *Explorations in Human Potentialities*, ed. H. A. Otto. Ill.: Charles C. Thomas, Inc., 1966.

———. "The Impact of Existential Phenomenology and Psychological Literature of Western Europe." *Review of Existential Psychology and Psychiatry*, Vol. 1, No. 3 (1961).

———. "Introspection and Transcendent Self-Presence." *Cross and Crown*, Vol. 26, No. 4 (1974).

———. "Life Situations as Life Directives." (Parts 1–3). *Cross and Crown*, Vol. 28, No. 5, 1–3 (1976).

———. "Motivation and Contemporary Anxiety." *Humanitas*, Vol. 1, No. 1 (1965).

———. "The Nurse in the Patient's World." *The American Journal of Nursing*, Vol. 59 (1959).

———. "Original Calling and Spiritual Direction." *Studies in Formative Spirituality*, Vol. 1, No. 1 (1980).

———. "Personality, Personal Unfolding and the Aesthetic Experience of Literature." *Humanitas*, Vol. 4, No. 2 (1968).

———. "Phenomenal Analysis Exemplified by a Study of the Experience of 'Really Feeling Understood.'." *Journal of Individual Psychology*, Vol. 15 (1959).

———. "Provisional Glossary of the Terminology of the Science of Foundational Spirituality." *Studies in Formative Spirituality*, Vol. 1, No. 1–3 (1980), Vol. 2, No. 1–3 (1981), Vol. 3, No. 1–3 (1982).

———. "Psychic Health and Spiritual Life," *New Catholic World*, Vol. 219, No. 1310 (1976).

———. "A Psychology of the Catholic Intellectual." *The Christian Intellectual*, ed. S. Hazo. Pittsburgh, Pa.: Duquesne University Press, 1963.

———. "A Psychology of Falling Away from the Faith." *Insight*, Vol. 2, No. 2 (Fall Issue 1963).

———. "Religion and the Existential Will." *Insight*, Vol. 1, No. 1 (1962).
———. "Religious Anthropology and Religious Counseling." *Insight*, Vol. 4, No. 3 (1966).
———. "Religious Counseling of Seminarians." *Seminary Education in a Time of Change*, ed. J. M. Lee and L. J. Putz. Notre Dame, IN.: Fides Publications, Inc., 1965.
———. "Review of the Divided Self by R. D. Laing." *Review of Existential Psychology and Psychiatry*, Vol. 2, No. 1, (1962).
———. "Sex and Existence." *Review of Existential Psychology and Psychiatry*, Vol. 3, No. 2 (Spring Issue 1963).
———. "Structures and Systems of Personality." *The New Catholic Encyclopedia*. Washington, D.C.: The Catholic University of America, 1966.
———. "The Threefold Path." *Studies in Formative Spirituality*, Vol. 2, No. 3 (1981).
———. "Transcendence Therapy." *Handbook of Innovative Psychotherapies*, ed. R. J. Corsini. New York: John Wiley and Sons, 1981.

Unpublished Materials

Byrne, R. "The Science of Foundational Human Formation and Its Relation to the Christian Formation Tradition." Doctoral dissertation, Institute of Formative Spirituality, Duquesne University, Pittsburgh, Pa., 1982.
Coulombe, J. "Presence to Culture: The Implication of Adrian van Kaam's Theory of Counseling for the Pastoral Counselor on an Indian Reserve." Master's thesis, St. Paul University, Ottawa, Canada, 1974.
Dunne, M. "Adrian van Kaam's View of Man: Some Basic Aspects of His Theory of Personality and the Implications of His Theory for Psychotherapy." Master's thesis, St. Paul University, Ottawa, Canada.
Girard, R. "A Study of the Existential Counseling of Adrian van Kaam as Applied to the Ministry of Pastoral Counseling." Master's thesis, St. Paul University, Ottawa, Ontario, 1974.
Leavy, M. "The Process of Reforming Dispositions: A Formative Approach to Habit Change." Doctoral dissertation, Institute of Formative Spirituality, Duquesne University, Pittsburgh, Pa., 1981.
Lewis, L. J. "The Formative Experience of Waiting: Moving from Living in Illusion to Living with Reality." Doctoral dissertation, Institute of Formative Spirituality, Duquesne University, Pittsburgh, Pa., 1982.
Lockwood, T. "The Formative Experience of Taking Responsibility for an Unfamiliar Task." Doctoral dissertation, Institute of Formative Spirituality, Duquesne University, Pittsburgh, Pa., 1981.
Maes, C. "The Silent Mode of Presence." Doctoral dissertation, Institute of Formative Spirituality, Duquesne University, Pittsburgh, Pa., 1978.
Reuter, M. "Formation through Encounters of Ordinary Life." Doctoral dissertation, Institute of Formative Spirituality, Duquesne University, Pittsburgh, Pa., 1982.
Vitaline, T., M.D. "Il Concetto di Presenza nella Teoria del Counseling di Adrian van Kaam e le sue Applicazioni nel Campo della Malattie Psicosomatiche." Master's thesis, St. Paul University, Ottawa, Canada.

Index

abandonment to formation mystery: and foundational formation option, 221–227; risk of, 227–242
action and disposition chart, 285
activism, pneumatism and, 182
actual life-form, 259–260
adolescence, sexual preformation and, 109–110
adoration, 160–161
affective prayer, 183
affirmation: of appreciative abandonment, 240–241; and basic reaction patterns, 131
ambitions, 5, 87, 100–101, 158
andragogy, 12
anger, vital expression of, 97
anonymous life directives, 71–72
anthropology of human formation, 218–220
anxiety, 64, 162
apparent form, 255–256
appraisal: body changes and, 128; and current and apparent life-forms, 255–256; of formation situation, 271; liberating, 271–272; of life experiences, 265–266; and sexuality, 108–109
appreciative abandonment: affirmation and implementation of, 240–241; consistent maintenance in daily life formation, 237–238; and negative experience, 236–237; obstacles to fidelity, 238; primordial formation disposition of, 235–236; reasonableness of, 238–240; and relationship of appreciative and depreciative appraisals, 241–242; risk of, 228–229. *See also* Primordial appreciative abandonment
art, spiritual-vital formation and, 101
articulation research, 19–20
articulations of functional dimension, 261–262
articulations of vital dimension, 133–138
artificial split in dimensions of forming presence and type of life, 60
asceticism: spirituality and, 81; of vital dimension of formation, 128
aspirations, 5, 261
assimilation of new directives, 61–62
atomic and subatomic formation, 208
atonement, 192
attunement, 192
autarchic pride-form, 188–190, 194. *See also* pride form
autarchic self-actualization, 53–54
autarchy of human formation, 53
autonomous self-actualization, 180–81
autonomous self-realization, 180
auxiliary sciences, 33; and formation technology, 65; and foundational theory, 247;

and reflection on formation, 10; potential contributions of, 35–36; and unifying theory of human formation, 282–283
awareness of formation mystery, 193
awe, 160–162

behavioristic formation, 178–179
behavioristic psychology, 280
biophysical dimension, 43–45
blind identification with formation situation, 273
bodily behavior, as manifold preformation question, 72
bodily limits, 128

centering, preformed need for, 81–82
centering spiritual presence, 159
centers of transformation, 24–25
central power of formation, 180
character traits, 84
charts of science of foundational formation, 284–298; action and disposition, 285; empirical, 284–285; foundational formative energy flow, 285–286; formation-polarity formation field diagram, 286; input, 286; integration, 286–287; structure, 285
Christian articulation research, science of foundational formation and, 14–15
Christian Association for Psychological Studies, 36–41
Christian form tradition; and divine preformation, 222–223; and foundational formation, 14–15, 16, 36–41; and importance of particular school versions of spirituality, 29–31; and mystery of trinity, 212; and pneumatism, 182; and transcendence, 167
Christian formation theory: and academic study of formative spirituality, 21–22; cultural-personal coloring of, 31–32; formative spirituality and, 20–23
cocreation of form directives, 246
commitment, spiritual, 148–149
communal-personal life formation, 210
communities, development of ideals and, 175–176
community consultants, formation scientists and, 117–118
compulsiveness, functional conscience and, 87
conceptual sciences, 279–280
conformity, 166
congenial life-form, 5, 267, 268
congenial compatibility, 268
congenial solution to transcendence crisis, 265
consonance, 46; of cosmic interformation, 205–206; of cosmos, 187; and creative dis-

Index

continuity, 62; and integration of spirituality and sexuality, 122–125; between preformation and formation, 6; and flow of world formation, 199; and preservation of vital vigor, 126; and sexuality, 103; and spirit, mind, body distinction, 63–64
consonant, 48
consonant contestation-ratification response, 274
consonant form directives, 5
consonant formation, 4, 6, 66, 179–180; and autarchic self-actualization, 54–56; and pneumatism, 183–184; as response to formation situation, 274; and self-preservation, 134; and virtue, 196
consonant life emergence, ideals and, 173
consonant life formation, 179
consonant living, 127
consonant society, 197
consonant spirituality, 142
contemplation, 183
contemplative presence, 207
contestation response, 274
contrast and complementarity, in cosmic interformation, 196
core form of life, 232–235, 253–255. *See also* heart
corresponding formation fields, 244–245
cosmic contemplatives, 206–208
cosmic epiphany of formation mystery: and autarchic pride-form, 188–190; awareness in spiritual form traditions, 193; of everyday formation, 191–193; functional formation in light of, 193–198; intrinsically dynamic and unifying, 198–208; and polar opposites, 196; primordial manifestations of, 201–202; and relationship of field and form, 203; and universal interformation, 190–191, 195–196
cosmic formation, 202–203, 207, 213–216, 234–235
cosmic interformation, 188, 196, 205–206
cosmic mysticism, 207–208
cosmic, organismic, and vital preformation, 209
counterfeit form structure, 206
creative delaying and distancing, 81
creative discontinuity, 61–62
crises of transcendence, 153–154
cultural directives, 183
cultural innovation, refusal of transcendent dimension and, 162
cultural-personal coloring, 31–32
culture, functional dimension, 86
current and apparent life-forms, 256–259
current formation situations, 273
current formative information, 255–256
current life-forms, 9, 255–256, 264; and integration of sexuality, 114
customs, 84

deformation: and appreciative abandonment, 236–237; and pneumatism, 183–184; and transcendentalist formation, 178–179
deformative dissonance, 157
deformative presuppositions of science of human formation: transcendental autarchic self-actualizing view, 53–56; vitalistic view, 50–52; vitalistic-functionalistic view, 52–53

deformative suffering, 189
denial, 157
depreciative abandonment, 232–235, 240
depreciative abandonment disposition, 232–235, 241–242
destiny, mystery of, 172
detachment, 81, 151
De Vries, Michael J., 36–41
dialectical ideal, 174–175
dialogical integrative research methodology, 12
dialogical movement of formation, 158
dimensions of formative consciousness, 262–263
dimensions of forming presence, 59–61
direction disclosures, fidelity to, 63
directive formation, vitalistic-functionalistic view and, 53
directives, new, 61–62
dispositions: secondary foundational lifeform, 274–275; toward mystery of formation, 226–227
dissonance: and creative discontinuity, 61–62; of sexuality and spirituality, 103–105
distinctively human formation, 93–102; and functional formation, 93–94; and historical formation, 94–95; and permeation of vital formation by spiritual formation, 96–102
distortions in vital dimension, 138–141
divine preformation, 161; ongoing, 222–223
dynamic formation triad, and consistent maintenance of appreciative abandonment, 237–238

Einstein, Albert, 201, 208
emergent human formation, 4–5, 65–66; disclosure and appraisal of, 63; and power of spirit, 79–80
empirical formation, 284–285
empirical life-form, 7, 251–253
emptiness, 201–202
emotions, expression potency of, 130–132
energy field, 209, 243; and centering spiritual presence, 159; and cosmic field of formation, 187–188; vital dimension as, 127–133
envy, 158
epiphanies of formation mystery, openness to, 80, 187–188. *See also* cosmic epiphanies of formation mystery
equanimity, and mystery of formation, 194
equilibrium, and mystery of formation, 194
evolution, 35
exclusive functional dominance, 87–89
existential psychology, 40
existentialism, 34–35, 53–54, 178
expansion, 135–136, 146
experiential-formative sciences, 281–282
experiential sciences, 280–281
expression potency, 130
extra- or outer formation, 250

faith: in daily call to formation, 210
faith, hope, and consonance, 230–231
fanaticism, 87
fear, dehumanization and, 161
feeling of abandonment, 239–240
fidelity to appreciative abandonment, obstacles to, 238
field and form relationship, 77, 243

final beneficial meaningfulness of enigma of formation, 229
flexibility, transcendent ideals and, 173
flow of formation, 266
focal consciousness, formation and, 250
form dimensions, 57–59; integration of, 259–260
form direction, 244
form directives, 6, 7, 265–266; cocreation of, 246; and cosmic consonance, 191; and functional dimension, 86–87; and spiritual formation, 183
form potency, 57, 166; of children, 239–240; and core form, 254–255; and functional dimension, 86; growth in receptive dimension of, 219–220; maintenance of, 247–248; and refusal of transcendent dimension, 162; and transcendence crisis, 264–265; transcendent character of, 166
form receptivity: and appreciative abandonment, 236; and autarchic self-actualization, 54–56
form tradition: foundational sexual directives of, 104–105, 114–117; and personalized tradition directives, 114–115
form traditions: differentiation in, 14; emerging, 246; and foundational formation, 19–20; and foundational theory, 124–125, 247; and heart as image for core form, 254; and spiritual formation, 182–183; and transcendence, 167
formability. See form potency
formation: defined, 66; ground of consonance between preformation and, 6; mystery of, see mystery of formation; primary foundation of, 7–8; and transcendent dynamic, 8–9
formation conscientization, 10, 263
formation-consonance, 205–206
formation consultants: and adolescent sexuality, 109–110; and distinction beween normal foundation problems and psychological disturbances, 121–122; impact of subcultures on, 118–119; preparation of, 120; and sexual security directives, 119–120
formation energy, and articulations of vital form dimension, 133–138
formation event, 199
formation field, 2–3, 57; current and apparent life-forms and, 256; daily formation of human life within, 65; and formative value directives, 51; human formation and, 248–249; interaction with, 9–10; interaction between vital life and, 84; mystery of formation and, 200–201; original obscure, 70; poles of, 248–249; and power of spirit, 79–80; sexual preformation within, 110; vital preformation of life and, 68–74
formation freedom, 214–216, 219–220, 224–225
formation guilt, 224
formation history: preselection of schools of spirituality from, 27; and reasonableness of appreciative abandonment, 238–238
formation impotence, 162
formation intuitions, 9
formation matter, 223–224
formation movements in human life, 267–269

formation mystery. See mystery of formation
formation phases, 9
formation poles, 47, 286; vital-functional, and female-male, 196–198
formation potential; and foundational formation movements of life, 267; of tradition, 113–114; and vital behavior, 105–106
formation powers, vital, functional, and transcendent, 65
formation questions, reflection and, 10
formation responsibility, preformative direction and, 8
formation situation, 3, 271–274. See also situational formation
formation symbols, 245
formation terminology, 64–66
formation theory of personality, and transcendent dimension, 150
formative anticipation, 35
formative appraisal, 231, 241–242
formative consciousness, 262–263
formative counseling, 140–141. See also formation counselors
formative decision, 215
formative dimensions of human life, 1–5
formative dispositions, 52
formative emergence, complexity of, 66
formative imagination, 253
formative life situations, 222
formative life-style, 129
formative meaning, 3, 4, 8
formative meditation, 183
formative memory, 35
formative mind, rationalist view and, 46
formative receptivity, crisis and, 153–154
formative repetition of functional vital directives, 84
formative responses to formative situations, 273–274
formative spirituality: academic study of, 21–22; basic questions related to, 17–18; and Christian formation, 20–23; definition of, 14; emergence of, 18; science of, xvii. See also science of formation
formative tendency of humanity, xix–xx
formative tending, 214
formative thinking, xvii–xix
formative transcendent mind, 252
formative transcendent process, 264–265
formative value directives, 44, 51
forming presence of the human spirit, 4, 93, 94
foundational, 34–35
foundational Christian formation, 23
foundational directives, misidentifaction of, 116–117
foundational dynamics of emergent human formation, 79–81
foundational dynamics of human formation, 57–67
foundational elements of universe, 199–200
foundational form direction, 212
foundational form potency, 244
foundational formation, 166; compared with field of spiritual theology, 27–29; compared with special theories of formation, 26–27; and importance of school versions of spirituality, 29–31; prereflective and scientific knowledge of, 8–9

foundational formation decision, 221–227.
See also primordial formation decision
foundational formation movement, 267
foundational formation option, 223–227
foundational formation theory, 243–275
foundational formation theory: and actual life-form, 259–260; and adaptive flexibility of foundationals, 271–272; and articulations of functional dimension of human formation, 261–262; and cocreation of form directives, 246; and core form, 253–255; and current and apparent life-forms, 255–258; and descriptive definition of four life-form dimensions, 260–261; and dimensions of formative consciousness, 262–263; and field theory, 243; and five incarnational sources of empirical life formation, 252–253; and five types of formative responses to formation situations, 273–274; and flow of formation, 266–267; and form directives, 265–266; and form potency, 244; and form-potency maintenance, 247–248; and formation field, 248–249; and formation movements in human life, 267–269; and formation and situation, 269; and formative transcendence process, 264–265; and human form directives and corresponding formation fields, 244–245; and human formation symbols, 245; and key formation situations, 272–273; overall structure of, 246–247; and periodical permanence of current and apparent life formation, 258–259; and phasic formation, 263–264; and secondary foundational life-form, 274–275; and situational formation situation as point of departure, 270–271; and situational formation transfer, 270; and structural effects of human formation, 250–252; and transcendent sources of empirical life formation, 252
foundational formative energy flow chart, 285–286
foundational formative spirituality, and human interformation, 123–124
foundational hope, 238
foundational human formation, 65–66, 167, 218–220
foundational human life-form, sexual directives and, 119–120
foundational human view of formation, 46–49
foundational life call, 80–81
foundational life direction, 7, 148
foundational life-form, 89–92, 189, 274–275
foundational question, 226–227
foundational response to formation mystery, 225–227
foundational sexual directives of form tradition, 114–117
foundational spirituality, 13–14, 144
foundational theory of proximate formation, 64–65
foundational tracing, 118
foundational triad, 230–231
foundationals, adaptive flexibility of, 271–272
free formation movement, 223–224
freedom, 213–216, 225–227, 233–235. See also formation freedom

Freud, Sigmund, 169
frustration, spirit-body dualism and, 64
full integration, 287
functional, use in science of formation, 64–65
functional achievement, 94
functional-aesthetic articulation, 262
functional ambitions, transcendent aspirations and, 93–94
functional bridges, 170–171
functional categorical thinking, 190
functional conscience, 87
functional dimension, 58–59; articulations of, 261–262; characteristics of, 90; concrete emergence in childhood, 85–89; emancipation of, 81–82; emergence of, 66; exclusive dominance by, 87–89; executive role of, 86; formation of, see functional formation; projecting and managing operations of, 171–172; quasi-transcendent experiences of, 150–151; relationship with vital dimension, 76–77. See also vital-functional dimension
functional ego, pride form and, 190
functional enlightenment, 86–87
functional form potency, 94
functional form potential, 261
functional formation, 83–92; cosmic epiphany and, 193–198; limits of, 156
functional formative anticipation, 253
functional formative intelligence, 252
functional formative memory, 253
functional formative will, 252–253
functional identity, 85–86, 148
functional mind, 83–84, 196
functional phase of personal-spiritual formation, 143
functional potency, dynamic balance and, 89–92
functional projects, 168–177
functional spirituality, 141–142
functional-transcendent life, 127
functional view of world, 193–194
functional vital directives, 84
functional willing, 89
functionalism, health and, 155–156
functionalistic stereotype, 197
functionalistic view of life, 85
functionalistic willfulness, 192–193
functionality, 170–171, 196–198
fusion, 139
fusion striving, 134

galaxies, formation of, 199
genetic inheritance, 62, 129, 148, 247–248
genetic preformation, primordial abandonment option and, 221
gentle style of life, 127
global convictions, 253–254
global directives, 253–254
global formative effects of heart, 255
global formative experience, 3–4
global love direction, 253–254
glossary, 299–308
graced formation, 21
greediness, 178–179
guilt, spirit-body dualism and, 64

heart, 253–257
historical form traditions, 95–96

historical formation, 94–96
historical pulsations, 94–95
historical situations, traditions and, 112
historical unfolding, 173
history, engagement in, 49
Holy Spirit, 144, 181, 183. *See also* spirit
horizon of the spirit, 80, 168, 170
horizontal interformation, 99
human dwellings, 99
human form directives, 244–245
human formation: and emergence of vital-functional dimension, 75–82; and form traditions, 124–125; foundational form direction in, 212; ideals and, 170–171, 176–177; as natural analogical concept, 216–220; phases of, 143–144; scientific fields of, 11–16; structural effects of, 250–252; temporality of, 124–125
human formation symbols, 217–218
human history, 141–142, 176–177
human life-form, 59–61; and cosmic formation, 202–203; emergent and transcendent, 65–66; and unity in diversity, 158–159
human life in formation, 1–16; universally valid theory of, xx–xxi
humility, 179
Huxley, Aldous, 169–170
hygiene, vital vigor and, 126
hysterical personalities, 271

ideal form of life, 213
idealist view. *See* rationalist view
ideals, 169–177
idolatry, 169
idolized forms of prayer, 170
idolized ideals, 169–170
idolizing, pride-form and, 189–190
idolizing appraisal, 271–272
idols, ideals becoming, 169
implementation of appreciative abandonment, 240–241
impulse-reaction circuit of vital life, disruption by spirit, 80
impulses, 5
impulsive feelings and desires, 83–84
impulsive reactions, 78
incarnation of ideals, 168
incorporation of vital form dimensions, 136–137
individualization of vital dimension, 128–129
informative thinking, xvii–xviii
infraconscious, 250, 263
initial formation, 6–7
initial integration, 287
inner formation, 4
input chart, 286
inspirations, 168, 261
in-spirited functional dimension, 169
instinct, 110
integration: and actual life-form, 259–260; of form dimensions, 259–260; and Holy Spirit, 144; and human formation, 61–64; and ideals, 173–174; of new directives, 61–62; of science of formation and theology, 36–41; of sexuality, 108–109, 114–115, 121–125; and spiritual-functional vital life, 63–64; and spiritual identity and direction disclosures, 62–63; and transcendent dimension, 147–148, 158–159;

and transcendent experiences, 150–151; and vital, functional, and transcendent formation powers, 65; of vital-sexual and transcendent life formation, 111–122
integration chart, 286–287
integrative thought and study, xix
interaction, preformative sensate meaning and, 73
interconsciousness, 262–263
intercultural knowledge, 18
interformation, 46, 167, 249, 250; and emergence of functional dimension, 85; foundational formative spirituality and, 123–124; and historical form traditions, 95; and primordial abandonment option, 221
interforming actions, universe and, 204
interforming oneness of universe, 195
interiorized form directives, 269
intermediate integration, 287
intermediate whole, transcendence and, 155
interpenetration of spirit, mind, and body, 60–61
intraformation, 46, 249; and situational formation, 269
intraformative dialogue, 66
intraformative dispositions and directives, 270
intraformative experience, 225
intraformative foundational decision, 225–227
intraformative process, vital formation and, 250
intuition, 10
inwardness, incorporation urge and, 137
isolationist tenderness, 82
issue-oriented thinking. *See* informative thinking

Jewish form traditions, and transcendence, 167
Jungian formation, and trancendentalist formation, 178

knowledge: of formation freedom, 224–225; sensate, intellectual, emotional, and spiritual-intuitive modalities of, 152–153
Kuhn, Thomas S., 34

laws of nature, 209
life-directing sensate experience, 72
life direction: and formation mystery, 216; knowledge of, 251–252
life directives, 114, 167
life experiences. *See* daily life
life-form, 4; descriptive definition of dimensions of, 260–261; vital functional dimension, 75–82; vitalizing force of ideal in, 174–175
life situation, and human formation, 50–52
logic, and mystery of formation, 186
love, and core form of life, 253–254
loving consonance, transcosmic dynamic of, 210–213

macro- and microcosmic formation process, 187
magic power, and pseudospirituality, 140–141
maintenance, and receptivity to transcendent dimension, 146
managing presence, 171–172

INDEX

Marx, Karl, 169
mathematics, and behavioristic psychology, 280
meditative prayer, 170
microcosmos, 187
mid-life crisis, 254
mineral, plant, and animal formation, human formation and, 19
misidentification of foundational directives, 116–117
de Montfort, 28
moral choice, 198
moral theology, 278
mortification striving, and articulation of vital form dimension, 135
mysterious whole, belief in, 162–163
mystery of formation, 6–7, 101, 138–139, 162, 169, 177, 185–220
mystery of personal formation, 210
mystery of Trinity, Christian form tradition and, 212

naturalism, and pneumatism, 182
nature mystics. *See* cosmic contemplatives
negative experiences, appreciative abandonment and, 236–237
negative stage in childhood, 86
Nietzsche, 169
nonself, and human formation, 47
nudity, 104

obedience to life's limitations, 137
obsessive-compulsive, 271
obstacles to fidelity to appreciative abandonment, 238
oneness in uniqueness, intuition of, 147
ontological discontinuity of formation, 216
organic formation, and preformation, 250
organic infraformation, 209
outer formation, 46

paradigm, new, 34
parents. *See* significant formation agents
participant life-form, 136
peace, and centering spiritual presence, 159
pedagogy, and problems of human formation, 12
perception, lasting patterns in, 2
perfectionism, and functional conscience, 87
periodical permanence of current and apparent life formation, 258–259
persistent situations, 273
personal assimilation, and interiorized form directives, 269
personal epiphany of the formation mystery, and transcosmic dynamic of loving consonance, 210–213
personal life, and vital form dimension, 127
personal-spiritual formation, 143–144
personality, foundational potential form of, 250–251
personalization of the common ideal, 177
personalized tradition directives, 114–115
phasic formation, 263–264
philosophy, and science of foundational formation, 12–13, 14–16, 33
physical epiphany of the formation mystery, 200–201
physical and experiential research, and spiritual-functional-vital formation, 101–102
physical-formative sciences, 279

physical sciences, 278
physicists: and mystery of formation, 206–208; and unification of various physical formation fields, 201
physics: and approximate knowledge of cosmic formation fields, 205; and consonance of cosmos, 187; and flow of world formation, 199; and mystery of formation, 195–196
physiology, and vital reaction patterns, 129–130
plants, animals, minerals, human formation processes and, 42–45, 49
pneumatic dimension, 144, 181–184
pneumatic phase of personal-spiritual formation, 144
pneumatist formation, transcendent form potency and, 181–184
pneumatists, 181–184
polar fields of formation, and mystery of formation, 191
polar opposites, functional mind at, 196
polarity paradigm of science of formation, 269
poles of formation field, 248–249; preformation of the human life-form and, 249–250; and structures of the current life-form, 258
polymorphous versatility of sexual preformation, 110
positivist view of formation, 42–45
poverty, 137
power of spirit, emergent human formation and, 79–80
praxis of formation, 20
prayer, idolized forms of, 170
preconscious, 250
preconscious attitudes, and integration of spirituality and sexuality, 113–114
preconscious field of vital preformation, 71
preconscious formation, 164
preconsciousness, 262
predisposition, to depreciative abandonment, 232–234. *See also* genetic preformation
preformation, 4, 6, 46, 62, 66, 106, 248–249, 250
preformation of the human life-form, and poles of the formation field, 249–250
preformation of sexual appeal, 108–109
preformative direction, 7–8
preformative sensate meaning, and interaction, 73
preformative vital life directives, 71–73
prehuman formation processes, 44
prehumanized vital dimension, 45, 77–78
prelogical language of the formative experience, 10
prereflective and scientific knowledge of foundational formation, 8–9
prereflective awareness, 10
prescientific presuppositions, science of foundational formation and, 12–14
preservation, and articulation of vital form dimension, 133–134
presuppositions of science of human formation, 42–49. *See also* informative presuppositions of human formation
pride-form, 54, 82, 204, 211, 266–267, 271–272
primal foundation of all formation, 7–8

primordial appreciative abandonment, formative appraisal and, 231. See also abandonment to formation mystery
primordial depreciative disposition, 232–235
primordial formation decision, unavoidability of, 229–231
primordial formation disposition of appreciative abandonment, 235–236
primordial formation disposition of depreciative abandonment, 232–235
primordial manifestation of cosmic epiphany, 201–202
professional dedication, 98
projecting functional dimension, 172
projecting and managing operation of functional dimension, 171–172
projects: overattention to, 175; and spirit, 172
provisional unity between vital and functional dimensions of life, 62
proximate directives of sexual life formation, 104
pseudospirituality, and distortions in vital dimension, 138–141; vital experience and magic component of, 140–141
psychology, and theological systems, 37–41
psychosomatic illness, 157
psychotherapy, and spirit-body dualism, 64
public potency affirmation, yearning for, 219
pulsations, 5
purity, 137, 200–201

quality of life, and transcendent formation, 165
quantum field, 200
quasi-foundational pride-form of life, and primal violence, 158
quasi-transcendent experiences, of functional and vital life dimension, 150–151

radical conservatism, 83, 134
radical detachment, 176–177
radical distancing of spirit, 177
radical reasonableness, 231
ratification of past or present formation situation, 273–274
rationalist view of formation, 45–46
readiness for deepening, 163
realism, and centering spiritual presence, 159
realistic ideal. See dialectical ideal
reasonableness of appreciative abandonment, 238–240
recollection, and incorporation urge, 137
reflection, 9–11, 76, 128
relationship of appreciative and depreciative appraisals, 241–242
religion: idols in, 169–170; transcendent dimension and, 159–160
repression, 157
respect, and reverence, 157, 160, 162, 164
restriction, 112–114
reverence, 160–164
revolt against directives of formation, 99
rigidity, and functional conscience, 87
risk of abandonment to formation mystery, 227–242
ritual dances, 101
robots, 44

root of appreciative abandonment, 230–231
rupture of vital impulse-reaction cycle, 80

Sartre, Jean-Paul, 178
school of spirituality, 26–27, 29–32
science of formation, xix–xxi; and the auxiliary science of theology, 36–41; deformative presuppositions of, 50–56; emergence of, 5–11; need for, 22–23; position within classification of sciences, 276–283; and reflection, 9–11; role of, 282–283; terminology of, 32–36, 299–308; and transcendent dynamic of human formation, 9
science of formative spirituality, 13, 243; and formation field, 201; ontological basis of, 216; point of departure of, 211
science of foundational formation, 11, 12–16, 23–26
science of foundational human formation, 11, 18–20, 42–49, 65
science, technology, and spiritual-vital formation, 99–101
scientific language, necessity of, 32–36
scientific reasoning, and mystery of formation, 186
scientific reflection on formation, 73–74
scrupulousness, and functional conscience, 87
Second Vatican Council, 38
security directives, 114
self-actualizing formation, 53, 65, 180–181
self-realization, 53
sensate form directives, 69–70
service, style of, 128
"sex appeal," 107
sexual directives: alien, 118–119; and foundational structure of human life-form, 119–120
sexual form potential, 107
sexual formation: and excessive security directives, 104–105; and formation scientists as community consultants, 117–118; and the foundational structure of human life-form, 119–120; normal problems of, 121–122; proximate directives of, 104
sexual preformation: adolescence and, 109–110; of life situations, people, and things, 107; polymorphous versatility of, 110
sexual security directives: excessive, 104–105; traditions and, 114–115
sexual virtue, 107
sexuality, dissonance of, 103–105
siblings. See significant formation agents
significant formation agents, and feeling of abandonment, 239–240
situation pole, 249
situational directives, 269
situational formation, 269
situational formation transfer, 270
social articulation, 262
social cohesion, and fusion, 134
social concern, 172
social or cultural pressure, and dissonant formative meanings, 8
social justice, and foundational formation, 19
social-personal development, and vital-functional life, 126–144
socio-historical form dimensions, 57–58; and dynamics of human formation, 66–67
socio-historical form directives sedimented, 266

socio-historical form potential, defined, 260–261
socio-historical form traditions, 57–59
socio-historical identity, 148
special theories of formation, 26–27
specialized formation, and foundational formation, 23–24
spirit, 13; awakening in children, 84–85; defined, 93; expansion of, 126; and emancipation of functional dimension, 81–82; and functional form potency, 94; and functional-vital life, 67, 172; and functionality, 170–171; power of, 79–80; and preformed sexual appeal, 107–109; radical distancing of, 177; and sexual articulation of vital dimension, 121–122
spirit-body dualism, 63–64, 68
spirit dimension, transcendent experience of, 151–152
spirit-mind-body dialectic, 60–61, 63–65
spirit potency, and functionalistic orientation, 88–89
spirit of poverty, 200–201
spirit power. *See* transcendence dynamic of human life
spiritual, meaning of, 68
spiritual attitudes, and intuition of oneness in uniqueness, 147
spiritual center, and vital, functional and transcendent formation powers, 65
spiritual conscience, and functional conscience, 87
spiritual dimension. *See* transcendent dimension
spiritual disclosures, 93
spiritual experience, transcendent dimension and, 145–146
spiritual form potency, 79–80
spiritual form traditions, and awareness of cosmic epiphany, 193
spiritual formation: form directives and, 183; as distinctively human, 93–102; and form-receptive potency in a functional society, 220; and pseudospirituality, 138–141; role of vital dimension in, 68–74; of world and immediate situation, 98–99
spiritual formation power, 19
spiritual-functional-vital formation, physical and experiential research and, 101–102
spiritual ideal, incarnation of, 168
spiritual identity, 62–63, 148; vital-functional identity and, 62–63
spiritual life, conditions for, 81
spiritual presence: and religious experience, 159–160; and reverence, 160, 162–164
spiritual theology, 27–29, 278
spiritual-vital formation, 99–101
spirituality: approaches of theology and science of foundational formation to, 28–29; and cultural personal coloring of Christian formation, 31–32; Marian school of, 28; meaning of, 68; permeation of vital formation by, 96–102
spirituality and sexuality, 103–125; and dissonance of sexuality, 103–105; and foundational structure of vital-sexual formation, 105–110; integration of, 121–125; and integration of vital-sexual and transcendent life formation, 111–112; and normalcy of formation problems, 121–122; and reserve of the formation scientists as community consultant, 117–118
spiritualization of vital formation, 97–98
spontaneous formation awareness, 10
stars, formation of, 199
static misconception of universal formation field, 198–200
stereotyped reactions, and refusal of transcendent dimension, 162
structural effects of human formation, 250–252
structure chart, 285
Structure of Scientific Revolutions, The, (Kuhn), 34
stubbornness, and functional conscience, 87
subcultures of formation scientists, 118–119
subhuman, and form genetics, 247–248
subjectivism, and rationalist view of formation, 46
subtheories of formation, 247
survival, and receptivity to transcendent dimension, 146
symbols, and human formation, 217–218, 222, 245

Tanquerey, 28
teachers. *See* significant formation agents
technical articulation, 261–262
technology: and informative thinking, xviii; and spiritual vital formation, 99–101
temperament, 131; formation of, 129–130; and vital dimension, 75
temporality of human formation, 124–125
tension, 5
terminology of science of formation, 32–36
theology, and science of formation, 12–13, 36–41
theoretical-formative sciences, 278
theoretical sciences, 277–278
total formative experience, 3
traditions: and science of foundational formation, 13; and sexual directives, 119–120; and sexuality, 111–112
transcendence, 65–66; and awe, worship and adoration, 160–161; and intermediate wholes, 155; as less common contemporary event, 155–156; refusal of, 162; and respect vs. violence, 156–158; and reverence, culture and humanization, 161–162; and reverence and respect, 160
transcendence crisis, 264–265
transcendence dynamic of human life, 19; use in science of formation, 64–65
transcendent aspirations, 2, 164; and expansion urge, 135–136; and functional ambitions, 93–94
transcendent call to consonance, and human mystery of formation, 211–212
transcendent dimension, 86, 93, 137, 145–165, 167, 178, 194, 196–197, 267–268
transcendent dynamic, 211; formation and, 8–9
transcendent enlightenment in childhood, 85
transcendent entities, absorption in, 134
transcendent experience, 149–159
transcendent form dimension, 59
transcendent orientation, and crisis, 154
transcendent form potency, 59, 148, 156, 166–184
transcendent form potential, defined, 261

transcendent formation, 51, 167–168; vital-sexual formation, integration with, 111–122
transcendent formative aspiration, 213
transcendent-functional dimensions of life-form, 80–81, 97–98
transcendent ideals, 168–177
transcendent openness, 163
transcendent participation, 80
transcendent phase of personal-spiritual formation, 144
transcendent self-emergence, 144
transcendent sources of empirical life formation, 252
transcendent spiritualities, 142–143
transcendent tendency of all human formation, 213
transcendent value directives, 182–183
transcendental, autarchic self-actualizing view of formation, 53–56
transcendentalist formation, 177–181
transconscious, 250, 263
transcosmic foundational formation, 213–216
transcultural form directives, 246
transforming power of transcendent dimension, 147
transition from periodic life-form to another, 264
transition crisis of children, 138–139

union, experiences of, 138–140
unity of transcendent, functional and vital dimensions, 173–174
universal directives of formation, 249
universal formation field, static misconception of, 198–200
universe: formative power in, 208–216; interforming actions and, 204; interforming oneness of, 195

vertical preformation and interformation, 99
vigor, depletion of, 127
violence, 157–158
virtue, 196
vital-bodily modes of preformation, 93
vital dimension, 66, 68–78, 86, 94, 127–133, 138–141, 168, 177–178, 217–218; See also vital-functional dimension
vital-emotional needs of body, and functional achievement, 94
vital field formation, sexual formation and, 106–107
vital form dimension, 58; articulation of, 133–138; summary of characteristics of, 131–133
vital form potential, defined, 261
vital formation: limits of, 156; permeation by spiritual formation, 96–102; and preformation, 250; spiritualization of, 97–98
vital and functional dimensions, 62, 81–82; and emancipation of functional dimension, 81–82; emergence of, 75–82; and emergence of transcendent dimension, 146; and energy for reflective attention, 67; and expression potency, 130–131; and formation of temperament, 129–130; and foundational dynamic of emergent human formation, 79–81; and individualization of vital dimension, 128–129; ongoing movements and interforming influence of, 126–144; and transcendent spirituality in humanity's formation history, 141–144; and vital dimensions, as energy, 127–133
vital-functional formation polarities, 196–198
vital-functional identity, and spiritual identity, 62–63
vital-functional life, social-personal development and, 126–144
vital growth, 51
vital health and energy, individualization of, 128–129
vital impulse-reaction cycle, rupture of, 80
vital impulses, and transcendent aspirations, 94
vital life, 50; and formation situations, 68–69; and functional formation, 84; and human sexuality, 110; quasi-transcendent experiences of, 150–151
vital phase of personal-spiritual formation, 143
vital pre- and coformation of world, 106
vital preformation, 69; original obscure field of, 70–71; scientific reflection on, 73–74
vital preformation of life: and formation field, 68–74; and preformative vital life directives, 71–73
vital preformative presence, 69–70
vital reaction patterns, 129–130
vital reactive life, participation in human formation, 79–81
vital sexual formation: and adolescence and sexual preformation, 109–110; foundational structure of, 105–110; integration with transcendent life formation, 111–112; and vital field formation, 106–107; and vital pre- and coformation of world, 106
vital-sexual preformation, and polymorphous versatility of sexual preformation, 110
vital strivings. See articulations of vital dimension
vital vigor, preservation of, 126
vitalism, and human health, 155–156
vitalistic form directives, and interaction between formation field and vital life, 84
vitalistic-functionalistic view of formation, 52–53
vitalistic stereotypes, females and, 197
vitalistic-functionalistic view of formation, 50–52
vitality: components, 75; dynamic balance between functionality and, 196–198
void. See emptiness

Western culture, and informative approach, xviii
wholeness, and Holy Spirit, 144
Wittgenstein, Ludwig, 33
world: as continuous flow of ongoing formation, 198–200; formative and deformative engagement in, 49; functional view, 193–194; as a human formation field, 47, 57; and mystery of cosmic formation, 208; spiritual formation of, 98–99; vital pre- and coformation of, 106
world pole, 249
worship, 160–161